Ethnic Groups in the City

Ethnic Groups in the City

Culture, Institutions, and Power

Otto Feinstein
Monteith College
Wayne State University

Heath Lexington Books
D.C. Heath and Company
Lexington, Massachusetts
Toronto   London

Copyright © 1971 by D.C. Heath and Company.

Published simultaneously in Canada.

Printed in the United States of America.

Standard Book Number: 669-73312-1

Library of Congress Catalog Card Number: 70-151775

Table of Contents

List of Figures

List of Tables

Preface

This book is one of the material products of the Conference on Ethnic Communities of Greater Detroit. It contains transcribed oral presentations from the conference and written papers which were either prepared specially for the conference or included in the kit which the participants at the conference received.

The idea for the conference came from the students in the 1969 classes of Science of Society at Monteith College. As part of the basic course they were studying their own communities and found it very difficult to get a collection of articles in this subject area. We thus invited people with special knowledge from the community and ethnic leaders to our class. As the course progressed, the students wished to discuss the important truths they found out from their own work with their parents, relatives, and friends. Miss Florence Cassidy, of the International Institute and of the Peoples of Detroit Project, one of the great experts of ethnicity who resides in Detroit, was of great help to the students. She pointed out that 1970 was the 25th Anniversary of the International Institute and that an ethnic conference in Detroit would be a fine thing. Plans slowly mushroomed and in November, 1969, we met Father Daniel Bogus, co-chairman of the Black-Polish Conference of Detroit, at the Chicago Consultation on Ethnicity sponsored by the American Jewish Committee at the University of Illinois. The idea thus grew again and with the help of Sherwood Sandweiss of the Detroit AJC and the many people already involved we decided on a general conference for June 11-13, 1970. Thus the conference developed into a conference for all the people of Detroit where without the suppression of our diversity we could find the unity which we so badly need for our individual and collective survival.

We would like to thank the thirty-nine ethnic organizations and twenty-three institutions that sponsored the conference. The ethnic organizational sponsors were:

American Arabic Council; American Jewish Committee; Armenian Studies Committee, W.S.U.; Black-Polish Conference; Can-American Council of Maltese Organizations; Croatian Singing Society—"Nightingale"; Czechoslovak National Council of America—Masaryk Chapter—Detroit; Dancers Hungaria; Detroit Highland Dancers Society; Detroit Lithuanian Organizations Center; Filarets Chorus; Finnish American Historical Society of Michigan; Friends of Polish Art.

Also: German American Cultural Center; International Afro-American Museum; Japanese American Citizens League, Detroit Chapter; Korean Society of Detroit; Latin Americans for Social and Economic Development; Lithuanian American Community of the U.S.A.—Detroit Chapter; Lithuanian Folk Dancers—"Silaine"; Lithuanian National League of America—"Sandra"; Maltese American Benevolent Society, Inc.; N.A.A.C.P.—Detroit; North American Indian Association of Detroit; Ravanica Mothers Club.

Also: St. Mary's College—Orchard Lake; Serbian National Federation—Lodge 98, "Beograd," Lodge 14, "Bratska Sloga"; Slovak League of America; Society for German Culture; Ukrainian Folk Dance Ensemble; Ukrainian Graduates; Ukrainian National Women's League—Detroit Regional Council; Ukrainian Youth Bandurist Ensemble of St. Vladimir Ukrainian Orthodox Church of Windsor, Ontario; United Belgian Societies; U.S. Highland Dancers Association —District #3; Wawel Dancers of Detroit; Payne Theological Seminary, Wilberforce University.

The institutional sponsors included:

Archdiocese of Detroit; Center for the Teaching about Peace and War; Center for Urban Studies, W.S.U.; Detroit Industrial Mission; Detroit Board of Education; Labor Education Division, Institute of Labor and Industrial Relations, W.S.U. and U.M.; Inter-Faith Action Council; International Brotherhood of Teamsters; International Institute of Metropolitan Detroit.

Metropolitan Detroit AFL-CIO; Metropolitan Detroit Council of Churches; Michigan Civil Rights Commission; Monteith College Ethnic Project, W.S.U.; Peoples of Detroit Project; Teamsters—Local 985; U.A.W.: Region 1A; U.A.W.: Region 1E; Urban Alliance; United Methodist Church—Detroit; United Presbyterian Church—Detroit; Wayne County Community College.

Part I
Ethnicity, Community and Culture:
Who are We?

1

Ethnicity as an Influence on Behavior

Andrew Greeley

One suspects that when the social historians of, let us say, the twenty-third or twenty-fourth century look back on the era that we now presume to describe as the modern world, they will find two or three social phenomena of extraordinary interest. One is certainly the demographic revolution—the astonishing increase in the population level of the world that has occurred in the past century and a half. The second will be the westernization and industrialization of the non-Western world, and the third, unless I miss my guess, will be the formation of a new nation on the North American continent made up of widely different nationality groups. The historians of the future will find it hard to believe that it could have happened that the English, Scottish, and Welsh, Irish, Germans, Italians, and Poles, Africans, Indians, both Eastern and Western, Frenchmen, Spaniards, Finns, Swedes, Lebanese, Danes, Armenians, Croatians, Slovenians, Greeks, and Luxemburgers, Chinese, Japanese, Filipinos and Puerto Ricans would come together to form a nation that not only would survive, but, all things considered, survive reasonably well. I further suspect that the historians of the future will be astonished that American sociologists, the product of this gathering in of the nations, could stand in the midst of such an astonishing social phenomenon and take it so much for granted that they would not bother to study it.

They will find it especially astonishing in light of the fact that ethnic differences, even in the second half of the twentieth century, proved far more important to men than did the differences in philosophy or economic system. Men who would not die for a premise or a dogma or a division of labor, would more or less cheerfully die for a difference rooted in ethnic origins. Chinese and Malay fight each other in Southeast Asia; Ibo and Hausa in Nigeria; Greek and Turk on Cyprus; Czech and Slovak in Czechoslovakia; Arab and Jew in the Middle East; black (at least so-called) fight white (at least relatively) in the United States[a]; and the French and the English, running out of colonial peoples with which to contend, now renew the feud that the Hundred Years' War never did settle. Finally, along the lines of the Shamrock curtain another feud

---

This paper was originally presented to the National Consultation on Ethnic America, convened by the American Jewish Committee, Fordham University, June, 1968. Rev. Greeley has expanded on this paper in "Why can't they be like us? Facts and Fallacies about Ethnic Differences and Group Conflict in America."

[a]Though I am sure that a visitor from Nigeria would be hard put many times to tell who was black and who was white in the United States.

3

simmers, and Frank O'Connor's immortal words, spoken from the secure position of his own agnosticism, are as true as ever: "The north of Ireland contains the best Protestants in the world and the south of Ireland, the best Catholics, and there is nary a single Christian in the whole lot."

In this paper I wish to cover four topics: (1) some remarks about the nature of ethnic groups; (2) comments on the present lack of information about the social correlates of ethnicity; (3) a summary of some tables on ethnic differences; and (4) certain recommendations for what might be very loosely called "policy."

Ethnicity in American Society

Ethnic groups, in the sense we are using the term, are to be defined as human collectivities based on an assumption of common origin, real or imaginary. As E.K. Francis points out, in commenting on this essentially Weberian definition, the ethnic collectivity represents an attempt on the part of men to keep alive during their pilgrimage from *gemeinschaft* to *gesellschaft*, from peasant commune to industrial metropolis, some of the diffuse, ascriptive, particularistic modes of behavior that were common to their past. One is not an ethnic in one's native village, but only when one has left one's village for the city or left one's country for the New World. In Ireland we were Mayo men or Cork men; in Italy, Baresi or Neopolitans or Sicilians; in Germany, Swabians or Bavarians or Saxons; we became Irish, Italian, German, only when the host society chose to define us as such, and we found that the primordial ties of soil and blood could best be described in such terms in the new setting in which we found ourselves. Our ethnic group provided for us a pool of preferred role opposites in various areas of our lives. It was perhaps necessary in the large corporate structures to interact with whomever the random possibilities of the economic system put at the workbench or the desk next to us. But when it came to choosing our wife, our poker or bridge partner, our precinct captain, our doctor, our lawyer, our real estate broker, our construction contractor, our clergyman, and even our psychiatrist, we felt much more at ease if we could choose those of whom we could say, "After all, they're our kind of people." Furthermore it was even a big help if, when we approached the personnel office of a large corporation, we could say, at least to someone in that office, "My mother knows your mother."[b]

---

[b]In the recent mayoral campaign in Chicago a Polish Republican was opposing the incumbent Irish Democratic mayor. In a television interview the Republican candidate went down the list of Democratic administrators of the city and indicated one by one why he would replace them. Only one name was omitted and that was the Director of the Commission on Human Relations, who was, curiously enough, of Polish origin. The interviewer asked what would be done with this administrator. The Republican candidate shrugged his shoulders and said that, after all, he and the administrator had grown up in the same neighborhood and that, as far as he could see, the administrator was doing a reasonably good job. That their mothers knew each other can be left to the future historians to determine.

It is assumed, I think, by people for whom ethnicity is a relevant variable, that members of ethnic groups share certain common values about the behavior of opposites in intimate role relationships. I would hypothesize, at least until further research proves me wrong, that the principal variations among ethnic groups will be found to be in the expectations one has of a parent or sibling or child or spouse or cousin or a niece or an aunt or a friend, and I would suggest that it is precisely this common core of assumptions about how one behaves in intimate relationships that is most difficult for any acculturation process to erase and is most likely to survive for generations, if not permanently, among the descendants of ethnic immigrants.

The sociological profession has assumed for the last three decades that ethnicity is not a relevant variable in American society, and that intermarriage is rapidly eliminating the ethnic groups. Curiously enough, little or no evidence has been provided to back up this assumption, and the evidence that does exist (much of it collected by my student, Harold Abramson) would indicate that while ethnic intermarriage does occur, it is generally a highly selective form of intermarriage, and that it has by no means eliminated the ethnic collectivities.

But if ethnic groups seem to the behavioral scientist to be unimportant, there are many other citizens of our republic who think differently—politicians, church administrators, real estate men, and the more sophisticated public educators, to name but a few such groups. The balanced ticket, the ethnic parish, the nationality suburb, are all too obvious on the American scene, even if the inhabitants of Cambridge, Hyde Park, Madison, Ann Arbor, and Berkeley haven't noticed lately.

The exact composition of ethnic groups, who belongs to a group, to what extent formal organizations are necessary or what role formal institutions play, the relationship between ethnic groups and the mother country, are all subjects for research—research which, alas, one must report simply has not been done. The questions at issue are fascinating, however. It is clear to anyone who has observed them closely that the American Irish are not the Irish Irish, nor are they the English Irish, and that all three groups have something in common with one another. Being Irish in the United States, for example, no longer involves, as it once did, deep concern about the politcal fortunes of the Irish Republic. No so long ago I was visiting a Catholic girls' college in the heartland of America and I noticed a sign on the bulletin board announcing that shortly the Irish Club of the college would hold its monthly meeting. I asked the young lady who was showing me through the college if she belonged to the Irish Club and she admitted that she not only belonged to it, but was its president. "Peggy," I said to her, "do you know what the six counties are?" She admitted that she did not, and I said, "Have you ever heard of the Sein Fein?" and she admitted that she did not know what it was. "And," I said, "have you ever heard of the Easter rising of the I.R.A.?" She admitted her ignorance. Finally, I said, "Peggy, do you know who Eamon de Valera is?" She brightened at that question. "Isn't he the Jewish man that is the Lord Mayor of Dublin?" she asked.

Information about Ethnic Groups

The basic response to the question about which this paper is concerned is that there isn't any demographic, socio-economic, or socio-psychological information about the latter stages of the acculturation processes of the American ethnic group; it simply does not exist and is not likely to exist in the foreseeable future. In all likelihood, no attempt will be made to collect such information until it is too late. The Census Bureau now provides only data on the foreign-born and tells us nothing about the second, third, or the fourth generation of the ethnic immigrant groups. If one looks under the title "Ethnicity" in the indices of the behavioral science journals , one can find articles about Eskimos and Navaho, about tribes in Africa and New Guinea, and even occasionally about black-white relationships, but precious little else. Ethnic questions are not routinely included in survey research questionnaires, and for all the wild assertions about ethnic voting patterns (based usually on the foreign-born percentages of the Census tract data), national samples of political behavior rarely break the American religious groups up into their ethnic components.

Even though graduate students are interested in writing dissertations on the subject (a strange application of Hansen's law), faculty members who feel qualified to moderate such dissertations are almost nonexistent. The sprightly Glazer and Moynihan book (*Beyond the Melting Pot*) offers interesting data and speculations about New York City, but New York City is not, as startling as it may seem in the present set of circumstances, the whole republic. Herbert Gans' book about the Italians of Boston (*The Urban Villagers*) is extremely suggestive, but one looks in vain for imitators of Gans. Fishman's book on language loyalty (*Language Loyalty in the U.S.*) is extremely valuable but quite narrow in its focus; it tells us nothing, for example, about ethnic groups like the Irish who speak only English, and that sometimes not too well. Gordon's book (*Assimilation in American Life*) is, as far as I know, the only serious attempt to state some general propositions about ethnicity in American society. When one attempts to persuade on the exigencies of ethnic research as important, one is told first that the question is quite irrelevent because of the workings of the assimilation process, and second that it is a highly sensitive issue which might offend people if pushed too vigorously. How something can be irrelevant and sensitive, no longer an issue and still offensive, is one of those great paradoxes that we sociologists must learn to live with. One can submit articles on ethnicity to even such respectable journals as *The Public Interest* and not even expect the courtesy of having the articles rejected; and proposals, even technically sound ones, to governmental agencies are likely to be rejected without even the formality of a visit from the site committee. Ethnic study is out and one wonders if there is any likelihood that it is not going to stay out.

I shall not speculate at great length as to the reason for this nonexistence of interest in research on ethnic groups, but one is truly hard put to know why the last serious sociological study of American Poles was done by Thomas and Znaniecki in the 1920s. It could be that ethnic material is not particularly suited for multiple regression analysis, or it could be, if one wants to take a very sinister interpretation, advanced to me by one middle-aged Ph.D. from Columbia, that those who have trained the present generation of younger American sociologists repressed the possibility of ethnic research from their consciousness because of their own profound ambivalence about their personal ethnic backgrounds.

Be that as it may, we do not have the information, and because we lack information it is hard to come to grips with the question of ethnic groups in either a meaningfully theoretical or practically operational way. Is everyone an ethnic? Do we all belong to some larger collectivity that stands between the family and society and is somehow based on common origins? Are Protestants an ethnic group? Are Texans? Are intellectuals? What is the relationship between ethnicity and religion? My own inclination is to say that almost all of us need some collectivity with which to identify ourselves, and that many, if not most of us, are still inclined to fall back on the primordial bonds of blood and land. In some sections of the country, to be a white Anglo-Saxon Protestant is definitely to be an ethnic, and I suspect that to be an intellectual and a Texan may well be to be an ethnic. However, it seems to me that the really relevant piece of research information that is not available to us is under what set of circumstances which kind of people find which ethnic values and behavior appropriate? We need to know, therefore, both the basic demographic information about the ethnic groups—who they are, where they are, what they are doing—and also what value and behavioral correlates of ethnicity have survived in modern society. Finally, it would help to know how these ethnic collectivities relate to more organized groups of society, either those which could be called formal ethnic institutions or those which are intimately connected with nationality origins such as political parties and churches.

Some Available Data

In this section of the paper I propose to comment on some tables gathered in secondary analysis of NORC research data. These tables are cited to show that ethnic differences still do persist in American society, and also to fulfill at least in part what is basically an impossible task—to report on the social and demographic correlates of ethnicity.[c]

In Table 1-1 we learn that the Irish are the most successful of the Catholic immigrant groups in terms of their education and their income, while the Italians and the Polish are the least successful. The Germans seem to have less education and less income than the Irish.

Poles are the most loyal to the Democratic party, while the Germans and the Italians are the least loyal, though even here two-thirds of the respondents were Democrats, and the spread of twelve percentage points between the Germans

---

[c]It should be noted that all the respondents represented in Tables 1 through 5 were Roman Catholic, and that the "French" were largely French Canadian.

and Poles is, one supposes, not terribly great. There is little difference in religious behavior between the Irish, the Germans, and the Poles, though the French and the Italians seem to be substantially less devout than the other three groups. The Irish and the French score highest on the happiness measure, and the Poles, with true slavic sobriety, score the lowest. Similarly, the French and the Poles have the highest scores on an index of religious extremism, and the Irish and the Germans, the lowest scores. The racism scores are highest among the Poles and lowest among the Irish and the Germans. The Irish are lowest on the anti-Semitism index; the French and the Poles are the highest. The Irish are also most likely to score high on open-mindedness and low on anomie, with the Germans just behind them, and the other three groups trailing.

In summary, as one might suspect, the earlier immigrant groups are the most tolerant, but there are enough differences, say, between the Irish and the Germans and between the Italians and the Poles to suggest that other factors are at work besides the time at which one's parents arrived on the American shores.

In Table 1-2 we devote some passing attention to regional differences among ethnic groups. The Eastern Irish are more likely to be Democratic than the Middle Western Irish, while exactly the reverse seems to be true of the Germans. All four ethnic groups seem to be more religious in the Middle West than in the East. The Middle Western Irish seem somewhat more liberal politically, as do the Germans from that region. The Middle Western Poles, on the other hand, seem to be more ethnocentric than their counterparts on the East Coast.

In Table 1-3 we attempt to see if education explains the differences we have

Table 1-1
Comparison of Five Catholic Ethnic Groups

(Percent)

Item	Irish	German	Italian	French	Polish
Duncan 8-10	32	31	13	22	17
High School Graduate	77	62	51	42	46
More than $14,000	24	19	17	7	18
High on General Knowledge Scale	18	9	7	5	3
Democratic	70	65	67	70	77
"Very Happy"	41	36	35	40	27
High on "Sacramental" Index	32	31	13	22	30
High on "Religious Extremism" Index	19	20	24	28	34
High on "Racism" Index	44	46	54	51	61
High on "Anti-Semitism" Index	29	47	43	54	52
High on "Open-mindedness" Index	52	48	42	40	43
Low on Anomie Scale	64	51	47	49	43
	(328)	(361)	(370)	(177)	(184)

Table 1-2
Comparison of Regional Differences Among Four Catholic Ethnic Groups

(Percent)

Item	Eastern[a]				Middle Western[b]			
	Irish	German	Italian	Polish	Irish	German	Italian	Polish
High on General Knowledge Scale	15	8	5	1	14	8	8	2
Democratic	76	56	67	70	64	67	69	80
"Very Happy"	45	36	33	32	34	35	37	29
High on "Sacramental" Index	28	16	10	13	44	37	22	21
High on "Religious Extremism" Index	23	20	26	35	15	22	19	39
High on "Racism" Index	44	51	50	54	41	48	48	64
High on "Anti-Semitism" Index	31	44	44	55	30	53	45	53
High on "Open-Mindedness" Index	53	42	43	47	49	47	35	39
Low on Anomie Scale	66	52	41	49	61	54	59	40

[a]New England and Middle Atlantic
[b]East North Central and West North Central
Other regions are excluded

Table 1-3
Comparison of Educational Differences Among Five Catholic Ethnic Groups

(Percent)

Item	Did Not Graduate from High School					High School Graduate				
	Irish	German	Italian	French	Polish	Irish	German	Italian	French	Polish
Duncan 8-10	5	4	2	1	5	30	25	18	22	21
Professional or Manager	5	5	0	4	5	46	37	32	18	24
More than $14,000	12	12	10	14	13	28	24	26	16	23
High on General Knowledge Scale	4	1	1	1	0	22	14	12	11	6
Democratic	79	69	79	75	83	67	63	59	63	70
"Very Happy"	28	29	30	39	22	44	40	40	40	32
High on "Sacramental" Index	5	4	2	1	5	36	33	15	35	15
High on "Religious Extremism" Index	27	31	29	36	44	15	14	20	17	25
High on "Racism" Index	55	54	58	56	64	43	36	48	28	60
High on "Anti-Semitism" Index	36	61	51	60	60	28	40	37	46	44
High on "Open-Mindedness" Index	52	42	38	37	39	52	50	45	45	47
Low on Anomie Scale	45	41	41	39	38	69	57	53	61	50
	(72)	(131)	(175)	(101)	(96)	(256)	(230)	(195)	(76)	(87)

observed among the five ethnic groups, and discover that even among high school graduates the Poles and the Italians and the French score higher on measures of racism, anti-Semitism, and religious extremism than do the Irish, and in most instances, the Germans. Interestingly enough, high school graduation seems to make less difference on the racial question for Polish respondents that it does for the members of the other four ethnic groups.

In Table 1-4 we try to determine to what extent the differences we have uncovered can be explained away by the different generational compositon of the ethnic groups, and see that, even holding generation as constant as we can with our relatively small sample, the Irish and the Germans tend to be more socially successful and less ethnocentric than do the Italians and the Poles, although later generation Italians have the lowest score on the racism scale. It is further worth noting that third generation Poles score higher on the racism measure than do earlier generation Poles, perhaps because the Polish population is at the present time in the first phase of the home-owning stage in American society, and hence the one most to be threatened by the migration of Negro population in the urban centers of the nation.

In Table 1-5 we try to combine controls for generation and education, though the case bases here in this table are so small that one can generalize from the table only with great risk. Even among the high school graduates who are at least the grandchildren of immigrants, the Irish, Germans, and Poles seem to be more successful in occupational prestige and income than the Italians or French. The Irish are the best informed, with the Germans and Italians taking second place on this measure; and the Italians are the most likely to have migrated out of the Democratic party. The Irish and the French are the happiest, hopefully putting to rest forever the notion that the Celts are a morose and melancholy lot, and I shall leave to others to explain why the descendants of sunny Italy seem so gloomy, though with only twenty-nine of them in the table, one could easily argue that the whole sample was made up of somber Milanese.

The Poles consistently score highest on the measures of ethnocentrism, the Irish being the lowest on anti-Semitism, and the Germans and French the lowest on racism. The Irish—or at least the Irish in our sample—are the least anomic and the Italians the most, and the Germans the most open-minded and the Poles the least open-minded.

Table 1-6 is presented not because one has a great deal of confidence in it, but simply because it gives some comparative information for non-Catholic ethnic groups. It should be remembered that the case bases here are very small and that the WASP group includes many southern whites. Table 1-6A does show, however, in comparison with the percentages for the Irish, Polish, and Italians in Table 1-1, a fairly close similarity in percentages claiming to be "very happy." It is reassuring to know that the laws of probability still do work.

Similarly, the differences between the Irish and the Polish on racial issues (at least in 1962 when the data were collected) are similar to those reported in Table 1-1. Furthermore, it would appear that the Irish were the least likely of the three Catholic groups to vote for their fellow Irish-Catholic, John Kennedy,

Table 1-4
Comparison of Generational Composition of Five Catholic Ethnic Groups

(Percent)

	First and Second Generation					Third or Later Generation				
	Irish	German	Italian	French	Polish	Irish	German	Italian	French	Polish
Duncan 8-10	21	14	5	10	12	25	20	12	16	16
Professional or Manager	21	17	10	26	18	24	29	17	27	9
More than $14,000	24	15	7	20	20	24	21	8	13	17
High on General Knowledge Scale	19	10	3	5	2	18	10	7	16	5
Democratic	69	64	74	70	77	71	66	72	51	76
"Very Happy"	30	36	49	34	27	45	37	43	37	24
High on "Sacramental" Index	32	23	26	13	19	32	33	23	11	16
High on "Religious Extremism" Index	16	20	26	26	38	17	20	27	12	20
High on "Racism" Index	53	55	45	53	51	43	41	35	54	67
High on "Anti-Semitism" Index	35	55	53	46	53	28	44	52	35	53
High on "Open-Mindedness" Index	55	42	34	40	47	51	50	44	45	37
Low on Anomie Scale	52	48	49	47	48	70	54	60	50	43
	(76)	(109)	(70)	(294)	(111)	(225)	(216)	(62)	(79)	(58)

for the presidency. One must note of Table 1-6C that the Jewish percentage is obviously quite inaccurate.

Table 1-6D would suggest that on certain matters of sexual morality the Irish and the WASP constitute a moderate group with the Jews being the more "liberal," the Italians more conservative, and the Poles ambivalent, approving of petting more than anyone else, and of having intercourse much less than the Irish and the WASPs.

Finally, in Table 1-6E, we note that Jews and Protestants are more abstemious in their dealings with John Barleycorn than are the Catholics, though by and large, the Irish are successful in confirming their reputation for being quite apt when it comes to "downing a few."

There is some other research material available which can be summarized in one paragraph. Ethnicity predicts, as we might expect, occupational choice. Germans, regardless of religion, are more likely to choose careers in science and engineering than any other group. Jews over-choose medicine and law. The Irish over-choose law, political science, history, and the diplomatic service. (In the

Table 1-5

Comparison of Generational Composition and Education Among Five Catholic Ethnic Groups

(Percent)

Item	Third Generation or Later, High School Graduates				
	Irish	German	Italian	French	Polish
Duncan 8-10	31	34	12	21	32
Professional or Manager	45	47	37	31	22
More than $14,000	26	22	3	11	21
High on General Knowledge Scale	26	17	20	9	11
Democratic	67	61	51	76	62
"Very Happy"	47	38	26	48	32
High on "Sacramental" Index	32	32	10	39	20
High on "Religious Extremism" Index	14	15	20	26	31
High on "Racism" Index	39	30	54	29	61
High on "Anti-Semitism" Index	25	38	32	43	59
High on "Open-Mindedness" Index	51	56	51	40	34
Low on Anomie Scale	74	60	44	60	61
	(131)	(102)	(29)	(31)	(24)
N's for other tables:					
Third Generation Did Not Graduate	(22)	(37)	(11)	(31)	(16)
First or Second Generation Did Not Graduate	(9)	(33)	(153)	(47)	(69)
First or Second Generation Did Graduate	(29)	(26)	(123)	(18)	(27)

Table 1-6
Comparative Information on Non-Catholic Ethnic Groups

A. Happiness

"Taken all together, how would you say things are these days—would you say that you are very happy, pretty happy, or not too happy?"

Item	Wasp	Irish	Polish	Italian	Jewish
Very	37	47	28	31	14
Pretty	47	38	59	52	55
Not too	16	18	13	17	31
	(227)	(64)	(39)	(59)	(43)

B. Attitudes on Race
(Percent)

Item	Wasp	Irish	Polish	Italian	Jewish
Negro children should go to separate schools	64	20	38	17	30
Negroes should be on separate sections of street cars and buses	22	5	21	14	8
Unfavorable to Negroes living in same block	41	25	46	36	30

C. Voting in 1960 Election
(Percent)

Item	Wasp	Irish	Polish	Italian	Jewish
Voting for Kennedy	43	76	82	88	57

D. Attitudes on Courtship Practices
(Percent Rating Practice as "Acceptable for Male When He Is Engaged")

Item	Wasp	Irish	Polish	Italian	Jewish
Kissing	96	95	97	94	92
Petting	63	55	70	42	63
Intercourse	18	22	13	5	49

(Percent Rating Practice as "Acceptable for Female When She Is Engaged")

	Wasp	Irish	Polish	Italian	Jewish
Kissing	95	93	95	95	92
Petting	57	53	63	41	63
Intercourse	14	14	8	5	45

E. Attitudes Toward Drinking
(Percent)

Item	Wasp	Irish	Polish	Italian	Jewish
Abstainers	33	11	10	10	23
Twice a Week	28	41	32	15	44
Neglect Meals	14	17	17	6	25
Don't Remember Next Day	14	12	11	4	17
Toss Down Fast	26	28	19	7	35
Make Socializing More Enjoyable	36	64	74	45	38
Make Less Self-conscious	19	27	18	11	14

June, 1961, sample, one-half of those who said they were going to take the foreign service exams were Catholic and one-quarter of them were Irish Catholic, suggesting that the Irish migrate from the precinct to the Embassy. Whether this be social progress or not is, one supposes, a matter of values.) Polish and other slavic groups are less likely to approve of bond issues. Irish react to sickness with fierce bravery that represses symptoms, while Italians react with an emotional intensity that, if anything, exaggerates the symptoms.

One could, I suppose, attempt to evolve explanations for the phenomena reported in the tables accompanying this article. But given the weak state of our theory on ethnic groups, the scarcity of data, and the general unreliability of the case bases on which the critical comparisons are based, one would probably be wasting one's time. These tables establish what they were intended to establish—ethnicity is still a predictor variable of some relevance in American society.

Policy Recommendations

I would suggest that there are two reasons which would justify research in American ethnic groups, even though the subject was not one which seems to me to be inherently interesting.

First of all, there are immediate social problems which our society faces that cannot be solved unless we understand more about the operation of the ethnic factor. One need not look at the statistics in my tables about Polish attitudes on race questions, to know that there is an acute problem here, not, at least, if one lives in Chicago. But beyond mythological explanations it is extremely difficult to attribute a cause for this phenomenon. It would be extremely helpful, not to say imperative, if we understood more about the antipathy of certain ethnic groups to other ethnic groups.

Secondly, since it seems likely that many of the problems existing in the

United States and in the whole world today are based on, or at least focus about the presumed differences in origin, one would want to know as much as possible about the ethnicity, the root of these differences, in order to understand how people of diverse origin and values can live with each other in peace—at least in relative peace. This may, in the final analysis, be the ultimate contribution that our multiple melting pot society is able to make to the rest of the world.

In my judgment, the first thing we must do is collect the basic demographic and socioeconomic information which simply does not exist now. We must know who and where and what the major ethnic groups are and not merely the large groups of which we have spoken in this paper, but also the smaller groups which may be even more instructive for understanding a multiple melting pot model of society. The Greeks, the Armenians, the Luxemburgers, the Lebanese are still very much with us and there might be a lot to be learned from them. Once we have the basic demographic information, then we could go on to attitude and value studies and the more complicated questions of the impact of ethnicity on social structure. I say, we could, because in all honesty, I don't really believe that we will. In fact, I don't even believe that we are going to start putting ethnicity on survey research questionnaires as a standard item.

Let me conclude with a story whose point I think I need not emphasize. I was standing in front of a church in the west of Ireland, camera in hand, attempting to record the church which I thought just possibly was the place of my grandfather's baptism. The parish priest who was out cutting his hedge despite the rain, approached me, noted that I was a new man around here, and introduced himself. I must say I was a bit surprised when, on hearing my name, he remarked, "Ah, yes, you'd be the sociologist fellow from Chicago," and then added, "Would you be wantin' your grandfather's baptismal record now?"

I admitted that the idea hadn't occurred to me, and he shook his head in discouragement. "Ah," he said, "fine sociologist you are." "Do a lot of people come seeking such records?" I asked. He shook his head gravely. "Indeed they do," he said, "indeed they do." Those poor people, you know, they've been in the States now for three generations and they come seeking roots; they want to know who they are; they want to know all about their past and their ancestors. The poor people, I feel so sorry for them. "Well," he continued, "the least we can do is be of some help to them. That's why I had all their baptismal records put on microfilm. It makes it a lot easier for people to find their roots."

2 Ethnic Pluralism in the Central City

Harold J. Abramson

About a half century ago, in his book *Character and Opinion in the United States*, the philosopher George Santayana described the social context of being an American. "If there are immense differences between individual Americans," he wrote, "yet there is a great uniformity in their environment, customs, temper, and thoughts. They have all been uprooted from their several soils and ancestries and plunged together into one vortex, whirling irresistibly in space... To be an American is of itself almost a moral condition, an education, and a career." Santayana saw the American as a symbol.

This is the theme that has predominated in interpretations of the American society by historians, journalists, and sociologists. In other phrases, and with other variations, this is the theme of the melting pot, and of Anglo-Saxon conformity, and of the Americanization movement. But one might also choose to turn this idea around, and say, if there is considerable uniformity among the masses of Americans, yet there is a history and a present of important differences. And one may choose to look at the American experience in terms of its differences as well as its uniformities, and *then* begin to wonder at the way in which it has all been put together. As we all know, the melting pot did not happen. Ethnicity, as a kind of distinctiveness defined by race, religion, national origin, and even geographical isolation, remains, even if little systematic work has been done on the subject in describing how and why ethnicity is maintained, and to what degree it is meaningful.

As with so many other aspects of the present, past, and future, the Black Movement of the 1960s and 1970s urges a reassessment of American society. We are indebted to America's blacks, because their social movement—their very

Data examined in this report come from a study of Connecticut cities, as research performed pursuant to a contract with the United States Department of Health, Education and Welfare, Office of Education, under the provisions of the Cooperative Research Program. Additional support was received from the University of Connecticut Research Foundation and the Connecticut Research Commission. For a description of the study, see Irving L. Allen and J. David Colfax, *Urban Problems and Public Opinion in Four Connecticut Cities* (Storrs, Connecticut: Institute of Urban Research the University of Connecticut, 1968).

For the preparation of this report, the author wishes to acknowledge the financial support made available by the American Jewish Committee, consultation with Irving L. Allen, and research assistance provided by Scott B. Cummings, Deena J. Steinberg, and David L. Metzger.

17

relevant revolution—forces us to be more aware of who we are and of what America has been, is, and will be. There is a history of violence and ethnic strife in the American past, as well as a history of social change and social mobility and progress. And what ties the past to the present, as a thread of national continuity, is pluralism—the diversity of different ethnic groups co-existing in some degree of accommodation under the roof of the same society. At times this ethnic pluralism can function positively, and can lead to harmonious and stable relationships. At other times this pluralism can function negatively, with conflict and tension among the groups and the values they seem not to share.

Before we can begin to understand the implications of ethnic pluralism for social behavior and attitudes, some idea of the extent of diversity among ethnic groups is necessary. Even if we cannot claim to grasp all the issues involved, a basic step would be some appreciation of just how much diversity there actually is among different ethnic groups in America. Toward this goal, we can provide a look at the ethnic groups that reside in the center of three of Connecticut's largest cities: Hartford, Bridgeport, and New Haven. The aim of this paper is to provide some hard facts by way of introducing some questions of ethnic life in Connecticut. How similar or dissimilar Connecticut's ethnic groups are in social characteristics, in economic and political terms, and in their attitudes toward the world around them. This will be a brief attempt to raise some basic questions about a very important idea—the fact of ethnic diversity in contemporary life.

A Profile of the Ethnic Factor

Religion and national origin frequently go together, and the survey shows just how related these two components of ethnicity actually are. The three largest religious faiths—Protestant, Roman Catholic, and Jewish—are identified, as are the largest independent nationality or ethnic backgrounds—Afro-American or black, Eastern European, English, French-Canadian, German, Irish, Italian, Polish, and Spanish-speaking.[a]

When the relation between religion and ethnicity is drawn (Table 2-1), we find what we expect, that a majority of the people who are of black, English, and German background, are Protestant, and the majority of the Eastern Europeans, French-Canadians, Irish, Italians, Poles, and the Spanish-speaking, are of course Catholic. We can turn the question around and also ask, which are the larger and which the smaller ethnic groups in these central city areas (Table 2-2). For all three cities in Connecticut, the blacks are the largest single group; they comprise 17 percent of this population. The Italians are the next numerous,

[a]For reasons of the number of cases per group in the survey, and for some ethnic similarities in background, certain groups were combined as follows: Eastern European includes Hungarians, Lithuanians, Latvians, Estonians, Slovaks, Ukrainians, Russians, Czechs, Rumanians, Bulgarians, Albanians, Serbs, and Croations; English includes English, Scottish, Welsh, and English Canadians; German includes German, Dutch, Austrian, Swiss, and Flemish; Spanish-speaking includes Puerto Rican, Latin American, Spanish and Portuguese.

Table 2-1
Percent Distribution of Ethnic Groups by Religion

Father's Ethnicity	Protestant	Catholic	Jewish	Total
Black	94	6	0	100(288)
Eastern European	13	59	28	100(163)
English	68	31	1	100(173)
French-Canadian	11	87	2	100(92)
German	51	36	13	100(143)
Irish	17	83	0	100(198)
Italian	2	98	–	100(268)
Polish	5	82	13	100(94)
Spanish-speaking	11	89	–	100(91)
Other	39	22	39	100(127)
Total	36	56	8	100(1,637

N	=	1,637
No religion	=	50
Other religion	=	42
NA, religion, ethnicity	=	54
Total N	=	1,783[a]

[a] N = 1,783 = the total number of respondents interviewed in Hartford, Bridgeport, and New Haven (central cities).

Table 2-2
Percent Distribution of Religious Groups by Ethnicity

Father's Ethnicity	Protestant	Catholic	Jewish	Total
Black	45	2	1	17
Eastern European	4	11	35	10
English	19	6	2	11
French-Canadian	2	9	2	6
German	12	6	14	9
Irish	6	18	1	12
Italian	1	28	–	15
Polish	1	8	9	6
Spanish-speaking	2	9	–	6
Other	8	3	36	8
Total	100	100	100	100
	(595)	(909)	(133)	(1,637)

being 15 percent, and the Irish are 12 percent of this urban population. The blacks also stand out when counted by religion; almost half of the Protestants in these three cities are Afro-American.

The remaining description will focus on the largest specific groups involved: the blacks (of all religions) and the whites, Protestants, Jews, and Roman Catholics, the latter as a total group and also viewed by ethnic composition. Because of the importance of social class, we can better understand the extent of diversity if we distinguish between white collar and blue collar occupations, for each ethnic group.[b] The percentage of workers in blue collar occupations varies considerably among all of these ethnic groups (Table 2-3). The membership of the blue collar working class runs from 95 percent of all Spanish-speaking Catholics to 25 percent of all Jews. Two facts stand out in this comparison: first, the fact that white collar and blue collar jobs vary a great deal in their distribution from one ethnic group to another, and second, that because of this, it is essential to look at both ideas when we talk of pluralism and diversity. Is diversity in Connecticut due to socioeconomic factors, such as the kind of occupation? Or are differences more complicated than that? Does diversity exist, regardless of one's white collar or blue collar employment?

Let us consider a few important ideas, especially those which are particularly germane to life in the central city. Home ownership, for example, is often an important characteristic in describing an urban neighborhood, but we usually lack information on which groups are more likely to own their home, and which are more likely to rent them. We would probably expect that relatively few in the central cities of Connecticut do actually own their homes, or live in houses where they are paying on a mortgage instead of some fixed rental. This is true; only one-third of all central city residents own their homes (Table 2-4). But the figures for the different ethnic groups show real diversity. As many as half of all Jews, and Eastern European, Italian, and Polish Catholics, own their homes, but all other groups are considerably more likely to rent theirs. And this diversity remains, even when we look at blue collar and white collar families. White collar job-holders are somewhat more likely to own than to rent, for all in the survey taken as a whole, but this is not always true for each ethnic group taken separately. German Catholics and Jews, for example, are more likely to own a home if they are blue collar, and there is no difference at all between white collar and blue collar Irish, or between Italians of different occupations. Regardless of their occupational status, the Irish are more likely to rent, and the Italians are more likely to own. Interests in home ownership, and the alternative prospects of owning or renting, are variable by ethnicity as well as class.

The idea of home ownership in the central city is important also for the sense of the neighborhood. Despite all the research into the large metropolitan or

---

[b]The occupational classification is based on U.S. Census categories, as follows: white collar jobs include all professional, managerial, clerical and sales workers; blue collar jobs include all craftsmen, factory operatives, private household workers, service workers, and unskilled labor.

Table 2-3
Percent Distribution of Religio-Ethnic Groups by Occupational Class

Religio-Ethnic Group	White Collar	Blue Collar	Total
Blacks, all religions	13	87	100(283)
Protestants, white	48	52	100(312)
Jews, white	75	25	100(129)
Catholics, white	36	64	100(878)
Total	37	63	100(1,602)
Specific Catholic Groups			
Eastern European	30	70	100(96)
English	50	50	100(54)
French-Canadian	25	75	100(79)
German	66	34	100(50)
Irish	49	51	100(162)
Italian	36	64	100(259)
Polish	22	78	100(78)
Spanish-speaking	5	95	100(73)

N   = 1,602
NA, occupation =   35
Total N   = 1,637

Table 2-4
Percentage of Home Owners, by Religio-Ethnic Group and Class

Religio-Ethnic Group	White Collar	Blue Collar	Total
Blacks	22(37)	13(245)	14(282)
Protestants	30(149)	24(163)	27(312)
Jews	48(97)	66(32)	53(129)
Catholics	40(312)	35(564)	37(876)
Eastern European	55(29)	45(67)	48(96)
English	26(27)	11(27)	19(54)
French-Canadian	40(20)	24(59)	28(79)
German	33(33)	41(17)	36(50)
Irish	32(80)	28(82)	30(162)
Italian	52(92)	54(167)	53(259)
Polish	59(17)	41(59)	45(76)
Spanish-speaking	—(4)[a]	9(69)	8(73)
Total	38(595)	29(1,004)	32(1,599)

N   = 1,599
NA, home owners =   3
Total N   = 1,602   [a]Too few cases for percentaging.

middle-size American city, under the traditional name of urban sociology, we know little about comparative ethnic behavior in the central city. We lack information, for example, on the ethnic neighborhood. To be sure, there are studies and reports which look at particular neighborhoods, individually. But until we emphasize *comparative* life styles, we cannot begin to talk about ethnic pluralism.

In this connection, it is valuable to have an idea of the ethnic relationships in urban neighborhoods. A question included in this survey which comes close to this idea refers to the number of close friends in the neighborhood who are relatives or in-laws of the family being interviewed. The question then taps not only the location, i.e., the immediate neighborhood, but also the nature of friendship choice and kinship. For all people in the survey, only 27 percent replied that most of their close friends are neighbors (Table 2-5). But the difference by social class is impressive. Blue collar workers are more than twice as likely to have these stronger ties of kinship than are white collar workers. And this is true for most of the specific groups mentioned as well.

Ethnic diversity on this question is also impressive. Of all the groups interviewed in Connecticut's central cities, the Italians, the Spanish-speaking, and the Poles stand out as reflecting this kind of ethnic kinship pattern and neighborhood. The white collar Protestants and German Catholics stand out too, at the other end, as exceptions to this pattern.

The implications of this are interesting. If one-third to one-half of a particular

Table 2-5
Percent Who Say That Most of Their Close Friends in the Neighborhood Are Relatives, by Religio-Ethnic Group and Class

Religio-Ethnic Group	White Collar	Blue Collar	Total
Blacks	18	34	32
Protestants	7	29	19
Jews	15	26	17
Catholics	21	36	31
Eastern European	34	28	30
English	26	19	22
French-Canadian	15	23	21
German	6	18	10
Irish	14	27	21
Italian	26	47	40
Polish	29	37	35
Spanish-speaking	—a	49	49
Total	16	34	27

aToo few cases for percentaging.

group in the central city claims that most of its friendship choices in the neighborhood are among relatives and kinfolk, then the idea of the urban neighborhood assumes a strength and a character which, perhaps, many have tended to ignore. The neighborhood can be an extended family, or so it can be defined if the three ideas of local vicinity, friendship choice, and family relations are more than randomly united. If this pattern varies, and is more important for some ethnic groups than for others, as it indeed is, it is crucial for urban planning and urban development. The problem of urban renewal seems all the more momentous because it so frequently tends to ignore this very kind of consideration.

Another important background factor, certainly, is the level of formal education one has reached. The findings on this question show, as might be expected, that education does correlate with occupation; people with white collar jobs tend to have more formal education (Table 2-6). But the fact of ethnic diversity is just as real, within each occupational category. The percentage of those who have at least some college experience or more covers a wide range among white collar job holders; 62 percent of the white collar Polish. The differences in this area may well be due to the influence of generation in the United States and Connecticut, since the Irish immigrated to America in periods before most of the Polish did. But it is precisely this kind of diversity which needs to be accounted for in understanding the pluralism of the United States.

A relevant economic factor is, of course, family income. Again, as with education, one might expect that white collar jobs produce more income on the

Table 2-6
Percent With Some College Education or More, by Religio-Ethnic Group and Class

Religio-Ethnic Group	White Collar	Blue Collar	Total
Blacks	27	6	10
Protestants	53	10	31
Jews	49	19	41
Catholics	40	11	22
Eastern European	20	14	16
English	48	18	33
French-Canadian	35	5	13
German	48	24	40
Irish	62	21	41
Italian	31	9	17
Polish	18	13	14
Spanish-speaking	_a	1	2
Total	44	10	23

aToo few cases for percentaging.

average, but this is actually not always true. It is true for the total population; 28 percent of the white collars in this study had family incomes over $10,000, but only 10 percent of the blue collars were this affluent. And, this pattern is most evident for the German Catholics and the Jews; their increase from blue collar to white collar is the greater, for all groups (Table 2-7). But, the blacks, the Eastern Europeans, the Irish, and the Polish show less gain in income between the two occupational categories. Thus, not only is there diversity within the total population when seen ethnically, but the patterns themselves are variable by ethnic group.

One aspect of income is the question of poverty in America, and attitudes toward the poverty issue are a most important segment of public opinion. The central city residents interviewed in Connecticut were questioned on how they felt about the government's role on the problems of poverty. They were specifically asked if the federal government should do more to fight poverty, should do less, or if they felt that the government is doing the right amount at the present time. Fifty-five percent of all those interviewed said that the government should do more (Table 2-8). Again, ethnic groups show some differences on this question. The blacks and the Spanish-speaking stand out as most supportive on more federal activity, and the Polish and Irish Catholics appear as less so.

Class differences, we would expect, might be obviously relevant here, and the data support our expectations. Blue collar workers are 61 percent in favor of

Table 2-7
Percent Whose Annual Family Income Is Over $10,000, by Religio-Ethnic Group and Class

Religio-Ethnic Group	White Collar	Blue Collar	Total
Blacks	13	7	8
Protestants	27	10	18
Jews	41	4	32
Catholics	26	13	17
Eastern European	26	22	23
English	33	19	26
French-Canadian	26	11	15
German	43	7	30
Irish	25	24	24
Italian	22	9	14
Polish	12	11	11
Spanish-speaking	—a	0	0
Total	28	10	17

aToo few cases for percentaging.

Table 2-8
Percent Who Feel the Federal Government Should Do More to Help the Poor, by Religio-Ethnic Group and Class

Religio-Ethnic Group	White Collar	Blue Collar	Total
Blacks	63	77	76
Protestants	44	51	48
Jews	51	43	49
Catholics	40	57	51
Eastern European	35	66	56
English	38	58	48
French-Canadian	33	65	56
German	44	67	51
Irish	33	54	44
Italian	48	51	50
Polish	33	41	39
Spanish-speaking	—a	63	62
Total	44	61	55

aToo few cases for percentaging.

greater government activity, while white collar workers are only 44 percent in favor. There are some ethnic differences here too. For the most part, blue collar workers from each ethnic group are more interested in seeing federal activity increase in poverty programs, with the exception of the Jews. The Jewish blue collars, like the Polish Catholic working class, are among the least supportive of more federal activity on this issue. For the Italians, there seems to be no class difference; half of each of the white collars and the blue collars among the Italian Catholics favor more government activity, rather than less or the status quo.

The interesting finding here, it would seem, is that a plurality of almost all of the groups are behind the idea of a greater government role in solving the problems of poverty. On the surface, one might expect a plurality in support of the status quo. This is not the case, however. Religious and racial and ethnic groups in Connecticut are fairly united on generalized support for the notion that the federal government not only has a role to play in poverty issues, but that its role should be even greater than it presently is.

Support of the government's role in poverty and welfare issues is historically linked to the Democrats, as opposed to the Republicans. What are the political party preferences of Connecticut's ethnic groups, as they emerged in this study? For total figures, 68 percent of all those interviewed in the central cities replied that they were Democrats or leaned toward the Democratic Party. Three-fourths or more of the blacks, the Jews, the Irish, and the Spanish-speaking, are Democrats, and a majority of every other group except the white Protestants tend to support this party (Table 2-9).

Table 2-9
Political Party Preference, by Religio-Ethnic Group and Class (in Percentages)

Religio-Ethnic Group	White Collar				Blue Collar				Total			
	Dem	Rep	Ind	Total	Dem	Rep	Ind	Total	Dem	Rep	Ind	Total
Blacks	83	9	8	100	87	7	6	100	86	7	7	100
Protestants	29	56	15	100	47	34	19	100	38	45	17	100
Jews	81	8	11	100	83	7	10	100	81	8	11	100
Catholics	59	24	17	100	76	12	12	100	70	16	14	100
Eastern European	76	19	5	100	67	14	19	100	70	16	14	100
English	54	31	15	100	60	24	16	100	57	27	16	100
French-Canadian	65	5	30	100	74	19	7	100	71	15	14	100
German	42	34	24	100	79	7	14	100	53	26	21	100
Irish	63	19	18	100	86	5	9	100	75	12	13	100
Italian	60	28	12	100	80	12	8	100	73	18	9	100
Polish	62	19	19	100	64	14	22	100	64	15	21	100
Spanish-speaking	—	—	—	—	88	8	4	100	87	10	3	100
Total	57	28	15	100	75	14	11	100	67	20	13	100

Class membership is important. For the total, there are twice as many Republicans among white collar workers as there are among blue collar job holders, and this of course supports the general and repeated finding that political party relates very strongly to social class and economic status. But the total figures mask ethnic diversity. The reality of ethnic politics is such that there are exceptions. White collar workers among the blacks, the Jews, those from Eastern European backgrounds, and the Polish Catholics tend to be Democrats as well, at least as strongly as they are represented among the blue collar counterparts in these groups. Other ethnic backgrounds show some change in the percentage Democratic between blue collar and white collar politics, but the changes are variable.

The last research to be reported here is a generalized subjective feeling about race relations between blacks and whites in Connecticut. Central city residents were asked for their perception of the race climate in their cities; was it getting better, staying the same, or getting worse, with reference to how they thought things used to be in the last five years or so? As the total figures emerge, there are no differences by occupational class position. Thirty-one percent of all respondents felt racial matters were getting better, 40 percent felt the climate was staying the same, and 28 percent said that race relations were getting worse (Table 2-10). This is about one-third in each category. By ethnicity, however, German Catholics and Eastern Europeans were more likely to feel things were deteriorating, blacks as a group were more likely to see things staying the same, and Jews were more likely to see the race climate as improving. All other groups

Table 2-10

Perception of Race Relations (Getting Better, Staying the Same, Getting Worse), by Religio-Ethnic Group and Class (in Percentages)

Religio-Ethnic Group	White Collar				Blue Collar				Total			
	Better	Same	Worse		Better	Same	Worse		Better	Same	Worse	
Blacks	52	45	3	100	39	53	8	100	40	52	8	100
Protestants	32	43	25	100	28	34	38	100	30	38	32	100
Jews	48	30	22	100	36	39	25	100	45	32	23	100
Catholics	27	38	35	100	27	39	34	100	27	39	34	100
Eastern European	22	33	45	100	20	36	44	100	21	35	44	100
English	38	43	19	100	33	46	21	100	36	44	20	100
French-Canadian	28	33	39	100	31	44	25	100	30	41	29	100
German	25	33	42	100	6	44	50	100	18	37	45	100
Irish	38	41	21	100	28	35	37	100	33	38	29	100
Italian	18	39	43	100	32	40	28	100	27	40	33	100
Polish	25	33	42	100	19	42	39	100	20	41	39	100
Spanish-speaking	–	–	–	–	24	41	35	100	24	41	35	100
Total	33	39	28	100	30	42	28	100	32	40	28	100

were, by and large, roughly divided by these three opinions, and class position makes a difference only for some groups, and not always in the same way. Being white collar suggests that blacks, Jews, German Catholics, and Irish Catholics were more likely to see improvements, but Italian Catholics were more likely to see race relations getting better if they were blue collar workers.

When summing up the implications of these various findings and ideas, I wish to make several points. It is difficult, if not impossible, to draw sufficiently clear and complete portraits of ethnic behavior in a short presentation. The data as presented here are merely suggestions of ethnic differences. We cannot explain, at this stage, as much as we would like to, because the complexity of the questions involves so much more than what meets the eye. We have a good deal more to do in research in this area of inquiry, and we need to account for many more factors than mentioned above. The length of time an ethnic group has been in the United States or in an urban area, the subjective identification one has with his own ethnic background, the historical experience of an ethnic group in this country and abroad, and the specific values and way of life which may characterize any particular ethnic group—all these are important to realize before conclusions can be reached that are surer of reality.

On the other hand, if ethnicity were not important in American life today, then politics and family life and urban neighborhoods, to name a few instances, would not show the ethnic diversity that they do show, and differences in surveys of the American population would not emerge. Most interpretations of America that do emphasize differences usually, up to now, have dwelled on sectional cleavage—the values and interests of the North, and the South, the Middle West, and the Far West, and regions within these sections, such as New England—or on the class conflict between the haves and the have-nots, and between labor and management.

But ethnic pluralism may still be another way of interpreting the United States, and especially those areas such as Connecticut, where everybody in fairly recent memory has come from somewhere else, and where accommodation to the social and economic and political system is always being negotiated. Our American history and society has been a constant exchange of the negotiation of power, for example, and ethnic groups in America have always been involved in conflict, and even frequently in violence, because of this negotiation.

The ethnic and economic interests in Black Power, now, among Afro-Americans in the United States, or the struggles in the Grape Strike in California among Mexican-Americans, are in the same tradition of the Molly Maguires among the down-trodden Irish coal workers in Eastern Pennsylvania, or the conflicts of Italian laborers in New Orleans and in the railroad towns of Colorado, or the efforts of the Chinese to ward off massacres and lynchings in the Far West. The tradition is one that combines ethnicity and economic necessity, and one that usually combines elements of powerlessness with ethnic differences. Some trends of the present may de-emphasize ethnic diversity, but the reality of the American past and persisting cultural variations suggest that ethnic pluralism is not just romanticism but a force in American society which has long had a role in shaping intergroup relations, and which we may be just beginning to understand.

3

Ethnicity in American Life: A Social-Psychological Perspective

Thomas F. Pettigrew

In the introductory remarks to my lecture at the Centennial Celebration of Loyola University, I said, "I am a second-generation Scots-American and a southern-born and reared Protestant. I now teach at a New England University. I was invited to speak by a national Jewish organization, the Anti-Defamation League, and a Mid-western Negro organization, the Chicago Urban League, in order to celebrate the one-hundredth anniversary of a Roman Catholic university!"

Therein lies my chief point. This is hardly evidence for the old idea of a melting pot, or at least a triple melting pot, society.[1] But it is certainly evidence against the popular and dangerous counter-myth to the melting pot notion that is current in America today. Just as incorrect as what it proposes to replace, *the new myth of complete pluralism* does not do justice to the complexity and subtlety of intergroup relations in the United States in the last third of the twentieth century. We have neither complete assimilation nor pluralism. But whereas Israel Zangwill's melting pot myth at the turn of the century was highly functional for the society,[a] the presently fashionable myth of complete pluralism is a dysfunctional retreat from the critical intergroup issues at hand.[b]

Definitions and Functions

Before pursuing this theme further, let us first agree on some basic definitions, for ethnicity is a vague term allowing many meanings. Following Max Weber's classic definition, an ethnic group is a human collectivity based on an assumption of common origin, real or imagined. It has at least some values which contrast with those of the larger society, and it maintains some separate institutions and rituals. In the American case, of course, these distinctive values, institutions, and rituals are not mere reflections of life in the "old country," even life at the time the immigrants left it. Rather they have been importantly

This article is based on a speech presented at Loyola University, and is used with the permission of the Anti-Defamation of B'nai B'rith.

[a] The term "melting pot" took on common currency after Israel Zangwill's 1908 drama by that name.

[b] Professor John Hope Franklin has already espoused this position. It is reassuring when the historical and social psychological perspectives can reach the same conclusion. Total independence of judgment cannot be claimed, however, since Professor Franklin's writings have strongly influenced my thinking for many years.

29

shaped and molded by the American experience, by the group's reception and history in the New World.

For our present purposes, however, this definition casts the net too broadly, for under it virtually all identifiable groups in America become ethnic groups; hence, the term loses its conceptual and analytical value. It is useful, then, in the American context to narrow the definition to nationality groups, in particular to post-1840 immigrant groups. Oscar Handlin[2] and others have argued that black Americans are just another ethnic group, distinguished largely by their late arrival to the nation's biggest cities as well as by their color. But such a view ignores the crushing effects of two centuries of degrading slavery and another of debilitating segregation. It is often useful to apply cautiously ethnic analogies to American race relations, but it is dangerously misleading to mistake black Americans as yet another ethnic group.

Defined in this manner, Father Andrew Greeley has neatly summarized the functions, positive and negative, of American ethnic groups:

They keep cultural traditions alive, provide us with preferred associates, help organize the social structure, offer opportunities for mobility and success, and enable men to identify themselves in the face of the threatening chaos of a large and impersonal society. On the other hand, they reinforce exclusiveness, suspicion, and distrust, and . . . serve as ideal foci for conflict. Finally, ethnic groups are something like the Rocky Mountains or the Atlantic Ocean—whether we like them or not really doesn't matter very much; they are concrete realities with which we must cope, and condemning or praising them is a waste of time.[3]

Indeed, "condemning or praising" ethnic groups *is* "a waste of time." Our national defensiveness, which we often betray in condemning them, is due in large part, I believe, to our failure to see how cultural diversity and richness can contribute to rather than detract from, a stable, unified American society. Perhaps, from our history of inter-ethnic conflict and our struggles to become "American" in every conceivable sense, many have come to regard ethnicity as somehow "un-American." But that was an earlier phenomenon. At present we are busy praising ethnicity out of all proportion and questioning the old concept of "American" as either a "white man's world" or "an Anglo-Protestant world." Ethnic Americans, we are told, are the forgotten Americans, the silent Americans, the little people whom the nation has ignored while concentrating on black America. While there is a kernel of truth to this reasoning, as we shall see shortly, it is often carried to such extremes as to become *the new myth of complete pluralism*, upon which I wish to concentrate for the remainder of the lecture.

Assimilation and Pluralism Form One Process

For a social psychological perspective on ethnicity, three central and interrelated points need emphasis. First, in a nation of immigrants, assimilation is not the opposite of but part of the same process as pluralism. The two conceptually-separate processes are in reality inseparable parts of the same ball of wax called American society. In such a society, any claims of complete pluralism are even more absurd than the melting pot metaphor.

Father Greeley, an important contributor to this field of study in social science, has proposed a fascinating, if speculative, six-step paradigm for the American acculturation and assimilation process which illustrates its interwoven quality with pluralism.

1. *Cultural shock*—among the new arrivals.
2. *Organization and self-consciousness*—and sometimes the actual initiation of a sense of nationalism for the "old country."
3. *Assimilation of the elite.*
4. *Militancy*—led by the elite and made possible by the accumulation of at least a modicum of power.
5. *Self-hatred and anti-militancy*—articulated most strongly again by the group's elite in reaction to the previous stage.
6. *Emerging adjustment*—signifying an easy acceptance of both the ethnic and "American" identities as completely compatible.[4]

Greeley further speculates that black Americans are currently moving as a group into the fourth stage of militancy; that the Italo-Americans and Polish-Americans are now in the midst of this stage; that both Irish-Americans and German-Americans have since World War II been largely operating in stage five—self-hatred and anti-militancy; and, he adds hopefully, that the first signs of true stage six behavior—emerging adjustment—can now be detected among young Irish-Americans in their twenties. He points out that if blacks seem unusually militant to white Americans at the moment, they might remember their own fathers and grandfathers when their group was at a similar time in their assimilation to the wider society. Finally, Greeley notes that regression is clearly possible, when an ethnic group under particular stress or threatened loss of power slips back to an earlier mode of behavior and outlook.

Like the Netherlands' complex and unique structural arrangements and "rules of the game" between religious, political, and social groups,[c] the United States has evolved its own unique intergroup structural arrangements and "rules of the game." Milton Gordon, in his valuable volume, *Assimilation in American Life*, distinguishes between two kinds of assimilation.[5] The first kind is behavioral or cultural assimilation, or, more simply, *acculturation*, which is the process of learning the manners and style of a new society. The second kind is structural assimilation, or, more simply, *assimilation*, which involves "large-scale entrance

---

[c]The Dutch system of *verzuiling* is as complex as it is fascinating, but it has led to an orderly, loyal, unified state by providing a separate *zuil*, or pillar, for each major religious and social class interest group. As the Dutch metaphor goes, separate *zuilen* are all important pillars in supporting the one national roof. See: Johan Goudsblom, *Dutch Society* (New York: Random House, 1967).

into cliques, clubs, and institutions of [the] host society" and the dissolution of group differences even at the most intimate primary levels of friendship and family. Gordon stresses the fact that acculturation can occur without significant assimilation taking place; but once assimilation at the structural level begins to take place it also marks a reduction in prejudice, discrimination, and intergroup conflict as well as the development of a sense of "peoplehood" within the ethnicity based exclusively on the host society.

Within this clarifying framework, Gordon argues that America today witnesses mass acculturation side by side with only moderate assimilation. Indeed, the society is intolerant of groups which refuse to acculturate, but is rather tolerant of structural separation within limits. Yet under this system, binding ties across groups develop on the job, etc., without necessarily breaking down segregation at the more intimate levels. In fact, this American tendency can lead to some situations which seem rather odd at first glance. Consider, for example, a neighborhood of white steel workers in East Chicago, Indiana.[6] These men were all members of the same racially-desegregated union and worked in thoroughly desegregated plants. Thus, Negroes held elected positions as shop stewards, executive board members, and vice-president of the union and shared with whites the same locker rooms, lunch rooms, showers, and toilets in both the union hall and the plants. Only twelve percent of the 151 whites who were studied evidenced "low acceptance" of Negroes in this work situation; and the deeper their involvement in union activities, the greater was their acceptance of Negroes as co-workers. But neighborhood acceptance was a vastly different matter. Bolstered by a neighborhood organization which opposed desegregation, 86 percent of the white steel workers rejected the idea of allowing Negroes to live near them, with those men most involved in the collective life of the neighborhood evincing the most adamant opposition. The effects of harmonious interracial patterns in employment, then, did not extend to housing. No relationship existed between acceptance of Negroes as fellow workers and acceptance of them as neighbors. Note, too, how the steel workers in each situation conformed to the norms of the positive reference group—either the union or the neighborhood organization, thus revealing the critical importance of institutional structures in determining the rate and degree of assimilation.

The Problems of Ethnic Solidarity

The second social psychological point deserving emphasis involves the problems of ethnic solidarity. Some spokesmen see in *the new myth of complete pluralism* a golden opportunity to advance personal and group aims. "Black power" is the most publicized version of this type of statement; but talk of "Irish power," "Italian power," "Polish power," "Chicano power," etc., or their equivalents are also on the upswing. But ethnic solidarity for the advancement of group aims is a two-edged sword in general, and in a nation such as ours in particular. While in the short run it is often an advantage for individuals to emphasize minority solidarity, it frequently works in the long run as a disadvantage for the *group* as a whole.[7]

Especially is this so when group solidarity entails resistance to even basic acculturation. But there are disadvantages, as well as advantages, too, when group solidarity sternly resists structural assimilation. In Greeley's fourth stage of militancy, the group grossly exaggerates the advantages of structural separation. This is the period when there emerges an array of substitute institutions—for instance, a Catholic Lawyers Guild, Catholic sociological, historical, and psychological societies, etc. But the fifth stage of self-hatred and anti-militancy is a sharp reaction to this trend, and often involves an overemphasis upon the disadvantages of structural separation. Greeley's optimism is expressed in his hypothesized sixth stage of emerging adjustment where a balance is struck between these two pulls.

Elsewhere the present writer has attempted to set down the pitfalls for black separatism within the American race relations context.[8] For ethnic groups directly, Greeley stresses the fourth stage disadvantage of what he describes as "the mobility trap." This trap entails rapid mobility for talented leaders and professionals within the ethnic group at the high cost of cutting themselves off from the less certain but more significant mobility in the wider society.[9]

Ethnicity Is Not Basically Causal in American Race Relations

The third social-psychological consideration of importance involves a correction of the widespread misconception that ethnicity is somehow a basic causal factor in generating white prejudice and discrimination against black Americans. To be sure, ethnicity is, like race, conspicuous in some parts of the country such as Chicago. Hence, it becomes easy to commit the error of assuming it to be causal when in fact other factors strongly associated with ethnicity, such as social class, are crucial. This phenomenon can be forcefully illustrated with voting and opinion survey data that are relevant to the alleged "ethnic backlash," which in actuality is a corollary to the more general *myth of complete pluralism* under discussion.

Consider the 1968 vote for George Wallace for president in three cities, Cleveland, Gary, and Boston, noted for their unusually strong maintenance of ethnic ties and structure. Even at the aggregate level, the mass media contention that angry ethnic Americans were the backbone of Wallace's northern following appears highly questionable. The salience of ethnicity in these cities led some political observers to inspect only the raw Wallace voting totals in heavily ethnic areas. When this is done naively without relevant controls, precincts with varying ethnic compositions tended to vote somewhat differently for or against the southern ex-governor in Gary and Boston but not in Cleveland. In general, Polish precincts in Gary and Irish precincts in Boston cast relatively more Wallace ballots, while the foreign-born districts in Gary and Jewish districts in Boston cast relatively fewer.[d] And when such social class variables as the areas' levels of education, income, rent, and house value are entered into the regression equations, these few trends are substantially reduced. Likewise, precincts with relatively large numbers of first-generation Americans tended to cast *fewer* votes for the Alabamian in Cleveland and Gary, while no trend at all is evident in Boston.[e]

It is dangerous, of course, to draw final conclusions about individuals on the basis of area data alone. To avoid this "ecological fallacy," my Harvard research project has also—with the invaluable assistance of the University of Chicago's National Opinion Research Center—conducted probability surveys of the white residents of Gary and Cleveland. When this is done, we find in Gary—where the aggregate data by precinct suggested some relationship between ethnicity and Wallace voting—a most revealing pattern. Those Polish-Americans and other ethnic Americans who intended to vote for Wallace tended to be *marginal* members of their ethnic communities at best. Those who indicated that they had no close friends of their group were twice as likely to support the candidate of the American Independent Party than comparable respondents who reported having close friends of their ethnic group.[f]

Wallacites were also more likely to be considering moving from their present neighborhood where they have not lived very long and which they tend to find only "fairly" warm and friendly. In short, Wallacites in Gary are not *self-identified* ethnic Americans. In any meaningful social psychological sense, they are not ethnics at all. To think of them as angry ethnics in revolt, as many mass media observers have unhesitatingly done, is to confuse a mere *social category* with a true *social group* which is referent for the individuals in question.

If Wallace voting in highly ethnic cities was not actually an ethnic phenomenon, what was it? What was the actual dynamic that the myth of complete pluralism and its corollary of ethnic backlash is attempting imperfectly to explain? Our data from Cleveland, Gary, and Boston lead us to construct a

---

[d]These results are not completely in line with the anti-Negro data presented by Greeley (Why Can't They Be Like Us?, pp. 46-51). Without applying the needed social class controls, he found Polish-Americans the most anti-black among his ethnic group comparisons, save for relatively tolerant Polish college graduates; and he found Irish-Americans unusually tolerant. Our data coincide with his first, but not his second, result.

[e]These results with the first-generation variable derive from nineteen-variable prediction regressions which in effect control for social class. Interestingly, these Cleveland and Gary findings for the foreign-born coincide with the results of van der Slik on congressional voting for Civil Rights laws in the sixties. Of twenty-one independent census variables measuring the constituencies of the members of the House of Representatives, percent foreign-born proved the best predictor of pro-Civil Rights voting (Spearman Rho correlation = +.643; for just Democrats = +.767; for just Republicans = +.230). Jack R. van der Slik, "Constituency characteristics and roll call voting on Negro rights in the 88th Congress," *Social Science Quarterly*, 1968, Vol. 49 (3), pp. 720-731.

[f]Those answering "don't know" to this query about the ethnicity of close friends were combined with those saying "none" since it implies a very low salience for ethnicity.

two-factor theory, each aspect of which is correlated positively with ethnicity and thus created the confusion over the basic cause of the phenomenon. The first factor is a specific social class effect. Indeed, Wallace support in Gary, we found, drew from one of the narrowest social ranges we have ever observed in American political data. Hence, the typical Gary voter for Wallace was a lower middle class male who had some high school education and was highly identified with the "working class." He was generally below forty years of age, a skilled craftsman, and making an annual family income between $7,500 and $10,000. Within this narrow social spectrum, our second explanatory factor is social psychological. Gary Wallacites, when compared with similar workers, are in an extreme state of relative deprivation. Thus, controlling for relevant social class variables, they were far more likely than their peers to agree that: "In spite of what some people say, the lot of the average man is getting worse, not better." Wallacites also tended to be more anti-black and more generally distrustful than others, but it was feelings of acute relative deprivation that most distinguishes them psychologically. They have typically done better than their fathers and are objectively fairly secure; but like black Americans, they have high aspirations without a sense of making progress toward their goals. Worse, they believe that Negroes and others are unjustly making rapid strides forward at their expense, helped out by a too generous federal government that has forgotten them. Spontaneous comments make it clear that more than others in their position, the American Independent Party's faithful believe that they are victims of a national effort to aid through public welfare and Office of Economic Opportunity programs those who "refuse to work" while heavily taxing those who "have worked hard all their lives to get where they are now."

The bitter irony for our nation is that the same powerful social psychological mechanism—relative deprivation—is leading to racial strife on *both* sides of the color line. Black Americans typically regard themselves as victims of injustice when they compare their still largely low status with that of other Americans. Yet the white Wallace voters in Gary shared much the same feeling. They understandably deduced from all the publicity about civil rights gains of the past decade that Negroes, in contrast with themselves, were in fact "making it big." Yet the hard truth is that most blacks are not "making it"—indeed, do not as a group approach the position of the threatened Wallacites.

This ironical situation, then, is a true measure of the extreme difficulty and madness of our times. Thanks in part to an unwelcome and draining foreign war, thanks in part to the politician's natural bent to publicize and hail progress before it has been achieved, we find ourselves as a society in the 1970s in a "worst of both worlds" situation. On the one hand, many aspiring young members of the white working class are threatened and angry in the manner one might have expected had the nation actually delivered on its high promises to its black citizens. And on the other hand, many aspiring young blacks are angry and frustrated because the nation did not in fact deliver to the black rank-and-file. The federal government, therefore, stands condemned as if it had actually made a lasting and significant difference for most black Americans, and equally condemned because it in fact did not make this difference. The United States finds itself thus caught in a vise of its own making, a vise which Adlai Stevenson in the 1950s accurately labeled as "the age of rising expectations."

Attention to "the forgotten Americans" *is* needed, and ethnic organization might well be one of the routes to pursue. But, as Irving Levine has indicated, truly effective governmental "attention" must be based realistically on the social structural and social psychological roots of the problem.[10] And given the comparable psychological feelings and economic concerns between those marginal ethnics "in revolt" and many young black Americans, political coalitions, at least at the leadership level, are obviously called for.

A Final Word

America can never understand herself or achieve full justice until she strips away the intergroup myths that cloud her thinking. And replacing one myth with another is hardly an improvement. We live now in a relatively anomic period of great change and vast disillusionment. Understandably, such a period has fashioned a myth of complete pluralism; that we are *not* only not what we have claimed to be but that our nation of immigrants remains a nation of largely *separated* immigrants. In resisting such views, we must be careful to avoid swinging the pendulum back to 1908 and the melting pot. Merely rejecting myths is not enough. We need to look at ourselves coldly and boldly, to ply the developing tools of social science to best advantage, and to learn more about the complexity and subtlety of our nation's intergroup relations that cannot be captured in memorable metaphors or dogmatic ideologies.

Let me end as I began, if I may, with a personal experience in American ethnicity. Father Greeley closes his sprightly monograph, *Why Can't They Be Like Us?*, with a poignant episode which occurred in front of a church in the west of Ireland where one of his grandfathers had been baptized in the nineteenth century. While preparing to take a photograph of the structure, Greeley was asked by the parish priest if he wanted his grandfather's baptismal record. Greeley replied he did not, but wondered if a lot of Americans came seeking such records. "Indeed they do," remarked the priest with sincere sympathy. "Those poor people, you know, they've been in the states now for three generations and they come seeking roots; they want to know who they are; they want to know all about their past and their ancestors. The poor people, I feel so sorry for them."[11]

But, alas, this story in the complete pluralist vein is incomplete. I, too, "returned" with my immigrant mother to "the old country"—Scotland. And we went to Inverness to check on our roots, and even found the Fraser homeplace still inhabited by Frasers. But I do not need the heartfelt sympathy of the Irish parish priest. For I learned how different I really was from my Scots relatives, whom I liked very much. In short, though proud to be of Scottish origin, what I really found was that my roots are in America, that I am disgustingly American.

Perhaps, the best way to dispel the myth of complete pluralism would be to have Americans, black and white, of all religions and nationality groups, return to their supposed "homelands" and learn the same thing.

Notes

1. See: R.J.R. Kennedy, "Single or triple melting pot?" *American Journal of Sociology*, 1944, Vol. 49, 331-339; and again in *American Journal of Sociology*, 1952, Vol. 58, 56-59. The "triple melting pot" of the three religions, rather than the older single melting pot notion, was introduced by Ruby Jo Reeves Kennedy after study of the intermarriage trends in New Haven from 1870 through 1940. Will Herberg later popularized the concept in his *Protestant-Catholic-Jew* (New York: Doubleday, 1955).

2. Oscar Handlin, "The goals of integration," in T. Parsons and K. Clark (eds.), *The Negro American* (Boston: Houghton Mifflin, 1966), pp. 659-677.

3. Andrew M. Greeley, *Why Can't They Be Like Us?* (New York: Institute of Human Relations Press, 1969), p. 30.

4. Ibid., pp. 31-37.

5. Milton Gordon, *Assimilation in American Life* (New York: Oxford, 1964).

6. J.D. Lohman and D.C. Reitzes, "Notes on race relations in mass society," *American Journal of Sociology*, 1952, Vol. 58, 240-246; J.D. Lohman and D.C. Reitzes, "Deliberately organized groups and racial behavior," *American Sociological Review*, 1954, Vol. 19, 342-344; and D.C. Reitzes, "The role of organizational structures: Union versus neighborhood in a tense situation," *Journal of Social Issues* 1953, Vol. 9 (1), 37-44.

7. H.M. Blalock, Jr., *Toward a Theory of Minority-Group Relations* (New York: Wiley, 1967), p. 84.

8. T.F. Pettigrew, *Racially Separate or Together?* (New York: McGraw-Hill, Inc., 1970), Chapter 13.

9. Greeley, *Why Can't They Be Like Us?*, pp. 29-30.

10. Irving M. Levine, "Government's role in meeting some important needs of America's lower middle class white ethnic citizens." Statement prepared for Chicago Consultation on Ethnicity, University of Illinois Chicago Center, November 17-18, 1969.

11. Greeley, *Why Can't They Be Like Us?*, pp. 74-75.

4

Adjustment vs. Assimilation: Immigrant Minority Groups and Intra-Ethnic Conflicts

Djuro J. Vrga

The Nature of Immigrant Minority Groups

No ethnic minority group, including a predominantly immigrant one, is homogeneous and undifferentiated although it may appear as such to the majority group and to other minority groups.[a] Moreover, "immigrant groups from different nations are neither fair samplings of their home population nor comparable among themselves," and their differential behavior "may simply reflect their former environmental background."[1] Furthermore, the immigration itself is a factor which greatly affects the immigrant's intellectual make-up, the organization and the direction of his emotional reactions. Finally, the contact situation in the new society is of crucial importance for the immigrant's successful adjustment to new conditions. This contact situation may be that of superordination, subordination, or equality, of intolerance, acceptance, or indifference.[b]

Most immigrants in America came from two major immigrations: old immigrants who immigrated before World War II, and new immigrants who came to America after World War II. While the old immigrants from Central and Eastern Europe represent a more homogeneous group, the new immigrants are sharply divided into three categories: the refugees, the escapees, and the recent immigrants who left their native countries legally.

Refugees and escapees or displaced persons represent the great majority of

---

[a]Kurt Lewin states, "Members of the majority are accustomed to think of a minority as a homogeneous group which they can characterize by a stereotype like 'the Jew' or 'the Negro.'" *Resolving Social Conflicts*, ed. Gertrude Weiss Lewin (New York: Harper and Brothers, 1948), p. 194.

[b]In his "A Societal Theory of Race and Ethnic Relations," *American Sociological Review*, XXVI (1961), 902-910, Stanley Lieberson distinguishes two types of superordination-subordinate contact situations: one in which the indigenous population is superordinate and the other in which the migrants are superordinate. See also R.A. Schermerhorn, "Polarity in the Approach to Comparative Research in Ethnic Relations," *Sociology and Social Research*, LI (January, 1967), 235-240.

39

the new or post-World War II immigration from several European countries.[c] Unlike the old immigrants, they came in groups. Besides their educational and occupational differentiation, these refugees exhibit other vertical and horizontal differentiations which make them the most heterogeneous immigrant group. They can be classified according to their activity during the war, when many of them were German war prisoners as Army officers and soldiers who had fallen into German captivity after the short war between the Axis powers and their native countries. A good number of refugees were either in German concentration camps or in forced labor camps during the war. There were also refugees from the countries allied with Nazi Germany; simply, from all countries which came under Soviet domination after the war. Refugee immigrants brought with them their hopes, desires, expectations, aspirations, disappointments, anxieties, and frustrations. Each refugee sub-group defined its situation in emigration in its own way.

Categorization should be used for distinguishing the old immigrants, the refugees, the escapees, the recent immigrants and their American-born descendants. Otherwise, the broader categorization of the old and the new immigrants, and the American-born is used most often. In addition, the categorization by the motivation for immigration—economic and political—as often used by the immigrants themselves in either an approving or derogatory sense, should also be used when issues of relevant importance come up for discussion.

Three Sets of Variables

Three sets of factors—the environmental background, the immigration itself, and the contact situation—are of essential importance for the understanding of the composition and functioning of a predominantly immigrant ethnic group which consists of several successive immigrations and their American-born descendants. The contact situation between the various successive immigrations appears to be of special significance. The kind and degree of mutual acceptance are conditioned by all three above mentioned sets of factors, each of which has its time dimensions.

The environmental background is a combination of several socio-cultural variables by which the successive immigrations, or more precisely the immigrant

---

[c] "'Refugee' means any person in a country or area which is neither Communist nor Communist-dominated, who, because of persecution, fear of persecution, natural calamity or military operations is out of his usual place of abode and unable to return thereto, who has not been firmly resettled and who is in urgent need of assistance for the essentials of life, or for transportation." *Refugee Relief Act*, PL83-203, Section 2 (a), approved August 7, 1953. "'Escapee' means any refugee who, because of persecution or fear of persecution on account of race, religion, or politcal opinion, fled from the Union of Soviet Socialist Republics or other Communist, Communist-dominated or Communist-occupied areas of Europe, including those parts of Germany under military occupation of the Union of Soviet Socialist Republic and who cannot return thereof because of fear or persecution on account of race, religion, or political opinion." Ibid., Section 2 (b).

categories, differ from one another. One of these variables, the province of origin with the political sovereignty over it, should be touched upon in the case of many immigrant ethnic minorities. It is usually taken as a cultural area with all its peculiarities, shaped in the course of historical processes.

The level of formal education, occupation, and age at the time of leaving the native country are also pre-emigration environmental variables which have a strong bearing on the immigrant's occupational opportunities in the new society. They also affect the acceptance of the successive immigrations by each other. While the old immigrants from many European countries came mainly from the peasant stratum, the new immigrants, especially the refugees, represent a cross-section of their native societies including peasants, factory workers, officials, proprietors, professionals, politicians, and intellectuals.

The immigration itself includes three main sets of variables: the motivation, the conditions under which immigration occurred, and the intervening history. In this respect, the difference between the successive immigrations or immigrant categories is of essential importance for the understanding of attitudes of the different immigrant categories toward each other, toward their American-born children, and toward the larger American society. These variables, in conjunction with the variables from the pre-emigration environmental background, set the boundaries of the immigrant's goal achievements and shape his self-perception. In reference to the adjustment of immigrants, Oscar Handlin strongly emphasizes the importance of background factors by saying, "In understanding the character of that adjustment, it is essential to know about the circumstances under which the newcomers departed from their lands of birth."[2]

The contact situation refers to the position which the host society deems proper for the immigrant and the subsequent treatment which it accords him. It also refers to the acceptance of the immigrants by the preceding immigration. A sizable later immigration may cause uneasiness and discomfort to an earlier immigration which has its organized communal life, especially if the differences between the two immigrations are significant in terms of their background. Thus, besides the need of minimal integration into the larger society, later immigrations are faced with the problem of integration into the preceding immigration of their nationals. Therefore, whether the preceding immigration can or cannot absorb the following immigration without drastic alterations of its stabilized structure and network of organizations is of crucial importance for their mutual adjustment.

Adjustment of Immigrants

Structural changes in many European ethnic minority groups were brought about after World War II by the influx of a great number of immigrants, admitted to the United States under the provisions of the Displaced Persons Act of 1948 and the Refugee Relief Act of 1953. Their entry was sponsored by their national organizations in America, their churches, and individuals who considered it their national and humanitarian obligation to help their nationals who had suffered in Nazi war prisons and/or concentration camps or had fought the Nazis and communist partisans, or whose country had fallen under Soviet domination.

As the number of new immigrants grew, differences between the old and new immigrants became more and more obvious. On both sides, the awareness of differences sharpened with the passing of time. The inclusion of new immigrants into the ethnic community was not an easy or smooth process. The limited number of existing organizations meant to satisfy the needs of the old immigrants and their American-born children could not provide a sufficient framework for the activities of the new immigrants with their diverse, often competing and mutually exclusive, political, social, and cultural interests and ambitions. While retaining membership in the organizations of old immigrants, the new immigrants soon launched new organizations with more or less inclusive programs. In the case of many immigrant minorities, their churches were the ground on which competing and antagonistic organizations tested their strength and measured their popularity in the ethnic community.

The changes in the predominantly immigrant ethnic community puts the organization of new associations and splits in churches in the perspective of social change which always results in greater or lesser strains and therefore requires a degree of adjustment on the part of those involved in them. The tendency of many members of immigrant ethnic minority groups to express their diverse needs within the framework of their ethnic community produces strains which culminate in conflict over the social function and role of their associations and churches and, in consequence, lead to a split of the whole group into two hostile parts.

In his analysis of socialization, Parsons maintains that "the mechanisms of adjustment are the processes by which the individual actor deals with elements of strain and conflict in his relations to objects, that is, to the situation of action."[3] In a modern complex society, the number of such situations is almost infinite. Therefore, the number of social situations in which an individual may be involved increases with social differentiation. While immigrants must make many adjustments within their own ethnic group, their minority status in the larger society is a source of additional strain. The latter requires a different type of adjustment which need not coincide with their intragroup adjustments. This is due to one's different orientation toward and attachments to his ethnic group and to the larger society. An immigrant finds himself in an especially difficult position when he is faced with conflicting role expectations in the larger society and in his narrow ethnic group.[d]

Therefore, when the question of adjustment of immigrants is raised, it does not imply that assimilation is neglected completely. For an understanding of the immigrant's life, it seems more fruitful and promising to explore the nature of a series of more or less painful adjustments imposed on him by his total social

---

[d]Internal conflict, in Parsons' interpretation, results from the actor's inability to solve his problem of conflicting role-expectations. *The Social System*, New York: The Free Press of Glencoe, 1964, p. 280.

situation. When the position of immigrants in a highly differentiated and pluralistic society, such as the American society, is in question, it seems more promising to address oneself to the problem of manifold intergroup adjustment, because no individual is completely adjusted to all segments of such a society.[e]

As the position of American Negroes cannot be adequately explained without reference to whites, so the problems of an immigrant ethnic minority in America—Jewish, Irish, Chinese, or any other—cannot be separated, in reality or analytically, from the group's position in the larger society. In this respect, the intragroup situation reflects, in a lesser or greater degree, what happens to the group as a whole or to its individual members in contact with other groups with which they are involved in a common social system. Reversely, from the point of sociological understanding of cultural pluralism, there is the need for a deeper insight into the dynamics and structure of racial, ethnic, and religious groups. Since these groups in America are not isolated and self-sustaining, their structure and function are affected by conditions in the whole society.

In the study of predominantly immigrant minority groups, the differential adjustment of immigrants should be taken as the main, although not the only frame of reference. According to Sheldon Stryker's definition, "the adjustment of the individual is a function of the accuracy with which he can take the role of the other(s) implicated with him in some social situation."[f] Adjustment, then, is a process by which the individual solves the problem of tension and acquires satisfaction, temporarily at least. Since the individual is constantly making adjustments due to changes in his own physical conditions or in the conditions of his total social and natural environment, the personality of an individual is considered "as his persistent tendencies to make certain kinds and qualities of adjustment," and the degree of coordination of "his various habits, perceptions, motives and emotions" determine whether an individual is adjusted or maladjusted.[4] Therefore, the greater the changes in the individual's life situation,

---

[e]Milton Gordon, *Assimilation in American Life* (New York: Oxford University Press, 1964), pp. 7-9. Yinger is very skeptical about the validity of the assimilation approach in the study of ethnic-religious groups because he agrees with Munch that two types of forces—one of assimilation and the other of differentiation—are at work simultaneously especially in a society which is composed of peoples of different ethnic and religious backgrounds. J. Milton Yinger, *Sociology Looks at Religion* (New York: The Macmillian Company, 1963), pp. 92-94.

[f]"Role-Taking Accuracy and Adjustment," *Sociometry*, XX (December, 1957), 286-296, reprinted in *Symbolic Interaction*, Jerome G. Manis and Bernard N. Meltzer (eds.) (Boston: Allyn and Bacon, 1967), p. 482. A definition implying social equilibrium as the most desired state of social relations can be found in *Dictionary of Sociology*, Henry Pratt Fairchild (ed.) (Ames, Iowa: Littlefield, Adams and Company, 1959), p. 4. According to this definition adjustment is "a condition or state of being in which the individual is in harmonious relations with a given social situation." Robert K. Merton prefers the term adaptation to adjustment, although he says that manifest functions refer to "those objective consequences for a specified unit (person, subgroup, social or cultural system) which contribute to its *adjustment or adaptation* and were so intended" (italics added). Robert Merton, *Social Theory and Social Structure*, (New York: The Free Press of Glencoe, 1956), p. 63.

the greater the efforts for effective adjustment. According to the situation-response approach to adjustment, "a maladjustment is always an inadequate response to present difficulties."[5] It is therefore possible to talk about various kinds of adjustments to a variety of situations in which an individual can find himself from time to time. From this perspective adjustment means, as Riesman suggests, "socio-psychological fit" rather than a kind of "adequacy in any evaluative sense," and thus, adjusted persons would be those who "reflect their society or class within the society with the least distortion" because they feel comfortable in their positions and in the roles assigned to them by the society.[6]

Although assimilation is most often the frame of reference in treating the immigrant's position in the host society, in the adjustment reference the attention is turned toward the immigrant and the ways he manages to overcome obstacles in finding satisfactory solutions to his problems in a new environment. In the adjustment reference, the immigrant's position in the new society, including his own ethnic group, is viewed as a combination of various situations in which he is engaged. Whether his response or reaction to a given situation is more cognitive or affective depends upon the combination of factors inherent in the situation on one hand and his dispositions and experiences on the other. As the newly-wed couple, the aged, the newly arrived people from rural areas to industrial cities and the convicted offenders on probation have to make changes in their habits and self perceptions so the immigrants must adjust to their new environment.[7] Many of these adjustments are similar to those made by a great number of native born citizens when they change their environment, especially in a large country whose population is highly differentiated occupationally and composed of peoples of different cultural, ethnic, and racial backgrounds.

The adjustment frame of reference in the study of predominantly immigrant minorities is proposed for reasons of analytical flexibility as well. Immigrant ethnic groups are predominantly composed of two large successive immigrations which differ from each other not only in the motivation for emigration, but in several other respects. Therefore, it is essential to the understanding of intragroup conditions to look at the problems which the two successive immigrations had to face in adjusting to each other. As all available evidence indicates, strains and conflicts in an immigrant ethnic group are likely to develop when the successive immigrations or parts thereof significantly differ in background, motivations or reasons for emigration, and in contact situations with the host society.

On the other hand, by taking adjustment as the frame of reference, it is possible to establish an approximate relationship between the two successive immigrations' adjustment to the larger American society and their adjustment to each other. The encounter of the post-war immigrants with their American-born ethnics who continue to identify with their ethnic group is of crucial importance for understanding different kinds and aspects of intra-ethnic group maladjustment.

For the above reasons, it is suggested that attention be focused on what may be called the dual adjustment of immigrants, i.e., first, the adjustment of successive immigrations to each other and, second, the adjustment of each immigration to the host society. The complexity of adjustment of new immigrants was recognized by President Kennedy when he said that "each new group was met by the groups already in America, and adjustments were often difficult and painful."[8] Oscar Handlin thinks that "the nature of the opportunities open to the immigrant and the length of time afforded him for adjustment" are more important for his adjustment than his cultural heritage.[9] The distinction between the two types of adjustment is especially prominant when one deals with ethnic minorities which are physically distinguishable, or belong to the cultural and linguistic stock significantly different from the majority of population of the host society.

Difference between the adjustment approach and the assimilation approach in the study of minority groups, predominantly immigrant ethnic minority groups, is manifold and of essential importance in the understanding of the position and roles of those groups. While the assimilation approach is socio-cultural in character from the viewpoint of the larger society or its dominant group, the adjustment approach is psycho-social in character from the viewpoints of both the dominant group and the minority group. In addition, the adjustment approach is existentialist in psycho-philosophical terms because the experience, expectations, hopes, and aspirations of members and segments of minority groups are of special significance for their acceptance of the host society. Therefore, the adjustment of immigrants can also be considered as the first stage of assimilation of immigrants.

Intragroup Conflict

The problem of intragroup conflict deserves serious attention in any systematic treatment of ethnic, especially predominantly immigrant, minority groups. Intragroup conflict becomes a significant theoretical issue when the adjustment approach is followed in the analysis of structure and dynamics of minority groups because this approach is psycho-social in its propositions and equal attention to the experienced internal strains by the socially imposed stresses on the individual members and segments of the minority group. The intraminority group conflict appears most often as a consequence of occupational displacement, role ambiguity, confusing expectations, unrecognized aspirations, and prestige frustration of many members or segments of the group. Quite often, latent aspirations may be an expression of differential perception of ethnic institutions and the tendencies of the dominant group. Although the intraminority group conflict does not often come to the attention of the dominant group, it definitely affects the structure and social role of the minority group and its members.

As a form of social process, conflict means "a struggle for power by contending forces, a clash of views, or a difference of opinion."[10] While having all of these characteristics, intragroup conflict, in its generic sense, is a social process which grows out of a series of lesser or greater disagreements concerning the common purpose of a group of people who minimize or disregard their similarities as the differences among their various segments become more accentuated. In conflict, unlike in competition, there is a mutual awareness among people involved in it.[11] In this sense, conflict is personal in character because of a strong emotional involvement of the participants.

Intragroup conflict is not necessarily a sudden, instantaneous break in group relations but rather an accumulation of prolonged tension which is manifested through sharpening competition between various subgroups. As soon as previously mild disagreements turn into antagonisms and when the group gradually becomes clearly divided on one or more issues relative to its structural arrangements and functions, conflict replaces competition. When this occurs, "the consensual basis of the relationship" or group life is disrupted and, in a relatively short period of time, previously small and isolated problem issues tend to fuse into one major issue of ideological proportions.[12] These issues call for a new self-identification by the proponents of both sides of the conflict. Small disagreements and apparently insignificant disputes which are contained in the major single issue, about whose consequences the conflicting sides cannot be fully aware, may be called "latent conflicts."[13]

It is these latent conflicts which indicate the direction in which the analysis of the main articulated issue should move. This analytical procedure is fruitful for the classification of overt conflicts which, as presented to the participants and to outsiders, may be either realistic or non-realistic, depending upon the motivation for the satisfaction of needs and socially valued aspirations.[14]

The degree of harmfulness of an intragroup conflict upon the group depends upon the structure of the group. "The closer the group, the more intense the conflict," Coser observes.[15] While an intragroup conflict may lead to the dissolution of the group, the conflict with out-groups increases its cohesion. While the "naturalness" of conflict is stressed and the integrating function of it emphasized, conflict is also considered "a kind of social problem," or as "a source of certain social problems."[16]

Intragroup conflict and group structure are tightly interrelated and act upon each other.[17] Other groups, singly or together, with which the group experiencing an inner conflict is in contact, have a strong bearing on its structure, function, and morale. Therefore, intragroup conflict may arise as a consequence of differential adjustment of various segments of the group to the conditions in the larger society. This situation may arise especially when the group experiences drastic structural changes while its functions remain unchanged or just slightly changed. While conflicts ensuing from that situation appear to be generated from within, their roots can also be traced in the total social structure.[18]

Intra-Ethnic Group Factionalism

Opposing sides in the controversies of ethnic minorities can be referred to as factions which have emerged after the injection of ideological issues into the conflict between various segments of the group. While the nature of intragroup conflict and the problem of immigrant adjustments were discussed separately, the treatment of factionalism is presented in the following pages. Not all intra-ethnic factionalisms grow out of intra-ethnic conflict over assimilation as Shibutani and Kwan suggest in their insightful discussion of factionalism in changing minorities.[19] Their contention that the basic issue in ethnic factionalism is that of identification holds true in all kinds of factionalism, but the problem of identification must not always be related to assimilation or acculturation. The reference group of the discontented must not be their whole ethnic group, but a narrow occupational group, political movement, or the provincial entity as well. It has been proved in several studies of ethnic cases that the manifest pronouncements of one or another faction may be in contradiction with their latent intentions.

Factionalism is a household concept in political science although its usage in the analysis of the American political scene has been replaced by concepts such as sectionalism, regionalism, blocs, cliques, and interest groups. In British constitutional history Edmund Burke warned against the danger of factionalism or a "politics of interest" in the struggle against oligarchy headed by the monarch.[20] The American Constitutional Convention worked in the shadow of the fear of factionalism[21] to which Madison devoted one of his essays in the *Federalist*. In his definition, a faction is composed of a number of citizens "who are united and actuated by some common impulse of passion, or of interest, adverse to the rights of other citizens, or to the permanent and aggregate interests of the community," and found the "latent causes of faction" in differences in opinion or in attachment to leaders or people of some other appealing characteristics.[22] He also suggested that the unequal distribution of property was most often the source of factionalism.

While the existence of political factions is deplored, factions in the American political system are considered as a natural resultant of the heterogeneity of the American population, a means to satisfy diverse needs and interest of people of different cultural background.[23]

Harold D. Lasswell defines a faction as a group "which works for the advacement of particular persons or policies."[24] Essentially, factions grow out of the struggle for power, although factional divisions may result from "divergent interpretations of the common goal or the efficious strategy."[25] Lasswell observes that factionalism appears when group members experience changes in their life situation, especially when the group is under external pressure. Similar observations were made by Siegel and Beals who distinguish external stress from internal strains.[26] Relevant to the subject of this study is Lasswell's conclusion that "the person may direct some of his aggressiveness against other members of the group" when his own group lacks opportunities in competition with other groups.[27]

The study of factionalism as a patterned type of intragroup conflict has been given much attention lately by Oscar Lewis, Raymond Firth, and others,[28] followed by Siegel and Beals' provocative typology of factions. A number of subsequent studies were carried on with reference to the theoretical propositions laid down by Lewis, Firth, and Siegel and Beals especially.

Although Siegel and Beals' typology is often criticized, it represents a valuable step toward a better understanding of intragroup conflicts. They distinguish two genuine types of factionalism: schismatic and pervasive. While schismatic factionalism is "conflict between well defined and cohesive subgroups within the larger group," pervasive factionalism is "conflict which occurs not only between larger sub-units of the group, but also within the sub-units."[29] Both kinds of factionalism most often result from changes in the situation of the group under external stress which affects the sub-units selectively and thus "tends to accentuate existing cleavage within the group."[30] The stress factor works in conjunction with strains which are already present, and refers to "acceptable techniques for the solution of either traditional problems or stresses."[31] Thus, factionalism appears as a maladaptive adjustment or reaction to stress and is therefore disruptive.

While concentrating on factionalism as a form of conflict, Siegel and Beals have paid little attention to the emergence and structure of factions and even less to the role of leaders who are considered, by some, the creators of factions.[32] However, the structure of factions is conditioned by the composition of the group, i.e., by its internal differentiation which may be economic, cultural, occupational, regional, or any other. While factions represent a cleavage in group relations, they differ from one another with regard to recruitment, internal solidarity, symbols, strategy, and leadership beside the difference in the conceptualization and interpretation of the main issue.

Permanent factional division in political parties leads to the organization of new parties. Therefore, it is said that the concept faction is not applicable when the factional split of the party becomes permanent.[33]

In the study of factionalism, internal strains and the effects of external pressure on group solidarity should be explored first through the analysis of group structure, and then the attitudes and beliefs of people involved in the controversy should be viewed in their relationship with the group structure and environmental factors.

The Status Group Struggle

The old immigrants from many European countries, with few exceptions, came from the peasantry. Their formal education did not go beyond elementary school or at best some kind of short craft training. In America, they almost all become unskilled factory workers. Only after years of hard labor, have some succeeded in starting small businesses or in moving up within the laboring class.

A small number of new immigrants from these countries were able to transfer their skills and specializations from the old country. More than any other occupational group, former army officers experienced more difficulties in adjusting to occupational changes regardless of their high military education. They had to accept the lowest ranking manual jobs, although many of them were already advancing in age.

In his analysis of achievements and adjustments of immigrants, Will Herberg emphasizes the opportunities for mobility in America but also recognizes that "Each new group, as it came, pushed upward the level of its predecessors, and was in turn pushed upward by its successors." He also admits that "this process of upward movement took place not without painful friction, not without conflict even . . ."[34]

Therefore, the occupational levelization of the great number of new immigrants with the old immigrants did not result in the feeling of the sameness of kind. Therefore, in their communal life, the status groups gradually appeared as a reaction to occupational levelization.[g] These status groups, in forms of various clubs and organizations, brought together people with similar experiences or former occupation. While the old immigrants accorded honors on the basis of the individual's class standing, the new immigrants, especially the refugees, could not accept the intragroup ranking on the basis of their class position in America, but on the basis of their pre-emigration social status. Consequently, these conflicting tendencies of different segments of various ethnic communities in ranking one another were soon felt even in their churches, the only institution in which they could find common ground for a minimal degree of cooperation.

Status Inconsistency and Factionalism

The differential adjustment of the various segments of different ethnic groups to one another on the one hand and to the American society on the other may be viewed as a result of reverse mobility direction experienced by various immigrant categories in America in comparison with their pre-emigration social status. In this study, a status inconsistant is considered mainly an immigrant whose occupational status in America differs from his occupational status in the native country. In this respect, one's status inconsistency refers to his social mobility in the two societies.

An immigrant's status becomes inconsistent especially when his ethnic group

---

[g]As defined by Max Weber, status groups are, unlike social classes, characterized by a "specific life style" and are distinguished from one another by a special honor which tends to express itself through social superordination and subordination regardless of economic situation. *Max Weber: Essays in Sociology*, trans. H.H. Gerth and C. Wright Mills (New York: Oxford University Press, 1946), pp. 185-190. In his *The Religious Factor*, pp. 363-364, Lenski suggests that socio-religious groups in America are replacing ethnic subcommunities which, as Weber proposed, had developed into status groups.

treats him in one situation according to his pre-emigration status and in the other according to his, most usually, degraded social standing in the adopted society. On the latent level of reaction against inconsistency, the frustration and hostility of an immigrant may be directed against both the larger society and his own ethnic group.

In this study, equal attention is paid to three types of mobility. First, the intergenerational mobility refers to changes in social status between the generation of fathers and the generation of their sons.[35] Second, generational mobility refers to the differences in the social standing of immigrants in the old country as compared with their achievements in the American society. In this study, special concern with generational mobility is what Sorokin calls "a degradation of a social groups as a whole" or an occupational group, like the military, which cannot transfer its skills or regain in the host society its pre-emigration social status and prestige.[36]

The third, or factual mobility denotes "the concrete mobility of an individual."[37] This type of mobility is of central importance in determining an immigrant's feeling of satisfaction with his position in the new society. Therefore, it is suggested that the greater the negative status inconsistency of an immigrant between his pre-emigration and the present social standing, the greater his tendency to look for a kind of compensation for his frustrated status expectations and aspirations. These compensatory tendencies may find expression in three general forms: first, political conservatism,[38] second, associational exclusiveness,[39] and, third, in the redefinition of the social role of associations and churches in the life of immigrants. In addition, the frustration resulting from the status discrepancy may also find expression in mental disorder if the immigrant's associational involvement is very low.

Status ambiguity, resulting from the incompatibility of expectations attached to a status, has, in the case of immigrants, its subjective and objective manifestations both of which result from status inconsistency of a great number of immigrants. A predominantly immigrant ethnic minority group often expects an immigrant to behave according to his pre-emigration status in one instance, but according to his present status in another. In actuality, status inconsistency results in serious strains when, as Lenski says, "the individual prefers to think of himself in terms of his higher status or statuses while others have a tendency to treat him in terms of the lower."[40] Similarly, many immigrants doubly assess their position in their ethnic community; first, in terms of their former or expected social position and, second, in terms of their present position in the larger society. Since the immigrational position of many immigrants represents a kind of occupational displacement and status degradation it can be said that the maladjustment of immigrants is directly related to their occupational dislocation, and to the degree of their frustrated status aspirations in both the larger society and the ethnic group. In other words, strains and conflicts in an immigrant ethnic group develop if a significant number of immigrants experience a drastic status discrepancy which represents the difference between their social standing in the native country and their achieved status in their adopted society.

In general, intragroup conflict and its concommitant factionalism are an inevitable consequence of internal group differentiations which tend to disrupt the previous group structure and function.

Anomic Factionalism

As already admitted, Siegel and Beals' typology of factionalism is very valuable. It is suggested, however, that a special category of factions should be recognized with regard to causes of deviancy and drastic social changes. If Lemert's proposition that *anomie* can also be a cause of social disruption and deviancy is accepted, it is then thought that anomic factionalism is an especially useful concept for understanding factionalism as an expression of maladjustment and as a manifestation of negative latent functionalism which represents reaction against the maltreatment and discrimination practiced by the dominant group and by one's own ethnic group.

The concept anomic factionalism was used first in the study of ethno-religious factionalism in the Serbian minority group which has about 150,000 members and is still predominantly immigrant in its origin and composition. A very brief presentation of the Serbian ethno-religious factionalism is meant to serve as an example of anomic factionalism which has occurred in many ethnic minority groups, even among Negroes in the North.

The internal tension in the Serbian ethnic group before the church controversy in 1963 had all the characteristics of the pervasive type of factionalism. With the break in the unity of the church, the intragroup conflict entered the phase which seems to have the apparent characteristics of schismatic factionalism because the church controversy appeared, at least to the outgroups, as a "conflict between well defined and cohesive subgroups within the larger group," as Siegel and Beals would say.[41] However, the most casual observation of the Serbian scene indicates that the proponents on either side of the church controversy do not constitute a cohesive subgroup, especially the unity faction.

Keeping in mind the fact that the status inconsistencies of a number of Serbs have resulted in their ambiguous position in the Serbian ethnic community, it is suggested that the present factionalism in the Serbian ethnic group is anomic rather than strictly schismatic in terms of Siegel and Beals' definition. For this schism is a manifestation of confused group values[h] and of the malintegration of group structure.[i] It is not the internal strain only which has produced the state

---

[h]"When values become confused, when they conflict with one another, or when they lose their immediacy to human beings," Robert A. Nisbet says "both individual behavior and the social order are affected." "The study of Social Problems," in *Contemporary Social Problems*, Robert K. Merton and Robert A. Nisbet (eds.) (New York: Harcourt, Brace and World, Inc., 1961), p. 17.

[i]Merton suggests that anomie results from the malintegration of the social structure and the cultural structure which he defines as organized normative values. *Social Theory and Social Structure*, (New York: The Free Press of Glencoe, 1956), pp. 162-163.

of anomie in the Serbian ethnic group. In fact, the external stress on the different segments of the group and individuals has produced a conflict between the norms of American society and the norms once held by many immigrants in a particular social structure regarding both the goals and institutional means for their achievement. Therefore, the schism as a form of factionalism was a consequence rather than a cause of anomie in the Serbian ethnic group.[j] The groups which are faced with acculturation are especially susceptible to anomic factionalism, because their members have to redefine the perception of themselves and to find new reference groups.[42] It should be recognized, however, that the occupational degradation and negative status discrepancy stimulate the immigrant against acculturation and cause his frustration because of prevention by the dominant group to realize his minimal expectations. Therefore, there is always more possibility for factionalism, as Lasswell suggests, "when large changes occur in the life situation of members of the group.[43] Furthermore, aggressiveness against one's own group or against some of its members is possible when he becomes aware that "the opportunities open to the group are limited, " either because of the group's minority status or because of his certain pre-emigration occupational and other social attributes.[44]

Since the personality structure and the life pattern of many immigrants of different ethnicity, especially the new ones, were well adjusted to life conditions in their native country, it became difficult for them to meet the social demands of their new status in the ethnic community and in the larger society because the acceptance of the new status had to be followed by more or less drastic changes in self-perception and role-playing. While they remained basically tradition or inner-directed they now tried to demonstrate the so-called "autonomous" other-directedness through indirect manifestations of dissatisfaction with their social status. Thus the striving of some immigrants for other-directedness aggravated their anomic conditions.[45]

Because of its many psycho-social causes originating in the ethnic minority group and the larger society, anomic factionalism appears to be the most serious and consequential type of factionalism.[46] The opposing anomic factions of minority groups operate in total opposition to one another and reach the line of warlike or revolutionary struggle which do not occur because of the social control exercised by the larger society.

In our systematic analysis of immigrant minority groups we are facing the question: Can the immigrants who experience occupational degradation, status discrepancy, and the social role ambiguity in the larger society and in their own ethnic group, be expected to assimilate in the host society rapidly and easily if they were not given the opportunity to adjust satisfactorily?

---

jIn "Social Structure, Social Control, and Deviation," *Anomie and Deviant Behavior*, Marshall B. Clinard (ed.) (New York: The Free Press of Glencoe, 1964), p. 77, Edwin M. Lemert says that "anomie may be a cause rather than an effect of circumscribed life chance."

Notes

1. Anne Anastasi and John P. Foley, Jr., *Differential Psychology* (New York: The Macmillan Company, 1956), p. 704.

2. *Immigration as a Factor in American History*, Oscar Handlin (ed.) (Englewood Cliffs, New Jersey: Prentice-Hall, Inc., 1959), Introduction to Chapter Two, p. 20.

3. Talcott Parsons, *The Social System* (New York: The Free Press of Glencoe, 1964), p. 203.

4. Lawrence Frederic Shaffer, *The Psychology of Adjustment* (New York: Houghton Mifflin Company, 1936), p. 282.

5. Ibid., p. 467.

6. David Riesman, Nathan Glazer, and Reuel Denney, *The Lonely Crowd* (Garden City, New York: Doubleday and Company, Inc., 1956), pp. 278-279. For the psychoanalytic interpretation of adjustment from the viewpoint of socio-cultural changes, see Allen Wheelis' provocative study *The Quest for Identity* (New York: W.W. Norton and Company, Inc., 1958), pp. 85-97.

7. See James A. Peterson, *Education for Marriage*, 2d ed. (New York: Charles Scribner's Sons', 1964), Chapter 13; Robert F. Winch, *The Modern Family*, rev. ed. (New York: Holt, Rinehart and Winston, 1965), pp. 662-674: Bernard S. Phillips, "A Role Theory Approach to Adjustment in Old Age," *American Sociological Review*, XXII (1957), 212-217; Ruth S. Cavan, Ernest W. Burgess, Robert J. Havighurst, and Herbert Goldhamer, *Personal Adjustment in Old Age* (Chicago: Science Research Associates, 1949); Otto Pollak, *Social Adjustment in Old Age* (New York: Social Science Research Council, Bulletin 59, 1948); Grace F. Leybourne, "Urban Adjustments of Migrants from the Southern Appalachian Plateaus," *Social Forces*, XV (December, 1937), 238-246; and Moris G. Caldwell, "The Adjustment of Mountain Families in an Urban Environment," *Social Forces*, XVI (March, 1938), 389-395; and Jay Rumney and Joseph P. Murphy, *Probation and Social Adjustment* (New Brunswick, New Jersey: Rutgers University Press, 1952), Chapter 5, 6, 7, and 8.

8. John F. Kennedy, *A Nation of Immigrants* (New York: Harper and Row, 1964), p. 63.

9. Oscar Handlin, *Race and Nationality in American Life* (Boston: Little, Brown and Company, 1957), p. 194.

10. Robert Lee, Martin E. Marty, "Introduction" to *Religion and Social Conflict*, op. cit., p. 4. Conflict is also defined as "the deliberate attempt to oppose, resist, or coerce the will of another or others." Arnold W. Green, *Sociology* (New York: McGraw-Hill Book Company, Inc., 1962), p. 63.

11. Reece McGee, *Social Disorganization in America* (San Francisco: Chandler Publishing Company, 1962), p. 23. In his *Conflict and Defense* (New York: Harper and Row, 1962), p. 5, Kenneth E. Boulding defines conflict as "a situation of competition in which the parties are *aware* of the incompatibility of potential future position and in which each party wishes to occupy a position

that is incompatible with the wishes of the other." George Simmel has observed that the conflict of impersonal interests is usually fought "with all the strength and resources of the whole personality." Nicholas J. Spykman, *The Social Theory or George Simmel* (Chicago: The University of Chicago Press, 1925), p. 117. See also Lewis A. Coser, *The Function of Social Conflict* (Glencoe, Ill.: The Free Press, 1956), p. 152; and McGee, *Social Disorganization in America.* For conceptual differences between competition and conflict, see Arnold M. Rose, "Voluntary Associations Under Conditions of Competition and Conflict," *Social Forces*, XXXIV (1955-1956), pp. 159-163.

12. Coser, Ibid., p. 152.

13. Talcott Parsons, "Social Classes and Class Conflict," *Essays in Sociological Theory*, rev. ed. (New York: The Free Press, A Division of the Macmillan Company, 1964), p. 329. Parsons uses the concept "latent conflicts" in his analysis of control mechanisms required for "the institution integration of the system." About latent activity as process, see Charles P. Loomis and Zona K. Loomis, *Social Theories* (New York: D. Van Nostrand Company, Inc., 1961), p. 122.

14. Coser, *The Function of Social Conflict*, p. 49. While Coser's classification of conflicts seems to be most pertinent, other classifications, especially those based on the type of scarred values for the possession of which the opponents in a conflict fight, should not be neglected. See Arnold M. Rose, *Theory and Method in Social Sciences* (Minneapolis: University of Minnesota Press, 1954), Chapter 6.

15. Coser, Ibid., p. 152.

16. Arnold M. Rose, *Sociology*, 2d ed. (New York: Alfred A. Knopf Publisher, 1965), p. 636. See also Mabel A. Elliott and Francis E. Merrill, *Social Disorganization*, 4th ed. (New York: Harper and Brothers, 1961), p. 6.

17. Coser, *The Function of Social Conflict*, p. 151. Coser holds that "types of conflict and types of social structure are not independent variables."

18. James S. Coleman, "Community Disorganization," *Contemporary Social Problems*, Robert K. Merton and Robert A. Nisbet (eds.) (New York: Harcourt Brace and World, Inc., 1966), p. 715-719. Coleman makes a distinction between internally generated and externally generated conflict. Relevant to this problem is Merton's analysis of anomie, *Social Theory and Social Structure*, Chapter IV.

19. Tamotsu Shibutani and Kian M. Kwan, *Ethnic Stratification* (New York: The Macmillan Company, 1965), pp. 502-533.

20. J. Ronald Pennock and David G. Smith, *Political Science* (New York: The Macmillan Company, 1964), p. 274.

21. Ibid., pp. 267-269. For factionalism in the major political parties, see also J.A. Corry and Henry J. Abraham, *Elements of Democratic Government* (New York: Oxford University Press, 1964), pp. 319-321.

22. "The Federalist No. 10", *The Federalist* (New York: The Modern Library-Random House, 1937), pp. 54-55.

23. See John M. Swarthout and Ernest R. Bartley, *Principles and Problems of American National Government*, 2d ed. (New York: Oxford University Press,

1955), pp. 125-126. Attention is called especially to James A. Riedel, "Boss and Faction," *The Annals*, CCLIII (May, 1964), pp. 14-26.

24. "Faction," *Encyclopedia of Social Sciences*, VI (1931), 49.

25. Ibid., p. 49.

26. Bernard J. Siegel and Alan R. Beals, "Conflict and Factionalist Dispute," *Royal Anthropological Society Journal*, XC (1960), 107.

27. Lasswell, "faction," p. 50.

28. *Group Dynamics in a North Indian Village*—A study of Factions (Delhi, 1954).

29. Siegel and Beals, "Conflict and Factionalist Dispute," pp. 108-109.

30. Ibid., p. 112.

31. Ibid., p. 112.

32. Jeremy Boissevain, "Factions, Parties and Politics in a Maltese Village," *American Anthropologist*, LXVI (1964), 1275. See also, Adrian C. Mayer, "Factions in Fiji Indian Rural Settlements," *British Journal of Sociology*, VIII (1957), 327; Riedel, "Boss and Faction," p. 19, and Ralph W. Nicholas, *What is Faction?*, mimeographed, p. 19.

33. Lasswell, "Faction," p. 50.

34. *Protestant-Catholic-Jew*, rev. ed., (Garden City, New York: Anchor Books, Doubleday and Co., Inc., 1960), p. 8.

35. See Pitirim A. Sorkin, *Social and Cultural Mobility* (New York: The Free Press of Glencoe, 1959), pp. 133-135; and Kaare Svalastoga, *Social Differentiation* (New York: David McKay Company, Inc., 1965), pp. 105-106.

36. Sorokin, *Social and Cultural Mobility*, p. 134.

37. Sabure Yasuda, "A Methodological Inquiry Into Social Mobility," *American Sociological Review*, XXIX (1964), 16.

38. Gerhard Lenski, "Status Crystalization: A Non-vertical Dimension of Social Status," *American Sociological Review*, XIX (1954), 405-413. Lenski finds that status inconsistent persons tend to be more liberal. See also Gerhard Lenski, "Status Inconsistency and the Vote: A Four Nation Test," *American Sociological Review*, XXXII (1967), 298-301. However, S. Lipset and some others suggest that status inconsistency may result in liberal and conservative political trends, depending upon the combination of measuring criteria; see K. Dennis Kelly and William J. Chambliss, "Status Consistency and Political Attitudes," *American Sociological Review*, XXXI (1966), 375-382.

39. See Elton F. Jackson, "Status Consistency and Symptoms of Stress," *American Sociological Review*, XXVII (1962), 469-480.

40. Siegel and Beals, "Conflict and Factionalist Dispute," p. 108.

41. "Status Inconsistency and the Vote: A Four Nation Test," p. 298.

42. Shibutani and Kwan, *Ethnic Stratification*, pp. 503-504. See also Siegel and Beals, "Conflict and Factionalist Dispute," pp. 111-112.

43. Lasswell, "Faction," p. 50. Siegel and Beals suggest that factionalism is especially a phenomenon of socio-cultural change." "Pervasive Factionalism," *American Anthropologist*, LXII (1960), 399. Ralph W. Nicholas also stresses social changes, especially if they are drastic and rapid, as a condition conducive

to factional cleavages. "Segmentary Factional Political System," *Political Anthropology*, Marc J. Swartz, Victor W. Turneer, and Arthur Tuden (eds.) (Chicago: Aldine Publishing Company, 1966), p. 55.

44. Lasswell, "Faction," p. 50. About self-hatred among Jews, see Kurt Lewin, *Resolving Social Conflicts*, ed. Gertrude Weiss Lewin (New York: Harper and Brothers, 1948), Chapter 12.

45. About the anomic consequences of overconformity or of effects to conform partially while still remaining dependent "on earlier forms of direction," see, Riesman, *The Lonely Crowd*, pp. 278-282.

46. Djuro J. Vrga and Frank J. Fahey, "The Anomic Character of a Schism," forthcoming in *Review of Religious Research*.

5

Ethnicity in Society and Community

Richard Kolm

I. The Meaning of Ethnicity in U.S.A.*

The part ethnic groups have played in the history of the United States is well known and recognized. In fact, as one historian stated, the history of the United States can be viewed as a history of its ethnic groups.[1] Yet, when it comes to the assessment of the standing of ethnic groups in the relational fabric of the American society, it is a different story. While their general contributions to the development of the new country are not denied, accusations abound of their exclusiveness and tendency to isolate themselves in their own communities and neighborhoods, of rigidity in their social patterns, of carrying over old world patterns of inter-group antagonisms; thus they are believed to generate suspicion and distrust, to harbor prejudices and tendencies for scapegoating and stereotyping, and generally are believed to be an obstacle to communication, cooperation, and harmonious relations in society.

These accusations are directed not so much against the individual members of the ethnic groups—descendants of immigrants or themselves immigrants—as against the groups as such. American society accepted immigrants but never approved of the ethnic groups.

There have been many attempts at formulating theories or rather ideologies of desirable ways to incorporate immigrants into the American society and of achieving unity and harmony. Essentially all these ideas or ideologies can be divided into two categories. The first one is the concept of absorption of immigrants involving abandonment of their cultural heritage and ways of life, and conformity as soon as possible to dominant, mainly Anglo-Saxon patterns. A variety of theories from the oldest one of assimilation through the concepts of melting pot, Americanization, triple melting pot, to the most recent one of the imminent disappearance of all ethnic groups from the American scene, can be put under this general category of the ideology of absorption. The second category, an opposite of the first one, is that of cultural pluralism, which promoted the idea of cultural diversities, believed to be the expression of the

*Originally prepared for the Committee on Education and Labor, Subcommittee on Education—as a statement in support of the Ethnic Heritage Studies Centers Bill (H.R. 14910) and published in the Hearings on the Bill by the G.P.O., 1970.

57

constitutional democratic ideas as applicable both to individuals and to groups. Under this category of cultural pluralism fell concepts such as "cultural democracy" and "integration", emphasizing cultural differentiation within the framework of social unity.

There is no doubt that both the above processes, assimilation and pluralism, existed and operated side by side and still do so. On the whole the assimilationist ideologies were dominant in American society as they usually are in countries receiving immigrants. The pressure towards absorption was at times very strong, as during the Americanization program before World War II, but it never exceeded the constitutional limits. As one writer puts it, "the American ethos forced society to tolerate religious and ethnic differences, even if it did not particularly like it."[2]

Despite the pressures, however, and despite the lack of acceptance and support from the society, the ethnic groups have shown an unusual resilience and capacity for preservation of their identity. The recent racial problems and some intergroup conflicts resulting from them have suddenly made the American society aware of the continuing existence of its ethnic groups, and of the fallacy of the accepted myth of the homogeneous American society. The final blow to the assimilationist ideology has been delivered by the black American. He could not disappear, and therefore did not fit into the concept of American adjustment; and consequently had to be put outside the Constitution.

The problem of the blacks and the subsequent chain reaction of conflicts involving other ethnic groups shattered another popular American myth, that of direct individual identification with the country, without the mediation of smaller units. As the report by the National Commission on the Causes and Prevention of Violence issued in June, 1969, states:

The myth of the melting pot has obscured the great degree to which Americans have historically identified with their national citizenship through their myriad subnational affiliations. This has meant inevitable group competition, frictions, and conflict.

The report gives as the reason for this mythology, "a kind of historical amnesia," and goes on to say:

As probably the most ethnically and culturally pluralistic nation in the world, the United States has functioned less as a nation of individuals than of groups.[3]

Whether a "nation of individuals" is at all possible remains an open question. There is no historical evidence of a larger society not being based on smaller ethnic units, mostly of some distant tribal origin. Through regrouping, fusing and blending of smaller groups, most of these units lost their biological base a long time ago; instead they evolved cultural bonds based on motivational consensus, and common language; on strong solidarity among members and loyalty to groups; on commonalities of beliefs, expressive forms, and of moral precepts—all of which are transmitted from one generation to another through time- and fire-tested methods of socialization of the young.

These are the elements constituting what is called "cultural roots" of a society or its "ethnicity." With regard to individuals or groups, "ethnicity" refers, then, to awareness and appreciation of cultural origins, to identification with distinct cultural content and with characteristic expressive forms.

In its essence, ethnicity signifies the unconscious, irrational elements of motivational involvement and commitment of individuals to their groups. It is the strength of this commitment that explains the survival of the presently existing old cultures of the world and that gives them the vitality in their historical struggle for existence and for identity.

It is also this aspect that explains the survival and "obstinate" tenacity of ethnic groups in the United States, still deriving their strength from their original cultures. And it is probably this tenacity of the immigrants in maintaining their ethnicity, from the first arrivals—Anglo-Saxons—to the successive later arrivals, that made the development and greatness of the United States possible. While the deeply instilled moral commitment of these immigrants to society could be taken for granted, the young society could devote its energies toward other goals.

And the ethnic groups, as they continue to cultivate their patterns of group life, are still the cultural taproots of the United States society. Two or even three hundred years of existence is hardly enough for a society to develop its own strong motivational patterns of solidarity and loyalty, of involvement and commitment to society, to a degree necessary not only for times of success and of dynamic growth and expansion, but also for times of difficulties and of crisis; the development of such new patterns is even more problematic for a heterogeneous society composed of elements derived from old established cultures.

The immense American achievements in science, technology, and economics have given the American people an affluence unparalleled in the history of mankind, and are an inspiration to the peoples of the world. They are, however, achievements based on moral commitments and on social responsibilities deeply rooted in the old cultures of the immigrants who brought them ready for use, and who also secured their continuation as they passed them on to their children.

But to re-enact continuously this meaning of their cultural heritage in their personal life, and especially in the socialization of their children, the immigrants, and later their descendants, needed their ethnic groups—for mutual support and for consensual validation of patterns. It is in this crucial matter that the relationship of society to its ethnic groups failed. Some already existing prejudices of the young society—religious, social, and political—reinforced by the anxieties and fears for its unity in times of the mass arrivals of new immigrants, gave rise to the myth of homogeneity, to theories of absorption, of individual citizenship, and to the rejection of ethnic groups. Thus, the old "fear of diversity" and the inter-group antagonisms known to the immigrants in their old countries were revived, in a different form perhaps, but with similar effects for them.

Perhaps the emphasis on the individual and the rejection of the ethnic group was necessary and desirable for the beginnings. It freed the individual from restrictive group bonds and released incalculable amounts of human energy, providing the new country with an explosive dynamism commensurate to the challenges of its resources and opportunities.

But there were also important negative effects both for the ethnic groups and for the American society. As with rejection of individuals in groups, the rejection of any group or groups in society must lead to negative developments. For the ethnic groups, the direct consequences were lowered group self-concept, weakening of group ties and subsequent attrition of membership, defensive withdrawal and stagnation of social and cultural life. These are, of course, also losses to the society, and especially to its relational climate. Lack of acceptance and the rejection of ethnic groups inevitably brought about general distrust and suspicion in relations of the society with its ethnic groups and of the groups with each other. Defensive reactions, stereotyping, scapegoating, prejudice and inter-group conflicts were only the logical consequences of such relations.

The general atmosphere of rejection and disapproval of ethnic groups can probably also be related to other contemporary social problems of American society. The intensity of the present racial conflict is probably best explained in terms of this general atmosphere; similarly, problems of juvenile delinquency and of youth alienation can be attributed to it. The general weakening of the ethnic socializing functions, caused by the negative attitudes of society towards ethnic groups, led to general weakening of the motivational commitment to society.

Blaming cultural diversity and ethnicity even partly for these negative developments is to confuse symptoms with causes. Though coping with diverse ethnic cultures requires greater efforts, diversity has also its important rewards to society. In addition to the previously mentioned values, ethnicity can be a catalyst of grass-roots cultural interest and involvement, and an effective antidote to the mass culture of our times, with its all-leveling mass media, shallowing human interaction, and the dehumanizing effects of material progress.

Furthermore, ethnicity may foster development of multiple-cultured personalities in society with capacities for increased awareness of self and others, and for better functioning in the complex modern world. The cultural ties of ethnic groups with their countries of origin can be viewed as a challenge and opportunity for cultural contacts and for intensified interaction of the American society with other nations. Finally, the pluralistic composition of American society can be viewed as an opportunity for developing intellectual, emotional and moral qualities necessary for its leadership role in the world, for effective coping with the dividing forces of the world, and for constructive use of diversity toward unity.

Above all, however, ethnicity provides many Americans with a deeper sense of self-identity and with greater satisfactions of communal living, and of meaningful interpersonal relationships, which in themselves are contributions to society.

The dissolution of ethnic groups would probably be a loss to society in many ways—in articulated identity, in social and cultural involvement, in organized life style, in colorful folkways, and in other areas. With all these positives, it would seem that the American society would be happy to have ethnic groups, to recognize them, and perhaps even to appreciate them. But old fears and negativism sanctioned by traditions die hard—as do all such sentiments. While other countries gave great attention to their ethnic elements, trying to save as much as possible before technological progress flattens everything into a gray sameness, and while some other immigrant-receiving countries already have learned to enjoy their only recently received immigrants, the American society has not yet recognized its old ethnic groups. The Irish are probably an exception, but it took them one hundred years to gain recognition. There are, of course, some noticeable positive changes in the attitudes of the American society toward its ethnic groups—except toward racial groups. The two world wars have proven to the American society the unconditional loyalty of its ethnic sons and this should be a sufficient cause for a change of heart. But the shallowness of this change was clearly shown by the reaction of the society to the "discovery" of white ethnic America and its presumed polarization in relation to blacks. The fear of ethnic diversity reappeared, showing that the real reason for mellowing of attitudes toward ethnic groups was rather the belief in the imminent disappearance of ethnic groups dutifully proclaimed and documented by researchers.

There is no doubt that the possibilities of negative developments related to ethnicity and cultural diversity are always present. Ethnocentrism, rigidity of traditional forms, and intergroup animosities can always become problems to society and, if not checked in time, may get out of hand. But, as recent events around the world have shown, conflicts arise also in most homogeneous societies and ethnic divisions are not the most frequent causes of conflicts in societies, even where these divisions are strong.

These negative tendencies in no way invalidate the positive values of ethnicity and of cultural diversity. Coping with these negative potentials is mainly a matter of prevention through alertness, flexibility, and the use of skills in human relations, all of which should not be lacking in the American society.

What is needed, at this point, is meaningful acceptance of its ethnic groups by the American society, involving genuine appreciation, interest, and support. The "fear of diversity" can be converted into acceptance and enjoyment of diversity as an important aspect of human life. On the other hand, ethnic groups on their part must recognize that all particularistic solidarities and cultural distinctions must be congruous, harmonious, and converging with the solidarities, ideals and values of the American society.

In view of the above framework "The Ethnic Heritage Studies Centers Act" of 1969 (H.R. 14910) is an important and most appropriate and desirable step in the direction of expressing formal acceptance and support of its ethnic groups by American society. The provision of opportunities "to all students of elementary and secondary schools of the Nation to learn about the differing and unique contributions to the national heritage made by each ethnic group" and about "the nature of their own cultural heritage and those in which they have an interest" will provide recognition and status to ethnic groups in the society and consequently will help them to enrich their cultural identity and their self-concept.

As a result, the ethnic groups will gain the psychological security needed for their positive relationship with other groups and with society, which, in turn, will diminish if not eliminate the main causes for defensiveness, exclusiveness, and intergroup conflicts; the increased security should also help the ethnic groups in their general participation and involvement in their communities and social affairs, and should enable them to make greater contributions to these communities and to society.

By promoting general interest in ethnic cultures the act will give evidence that American society has overcome its "fear of diversity" and may lead to "enjoyment of diversity," thus increasing mutual acceptance and improving the rational climate in society. The interest and grass-roots involvement in cultural affairs may also be a positive factor in combatting social ills such as alienation and delinquency.

Finally, by including all ethnic groups on an equal basis, the act may become instrumental in equal status involvement and interaction of all ethnic groups, including those who at present still struggle for equality and recognition as well as those already established, and in this way the act may contribute significantly to the stabilization of human relations in American society.

II. Community and Ethnicity*

The racial crisis of recent years in the United States has made a deep impact, not only directly on the black/white relations, but also on the total social fabric of the U.S. society. While it exposed dramatically the basic "American dilemma" of the black/white relationship, defined by Myrdal as early as 1944[4] the crisis opened up again the whole problem of ethnic groups and ethnic relations in the American society with all its concommitant philosophical, theoretical, political, and other aspects. With particular reference to American social philosophy regarding its cultural subgroups, the racial crisis and its reverberations have exploded a number of myths born of faulty premises and, frequently, of simple wishful thinking such as the myth of imminent disappearance of the ethnic groups and of the almost complete—except for the racial groups-homogeniety of American society, the myth of the melting pot and other absorption theories, and the myth of the direct identification of the individual with his society, without the mediation of the intervening groups (cultural, religious, occupational, and others).

*An adaptation from a presentation at the Conference on Ethnic Communities of Greater Detroit at Wayne State University, Detroit on June 12, 1970.

At the same time, the racial crisis also brought about conflicts between the expanding blacks and the immediate neighboring white populations which happened to consist mainly of ethnic working class groups. Threatened in their economic and communal interests, these groups often reacted defensively to the expanding blacks, creating confrontation and situations of conflict which aroused anxieties and fears of polarization and of large scale unrest. It was also this situation which made the society rediscover the continuing existence of its ethnic groups and their relationship to society.

The confrontation of ethnic groups with the blacks caused also the rebirth of interest, among the ethnic groups themselves, in their identity, their distinctness, and their relationships to the society and to other groups.

The persistence of ethnicity in American society is, in itself, nothing unusual. History provides many examples of such persistence, frequently under the most adverse circumstances, including political suppression, persecutions and even consciously planned annihilation. The example of the Jewish people, who retained their identity despite nearly two thousand years of dispersion, discrimination, and often severe persecution, is the most convincing.

The ethnic groups in the United States differ, of course, from those in most of the old societies where they usually have had a longer historical relationship with the dominant society and are also, most frequently, territorially defined. The dispersal of the ethnic groups in American society, with the exception of a few larger concentrations in the Eastern urban centers, would seem to make them easily subject to total absorption. Other factors, such as general mobility and the process of rapid suburbanization, economic affluence, and increased education, were generally thought to contribute to the process of assimilation of ethnic groups.

However, a number of recent studies have shown that some ethnic groups may even have increased in their awareness of identity in the second and later generations[5] and that occupational mobility and suburbanization do not preclude the maintenance of ethnic identity.[6] Similarly, it was found that other factors such as lack of ties with the mother country, the absence of prejudice and discrimination by the dominant groups, may not prevent the sustenance of ethnic awareness and identity.[7]

Altschuler, after reviewing some of the studies and analyzing the factors of persistence of ethnicity, concludes that "This is not to deny that ethnicity as a social and political factor may decline in importance over the next two or three generations."[8] Gordon Allport, on the other hand, in discussing the resolving of intergroup tensions, is of a different opinion:

Meliorism must be our guide. People who talk in terms of the ultimate assimilation of all minority groups into one ethnic stock are speaking of a distant utopia. To be sure, there would be no minority group problems in a homogeneous society but it seems probable that, in this country, at least, our loss through homogeneity would be greater than our gain. In any case, it is certain that artificial attempts to hasten assimilation will not succeed. We should improve human relations only by learning to live with racial and cultural pluralism for a long time to come.[9]

The above quotation raises another well-known issue from the past, that of cultural pluralism versus homogeneity and its consequent ideologies of assimilation and absorption. While the total absorption or assimilation theories, also called Anglo-conformity ideologies, were most widely acclaimed throughout the history of the new nation, the best known was probably the melting pot idea, developed by Israel Zangwill in 1909, which postulated the ongoing process of blending of the best traditions and traits of all the ethnic groups into a new dynamic unity.[10]

The most outspoken philosopher of cultural pluralism is Horace Kallen who, together with his contemporaries I.D. Berkson and Julius Drachsler, formulated and reformulated the idea of cultural pluralism to its final conclusion.[11] Using as a basis Dewey's ideas of the democratic man and democratic society, inevitably associated with individualism and pluralism, they asserted that immigrants coming from different cultures have not only the right to retain their cultural background but that society has an obligation to support and promote these various cultural affiliations for the sake of individual fulfillment and of democratic diversity. However, while Berkson and Drachsler looked at cultural pluralism rather from the functional point of view and as a reality which should be recognized and used to its full potential for the development of society and individuals involved, Kallen went much further with his conclusions. To him, pluralism becomes an end in itself; his dream is a nation based on cultural enclaves, a sort of federation of nationalities with no need for administrative, regional, or politcal divisions. Cultural diversity is to Kallen not only a direct implementation of democracy, it is to him also a direct expression of human nature and one of its primary needs; the strong tendency of immigrants to maintain their culture is a sacred human right; "Men may change their clothes, their politics, their wives, their religions, their philosophies to a greater or lesser extent: but they cannot change their grandfathers."[12]

As sound as these ideas about man's tendencies toward diversity and toward retaining his cultural background upon transplantation may have been, Kallen was not able to provide the basic theoretical framework for his insightful observations; regarded by many as an ideal and distant goal rather than a realistic structural and functional model for society, cultural pluralism had, however, little impact on the existing status-power patterns in intergroup relations in the society. With its exclusive reliance on cultural interpretations, and its failure to recognize the reality of social, economic, and situational factors of human relations, it became little more than a moralistic epigram, popular in liberal intellectual circles.

As a result, it was the political mode which provided the social framework of the American society, with its patterns of dominant and minority status and the consequent competition for recognition and power. The assuming of a dominant status position by the Anglo-Saxon group, who based their claims on seniority in arrival and on providing of the foundations for the institutional framework for the young society, created, of necessity, a hierarchical structure for the next arrivals, ascribing to them the status of descendingly ranked minorities. The acceptance-rejection dichotomies related to degrees of behavioral adjustment to dominant patterns and differentiated by public and private spheres, inevitably led to intergroup tensions, to mutual suspicion and social exclusiveness, to inequality of treatment, of opportunities and of life chances; to prejudice and discrimination, and eventually to hostilities and conflict.

It was this conflict between the moralistic-idealistic and the political-realistic concept that created the wishful ideas of the melting pot, of a new amalgamation of all elements—the dominant and the minority groups—into a new superior blend. The attractiveness of this idea lies in the deceptive metaphor, similar to the alchemist dream of the philosophical stone. It assumes, correctly, the impact of even small ingredients on the resulting amalgam but denies the reality of power relations in intergroup relations. It also overlooks the tenacity of cultural patterns and the essential differences between cultural and psychological processes on one hand the mechanical or chemical processes on the other. In practice the melting pot theory becomes only a semantic varient of the total absorption theories.

Recent events have shown repeatedly, however, the persistence of the pluralistic ideas, attesting to their relevance and validity for the American society and American values. These ideas may yet prove to be the most realistic basis for a viable American society.

Essentially, cultural pluralism derives from two basic precepts:

1. The value of ethnicity for individual development and the right of individuals, and especially of transplanted individuals and groups, to retain and cultivate their ethnic culture, and
2. The value of cultural diversity to a democratic society. Though related intrinsically to each other, these two theses have also their independent essential content.

With regard to its meaning, ethnicity refers to cultural roots, either of whole societies or of subgroups or of individuals. The term is derived from the Greek word "*ethnos*" meaning tribe, race or nation, or simply people. Recently the term has come to be more closely associated with the Greek concept of "*ethos*" or custom, which is now understood in terms of socialization and cultural patterns rather than in former conceptions of biological and genetic origins.[13] In this second sense, ethnicity refers more or less to the homogeneous, cultural base of a social group as developed and cultivated throughout its history. Applied to modern societies or cultural subgroups, ethnicity usually takes on the generalized meaning of cultural distinctness derived from historical origins and is usually associated with some folkcultural elements related to basic areas of life—family and communal relations, birth and death, love and procreation, work and play, aesthetic interests, manners, spiritual life, and so on.

However, these elements all refer in essence to the relational patterns within the group, among individuals, between the individual and his group, and to associated aspects such as solidarity, loyalty, social responsibility, communication, participation, belonging, and others. In this respect, one could probably regard ethnicity as the culture of basic human relations and of group survival, to which all other aspects of life are subjugated and directly supportive. It is safe to assume that in the past the relational stability provided by the ethnic cultures was the main condition for further social, cultural, and other developments of social groups.

The tenacity of ethnic patterns can be easily explained by the conditioning process of the slow and gradual development of these social groups from their dark beginnings to the present; by the tedious process of developing language and relational patterns of cooperation and the collective strength needed for the survival and development of the groups. Through the process of socialization, the patterns, confirmed in successful experience, were transmitted to the successive generations and accumulated over centuries, forming the web of life for the given social group. These are Sumner's folkways or mores which, according to him, were formulated and maintained largely unconsciously and operate in moments of need, securing proper reactions to most situations in the life of the individual and of the group.[14]

From these folkways and mores develop later new patterns institutions, philosophies, norms and laws, science, art, and in general the culture of the group. Folkways can be defined then as specific aspects or as products of ethnicity,

.... which are developed out of experience, which reach a final form of maximum adaptation to an interest, which are handed down by tradition and admit of no exception or variation yet change to meet new conditions, still within the same limited methods and without rational reflection or purposes.[15]

Similarly, Gemeinschaft in any specific form, or as a social category, is the product and expression of ethnicity, subject to change and discontinuity. Ethnicity is understood here as the fundamental human bond in historical social groups or societies, and as a process of largely unconscious transmission reflecting the historical experiences and cultures of these groups.

It is the central premise of this paper that ethnicity, in the above sense, constitutes the foundation and bonding substance of all societies and cultures and that, with the weakening of their ethnic content, societies may be subject to increasing disorganization and disintegration.

Like all human attributes, ethnicity has both its functional and dysfunctional aspects which, in the case of ethnic subgroups in a society, must be related both to the individuals in ethnic groups and to the society as a whole. The positive aspects of ethnicity to members of ethnic groups can be briefly summarized as follows:

1. The contribution to personality development, and particularly to self-identity, fostered by the richness, variety, and organic consistency of patterned motivational orientations and values, conveyed during the formative years of the individual.

2. The facilitation of mutual trust, direct response, and dependability in interpersonal relations, based on motivational consensus, mutual understanding and implicit patterns of mutual role expectations.
3. The patterning of motivational orientations conducive to creating an atmosphere of security beyond the family unit, to emphasis on "whole person" response and on acceptance within a diffused affective relationship.
4. The patterns of mutuality in expectations and behavior basic to the development of moral norms, of informal social controls, of social responsibility as well as of patterns of involvement, of commitment, of loyalty and solidarity.
5. The richness of historically accumulated spontaneous and creative expressions in folk arts, music, songs, dances and festivities, creating a medium of direct cultural involvement for all members of an ethnic group, young and old, and particularly important in the socialization process and the developing of spontaneous creativity and expressiveness.
6. The established and integrated life patterns of an ethnic culture, providing the essential guidelines for the organization of individual and group life, for a hierarchy of values, for priorities of needs and goals, for patterned reactions to stress and, above all, for patterns of socialization of the young.[16]

All the above-mentioned positive aspects of ethnicity can become also positives to the society as a whole, by the sheer weight of individual characteristics shaped in the ethnic cultures and of the group attributes in their interaction with groups and with society. All these qualities are most likely to extend from the ethnic groups to the larger society, providing that a generally positive relationship exists between the ethnic group and the general society.

The attitudes of American ethnic groups toward the general society were, on the whole, very positive despite the general covert, and sometimes overt, rejection by the society of the ethnic groups as groups. Except for some specific cases, such as that of the Bund during World War I, and perhaps some splinter groups of black separatists of today, there was, and is, no conflict between ethnic and societal loyalties; and there is enough evidence to assert that ethnic loyalty reinforces loyalty to society. The two world wars should be sufficient proof of the loyalty of the ethnic sons who excelled in their willingness to serve and in their behavior on the battlefield. And even such an overt hostile action as the infamous relocation of the Japanese-Americans during World War II did not shatter their loyalty to the new country.

There are also other general advantages of ethnicity to society: with the variety of expression, traditions and customs, ethnic groups provide added color and spice to cultural expression in society which, under propitious conditions, stimulate cultural interaction and involvement on the grass-roots level and can be an endless source for literary, musical, and other aesthetic inspiration. Thus they constitute an invaluable means of maintaining cultural interest in society and are probably one of the most effective antidotes to the deadly effects of mass culture and alienation in all its forms: meaninglessness, social atomism, uprooted individualism, false rationalism and objectivity irrelevant to life. It also may become a significant factor in combatting other social ills, particularly juvenile delinquency.

The cultivation of interest in diversified and living subcultures based on deeply rooted human relational motivations and on diversified aesthetic and intellectual interests, can only enrich and add meaning to life in an industrial, mechanized, megalopolized modern world with its leveling mass media, shallowing human interaction, and its dehumanizing impacts of raw materialism.

Furthermore, there are also some more intangible and broader aspects of ethnicity which may become an invaluable asset to the American society—the fostering of the development of bi-cultural or multi-cultural personalities, the use of cultural ties of ethnic groups with their countries of origin, and the inter-ethnic experience in society, can be turned to incalculable advantage to the American society and strengthen its leadership role in the world. It is the unique opportunity of the American society to use its pluralistic composition as a laboratory for developing the intellectual and emotional orientation, knowledge, skills, and methods necessary to its leadership role in the world, for coping effectively with the divisive forces in it and for constructive use of diversity toward unity and peace.

The negative aspects of ethnicity as referring to ethnic groups and individual development can be summarized in three categories. First, the static tendencies and certain rigidity in internal structure and the functioning of ethnic groups. Second, the isolationism, clannishness, and insularism creating obstacles to communication and to cooperation with other groups and leading to scapegoating, stereotyping, distrust, prejudice, and intergroup conflict. Third, certain cultural primitivism, tenacious clinging to traditional patterns and particularly some folkloristic activities and folkways which exclude the development of new patterns in society and of innovative efforts. The social and cultural limitations imposed by the above negative forms of ethnicity on individual development and life can easily be posited.

These are also potentials for negative developments in society which, as always with human problems, need careful attention and genuine efforts in preventive and in rehabilitative action. The negative aspects of ethnocentrism can become obstacles to the integration of society. They are also potential sources of open intergroup conflicts leading to confrontations and even violence, and of general balkanization of society, which refers to atomization into innumerable groupings hostile to each other, or at least not communicating or interacting sufficiently with each other. These intergroup problems may cause serious strains and conflicts in society, may create a disabling atmosphere of anxiety and fear, and may divert valuable energy of the society toward control functions at the cost of cooperative effort and productivity.

It is, however, unreasonable and unfair to put the blame for these negative symptoms of ethnicity, or the potentials of such symptoms, at the doorstep of the ethnic groups or ethnicity itself. As mentioned before, it can be argued that the main reason and source of intergroup problems in the United States, including the recent racial problems, is the lack of acceptance and recognition by society of its ethnic groups and the subsequent establishment of status-power systems in intergroup relations, relegating differential minority status to non-Anglo-Saxon groups by sequence of arrival, color of skin, rate of adjustment or "cultural affinity." This rejection of the immigrant groups was thought to be compensated by the general acceptance of the immigrant as an individual. Ideological, historical, as well as direct economic motives combined for the formulation of this approach, but essentially the individual immigrant was accepted because of his potential for conformity to the dominant group and for disavowing his distinct ethnic identity. As mentioned above, this brought about the problem of the blacks who could not disappear as individuals, even if they desired to do so, and exposed the iniquity of ethnic relations in the American society.

The "fear of diversity" on the part of the dominant group and its lack of acceptance of the ethnic groups and their cultures inevitably brought about a general erosion of the relational climate in society, and the consequent defensive reactions. The cultural heritage of the new arrivals was, in fact, their most valuable possession and their greatest gift to the new country. It enabled them to join immediately the new society as productive members, even if mostly only on the lowest level of economic functioning; but, most important, they were able to join the new society as fully responsible and willing citizens socialized in ethical behavior and in social order, and as devoted socializers of their children.

Nowhere is the problem of ethnicity and of intergroup relations more visible than in community life. In general, it is in the communities that real people live and love, work and play, and also hate, quarrel, and fight, become unemployed and suffer their daily frustrations and sorrows; above all, community is a place where people raise their families and where they have most, if not all, of their friends, where they spend most of their earnings, where they worship, belong to groups, and are directly involved in the making and breaking of the social order.

It is also in the communities, and particularly in the larger cities and metropolises, where ethnic groups cultivate their distinct patterns and develop their own communal life by communicating, and meeting even if dispersed in larger areas, or by having their own neighborhoods, districts, and even whole autonomous communities as in the case of Hamtramck. To paraphrase a statement quoted elsewhere: even if the American society did not accept the ethnic groups as distinct units, it did not interfere with their internal life. Though, by and large, the ethnic groups managed to live peacefully with each other and, as the International Institute and other agencies have shown, can be goaded into exemplary cooperation, there was also, at times, some neighborly bickerings, some youth gang warfare and open hostilities.

The recent confrontation between the blacks and the white ethnic groups in changing neighborhoods is probably one of the more serious problems having implications beyond the immediate conflicts between specific groups. Even if the problem is a societal one, it is the community which has to face it directly and which has to take immediate action. The federal authorities, the legislature, the executive government, and the judiciary system have, of course, an important role in the process of promotion and rehabilitation of general human relations in society, but essentially it remains the primary problem of the communities.

By its very origin from the Latin term *"munis"* to bind, community has the meaning of people being bound together with the obvious implication that they have something in common-needs, goals, interests, or ideas. As Ortega y Gasset puts it "people don't live together merely to be together. They live together to do something together."[17] Or, as paraphrased by Nisbet "People do not come together in significant and lasting associations merely to be together, they come together to do something that cannot easily be done in individual isolation."[18]

There are certainly enough common needs and problems in a community that call for common action and the cooperation of all concerned. Three main areas are suggested as main functions of community: (1) safety, involving protection, traffic regulations, health, sanitation, building norms, and many others; (2) socialization, involving schools, recreation, museums; and (3) convenience, involving utilities, transportation, housing, streets and sidewalks, parks, and so on.

Then there always remains the big issue of how to do things together and how to solve these common problems. Even taking the democratic framework for granted, there are the type of management and administration, of distribution of power, of organization, of districts and neighborhood boundaries and functions, of type of elections, of financing, of cooperation with state and federal agencies, and many others. In general, these are questions of community government of, by, and for the people, or of human welfare and human relations both in the broadest and in the concrete sense.

This is also the point at which the intergroup relations in community, and the role and function of the ethnic groups in community are most relevant. The general conversion between the community and the ethnic groups regarding the human relations aspects is evident. The ethnic groups, wherever they exist in communities, constitute cohesive, independent social units, which should be able to play a functional role in the human relations of the community. However, probably because of the ideological rejection of ethnic groups in American society, they are not included in the functional structure of their communities, and are seldom considered as entities except, perhaps, for political purposes at times of elections. The blacks raised the problem of their participation as a group in community control and functioning, and in that way they opened up the whole question of ethnic groups in community functioning in general. However, before the above issues can be discussed directly, a brief analysis of the general framework of community functioning and of the main dilemmas involved is in order.

There are many excellent formulations of criteria for optimal community structure and functioning or, more directly, for community control or for the distribution of power in the community. To cite a few: Warren proposes autonomy, viability, and broad distribution of decision-making power.[19]

Altschuler argues for "social peace and . . . legitimacy, not abstract justice or efficiency" as central issues;[20] and he specifies further that "the keys to legitimacy in the modern world are equality and self determination".[21] Nisbet emphasizes participation and self-determination: "community is the product of people working together on problems of autonomous and collective fulfillment of internal objectives and of the experience of living under codes of authority which have been set in large degree by the persons involved."[22] As can be easily seen, participation, and autonomy are directly or indirectly involved in all three of the above formulations. They are also probably the most generally recognized essential values in democratic community functioning and could provide a sufficient basis for discussions of the role of ethnic groups in the community. However, Nisbet's analysis of community provides a much more detailed and relevant framework. He uses society and community interchangeably and sees power, its distribution and its control, as a central problem in society and community; in the analysis of this problem he focuses on the concept of state, and juxtaposes two types of state:

The first type of state is inherently monolithic and absorptive and however broad its base in the electorate, and however nobly inspired its rulers, must always border upon despotism.

The second type of state is inherently pluralist and, whatever the intentions of its formal political rulers, its powers will be limited by associations whose plurality of claims upon their members is the measure of their members' freedom from any monopoly of power in society.[23]

For the community, the corresponding concepts to these two types of states are the moral community, based on a sense of identification, on security, and on membership in intermediary small groups, and the political community with its emphasis upon direct relationship of individuals to government, and on centralization of adminstration.

To Nisbet, the need for community is a powerful human drive:

The quest for community will not be denied, for it springs from some of the powerful needs of human nature—needs for a clear sense of cultural purpose, membership, status, and continuity. Without these, no amount of material welfare will serve to arrest the developing sense of alienation in our society and the mounting preoccupation with the imperatives of community.[24]

The absence of weakening of this drive causes alienation, the very antithesis of community: "one of the determining realities of the contemporary age" and the "essential tragedy of modern man's quest for community."[25] Alienation has essentially two meanings: as a state of mind and as the individual's relation to social function and social authority.

Alienation as a state of mind means finding "a social order remote, incomprehensible, or fraudulent; beyond hope or desire; inviting apathy, boredom, and even hostility. The individual not only does not feel a part of the social order—he has lost interest in being a part of it.[26] It involves alienation from the past, from physical place and nature, and alienation from things.

As a matter of the individual's relation to social function and social authority, alienation means functional disassociation from all intermediary groups in society, from local communities and neighborhood, extended family, church, cultural, professional, economic, academic, recreational groups, and so on. Disassociation from the functional significance of intermediary groups leads to the disengagement from the constraints of authority rooted in the statuses, functions, and allegiances of these groups. Together with Toqueville, Acton, and even the great anarchists, Nisbet asserts that freedom can be found only in the multiplicity of these intermediary associations, in the interstices of their authority, and in their competition for authority.

It is also the function and authority of these associations that give the individual status and, through it, vital relationship to society, as well as meaning, depth, and inclusiveness to individual life. This function and authority constitutes also the essential organization of society and provides opportunities for manageable social differences and conflicts and cultural frictions on which cultural development and even intellectual energy thrive.

Nisbet's central thesis is that the centralization of power in the modern world has "destroyed or weakened many of the established contexts of function and authority—and by its existence choked off the emergence of new contexts and thus created a great deal of the sense of alienation that dominates contemporary man."[27]

He traces the loss of community from ancient times through the French Revolution and the Napoleonic Empire, all characterized by collectivization of authority and centralization of administration and power, and derives from them most of the later developments in Europe, including such diverse phenomena as the modern nationalistic state, Prussian militarism, capitalism, Marxism, welfare state, and the total states of Communism and Nazism, and even certain trends of modern democracy, with its

general levelling of local, regional, and associative differences, nationalization of culture and taste, a collectivization of mind, and a continuous increase in the real powers of government over management, labor, recreation, religion, and social welfare.[28]

He attributes to Rousseau the most radical formulation of the power of the State. For the sake of liberation of the individual from the feudal class system, Rousseau denounced also the family, the church, the guilds, the community. To be free the individual must surrender completely and totally to the omnipotent state. Communism and Nazism are only logical applications, in various forms, of these radical ideas. The atomization of the intermediary groupings, including even the family, finally rendered the whole society a mindless, soulless, traditionless mass.[29]

Nisbet does not want his observations to be seen as a "lament for the old." Technological and scientific developments and population increase suffice to render much of the old order inadequate. But, assuming unabashedly the Utopian stance, he denounces soundly all present trends of "unitary democracy" in American society—trends of social atomization and political centralization—as the unmistakable symptoms of growing mass society. He repeatedly emphasizes that the most powerful resources of democracy lie in the cultural allegiances of citizens as they are nourished psychologically in the smaller internal areas of family, residential community, and association—ethnic, religious, occupational, etc. And he chooses the concept of liberal democracy for the representation of the free society built upon values of autonomy and freedom of personal choice which, however, can be achieved and maintained only under conditions of cultural diversity, plurality of association, and division of authority.

The above discussion of Nisbet's theories clearly points toward the direct relationship between community and ethnicity. On one hand community, like society, is subject to disintegrating forces of mass culture and alienation and trends of increasing political centralization and bureaucratization which threaten our values of autonomy and freedom. Decentralization, cultural diversity, and pluralism of autonomous associations are seen as the best guarantee against these trends.

On the other hand, the ethnic groups in American communities are autonomous, strong associations which, for their fostering of social and cultural participation and involvement and, above all, for their integrated socialization patterns, can make valuable contributions to society and may become one of the strongest elements of the envisioned pluralistic structure in community. However, being subject to the historial patterns of rejection by society, the ethnic groups have seldom assumed any formal functional roles in general community life, unless they formed their own communities, and the strong pressures by society toward assimilation have greatly affected their strength and particularly their socializing capacity. The inclusion of the ethnic groups in the decentralized functional social system of the community would be for them an expression of acceptance by the society and would, no doubt, revitalize their internal and external functioning and would allow them to unfold their full contributory capacity to society.

The question whether the ethnic groups should be included in the formal functional structure of the community or its sub-units is, however, to be analyzed, above all, in terms of its functional and dysfunctional aspects to the community itself.

Altschuler addresses himself directly to that question and, though he mainly refers to the blacks, he includes race into the ethnic dimension, along with religion and national origin. On the other hand, he denies the analogy between the present situation of the blacks and the adjustment problems of the white immigrants as they arrived in this country. The focus of his discussion is political participation which he defines as sharing in the exercise of political power, and which at present involves claims on the part of minorities to larger shares in political authority, in group representation in public bureaucracy, and in the private income (wages and profits) generated by governmental activity.[30] Altschuler sees political participation as the most pervasive issue in present-day American politics, a movement whose roots reach deep into American history with its strong traditions of citizen participation in politics, the preference of Americans for decentralized government, and their unwillingness to forego political representation in dealing with public bureaucracies, and, in addition, with its structural aspects of ethnic groupings, and the long exclusion of blacks from American politics.[31]

With reference to community, political participation is identified with community control, defined as "the exercise of authority by the democratically organized government of a neighborhood sized jurisdiction" . . . . denoting a "category of proposed reforms: transfers of authority from the governments of large cities to the governments of much smaller sub-units within them."[32]

In discussing a number of commonly posed questions regarding community control, Altschuler concludes, on the basis of a number of empirical studies, that community control does not necessarily mean increasing racial separatism and intensifying social frictions, nor is it irreconcilable with honest and efficient professionalism in government, but that it would, in the long run, be a vital step in developing ethnic pride, political skill and organization and, consequently, social responsibility.

To the important question of whether the participation of ethnic and racial associations, churches, and labor unions, should involve formal delegation of public authority, he answers positively, arguing that by treating groups as functional, significant units and as responsible participants in collective decision-making, their sense of unity and responsibility can be increased; that the sharing by these groups in the decision-making process in areas of their intensive concern will touch a responsive chord in them and, finally, that these are people who really care what happens in their neighborhoods.[33]

Altschuler goes on to discuss the "pluralistic options" of some aspects of the proposed "multi-purpose neighborhood government" such as: (1) the definition of neighborhoods, (2) mechanisms of representation and accountability, (3) financial, (4) personal, (5) contracting, and (6) the federal role.[34]

He finds that all these problems can be constructively analyzed and solved within the framework of social peace and political legitimacy based on equality and self-determination—the crucial problems of American society today. Justice or efficiency cannot be formulated in abstract, mechanical terms but have to be gauged in long-term, broad implications for stabilizing human relations and ensuring continuity of basic values.

As mentioned above, Altschuler argues that social peace and political legitimacy, based on equality and self-determination, are the crucial issues of American society today, and he expresses his personal belief that the participatory form would transform the bureaucratic subcultures and would provide a focus for black political organization, helping them to develop skills and self-respect and giving them a tangible stake in the American political system which, consequently, would enhance the legitimacy of the whole system in their eyes. And it may help cement the American union by providing an adequate outlet for racial pluralism, even if at the cost of some efficiency, but "efficiency is a word with little meaning where values are problematic."[35]

All the above remarks can be literally applied to any other ethnic group in American society, whether racial or cultural. Giving them functional status in neighborhood government—an area which matters most to them and with which they are most familiar—would not only enhance their self-respect and their group functioning, and through it their contributory capacity to society, but would also, no doubt, increase greatly their sense of social responsibility and their contribution to human relations in the community. These discussions of the decentralization of community control assume that the sub-units would remain in functional relationship with the higher levels of community government and would be subject to modification by demands of participation and cooperation in them and contribution to them. There is also the possibility of further involvement of the ethnic groups on the higher levels of community government in the form of advisory bodies in areas relevant to their intrinsic functions.

In order, however, to maximize the functional use of ethnic groups and minimize the negative potentials, some general rules derived from tested knowledge and experience in intergroup relations must be observed. Three such basic conditions can be suggested as the most important ground rules: (1) acceptance of equal status in formal and informal situations in communal intergroup relations. However, if the concept of decentralized neighborhood units were to succeed, the acceptance of equal status as a general principle would have to extend considerably beyond Altschuler's dimensions of equality of opportunity and equality before the law. More often than not these neighborhoods would be ethnically mixed. In any case, the groups would constantly be in some kind of contact with each other and nothing less than general acceptance, at least on the group interaction level, will suffice. This involves not only equal status in neighborly interaction but must aim at: (2) acceptance and enjoyment of cultural diversity as a basic and important pattern of general human relations, and (3) the unequivocal recognition that all particularistic solidarities must, despite their emphasis on differentiation, be congruous and converging with higher level solidarities, ideals and values of community, society, and mankind.

Within the framework of the premises underlying the above discussion, as derived from philosophical and theoretical formulations, we may summarize the foregoing in the form of three propositions: (1) The community is a very basic unit in society and its autonomy is most essential to the survival of liberal democracy. Its strength lies in the emphasis on decentralization of authority, on cultural diversity, and on pluralism of association—ethnic, religious, professional, business, labor, etc.; (2) the ethnic groups are still the cultural taproots of American society and can, through their distinct cultural patterns fostering personal and social strength, continue to make an invaluable contribution to the society as a whole; and (3) in recognition of their potential for contribution to society, as well as of their functional capacities in community, the ethnic groups could be recognized as significant functional elements of the communities, where they exist and could be given functional roles in the community, assuring them of direct participation in the political, social, and cultural responsibility in the community.

It is well recognized that the above proposals, involving changes in entrenched status relationships, are not easily introduced and implemented. As is well known from historical experience, changes of status are the most difficult human problems. Practically all revolutions in the past centered around that issue. But we also know that it is possible, using historical experience and available knowledge, to introduce even difficult changes if we can mobilize the motivational forces of purpose and of acceptance of reality.

Notes

1. Paraphrased from Oscar Handlin (ed.), *Immigration as a Factor in American History* (Englewood Cliffs, N.J.: Prentice Hall, 1959), 1.

2. Andrew M. Greeley, *Why Can't They Be Like Us?* (New York: Institute of Human Relations Press, 1969), 4.

3. As quoted in *White Ethnic America, A Selected Bibliography* (New York: Institute of Human Relations , October, 1969), 1.

4. Gunnar Myrdal, *An American Dilemma* (New York: Harper and Brothers, 1944).

5. Raymond Wolfinger, "The Development and Persistence of Ethnic Voting," *American Political Science Review* (December, 1965), 904-906.

6. Michael Parenti, "Ethnic Politics and the Persistence of Ethnic Identification," *American Political Science Review* (September, 1967), 721-722.

7. Wolfinger, "Ethnic Voting," 906.

8. Alan A. Altschuler, *Community Control* (New York: Pegasus, 1970), 96.

9. Gordon W. Allport, "Resolving Intergroup Tensions," in *Toward Better Human Relations,* by Lloyd Allen Cook (ed.), Detroit: Wayne University Press, 1952), 67-68.

10. Israel Zangwill, *The Melting Pot* (New York: The Macmillan Co., 1909).

11. Horace Kallen, *Culture and Democracy in the United States* (New York: Boni & Liverright, 1924); Isaac B. Berkson, *Theories of Americanization* (New York: Bureau of Publications, Teacher's College, Columbia University, 1920); Julius Drachsler, *Democracy and Assimilation* (New York: The Macmillan Co. 1920).

12. Horace Kallen, "Democracy Versus the Melting Pot," *The Nation* C (1915), 219.

13. Melvin M. Tumin, "Ethnic Group," *A Dictionary of the Social Sciences*, Julius Gould and William M. Kolb, (eds.) (New York: The Free Press, 1964), 244.

14. William Graham Sumner, *Folkways* (New York: Ginn and Co., 1906), 1-7.

15. Ibid., 4.

16. The discussion of the positive and negative aspects of ethnicity is largely based on another paper by this writer "Ethnicity and Mental Health" presented to the World Mental Health Assembly on November 18, 1969, in Washington, D.C. (mimeographed).

17. As quoted in Robert H. Nisbet, *The Quest for Community* (New York: Oxford University Press. Re-issued edition, 1969), 61.

18. Ibid., xvl.

19. Roland L. Warren, "Toward a Non-Utopian Normative Model of the Community," *American Sociological Review* (April, 1970), 223.

20. Altschuler, *Community Control,* 191.

21. Ibid., 201.

22. Nisbet, *Quest*, xvi.

23. Ibid., 283-284.

24. Ibid., 73.

25. Ibid., viii-ix.

26. Ibid.

27. Ibid., xiv-xv.

28. Ibid., 259.

29. Ibid., 203.

30. Altschuler, *Community Control*, 64.

31. Ibid., 71.

32. Ibid., 64-65.

33. Ibid., 125-127.

34. Ibid., 123-189.

35. Ibid., 192.

**Part II
Ethnicity in Detroit**

6 Ethnicity in Detroit

Carol Agocs

Detroit, like many American cities, was built by people on the move. They came from the east, from the south, from the north, from the countryside, and from all parts of Europe and the Middle East. Included in the legacy of these immigrants are the more than fifty well-defined ethnic communities that today make greater Detroit one of the most ethnically diverse and cosmopolitan of American cities. Yet relatively little is generally known about the present circumstances of Detroit's ethnic groups. This paper will discuss some illustrative information that is readily accessible, much of it from United States Census reports, and some problems these data present, in the hope of stimulating interest in Detroit ethnic studies.

The United States Census of 1960 found that 28.9 percent of the people of the city of Detroit were black, and another 32.2 percent were of foreign birth or parentage (Table 6-1). In addition, approximately 7 percent of the city's population were whites who moved to Detroit from the South within the past five years.[a] A 1958 survey documented the city's religious diversity: 56 percent of the population of greater Detroit were Protestants, 35 percent Catholics, and 4 percent were Jews.[1]

Religion as well as race or national origin, or some combination of these categories, may define an ethnic group, according to the sociologist Milton Gordon.[2] Members of an ethnic group often share a sense of common origins and a common fate as a people, which gives meaning for the present and future to group traditions inherited from the past. In some individuals or groups this feeling of attachment may not be strong enough to make them part of an "ethnic community," but the larger society may nevertheless define them as members of a particular ethnic group.

Gordon's definition of an ethnic group as a people set off by race, religion, and national origin is broader than the interpretation implicit in the U.S. Census, which does not take account of religion or of the nationality backgrounds of whites beyond the second generation after immigration. But even in terms of the census' restricted definition, over 60 percent of Detroit's population in 1960

---

[a]The census counted 12,149 whites who moved from the South in the last five years. In 1958, about 7.6 percent of the University of Michigan's Detroit Area Study sample were white Protestants born in the South. (Gerhard Lenski, *The Religious Factor: A Sociologist's Inquiry*, Garden City: Anchor, 1963, pp. 45-47).

Table 6-1
Detroit Population by Race and Nativity, 1960

	Detroit SMSA	Detroit	Detroit plus enclaves*	Detroit Suburbs (excluding enclaves*)
Total Population	3,762,360	1,670,144	1,742,344	2,020,016
White Population	3,195,372	1,182,970	1,242,069	1,953,303
as % of total	84.9	70.8	71.3	96.7
Black Population	558,870	482,223	495,078	63,792
as % of total	14.8	28.9	28.4	3.2
Other Races	8,118	4,951	5,197	2,921
as % of total	.2	.3	.3	.1
Foreign Stock	1,133,986	537,446	568,051	565,935
as % of total	30.1	32.2	32.6	28.0
as % of white population	35.5	45.4	45.7	29.0
Foreign Born	364,575	201,713	214,032	149,543
as % of total	9.7	12.1	12.3	7.4
as % of white population	11.4	17.1	17.2	7.7
as % of foreign stock	32.1	37.5	37.7	26.4
Native of Foreign or Mixed Parentage	769,411	335,733	353,019	416,392
as % of total	20.4	20.1	20.3	20.6
as % of white population	24.1	28.4	28.4	21.0
as % of foreign stock	67.9	62.5	62.1	73.6
Puerto Rican Birth or Parentage	2,161	1,549	1,553	608
as % of total	.1	.1	.1	.0
Native American Whites 3rd Generation or More	2,072,687	NA	NA	NA
as % of total	55.1	NA	NA	NA

Sources: *U.S. Census of Population, 1960, Michigan, General Social & Economic Characteristics* PC (1)-24C, and *Detailed Characteristics*
*Highland Park and Hamtramck

could be identified as members of some ethnic group. The old-stock, white-Anglo-Saxon-Protestant "majority" is definitely a minority in Detroit, as it is in most large American cities.

The census data summarized in Table 6-2 indicate that the largest nationality

Table 6-2
Countries of Origin of Foreign Stock, Detroit Area, 1960

	Detroit SMSA No.	%	Detroit No.	%	Detroit plus enclaves* No.	%	Detroit Suburbs (excluding enclaves*) No.	%
Canada	256,707	22.6	98,803	18.4	102,498	18.0	154,209	27.2
United Kingdom	114,466	10.1	46,493	8.6	48,776	8.6	65,690	11.6
Ireland	21,589	1.9	11,604	2.2	11,856	2.1	9,733	1.7
France	7,445	.7	3,412	.6	3,579	.6	3,866	.7
Norway	6,337	.6	2,349	.4	2,466	.4	3,871	.7
Sweden	13,289	1.2	5,338	1.0	5,563	1.0	7,726	1.4
Denmark	5,360	.5	1,839	.3	1,915	.3	3,445	.6
Finland	13,118	1.2	5,741	1.1	6,196	1.1	6,922	1.2
Austria	28,123	2.5	13,251	2.5	13,993	2.5	14,130	2.5
Switzerland	3,520	.3	1,449	.3	1,502	.3	2,018	.4
Germany	115,059	10.1	54,256	10.1	54,641	9.6	60,418	10.7
Netherlands	7,676	.7	2,876	.5	2,937	.5	4,739	.8
Poland	190,997	16.8	106,739	19.9	120,347	21.2	70,650	12.5
Czechoslovakia	19,141	1.7	8,888	1.7	9,221	1.6	9,920	1.8
Hungary	32,582	2.9	14,202	2.6	14,409	2.5	18,173	3.2
Rumania	12,054	1.1	5,788	1.1	6,242	1.1	5,812	1.0
Lithuania	13,581	1.2	8,116	1.5	8,434	1.5	5,147	.9
USSR	55,480	4.9	33,142	6.2	35,074	6.2	20,406	3.6
Yugoslavia	20,435	1.8	9,873	1.8	10,395	1.8	10,040	1.8
Greece	13,262	1.2	7,489	1.4	7,834	1.4	5,428	1.0
Italy	95,077	8.4	47,689	8.9	48,666	8.6	46,411	8.2
Portugal	416	.0	177	.0	185	.0	231	.0
Other Europe	32,552	2.9	16,720	3.1	16,986	3.0	15,566	2.7
Mexico	11,731	1.0	7,276	1.4	7,354	1.3	4,377	.8
Other Central- S. America	5,650	.5	66	.0	252	.0	5,398	.9
Asia	27,644	2.4	15,498	2.9	17,088	3.0	10,556	1.9
All other and Not Reported	10,695	.9	4,070	.8	4,340	.8	6,355	1.1

Sources: U.S. Census of Population, 1960, *Michigan, Detailed Characteristics*, Table 79
*Highland Park and Hamtramck

groups in Detroit in 1960 came from the United Kingdom, Canada, Germany, Austria, Poland, Hungary, the USSR, and Italy. These countries were the original homelands of over three-quarters of greater Detroit's population of foreign birth or parentage. The city's people of Polish stock alone account for about 16 percent of the total population, making Detroit second only to Chicago as a Polish center in the United States.

Since 1960, the most recent year for which census data are available, many changes have probably taken place in the ethnic composition and distribution of Detroit's population. For example, the 1970 census may show a significant increase in the numbers of Spanish-Americans, Southern whites, and American Indians in Detroit. Recent estimates have set the Detroit area Spanish-American population at anywhere from 35,000 to 90,000, and its Indian population at 3,000, as compared with the 1960 census figures of 19,542 Spanish-Americans and 2,195 Indians.[3] An estimated 40 percent of Detroit's population is now black;[b] the significant increase in the proportion of blacks since 1960 is a result both of natural population growth and of white movement to the suburbs.

Many white ethnic groups have joined in the exodus. Table 6-3 shows the proportion of each ethnic group that lived in the suburbs of Detroit in 1960, but the 1970 census will undoubtedly show many changes in those residential distributions. There are indications that the centers of Italian, Polish, German, and Jewish concentration, for example, have shifted outward in a "corridor" pattern, to some of the northern and northeastern suburbs.[4] Members of ethnic groups that move to the suburbs, even those whose income and life style have become middle class, may retain ties with their ethnic communities. In fact, the ethnic community may simply shift its location outside the city limits.[c]

Detroit and its suburbs continue to bear the marks of the city's major ethnic groups. They have played a significant role in shaping many aspects of local economic and cultural life, including residential patterns. It has been said, for example, that Detroit has one of the largest proportions of homeowners of any major American city. While relatively high wage levels have undoubtedly contributed to this pattern, so did the fact that many of Detroit's people have roots in the rural Central European tradition which places a high value on land ownership.[d]

---

[b]*Detroit Free Press*, June 15, 1969. Of the nation's twenty largest cities, only Baltimore, Washington, and New Orleans have larger proportions of Negroes than Detroit (Detroit Urban League, "A Profile of the Detroit Negro, 1959-1964," 1965, p. 1).

[c]Stanley Lieberson, ("Suburbs and Ethnic Residential Patterns," *American Journal of Sociology*, 67, 1962, pp. 673-81), in a study using census data, found that foreign born and second generation residents of suburbs tend to be segregated from native white groups. Also see Bennett M. Berger, "Suburbia and the American Dream," in Sam Bass Warner (ed.), *Planning for a Nation of Cities* (Cambridge, Mass.: MIT Press, 1966).

[d]This point is suggested by Frank Angelo in "The Peoples of Detroit Project," and with regard to Hamtramck, in Arthur Wood's *Hamtramck, Then and Now* (New York: Bookman Associates, 1955). Albert Mayer reports that the 1940 census showed that 47 percent of all Detroiters of foreign stock, and 46 percent of the foreign born, owned their own homes, compared with 40 percent of the total population. (Albert Mayer, "A Study of the

Table 6-3

Percent of Ethnic Populations Living in City and in Suburbs, Detroit SMSA, 1960

Group or Population	% in Detroit plus enclaves*	% in Suburbs excluding enclaves*
White Population	38.9	61.1
Black Population	88.6	11.4
Other Races	64.0	36.0
Puerto Ricans	71.9	28.1
Foreign Stock	50.1	49.9
United Kingdom	42.6	57.4
Canada	39.9	60.1
Ireland	54.9	45.1
France	48.1	51.9
Norway	38.9	61.1
Sweden	41.9	58.1
Denmark	35.7	64.3
Finland	47.2	52.8
Austria	49.8	50.2
Switzerland	42.7	57.3
Germany	47.5	52.5
Netherlands	38.3	61.7
Poland	63.0	37.0
Czechoslovakia	48.2	51.8
Hungary	44.2	55.8
Rumania	51.8	48.2
Lithuania	62.1	37.9
USSR	63.2	36.8
Yugoslavia	50.9	49.1
Greece	59.1	40.9
Italy	51.2	48.8
Portugal	44.5	55.5
Other Europe	52.2	47.8
Mexico	62.7	37.3
Other Central-S. America	4.5	95.5
Asia	61.8	38.2
All other and Not Reported	40.6	59.4

*Highland Park and Hamtramck

Foreign-Born Population of Detroit, 1870-1950," Wayne University, Department of Sociology and Anthropology, August, 1951, pp. 60-61). Comparable data for 1960 were not located.

But despite many signs that ethnicity is alive and well, Detroit and other large American cities are regarded by many as "melting pots" in which ethnic groups are losing their separate identities and blending into a homogenous middle class American mainstream. Although the melting pot idea has lost some of its scholarly respectability, it is still widely believed that the majority of members of most ethnic groups are being "assimilated," absorbed with hardly a trace, into the dominant American lifestyle.[5]

Blacks, Spanish-Americans and American Indians are frequently viewed as recent immigrants to the city who remain predominantly lower class, and retain a strong ethnic identity, partly because they still lack the necessary education or skills to assimilate and become upwardly mobile. But it is believed that they will acquire them given sufficient exposure to urban and middle class lifestyles, and that they will find more opportunities open to them as their political power grows, and as discriminatory practices in hiring and housing face increasing challenges.[6]

The belief that "anyone can make it if he tries"—a deeply ingrained American faith in the possibility of upward mobility—is closely tied to the melting pot idea in ways that have perhaps been insufficiently studied.[7] Acculturation, or the learning of a new culture and language, and assimilation, or full participation in the institutions and social relations of a new society, are analytically distinct from social mobility. It is one thing to become acculturated, another to assimilate, and still another matter to move upward in the social hierarchy. Yet acculturation and assimilation have often been considered prerequisites to upward mobility, which in turn has been viewed as a natural consequence of assimilation and acculturation. Mobility, it appears, has frequently been considered a partial test of the effectiveness of the melting pot.[e] Thus, for example, Otis Dudley Duncan and Stanley Lieberson justified their practice of treating indicators of socioeconomic status as measures of immigrant "adjustment" with the statement that "ethnic differentials in socioeconomic status are indicative of incomplete absorption and assimilation."[8]

A link between assimilation and upward mobility is also implicit in the writings of the social stratification theorists W. Lloyd Warner and Leo Srole, who maintained that:

Each group enters the city at the bottom of the social heap . . . and through the several generations makes its desperate climb upward. The early arrivals, having had more time, have climbed farther. . . . . It seems likely that oncoming

---

[e]For an example see W. Lloyd Warner and Lee Srole, *The Social Systems of American Ethnic Groups* (New Haven: Yale University Press, 1945), p. 284. This linkage of mobility with assimilation may have a source in the tendency of many American stratification theorists to view stratification in terms of differences in values and lifestyle (status) rather than in economic or political power (class), and to take equality of opportunity for granted. See John Pease, William Form, and Joan Rytina, "Ideological Currents in American Stratification Literature," *American Sociologist*, 5, 1970, pp. 127-37.

generations of new ethnics will go through the same metamorphosis and climb to the same heights that generations of earlier groups have achieved.[9]

Seymour Martin Lipset and Reinhard Bendix later observed that:

Traditionally, immigrants entered American society on the lowest rung of the occupational and status ladder. However, the native-born children of the immigrants, who generally received a better education than their parents and who were assimilated to American speech and behavior, were able to rise economically and socially as the national economy expanded. Consequently, it has been argued that low status and income in American society has been the plight of groups which are 'in the society but not of it'.[10]

Lipset and Bendix suggest, as do other stratification theorists, that the persistence of ethnic characteristics and identity—that is, a failure of the processes of assimilation or acculturation—partially accounts for failures of individuals or groups to be upwardly mobile. Upward mobility, it is implied, is at least in part a concommitant of a loss of ethnic characteristics and community ties. This melting pot style formulation of the mobility process has little appeal for many members of ethnic groups who prefer to think in terms of integration within a pluralistic social structure, and who may be sensitive to the role of prejudice and discrimination in retarding upward mobility. Perhaps from their point of view a meaningful definition of "assimilation" would entail free and unhindered access to employment opportunities, education, political power, and the material standard of living enjoyed by the majority.[f] Such a definition, contrary to the melting pot concept, need not mean the disappearance of ethnicity in all spheres of the life of the individual.[g]

The idea of the melting pot has been called into question in an increasing number of studies and publications.[11] There are at least three reasons to doubt this theory, and especially to question its implications for black and Spanish-Americans, who are sometimes considered the "newest immigrants" by melting pot theorists. These reasons include changed economic conditions since the time of the great immigrations, racial discrimination, and the probability that the melting pot failed to work effectively even for white ethnic groups.

Social and economic conditions in American cities have changed drastically since the melting pot idea gained widespread adherence during the first quarter of this century, when the last great wave of immigrants arrived from Europe. Detroit's automobile manufacturing and other industries needed a large supply

---

[f]Such concerns were expressed, for example, at a recent conference of white ethnic leaders (*New York Times*, July 17, 1970).

[g]"Assimilation" implies the disappearance of ethnicity, while "integration" suggests participation in the larger society without a necessary loss of ethnic or group identity. (Ralph Conant, Sheldon Levy, and Ralph Lewis, "Mass Polarization: Negro and White Attitudes on the Pace of Integration," *American Behavioral Scientist*, 13, 1969, p. 262.)

of unskilled labor in their early stages of development, and they recruited workers from many parts of the country and the world.[h] The demand for unskilled labor has since waned, however, and more recent immigrants, often black, Spanish or Southern white Americans, who came to Detroit to seek jobs and join relatives, may have found far fewer opportunities for steady and well-paying factory work than the groups who preceded them.[i]

The melting pot theory also fails to recognize that the large and growing black population of Detroit, together with the small Indian population, probably faces a depth of prejudice and discrimination that far exceeds that experienced by other ethnic groups. The 1960 census provided information about non-white ethnic groups in urban parts of Michigan but not disaggregated for cities. These data, shown in Table 6-4, indicate that 39 percent of urban Michigan's employed white males had white collar occupations in 1960, compared with New York State's 45.5 percent and Illinois' 41 percent. But only 12 percent of urban Michigan's employed black males, and 10 percent of its Indian males, had white collar jobs, compared with 21 percent of black males living in New York and 15.5 percent in Illinois. The proportion of employed black and Indian males in service and labor occupations in 1960 was more than twice that of white males in urban Michigan.[j] The income differential between whites on the one hand, and blacks and Indians on the other, was also marked. And in 1960, blacks and Indians were two years behind the median educational level of whites, and three times as likely to be unemployed.[k]

---

[h]John Leggett, *Class, Race and Labor, Working Class Consciousness in Detroit* (New York: Oxford University Press, 1968), p. 46. Many of the Detroit area's foreign-born residents may have moved here during those years from other parts of the U.S.A. rather than directly from abroad. Arthur E. Wood reports a survey suggesting that Hamtramck was not an area of first settlement for Poles. Most were attracted from New York, Pennsylvania, Ohio, and Massachusetts by Hamtramck's reputation as a Polish town, and by the prospect of production jobs; 45 percent of the fathers of Hamtramck school children were auto workers in the late 1930s. (Wood, *Hamtramck*.)

[i]The fact that in 1960, 33 percent of greater Detroit's employed Negro males worked in auto manufacturing jobs, compared with 22 percent of employed white males, may seem to contradict this statement. But it should be remembered that 17 percent of black males were then unemployed, compared with 6 percent of white males.

[j]White collar occupations include the census classifications of professionals, technicians, proprietors and officials, and clerical and sales occupations. Service and labor occupations include private household workers, other service workers, and all laborers' jobs. The term "blue collar" here refers to operatives, craftsmen, and foremen. Following Lipset and Bendix (*Social Mobility*, pp. 14-15), it is assumed here that a move from a manual to a nonmanual job would constitute upward mobility for males.

[k]There are some indications that the 1970 census will show a tendency toward equalization of the median educational levels of whites and blacks. (U.S. Departments of Labor and Commerce, "Recent Trends in Social and Economic Conditions of Negroes in the United States," Washington, D.C.: U.S. Government Printing Office, 1968.)

Table 6-4
White, Black, American Indian, Japanese, and Chinese Males, Selected Characteristics, Urban Michigan, 1960

	Population (both sexes)		Males: Median Age	Median School Years Completed	Median Income	% White Collar	% in Service-Labor Occupations	% Unemployed
	Detroit SMSA	Urban Mich.						
Whites	3,195,372	5,038,687	28.1	11.0	$5,286.	39.1	10.3	5.8
Blacks	558,870	686,491	25.0	9.0	3,848.	11.8	26.4	17.1
American Indians	2,195	5,064	28.3	9.0	3,130.	10.2	21.3	17.5
Japanese	1,815	2,650	23.3	13.9	5,301.	53.5	9.9	4.1
Chinese	2,242	3,135	28.2	12.9	3,579.	60.0	21.6	4.6

Sources: U.S. Census of Population, 1960, Subject Reports: *Non-White Population by Race*, PC(2) IC, Tables 50, 51, 52, 55, 56, and *Michigan, General Population Characteristics*, Tables 21, 47, 49, 67, 94, 96, 133.

Note: Data on social characteristics of Indians, Japanese, and Chinese were unavailable for Detroit separately, or for urban Michigan before 1960.

The tiny Japanese and Chinese populations of urban Michigan have fared better than whites with respect to educational level, unemployment rates, and representation in white collar occupations. The Chinese, however, shared the blacks' and Indians' low median income and high proportion of service workers and laborers.

To describe these social facts, of course, is not to explain them. Various strands in the tangled skein of discrimination, cultural heritage, social custom, and individual preference might be drawn upon to account for them. A brief discussion of the situations of several white ethnic groups in Detroit will again illustrate the impossibility of basing explanations or generalizations on the meagre evidence that is available, and the need for more and better information about the life conditions of Detroit's ethnic groups.

The evidence, however, is sufficient to call into question the belief that the melting pot has worked effectively for Detroit's ethnic groups. It is probable that the extent of social mobility even among white groups has been overstated, although the fact remains that in general they do enjoy better occupational conditions than most "non-white" groups.

Table 6-5 presents occupational and educational indicators for white ethnic groups in the North Central region in 1960. These data illustrate how misleading aggregate data on "whites" can be. The indicators for "whites" shown on Table 6-4 for purposes of comparison with non-white groups mask the wide variations within that category that emerge on Table 6-5, and like aggregate data on "non-whites," tend to lead to misconceptions and stereotyped thinking about color differences.

The 1960 census data are also of interest because they provide information about the position of Mexicans for the first time. It is evident that Mexican males, both first and second generation, were in a distinctly disadvantaged position in 1960 compared with other white ethnic groups—their median educational level was lower, and they were poorly represented in white collar jobs and disproportionately found in service and labor occupations. Their low median age may provide a partial explanation; second generation Mexicans tended to be young men who had perhaps not yet completed their educations or settled into their permanent occupations. However, the position of first generation Mexican males appears considerably worse than other first generation groups, and this handicap may hinder the progress of the second generation.

Mexican males of the second generation in 1960 were at about the same educational and occupational level as black and Indian males, while all other white groups had exceeded this level. However, this comparison must be made with caution because of the difference in geographical units for which the census data on white and non-white groups were tabulated.

Because the 1960 census data on white groups were tabulated by regions, their relevance for Detroit is questionable. The 1950 data presented in Table 6-6 are more pertinent to a study of Detroit ethnic groups, despite their age, because they apply directly to the metropolitan area. The 1950 census also provided an additional indicator of income. This information, unfortunately, is of little

Table 6-5

Characteristics of Foreign White Stock, Males, Age 14 Years and Over, by Nativity and Selected Country of Origin, North Central Region, 1960

	Median Age		Median School Years Completed	% White Collar	% in Service-Labor Occupations
	N. Cen. Region	Michigan			
United Kingdom					
1st gen.*	58.2	58.1	9.7	41.6	9.6
2nd gen.**	47.7	38.6	11.1	44.7	9.8
Canada					
1st gen.	49.6	50.9	10.5	46.4	7.8
2nd gen.	38.8	35.8	11.0	43.5	10.8
Germany					
1st gen.	57.6	56.0	8.7	28.6	12.0
2nd gen.	57.5	55.3	8.7	30.8	11.4
Poland					
1st gen.	63.9	65.5	7.0	26.4	14.4
2nd gen.	42.3	41.1	10.3	30.9	10.3
USSR					
1st gen.	62.1	63.0	8.1	44.8	12.3
2nd gen.	41.0	37.8	12.2	56.1	6.8
Italy					
1st gen.	61.0	58.8	6.0	21.4	24.6
2nd gen.	37.7	35.4	11.3	38.0	12.6
Mexico					
1st gen.	42.7	48.4	6.5	9.8	37.0
2nd gen.	21.8	22.7	9.0	16.3	27.1

Source: U.S. Census of Population, 1960, Subject Reports: *Nativity and Parentage* PC(2) 1A, Tables 4, 5, 8, 9, 10.

*Foreign Born

**Native of Foreign or Mixed Parentage

value; it is included here merely to illustrate a problem often encountered in working with census data. The median income statistic is based on the incomes of both men and women. It is thus of no use in comparing ethnic groups, because of the many group differences and cultural preferences surrounding the questions of whether women should work, how much, and at what kinds of jobs. It would be much more useful—in fact, of primary importance—to know the median male income.[1] It is unfortunate that the median shown on Table 6-6

[1] In this case it would be necessary to control for age. The low median ages of second generation males in some ethnic groups indicate that they have not yet reached the peak of their earning power, while other groups may have reached this maximum.

Table 6-6

Characteristics of Foreign White Stock, 14 Years and Over, by Nativity and Selected Country of Origin, Detroit Standard Metropolitan Area, 1950

	Population (both sexes)	Males: Median Age	Males: Median School Years Completed	Both Sexes: Median Income	Males: % White Collar	% in Service Labor Occupations	% Unemployed
England & Wales							
1st gen.*	28,530	NA	10.0	$3,152.	33.0	8.7	4.0
2nd gen.**	36,785	NA	11.2	2,887.	41.8	8.5	4.2
Ireland							
1st gen.	7,565	50-54	8.8	3,021.	25.8	15.8	4.6
2nd gen.	21,995	45-49	10.8	2,778.	43.3	11.5	5.8
French Canada							
1st gen.	11,131	45-49	9.3	3,086.	26.8	9.1	5.3
2nd gen.	11,620	25-29	10.0	2,821.	33.4	10.3	6.2
Other Canada							
1st gen.	87,135	45-49	10.6	3,098.	40.2	7.3	4.0
2nd gen.	86,615	20-24	11.2	2,782.	42.1	8.5	5.5
Germany							
1st gen.	25,270	50-54	8.7	2,977.	24.8	7.8	3.9
2nd gen.	98,145	45-49	9.0	3,013.	33.8	9.6	5.4
Poland							
1st gen.	62,000	55-59	5.8	2,853.	18.0	17.1	6.2
2nd gen.	133,825	30-34	10.4	2,899.	26.7	9.0	6.6
USSR							
1st gen.	20,360	55-59	8.2	3,228.	46.4	12.6	3.6
2nd gen.	29,155	25-29	12.4	3,166.	61.4	5.0	3.2
Italy							
1st gen.	29,995	50-54	5.8	3,081.	18.1	22.2	5.8
2nd gen.	45,960	25-29	10.7	2,744.	31.2	11.4	8.8

Source: U.S. Census of Population, 1950, Special Report, *Nativity and Parentage*, PE-3A, Table 22.

*Foreign Born

**Native of Foreign or Mixed Parentage

cannot be used, for it can be argued that income is the most significant factor to examine in a study of the life conditions of various ethnic groups. The median male income is probably a more important indicator for ethnic group comparisons than education or occupation, because these characteristics are more vulnerable to the formative influence of cultural preferences and traditions. Abstractly speaking, income might be less affected by differences in ethnic cultural heritage, and may thus provide a potential indicator of ethnic discrimination.

The variables of occupational distribution and median educational level shown on Table 6-6 for males of eight ethnic groups can be studied in two ways—by comparing the relative positions of the groups in the first and second generations, and by comparing the degree of mobility in each group from the first generation to the second.

When making either kind of comparison it would be highly desirable to take account of the recency of immigration of the various groups, their relative sizes and age structures, and of such factors as the rural or urban origin of the group, the resources of compatriots already established in the American city, and the content of the group's cultural heritage. The Germans and Irish, for example, have been in the Detroit area longest, and their median ages are highest in both the first and second generation. The other groups arrived more recently and are younger, probably of approximately the same median age as the general white population.

It might also be important when making comparisons between groups or generations to consider the difference between educational systems and values among the various countries of origin. In some countries only eight years of education may have been compulsory; thus the social value of eight years of education in such countries may be equivalent to twelve years in the United States, and more than eight years of education might indicate middle class status. Or men may receive advanced formal technical training for a skilled trade, studying for many years to prepare for a blue collar job. The meaning of education in countries with a high level of general culture may differ from countries where education beyond the compulsory level is relatively rare and assures upper middle class status. Such variations, which may influence views about education among members of ethnic groups, might be fruitfully examined in studies of educational mobility between generations.

Figure 6-1, which is based upon Table 6-6, illustrates profiles of the relative ranks of the second generation of eight ethnic groups in terms of selected educational and occupational indicators. The figure shows a clear split: males of Russian, English, and British Canadian origin rank high on every variable, while the French Canadians, Poles, and Italians rank low. The Irish and Germans show mixed profiles.

In terms of gains made by the eight groups from the first to the second generation, the Russians again, together with the Poles and Italians, made the greatest progress in education and in increasing their representation in white collar occupations and decreasing their proportions of service workers and

94

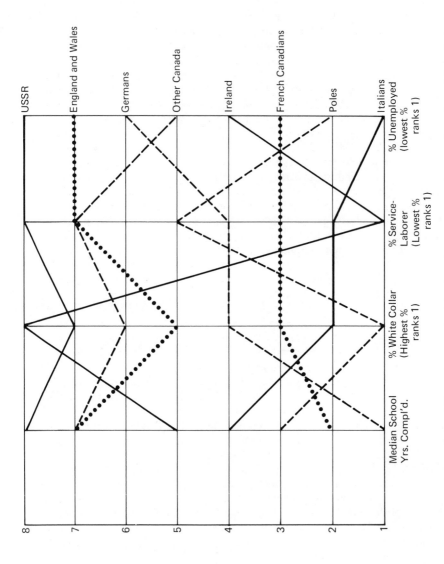

Figure 6-1. Ranking of Second Generation Males of Eight Ethnic Groups on Four Variables, (1=highest, 8=lowest).

laborers. These three groups tended to start from the most disadvantageous position in the first generation, while the English, Irish, and British Canadians started from a position of greater advantage, and made less progress. The position of the French Canadians and Germans was relatively low in the first generation, and generally remained so in the second.

The greatest gains were made and the highest ranking position achieved by men of Russian origin, who are probably predominantly Jewish.[m] Many studies, done both in Detroit and in other cities, have demonstrated and attempted to explain the cultural factors behind the consistent success of the Jews as a group in attaining a high educational level and an extremely high proportion of white collar workers.[12] The British Canadians and English, whose profiles are virtually identical, are next: their position probably closely resembles that of native white Americans of three generations or more.

The occupational distributions of the Irish, Germans, and to some extent the Poles appear somewhat irregular when education is taken into account. The Poles and especially the Germans appear to be concentrated in operatives', craftsmen's and foremen's occupations along with the French Canadians. On the other hand, the Irish, who are among Detroit's oldest immigrant groups, have disproportionately few of these blue collar workers. They appear to have found a niche for themselves in white collar and service fields. The Germans might be expected to have a much higher median educational level and proportion of white collar workers than they do, inasmuch as they also were among the first and most influential immigrant groups. But it has been observed that Detroit's German population continues to include a relatively large number of recent arrivals that have not taken their citizenship.[13] The census also provides evidence that second generation men are following the German tradition of choosing highly-paid, high-prestige skilled trades as their occupations. Local labor market conditions in the post-war decades, notably the relatively secure jobs and high pay enjoyed by blue collar workers in Detroit, may have reinforced the tendency of some groups to prefer such jobs, and lessened the pressure toward college education and white collar jobs for their children—although in general, of course, this pressure is strong.

What does this cursory examination of indicators of the educational and occupational positions of several ethnic groups tell us about how effectively Detroit's melting pot has functioned? What implications can be drawn for social policy?

The census data that served as the basis for Tables 6-5 and 6-6 cannot in themselves provide a basis for evaluating the extent of ethnic social mobility in Detroit. Those who subscribe to the melting pot theory believe that ethnic differences will weaken and eventually disappear, but this process is usually visualized as taking at least three generations. The small amount of available

---

[m]The decennial census does not count the Jews or other religious groups, but it has been estimated that about half of Detroit's Jewish families were originally of Russian nationality. The remainder are mostly of Polish and other Central European backgrounds. (David

census data about white ethnic groups covers only the immigration and second generations.

There are some limited sources of information about ethnicity in Detroit that take account of religion and nationality background beyond the second generation, thus providing a valuable supplement to what can be learned from the census. The 1958 Detroit area survey findings reported by Gerhard Lenski indicated marked differences among Detroit's major religious groups in life conditions and in attitudes which may influence mobility. In fact, Lenski's findings suggested that differences among Protestants, Catholics, and Jews tend to increase, not decrease, over the generations, and that they are greater among middle class people than among members of the working class.[n]

In focusing his investigation on the role of religion and neglecting that of ethnicity, Lenski was consistent with his belief in a version of the melting pot theory—the "triple melting pot" model—which holds that American society is not a single melting pot, but a tri-partite structure divided along religious lines.[14] According to this model, the three major religious groupings tend to remain structurally distinct, while ethnic differences within each group tend to disappear over time. The ethnic group, Lenski maintains, is destined to disappear; it is gradually blending into and being superseded by the "socio-religious sub-community, a group united by ties of race and religion."[15] Thus blacks and other non-white groups are excluded from the "triple melting pot" scheme—they are considered to be in a "pot" by themselves.

Edward O. Laumann's findings from a 1966 Detroit area survey suggest that social reality is more complicated than the triple melting pot theorists imply.[16] His report presents evidence that important ethnic differences do persist among native-born men within a single religious group, or even a single denomination. Marked differences were shown among various religious denominations and ethnic groups in median family income and median occupational status and educational levels of white males. For example, there was a tendency for "Anglo-American" groups, whether Protestant or Catholic, to have somewhat higher socioeconomic statuses than groups of other nationality backgrounds. Tables 6-7 and 6-8, based upon data presented by Laumann, give concrete illustrations of some ethnic differences in life circumstances within major religious groups, and of differences between various religious denominations within a single ethnic group.[o] Laumann also found that while Detroit men

Goldberg and Harry Sharp, "Some Characteristics of Detroit Area Jewish and Non-Jewish Adults," in Marshall Sklare (ed.), *The Jews: Social Patterns of an American Group*, New York: Free Press, 1958, p. 111.)

[n]Lenski, *The Religious Factor*, pp. 322-26. Lenski has been criticized for not taking account of differences in nationality background, especially in his Catholic sample. He replied that "it seems clear that with increasing intermarriage across ethnic lines, these differences will disappear and a common American Catholic subculture will emerge" (p. x). The triple melting pot assumption, however, must be adequately tested before it can be accepted.

[o]This illustration is limited by the fact that Laumann had to group Protestant nationalities, and the "Anglo-Americans" among the Catholics, into general categories because of the small number of individuals in each nationality group. "Scandinavians," for example, include Norwegians, Danes, Swedes, and Finns. In Detroit we would expect to find considerable differences among these four nationality groups.

tended to choose their closest friends from the same religious group as themselves, and secondarily from the same social status group, ethnicity, or depth of religious involvement, or both, were also involved in the selection of close friends.

Laumann's conclusions suggest that neither religion, nor ethnicity, nor social

Table 6-7

Income, Occupational, and Educational Characteristics of Lutheran and Catholic Males of Several Nationality Backgrounds, Detroit Area, 1966

Religion & Nationality	No.	Median Family Income	Median Occupational Status*	Median School Years Completed
Lutherans:				
Germans	57	$11,635.	43.1	11.8
Anglo-American	29	9,100.	27.5	11.7
Scandinavians	12	8,500.	46.7	12.5
Catholics:				
Anglo-Americans	33	12,167.	37.0	11.8
Irish	65	12,054.	56.9	12.6
Germans	81	9,944.	45.3	12.1
Poles	111	9,917.	33.8	11.7
Italians	55	9,700.	40.8	12.1
French	51	9,675.	37.5	12.1

Table 6-8

Income, Occupational, and Educational Characteristics of German Males of Several Religious Groups, Detroit Area, 1966

Religious Affiliations of German Males	No.	Median Family Income	Median Occupational Status*	Median School Years Completed
Presbyterians	25	$14,999.	58.8	13.6
Lutherans	57	11,635.	43.1	11.8
Methodists	32	11,154.	52.5	12.8
Baptists	27	9,250.	29.2	11.5
Catholics	81	9,944.	45.3	12.1

Source: Adapted from Laumann, "The Social Structure of Religious and Ethnoreligious Groups," Table 4.

*Duncan's Index of Socioeconomic Status, as described by Otis Dudley Duncan in "A Socioeconomic Index for All Occupations," in Albert J. Reiss, Jr. (ed.), *Occupations and Social Status*, New York: Free Press, 1961, pp. 109-161.

class alone accounts for variations in life circumstances or choice of friends. All three factors play a role, even in a population that includes third and later generations of descendents from immigrants. Support is thus provided for the idea that the ethnic factor does continue to play a role in the social and economic situations of Detroiters.

Thus the melting pot metaphor is not descriptive of Detroit's population. There are indications of differing patterns of association, social mobility, and occupational distribution among the city's ethnic groups, although more research taking at least the third generation into account is needed. But even if these differences were not evident, the metaphors of the melting pot and the triple melting pot must be rejected on the grounds that they exclude non-white groups from serious theoretical consideration. A model that fails to take account of 40 percent of Detroit's population is of no value.

What of the melting pot model as a goal for social policy? It might be argued that although Detroit cannot at present be described as a melting pot, the city might succeed in becoming one in the future. The melting pot idea has held an important place in the American ideology of egalitarianism in the past; the Canadian sociologist John Porter has suggested that the melting pot myth has been a significant stimulant to social mobility in America.[17] Immigrants to America were promised a good living, at least for their children, if only they would "Americanize"—reject their origins and heritage. Porter suggests that Canada's more conservative ideology concerning its immigrants focuses on the pluralistic ideal of the "ethnic mosaic," which makes intense loyalty to one's own ethnic group acceptable and customary, and minimizes the importance of social mobility.

But the Detroit data have shown the outlines not of the melting pot that Porter would expect to find, but tendencies toward a "vertical mosaic" of the kind he found in Canada. Northern European groups consistently seem to be overrepresented in high status positions, and blacks underrepresented, with Central and Southern European groups occupying varying ranks in between.[P]

Would it be a desirable goal for social policy to try to make the "vertical mosaic" into a "melting pot"? What would this mean, for example, for the occupational structure of various ethnic groups, a matter about which there is some, albeit inadequate, information? Should it be assumed that all groups should have the same proportion of white collar workers as white Anglo-Saxon groups, or at least the same as the general population? This is usually the sort of concept of mobility that is implied in the melting pot ideal, which emphasizes the homogenization of all ethnic characteristics. Should it be assumed that many more Poles, Italians, and French Canadians, for example, would prefer white

---

[P]Leggett's 1957-58 Detroit study involved asking ethnic group members to rank several groups, including their own, in terms of status. Regardless of their own group membership, all raters agreed that the English had highest prestige, followed by the Germans, Poles, and Negores. This rating parallels that made by Grosse Pointe real estate interests, who sought to exclude "undesirable" ethnic groups through the use of a point system. (Leggett, *Class, Race and Labor*, p. 109, and N.C. Thomas, *Rule Nine*, New York: Random House, 1966.)

collar jobs than had them in 1950? Perhaps they have already gained them; available published data do not make this clear. Or it may be that their cultural heritages emphasize other values, and that the color of the Polish or Italian breadwinner's collar is of relatively minor importance.

From one point of view it would be in the interest of every ethnic group to have as large a proportion of white collar workers as possible, inasmuch as the generation of new jobs in the future will largely take place in the white collar and service fields. The effects of automation, and the unemployment it sometimes gives rise to, have been and will be most strongly felt by blue collar workers.[q]

It goes without saying that ethnic discrimination in employment is undesirable from both an individual and social point of view, and should be eliminated. But our present state of knowledge does not make it possible to distinguish, either analytically or empirically, to what extent ethnic differences in occupational distribution are attributable to discrimination, and to what extent they are caused by ethnic differences in cultural values, or a variety of other factors. Even if there were no ethnic discrimination—that is, if men could gain access to any occupation they desired—could it be assumed that 40 percent of every group would choose white collar occupations?

If both the "melting pot" and the "vertical mosaic" models were to be rejected in favor of a model, as yet undeveloped, that is both pluralistic and equalitarian, ethnic differences in occupational choice would still be expected. Such a model for social policy would give social science the task of inquiring into the occupational preferences or goals of members of various ethnic groups, and showing the ways in which ethnic discrimination stands between the individual's occupational aspirations and his real prospects.

A pluralistic model for social policy would also point in the direction of eliminating vast differences in compensation for various jobs by placing a floor under income and compressing the range of financial rewards. If a man could be sure of making enough money to support his family no matter what occupation he selected, he could afford to exercise a greater degree of personal choice and cultural preference in selecting his occupation. He could weigh the relative costs in personal terms of investing his time and money in higher education or learning a trade, or of maximizing his opportunities for sociability with his family and friends, or of continuing in the traditional occupation of his family or group.[r]

---

[q]Beginning in 1957, the number of white collar workers has exceeded the number of manual workers in the U.S. (Lipset and Bendix, *Social Mobility*, p. 85). Since that time many new white collar jobs have been created in Detroit, while many blue collar jobs in the city's auto industries have been eliminated by automation. This, together with the persistence of a relatively high level of unemployment, has hit black workers especially hard. See Leggett, *Race, Class and Labor*, pp. 55 ff.

[r]Many studies have shown ethnic differences in values placed on social mobility, educational achievement, consumer goods, peer-group life, and the preservation of traditional culture—values that may often conflict with each other. These studies suggest that individual upward mobility is only one of many desirable lifestyles within the ethnic community. For examples see Gerald Suttles, *The Social Order of the Slum: Ethnicity and Territoriality in the Inner City* (Chicago: University of Chicago Press, 1968); Herbert Gans, *The Urban Villagers* (New York: Free Press, 1962); and Charles Keil, *Urban Blues* (Chicago: University of Chicago Press, 1966).

The maximization of personal preference in occupational choice would of course be only a secondary effect of income redistribution. The primary effect would be the elimination of the poverty that now most directly affects black residents of American cities. The benefits of such a program for other ethnic groups that have attained greater economic stability, however, are usually overlooked. There has been insufficient recognition of the substantial advantages to all ethnic groups of working together for a more equitable distribution of wealth and other social goals.

Selected Bibliography on Ethnicity in Detroit

A. Ethnicity in Detroit: Data Sources and Historical and General Readings

Annis, Sheldon. *Detroit: A Young Guide to the City*, Detroit: Speedball Publications, 1970.

Detroit Public Schools, Department of Intergroup Relations, Division of School-Community Relations. "Racial-Ethnic Distribution of Students and Employees in the Detroit Public Schools, October, 1969," mimeo.

_____. "Racial Distribution of Students and Personnel in the Detroit Public Schools as of October 19, 1967," mimeo.

Eldersveld, Samuel. *Political Parties*, Chicago: Rand McNally, 1964.

Glazer, Sidney. *Detroit: A Study in Urban Development*, New York: Bookman, 1965.

Graff, George P. "The People of Michigan: A History and Selected Bibliography of the Races and Nationalities Who Settled Our State," Lansing: Michigan Department of Education, Bureau of Library Services, 1970.

International Institute of Metropolitan Detroit, *Progress Report*, serial.

_____. *Newsletter* serial.

Laumann, Edward O. "The Social Structure of Religious and Ethnoreligious Groups in a Metropolitan Community: A Smallest Space Analysis," *American Sociological Review*, 34, 1969, pp. 182-97.

Leggett, John C. *Class, Race and Labor: Working-Class Consciousness in Detroit*, New York: Oxford University Press, 1968.

Lewis, Charles Alonzo. *Communication Patterns of Recent Immigrants: A Study of Three Nationality Groups in Metropolitan Detroit*, University of Illinois, Ph.D. dissertation.

Mayer, Albert J. "Ethnic Groups in Detroit: 1951," Wayne University, Department of Sociology and Anthropology, June, 1951, mimeo.

_____. "A Study of the Foreign-Born Population of Detroit: 1870-1950," Wayne University, Department of Sociology and Anthropology, 1951, mimeo.

Rankin, Lois. "Detroit Nationality Groups," *Michigan History Magazine*, 23, 1939, pp. 129-211.

Sellers, Donald. *Hamtramck: A Sociological Paradox*, Wayne State University, Department of Sociology and Anthropology, M.A. thesis, 1957.

Sigel, Roberta S. "Race and Religion as Factors in the Kennedy Victory in Detroit, 1960," Wayne State University, Department of Political Science, Reprint Series no. 6, n.d.

Thomas, Norman C. *Rule Nine: Politics, Administration and Civil Rights*, New York: Random House, 1966.

U.S. Census of Population, *Michigan, Detailed Characteristics*, and special reports on Nativity, Mother Tongue, Nonwhite Population, decennial.

Wood, Arthur E. *Hamtramck, Then and Now*, New York: Bookman Associates, 1955.

Woodford, Frank and Arthur Woodford. *All Our Yesterdays: A Brief History of Detroit*, Detroit, Wayne State University Press, 1969.

B. Race Relations and Detroit's Black Community

Anderson, Marc B. *Racial Discrimination in Detroit: A Spatial Analysis of Racism*, Wayne State University, Department of Geography, M.A. thesis, 1969.

Boggs, James. *The American Revolution: Pages from a Negro Worker's Notebook*, New York: Modern Reader Paperbacks, 1963.

Boykin, Ulysses. "A Handbook on the Detroit Negro, A Preliminary Edition," Detroit: Minority Study Associates, 1943.

Caplan, Nathan S. and Jeffrey Paige. "A Study of Ghetto Rioters," *Scientific American*, 219, 1968, pp. 15-21.

Cleage, Albert. *The Black Messiah*, New York: Sheed and Ward, 1968.

Detroit Bureau of Governmental Research, Inc. *The Negro in Detroit*, Detroit: Mayor's Interracial Committee, 1926.

Detroit Commission on Community Relations, "Detroit Area Setting: Population Changes and Characteristics," Detroit, June, 1962.

_____. "Employment and Income by Age, Sex, Color and Residence," Detroit, May, 1963.

Detroit Urban League, Research Department. "The Detroit Low-Income Negro Family," Detroit, 1966.

_____. "A Profile of the Detroit Negro, 1959-1964," Detroit, 1965.

Green, John M. *Negroes in Michigan History*, 1968, a reprint of Francis H. Warren (ed.), *Michigan Manual of Freedmens' Progress*, Detroit: Freedmens' Progress Commission, 1915.

Haughton, Ronald, Charles Remus and Frances Cousens. "A Study of Discrimination in Employment for the Equal Opportunity Commission," Wayne State University–University of Michigan Joint Institute of Labor and Industrial Relations, Sept., 1966.

Henderson, George. "Twelfth Street: An Analysis of a Changed Neighborhood," Detroit: Detroit Urban League, 1961.

Hersey, John. *Algiers Motel Incident*, New York: Bantam, 1968.

Isajiw, Wsevolod, Don Stewart, and Norbert Hartman. "Attitudes in the Inner-Core Area of Detroit," Wayne State University—University of Michigan Joint Institute of Labor and Industrial Relations, June 30, 1969.

Lee, Alfred N. and N.D. Humphrey. *Race Riot*, New York: Dryden, 1943.

Locke, Hubert. *The Detroit Riot of 1967*, Detroit: Wayne State University Press, 1969.

Meyer, Albert J. and Thomas F. Hoult. "Race and Residence in Detroit," Wayne State University, Institute for Urban Studies, Aug., 1962.

Meyer, Philip. "The People Beyond Twelfth Street: A Survey of Attitudes of Detroit Negroes After the Riot of 1967," Detroit Free Press and Detroit Urban League, 1967.

Michigan Civil Rights Commission. "Employment Distribution Study of the Construction Industry in Michigan," July, 1966.

_____. "Report and Recommendations on the Status of Migratory Farm Labor in Michigan, 1968," 1968.

_____. "Vocational Preparation and Race in Michigan Higher Education," n.d.

_____. "Women in Higher Education," 1969.

Musial, John. "The Analysis of Residential Segregation Trends in Metropolitan Areas," Wayne State University, Center for Urban Studies, March, 1968.

National Advisory Commission on Civil Disorders, *Report*, New York: Bantam, 1968.

New Detroit Committee, *Progress Report, April, 1968*, Detroit: Metropolitan Fund, 1968.

Sauter, Van Gordon. *Nightmare in Detroit: A Rebellion and Its Victims*, Chicago: Regenry, 1968.

Shogan, Robert and Thomas Craig. *The Detroit Race Riot: 1943*, Chicago: Chilton, 1964.

Terry, Robert. *For Whites Only*, Grand Rapids: Wm. B. Eerdmans, 1970.

Wolf, Eleanor P. and Charles Lebeaux. *Change and Renewal in an Urban Community: Five Case Studies of Detroit*, New York: Praeger, 1969.

_____. "On the Destruction of Poor Neighborhoods by Urban Renewal," *Social Problems*, 15, 1967, pp. 3-8.

C. Studies of Detroit Nationality and Ethnic Groups

Aprahamian, Ashod. *The Armenians of Detroit*, Wayne State University, Department of History, M.A. thesis, 1959.

Beynon, Erdmann D. "The Hungarian Population of Detroit," *Michigan History Magazine*, 21, 1937, pp. 89-103.

Ford, R. Clyde. "The French Canadians of Michigan," *Michigan History Magazine*, 27, 1943, pp. 243-57.

Helling, Rudolph A. *A Comparison of the Acculturation of Immigrants in Toronto, Ontario, and Detroit, Michigan*, Wayne State University, Department of Sociology and Anthropology, Ph.D. dissertation, 1962.

Johnson, Clarence. *Origins, Population, Locations, Occupations, and Activities of the Swedes in Detroit*, Wayne University, Department of History, M.A. thesis, 1940.

Kistler, Mark O. "The German Language Press in Michigan: A Survey and Bibliography," *Michigan History Magazine*, 56, 1960, pp. 321 ff.

Mayer, Albert J. and Sue Marx. "Social Change, Religion and Birth Rates," *American Journal of Sociology*, 62, 1957, pp. 383-90.

Miljeric, June. "The Yugoslav People," *Michigan History Magazine*, 25, 1941, pp. 358-64.

Napolska, Mary. "The Polish Immigrant in Detroit to 1914," *Annals of the Polish Roman Catholic Union Archives and Museum*, 10, 1945-46.

Ohnuki, Emiko. *Detroit Chinese: A Study of Socio-Cultural Changes in the Detroit Chinese Community from 1872 through 1963*, Madison: University of Wisconsin, Department of Anthropology, M.S. thesis, 1964.

Ostafin, Peter. *The Polish Peasant in Transition: A Study of Group Integration as a Function of Symbiosis and Common Definitions*, University of Michigan, Ph.D. dissertation, 1948.

Pawlick, Tom. "The Abandonment of the Indian in Detroit's Red Ghetto," *Detroit News*, "The Other Section," March 5, 1970.

Poles in Michigan, Detroit: Glow Press, 1953, 2 vols.

Russell, John A. "The Germanic Influence in the Making of Michigan," Detroit: University of Detroit Press, 1927.

Sengstock, Mary. *Maintenance of Social Interaction Patterns in an Ethnic Group*, St. Louis: Washington University, Ph.D. dissertation, 1967.

Stavros, Denny, *The Assimilation of Southern White Factory Workers in Detroit*, Wayne State University, Department of Sociology and Anthropology, M.A. thesis, 1956.

Stephanides, Marios. *Problems of Survey Research Encountered During the Process of Conducting a Study on Attitudes of the Greek Community in Detroit: A Methodological and Sociological Investigation*, Wayne State University, Department of Sociology, M.A. thesis, 1969.

Tait, John. *The Social Participation of the Polish Immigrant Professional in the Detroit Metropolitan Area: A Study in Assimilation*, Wayne State University, Department of Sociology, M.A. thesis, 1948.

Vismara, John. "Coming of the Italians to Detroit," *Michigan History Magazine*, 2, 1918, pp. 123 ff.

Wargelin, John. "The Finns in Michigan," *Michigan History Magazine*, 24, 1940, pp. 179-203.

Zeitlin, Irving. *The Sephardic Community of Greater Detroit*, Wayne State University, Department of Sociology and Anthropology, M.A. thesis, 1961.

104

D. Religious Groups in Detroit

Besanceney, Paul. "Unbroken Protestant-Catholic Marriages Among Whites in the Detroit Area," *American Catholic Sociological Review*, 23, 1962, pp. 3-20.
Fauman, S. Joseph. "Occupational Selection Among Detroit Jews," in Marshall Sklare (ed.), *The Jews: Social Patterns of an American Group*, New York: Free Press, 1958, pp. 119-37.
Franklin, Leo. "Jews in Michigan," *Michigan History Magazine*, 23, 1939, pp. 77-92.
Goldberg, David and Harry Sharp. "Some Characteristics of Detroit Area Jewish and Non-Jewish Adults," in Marshall Sklare (ed.), *The Jews: Social Patterns of an American Group*, New York: Free Press, 1958.
Jewish Historical Society. *Michigan Jewish History*, Semi-annual.
Lenski, Gerhard. *The Religious Factor*, Garden City: Anchor, 1963.
Moss, L.W. "Folklore Among Detroit Jews," *Michigan Jewish History*, 3, 1963, pp. 2-10.
Wilensky, Harold and Jack Ladinsky. "From Religious Community to Occupational Group: Structural Assimilation Among Professors, Lawyers and Engineers," *American Sociological Review*, 32, 1967, pp. 541-61.

Notes

1. Gerhard Lenski, *The Religious Factor: A Sociologist's Inquiry*, (Garden City: Anchor, 1963) p. 21.

2. Milton Gordon, *Assimilation in American Life: The Role of Race, Religion and National Origins*, (New York: Oxford University Press, 1964), p. 27.

3. Estimates by Tom Pawlick, "The Abandonment of the Indian in Detroit's Red Ghetto," *Detroit News*, March 5, 1970, "Other Section"; and Beverly Eckman, "Mexican Life Grows Out W. Vernor Way," *Detroit News*, Sept. 22, 1969.

4. Frank Angelo, "The Peoples of Detroit Project," Wayne State University, Center For Urban Studies, May 13, 1969, mimeo.

5. Andrew M. Greeley, *Why Can't They Be Like Us?* (New York: Institute of Human Relations Press, 1969), p. 5. A good example of the tenacity of the melting pot idea may be found in the U.S. Census, with its implicit assumption that nationality background is of no importance after the second generation. The melting pot idea, and its implied analogy for blacks, is still repeated in textbooks used in the public schools. (See Louis L. Knowles and Kenneth Prewitt, *Institutional Racism in America*, Englewood Cliffs, N.J.: Prentice Hall, 1969, p. 51.)

6. For examples see Oscar Handlin, *The Newcomers: Negroes and Puerto Ricans in a Changing Metropolis* (Garden City: Anchor, 1959), pp. 120-121;

Philip M. Hauser, "Demographic Factors in the Integration of the Negro," *Daedalus*, Fall 1965, pp. 847-77, and arguments criticized by Charles Silberman, *Crisis in Black and White* (New York: Random House), 1964, pp. 19-20, 36-42, and 124.

White (New York: Random House), 1964, pp. 19-20, 36-42, and 124.

7. Seymour Martin Lipset and Reinhard Bendix, *Social Mobility in Industrial Society*, (Berkeley: University of California Press, 1967), pp. 78-79. Also see Howard Schuman, "Sociological Racism," *Transaction*, Dec., 1969, pp. 44-48.

8. Otis Dudley Duncan and Stanley Lieberson, "Ethnic Segregation and Assimilation," *American Journal of Sociology*, 64, 1959, p. 370.

9. Warner and Srole, *Social Systems of American Ethnic Groups*, p. 2.

10. Lipset and Bendix, *Social Mobility*, p. 104.

11. For examples of recent challenges to the melting pot concept see Nathan Glazer and Daniel P. Moynihan, *Beyond the Melting Pot. The Negroes, Puerto Ricans, Jews, Italians, and Irish of New York City* (Cambridge, Mass: MIT Press, 1963); Greeley, *Why Can't They Be Like Us?*; Colin Greer, "Public Schools: The Myth of the Melting Pot," *Saturday Review*, Nov. 15, 1969, pp. 84 ff; Sidney Willhelm, "Black Man, Red Man and White America: The Constitutional Approach to Genocide," *Catalyst*, Spring, 1969, pp. 1-62.

12. See for example Goldberg and Sharp, "Some Characteristics of Detroit Area Jewish and Non-Jewish Adults"; S. Joseph Fauman, "Occupational Selection Among Detroit Jews," in Sklare (ed.), *The Jews: Social Patterns of an American Group*, pp. 119-137; Lenski, *The Religious Factor*; Glazer and Moynihan, "The Jews," in *Beyond the Melting Pot*; and Fred L. Strodtbeck, "Family Interaction, Values, and Achievement," in David C. McClelland, et al., *Talent and Society*, (New York: Van Nostrand, 1958), pp. 135-94.

13. Angelo, "The Peoples of Detroit Project."

14. For influential examples of this argument see Lenski, *The Religious Factor*, and Will Herberg, *Protestant-Catholic-Jew*, (New York: Doubleday, 1955).

15. Lenski, *The Religious Factor*, p. 363.

16. Edward O. Laumann, "The Social Structure of Religious and Ethnoreligious Groups in a Metropolitan Community," *American Sociological Review*, 34, 1969, pp. 182-97.

17. John Porter, *The Vertical Mosaic: An Analysis of Social Class and Power in Canada*, (Toronto: University of Toronto Press, 1965), pp. 70-71.

7

Reflections of the Black Detroiter

Reginald R. Larrie and Margaret L. Larrie

Of all the ethnic groups which reside in Detroit, Michigan, the Afro-Americans have received very little recognition for their memorable deeds. In an attempt to fill a great void in Detroit's history, this article about its largest ethnic community has been written.

Every effort has been made to compile enough factual data which experienced researchers as well as students may find helpful. It is anticipated that this study will also dispel some of the myths which have haunted the Afro-American—regardless of his endeavor to prove himself as a human being among other men.

Introduction

Among all of the groups described in this book, the Afro-American is statistically and physically one of Detroit's oldest members. At the present time (1970), the Afro-American population is well over 700,000 and many historians believe that the black man arrived in Detroit "at or about" the same time as Antoine de la Mothe Cadillac (July, 1701). However, for some unexplainable reason, the early history of the black man has become "lost, stolen, or strayed" and very little information has found its way into the history books.

Nevertheless, the Afro-American's contribution to Detroit's history is a record he can be proud of and every Detroiter should be made aware of it.

Early Detroit and Slavery

Dating back to the earliest days of Cadillac, slavery existed in Michigan territory. Its first slaves were not Africans, but the Panis Indians, and many of them had been transported as captives from Kentucky to Michigan by other Indian tribes. Usually the Panis did not remain in captivity for very long because they knew which trails to take in order to escape bondage. Consequently, the white men decided that it would be cheaper to buy Africans as slaves; mainly because blacks presumably had little knowledge of this country and its terrain. Without this knowledge, black slaves would resist the temptation to run away from their masters.

Perhaps it is difficult to imagine that Michigan, a northern state, would practice slavery, but most of its leading citizens owned several slaves. Men such as George McDougall, Joseph Campau, James D. Baby, James Abbott, and John R. Williams (Detroit's first mayor, from 1824 to 1825) are just a few of the white men who not only bought slaves but sold them as well.

In spite of the "buying and selling," however, slaves did not appear as figures in the Detroit census until 1773. By then, the following number of people were being held in servitude.

Male Slaves	46
Female Slaves	39

A property list composed by John Askin on January 1, 1787, showed that he owned both African and Indian slaves.

Jupiter, a Negro man	150 pounds
Tom, a Negro man	140 pounds
George, a Negro boy	90 pounds
Sam, a Panis Blacksmith	150 pounds
Susannah, a wench, and two children	130 pounds
Mary, a wench	100 pounds
Total	760

According to one author, "these slaves were well treated by their masters." An example of being "well treated" was pointed out when a black slave woman was hanged for the theft of six guineas (around forty dollars in today's money). Slaves were also sold like animals at auctions in the city square and during the year of 1793, a black boy of only twelve years was separated from his mother and sold for $532.50.

A 1794 copy of a bill of sale for a black slave reads: "That I, James May of Detroit, for and in consideration of the sum of forty-five pounds, New York currency, to me in hand paid by John Askin of Detroit, the receipt whereof I do acknowledge to be fully satisfied and paid, have sold and delivered unto the said John Askin a certain Negro man, Pompey by name, to have and to hold the said Negro unto the said John Askin, his heirs, executors, administrators and assigns forever."

Another slave by the name of Mullett served Joseph Campau as his confidential secretary. Maintaining a slave in this position was good business because he could not testify against a white man in court. Even though Mullett was a slave, he was greatly respected throughout the community and when he died at an age of over ninety years, many white mourners stood among the gathering for his funeral.

As late as 1807, Judge Augustus B. Woodward refused to free a Negro man and woman while declaring that they were legally slaves because of an old treaty.

It has also been noted that Governor Stevens T. Mason brought slaves with him from Virginia to Michigan.

Although slaves were generally used as laborers, houseboys, and personal attendants; if one was ever caught stealing, he was usually hanged. Furthermore, some of them went to war (1812) and fought alongside their masters, while others went in lieu of their masters.

The Ordinance of 1787 was passed by the U.S. Congress and it forbade slavery in the Northwest Territory. But Michigan continued to hold slaves in spite of the law. The state congress finally prohibited slavery in Michigan after what was called "The First Negro Insurrection in Detroit (1833)."

Eventually, Detroit became a city where thousands of runaway slaves found refuge until they were able to cross the Detroit River into Canada.

The Struggle for a Black School

Urban education for the white child in greater Detroit is probably one of the few things being taken for granted today (1970). However, this assumption has not always been valid for the black child who desired a better education. The Afro-American had to fight for the right to be educated and this struggle began over one hundred years ago.

Second Baptist Church, the oldest black church in the state, played an important role in this battle for equal schooling. Members of Second Baptist held several meetings and one of these resulted in the organization of a committee to fight for an Afro-American school.

According to Judge Ross Wilkins, a number of men, including John Biddle and John R. Williams, petitioned the legislature for the establishment of a separate school for black children. In 1839, the legislature enacted a law for the school, but no money was appropriated to pay for a teacher.

It was not until the following year (1840) that funds became available for the payment of a teacher's salary. Reverend William C. Monroe was employed as the first black teacher in Detroit's colored school and two years later, in 1842, the Board of Education opened a school for blacks in the Methodist Church on E. Fort Street. The lessons were taught by Reverend J.M. Brown, who later became a Bishop and left the school system in 1851.

The school was then moved to the Episcopal Church which stood at Congress and St. Antoine. Once again, the Reverend W.C. Monroe became the teacher in charge.

While black people fought for a grade school to accommodate thirty-six children, the whites were planning a college for their own. Finally, in 1860, a building was erected to house two grades for black children. The classes were taught by two white teachers, John Whitbect and a Miss Scott. She later resigned and went to Africa as a missionary.

In 1865, a second black public school was opened at the corner of Riopelle and Macomb. Within these walls, Fannie M. Richards became Detroit's first official Afro-American teacher and it has been reported that Miss Meta Pelham was her assistant.

Although both schools continued to operate under the separate-but-equal doctrine, in 1867, the state legislature of Michigan passed a law to provide that all children in a school district should be admitted to the school in their particular district. However, this law was ignored until a group of black citizens led by William Lambert (an early black leader) brought it to the attention of the Supreme Court in 1869. Those who encouraged Lambert to take the matter to the Supreme Court were Dr. S.C. Watson, John Cullen, J.D. Carter, George Parker, C.A. Jeffrey, William Webb, James Benga, Obadiah Wood, Robert Warren, J.L. Morten, Richard Gordan, and John Richards (the brother of Fannie Richards).

Through the actions of this group, Afro-American children have enjoyed the opportunity of attending any school in their Detroit school district since October 11, 1869.

The Afro-American's Military Involvement

During the War of the Rebellion (Civil War), more than 200,000 Afro-American men were mustered into military service. They served with honor and distinction in both the federal army and navy. Thus, the Afro-American becomes a rather unique creature because only a few ethnic groups in Detroit can trace their participation as far back as this great struggle toward changing the system.

From the very beginning (1861), Afro-Americans were among the first to respond, but the practice of "not accepting blacks" was upheld by the man who later became known as "The Great Emancipator." Prior to the time that Afro-Americans were permitted to fight for their own freedom, they were allowed to serve as cooks and waiters for high-ranking military personnel.

One of these black men who served as a cook—before he could obtain the rank of combat soldier—was an Afro-American by the name of Parker Bon. When the war started, Bon was twenty-five years old and he lived in Detroit. He went to Fort Wayne to enlist, but he was refused enlistment into the regular army. Yet, he was asked to serve as a cook for the officers and he accepted.

Shortly after he began to carry out his chores as a cook, Bon realized that he could learn a lot about military tactics by listening to the conversations among white officers. He was also in a position to make observations of various army maneuvers and he studied books written by the best military authors whenever he finished his assigned duties.

When the North began to lose one battle after another, President Lincoln made a decision to free the slaves in the south. Although this emancipation was actually a military move to preserve the Union, black men were accepted for service in the Union forces with pay. The blacks, of course, were paid only half of the salary received by white soldiers.

In Michigan, a Colonel Barnes was commissioned to raise a regiment which was originally identified as the First Michigan Colored Infantry. However, the unit was later recommissioned as the 102nd Regiment of the United States Colored Troop. The recruiting for this unit began on August 12, 1863, and 895 men were mustered into service. The total of blacks from Michigan eventually exceeded the 1,600 mark.

Some of the white officers recognized the need for a black man who could act as drill master and they made inquiries among the black citizenry. While they were seeking a man who could function in this capacity, a group of Afro-Americans were preparing a petition to appoint Parker Bon as drill master. They submitted the petition to Colonel Barnes who, in turn, sent for Bon. The eligible black male was examined by a board which found him mentally efficient and physically fit.

Sometime after Bon was accepted into service, he was promoted to the rank of sergeant major of the regiment. Subsequently, the 102nd U.S. Troop was assigned to the Ninth Army Corps, under the direction of General Ambrose Everett Burnside. The black men were later transferred to General Refus Saxton's division and this unit made history by taking Harper's Ferry from the South. At the close of the war, the 102nd had distinguished itself many times during the battles.

Along with the close of the war, black soldiers returned to their homes and Michigan farms where they resumed a struggle for the freedom they had dreamed of during the years of military service. But once again, they were confronted with the problems so often perpetuated by bigotry and hate.

Black Survival in an Urban Setting

On January 25, 1865, the second State Convention was held and the legislature was petitioned to grant black people the right to full citizenship. But again, blacks were refused and ignored. However, the Fifteenth Amendment of the Constitution of the United States was finally ratified on March 30, 1870, and it gave Afro-Americans their citizenship rights. On November 8, 1870, the black people of Michigan voted for the first time.

After receiving the right of suffrage, The Afro-American soon gained considerable confidence in the system. In 1876, John Wilson—a musician, barber, and leader in the black community—was elected coroner of Wayne County on a Democratic ticket. He was one of the first blacks elected to a public office in Michigan. Closely following Wilson into office was Thomas D. Owens, who also held the position of Wayne County coroner.

Early in the 1880s, Thomas Crisup became the first Afro-American to appear as an attorney in a Detroit court room. Later, D. Augustus Straker, a university graduate, opened his law office and displayed such competence that he became a popular idol of Detroit's white society. As a result of his popularity, Straker was elected as Circuit Court Commissioner during the 1890s. After serving two terms, he was later nominated as a delegate to the State Constitutional Convention in 1908.

The social life of the Afro-American in Detroit centered mainly around the churches, especially the Baptist and Methodist Episcopal Churches. Although there were clubs and societies which occasionally brought black people together, the church remained as the nucleus of most activities.

One of the major businesses for blacks was the barbering profession and some of the Afro-Americans owned and operated the largest shops in the city. One of the rather exclusive shops was located in the Russell House, Detroit's finest hotel. Black people also owned a number of saloons, a few small grocery stores and confectionaries. In the trades, there were a number of black carpenters, plasterers, blacksmiths, tailors, painters, and one cooper (a man who made and repaired barrels, casks, etc.).

All of the hotel and steamship owners hired blacks and the railroad lines had a considerable number of laborers, porters, red caps, and dining car waiters. Many of the Afro-Americans were forced into these positions because they were not allowed to compete for the "better and more highly respected positions."

Black women, much like most of the foreign and poor white women, generally engaged in domestic work. In several exceptional cases, they were able to get sewing jobs or else their husbands could make enough money to support the family without a second income. There were also the few black women who functioned as members of the teaching pprofession.

Table 7-1, taken from the Detroit City Directory for 1870 indicates that a number of Afro-Americans were engaged in gainful employment.

From a Detroit population figure of less than 500 Afro-Americans just prior to the Civil War, the black citizen count increased to more than 6,000 by 1910. With the inclusion of Hamtramck, Highland Park, and other suburbs adjacent to Detroit; the number of blacks is currently estimated at 715,000 (by *Standard Rate and Data*—1969).

By keeping in step with the development of Detroit, the Afro-American has grown numerically as well as socially. At the time of the Emancipation Proclamation (1865), most blacks in Detroit were domestic workers or servants and many were surviving under very meager conditions. In spite of considerable odds, however, the Afro-Americans have worked their way into almost every kind of profession, trade, and business in Detroit. Therefore, if the black man's progress is viewed with judiciousness, where would the Afro-American be today—if he had been permitted to function with the same degree of fairness allotted to the white man?

According to *Standard Rate and Data*, the black population in 1969 was 715,000. Of this number, there were 195,000 black families with incomes ranging from five to eight thousand dollars or more.

> 58.7% with incomes of $5,000
> 40.5% with incomes of $5,000 - 8,000
> 18.2% with incomes of $8,000 and over

Detroit's Afro-American banking power exceeded $827,793,000, which was more than the combined totals of the black ethnic markets in Kansas City, Atlanta, Cincinnati, and St. Louis.

Table 7-1

Negroes Engaged in Gainful Occupations in Detroit as Listed in the Detroit City Directory for 1870

Agriculture	6	Caterer	1
Farmers	4	Coachmen	3
Gardeners	2	Cooks	34
Manufac. and Mechanical	106	Hairdressers	2
Baker	1	Janitors	5
Brick and stone masons	9	Laborers	102
Builder	1	Laundresses	2
Carpenters	12	Laundryman	1
Cigar makers	1	Lunchroom keeper	1
Confectioner	1	Sleeping car janitor	1
Coopers	7	Stewards	5
Currier and tanner	2	Waiters	59
Dressm'k'rs & seamstresses	10	Warehousemen	2
Engineers	4	Washerwomen	17
Fireman	1	Professional service	12
Painter	1	Artist	1
Plasterers	15	Dumas Watkins	
Sawyers	3	Clergymen	3
Ship carpenter	1	J.S. Booth	
Shoemakers	3	Hezekiah Harper	
Stripper (tobacco)	2	Joseph Hurlburt	
Tailors	3	Druggist	1
Tobacconists	4	S.C. Watson	
Whitewashers	25	Horse trainer	1
Trade	32	Eugene Tunison	
Clerks (in stores)	3	Music teacher	1
Fruit dealer	1	Charles Thompson	
Grocer	1	Physicians	2
Hucksters and vegetable		B.L. Clark	
dealers	3	Joseph Ferguson	
Meat market	1	Teachers	
Intelligence office	1	Mrs. J. Cook	
Peddlers	3	Miss Sarah Webb	
Porters (in stores)	19	Miss Fannie Richards	
Transportation	47	Public service	3
Hack driver	1	City scavenger	1
Hostlers	3	John Logan	
Sailors	27	Inspector (Custom service)	1
Livery stable	1	John D. Richards	
Teamsters and draymen	15	Letter carrier (P.O.)	1

Table 7-1. (cont.)

Domes and personal service	321	John C. Ferguson	
Barbers	71	Clerical service	3
Bartenders	4	Messengers	2
Bell boy	1	Stephen Copper	
Billiard parlor or saloon	8	John L. Martin	
Boarding house keeper	1	Traveling agent	
Carpet shaker	1	Harvey Webb	

Undoubtedly, it is also wise to recall the fact that there have always been some white Detroiters who exhibited loyalty toward their black counterparts. And in most instances, both blacks and whites have lived peacefully together. Each group has helped the other and because of this working relationship, Detroit has developed into one of the finest cities in the nation today (1970).

Bibliography

Burton, Clarence M. *The City of Detroit, Michigan*, Detroit: The S.J. Clarke Publishing Company, 1922.

_____. *The City of Detroit, Michigan*, Detroit: The S.J. Clarke Publishing Company, 1922. Volume 2.

_____. *When Detroit was Young*, Edited by M.M. Qualife. Detroit: Burton Abstract and Title Company.

Catlin, George B. "The Story of Detroit," *The Detroit News*, 1926.

Colored Population in the Detroit Annual Report, 1917.

Detroit Journal and Advertiser (semi-weekly newspaper), July 19, 1833.

Farmer, Silas. *History of Detroit and Wayne County and Early Michigan*, 1890.

Mallas, Aris Jr. *Forty Years in Politics*, Detroit: Wayne State University Press, 1959.

8 Detroit's Greek Community

Marios Stephanides

The Greeks, along with other Southern European groups, came to Detroit mainly after the beginning of the twentieth century. By 1919, the core of the community was estimated at 30,000-35,000 people.[1] Rather than living in a particular place, they were scattered throughout the city and the suburbs.[a]

The Greeks in Detroit in many respects went through the same historical process as the rest of the Greeks in the United States. The first Greeks arrived in the United States in the late nineteenth and early twentieth centuries.[2] They came primarily from the "Kingdom of Greece," that is, the very early Greeks of 1890-1900 came mainly from the mainland of Greece. Later the immigration included Greeks from Cyprus, Turkey, Egypt, and Epirus. Since the island of Crete was not united with Greece until 1910, it was therefore not considered part of the Greek Kingdom prior to that time.

According to Saloutos, a small number of immigrants arrived in the nineteenth century. There were three specific periods of immigration in the nineteenth century. Encouraged by American missionaries in the 1820s and 1830s a small number arrived during this period. The second immigration occurred in the 1850s and revolved around the representatives of Greek-owned commercial firms. The third occurred among the Spartans in the late 1870s and 1880s and was mainly the result of economic problems.[3]

In the twentieth century the first major immigration took place between 1900-1910. This immigration was the result of limited economic opportunities, the unstable political situation, and lastly the coming of war against the Turks in 1912, which led some youths to leave Greece before they could be drafted, although others later returned to fight in the Greek army. The peak year for immigration during the decade was 1907, with the quota reaching 36,580 people. During this span of ten years, 167,579 people immigrated to the United

This paper is a revised edition of chapter 2 of the Master Thesis, by Marios Stephanides, Wayne State University, Sociology Department, 1969.

[a]However, U.S. Census figures of 1960 placed the Greek population in Detroit at only 13,262, and 18,221 for the whole state of Michigan. The discrepancy was due to the different way of defining "Greekness." Church records show first, second, third, and possibly fourth generation immigrants as Greeks if they identify themselves as such or attend church. In contrast, the U.S. Census only classify as foreign the first and second generation immigrants. For statistics see Census of Population, Part 24, Mich., U.S. Dept. of Commerce, Bureau of the Census.

States. The next two most important decades for Greek immigration are 1910-1920, with 184,201 and 1920-1930, with 51,084 people arriving in this country.[4]

The Greeks that immigrated to Detroit had much in common with those Greeks who settled in other areas of the country. They faced similar difficulties, had similar low educational backgrounds, and strangely the majority of them engaged in the restaurant businesses. This is surprising since their background was mainly rural and the only professional skills they possessed were those of farming. One possible explanation may lie in the emphasis placed upon individuality in the Greek culture.

Historically, the Greeks have been described as being clannish and uncooperative.[5] Saloutos states that the multiple existence of Greek organizations reflect the "localism" and "provincialism" of the Greeks.[6] In Detroit this factionalism, and provincialism was manifested among the Greeks mainly in the year 1914. Past political animosities in Greece between Royalist and Liberals had an impact on the life of the immigrants. The Greeks in the United States were divided into two groups, each hostile to the other. According to Politis, the hostility between the two groups at times led to bloodshed. She reports one such incident where a Cretan who had supported the Venzelos party was killed in the Greek Town area of Detroit.[7]

The social life of the Greeks centers around the church, its affiliated organizations, and the regional societies. Usually first generation Greeks place more emphasis on regional organizations in contrast to the second and third generations who tend to join national and religious groups. Originally, first generation Greeks from the same area of Greece had their own organizations and a particular coffee shop that they always visited. Usually, friends of similar origins visited among people of the same region.

As late as 1969, the entire community in Detroit was broken down into twenty-two regional organizations, around which most of the social interaction of the first generation Greeks took place. In contrast, for the second generation Greeks the parochial afternoon Greek schools and church organizations promoted national consciousness.

Historically, the Greeks in Detroit began to arrive in 1886.[8] Specifically, immigrants from Greece to Michigan numbered one native in 1850, four in 1880, 1,196 in 1910, and 8,989 in 1940. Thus, the largest immigration did not take place until the period of 1910-1940.[9] According to the official figures of the United States Census, in 1910 the number of foreign born Greeks in Detroit was 884. In 1920, the number increased to 4,628.[10] Thus, there was a net increase of 4,044 or approximately an 800 percent increase over the Greek population in Detroit in 1910. Church reports showed that the majority of the Greeks came from the city of Sparta in the Peloponnesus and related areas.[b]

[b]Annunciation Greek Orthodox Church, *Golden Anniversary Booklet*, (Detroit, Mich.; Eagle Printing Co., 1908). According to the results of the writers Masters Thesis Study, Greeks immigrate at young ages. Specifically, 56.3% came before age 24, 25.2% before age 34, 8.7% before age 44, and 6.8% before the age of 64.

The Greek immigration was the result of economic necessity. They were mainly uneducated and heavily represented the countryside.[c] The rural background of the Greek immigrants to the United States was very well described by a 1969 issue of *Time* magazine.[11] In this article, Greece was described as a nation of small poor towns, most of them located in isolated mountains away from modernization and progress. The people were described as "independent," "suspicious," and "resentful." According to the same report, the main values of the people were grounded for centuries on the foundations of church, the coffee houses, and the code of ethics based in turn on family loyalty and honor. This honor was based on the cultural belief that women should stay at home and never talk to the men or go to the coffee houses. Finally, the report states that other characteristics of their code included the extreme patriotic feelings that were fostered around school and church.

Thus, the majority of the early Greek immigrants (before 1948) had no work experience other than farming, and no specific training prior to coming to the United States. Consequently, they were not prepared to resume their positions in the American industrial society and environment. As a result of this inadequate training and ignorant of English, the Greeks found themselves ill-equipped and without a trade or profession. In view of this, it is understandable why times were hard for these first Greek immigrants in their adjustment to life in Detroit. It was especially difficult to secure employment with adequate income in American-owned businesses at about 1890. Reports indicate that the first Greeks in Detroit in the 1890s were forced to go into businesses of their own. Another relevant factor may have been the special characteristics of the Greek immigrants which were fundamental, such as individualism, pride, and aggressiveness. A common initial business was peddling, traveling through the neighborhoods of Detroit in small groups selling fruits and cakes. Possible explanations for their tendency to work in groups were the need for companionship and to help each other at work because of the language difficulty, and unfamiliarity with the city environment.

Later, when circumstances and time allowed, because of their great desire to enlarge their businesses and to avoid unnecessary expenses, they managed to save a small amount of money and open up small stands instead of practicing peddling around the city. Following the opening of the small stands, the first Greek coffee house appeared in the beginning of 1900 at 40 Macomb Street, modeled after the coffee shops in Greece.[d] This place served as a meeting place,

---

[c]According to the results of the writer's Master's Thesis, study based on a sample of 103 people mostly representative of the Greek-Cypriot community conducted in Detroit, 72% came from villages, while 28% came from cities in Greece.

[d]Annunciation Greek Orthodox Church, *Golden Anniversary Booklet*, Detroit, Mich.: Eagle Printing Co., 1908, one interesting study mentions that the Greeks of Boston in 1903 were engaged in the same profession. Strangely, the Greeks in Boston had a crime rate of 352 percent because of practicing peddling without a license; see F. Bushee "Ethnic Factors in the Population of Boston," 1903, published by the Economic Association, MacMillan Co., N.Y., 1903, pp. 98-121.

for relaxation, discussion of politics, playing cards, and the recollection of "the good old times" with their fellow compatriots. It also served as a local mailing address for new arrivals, an employment agency for newcomers, the place for receiving news from home, and a place where the priest or the few educated people would write letters, and advise people on their problems. As immigration increased and the number of Greeks multiplied, more coffee houses appeared, usually representing a specific region, and, more rarely, a political ideology of Greece.

The period of 1912-1913 was important for Detroit Greeks because Henry Ford, a leading automobile manufacturer even at that time, began paying a wage of five dollars a day, and the news spread all over the country and as a result, a great number of Greeks migrated to Detroit from other areas of this country in order to obtain employment. As one of them later explained, approximately 60-80 other people at that time were employed in the railroad business, constructing railroad truck lines in Colorado, Iowa, and Kentucky, but when they heard of the Ford salaries they left their jobs and came to Detroit, and they have remained in the city since then.[e]

Even this group did not remain in the factories for a long time; as soon as they saved some money, they took advantage of their economic welfare and started their own businesses. Again these businesses were mostly groceries, confectionaries, restaurants, coffee houses, shoe-shine and hat-cleaning stands. This pattern of food service occupation has survived until today with the main emphasis on restaurant business, although the number has decreased. In a survey conducted by the writer, which incorporated data and samplings of 103 Greeks 57 percent of them showed that either they owned a restaurant themselves, or worked in a restaurant owned by a Greek. Other important occupations include: 7 percent owners of grocery stores, and 11.6 percent laborers. However, the Greek community between 1949 and 1969 had produced a great number of doctors, lawyers, and engineers, educated mostly in the United States. Generally, although the parents were in the restaurant business, the children usually went to college and did not follow their parent's profession, although it was very profitable. According to data presented by Maroudas and Tassis,[12] in their random sample study, 45 percent of the first generation Greeks were self-employed, while the rate for the second generation declined to 31 percent. In addition, the second generation Greeks were mainly occupied in white collar professions at the rate of 56 percent, as compared to only 17 percent of the first generation. Most of the graduates came from the University of Michigan or Wayne State University. At Wayne, according to the records of the Eastern Orthodox Fellowship,[f] by 1970 there were one hundred and fifty students, including both Greek and Greek-American students.

Religiously, the old Greeks were very devoted Greek Orthodox Christians.[g]

[e]Interview, March, 1959, Detroit, Mich. In those states he mentioned that jobs were low paying, required them to move around, and were irregular.

[f]A religious student organization at Wayne State University.

[g]According to the Master's Thesis study, 78% of the Greeks did not approve of intermarriage; study conducted by writer.

With the increase in the Greek population in 1909,[h] which according to sources had reached a total of 250 people, the need was felt to create a church to be used not only as a religious but also as an educational and social institution.[13] So this initiated the first attempts to build a church, and for this purpose a committee was formed to collect money and make the necessary arrangements for finding a temporary place to be used as a church. After a year of hard work, some money was collected and the committee achieved the rental of a hall, on Broadway Street, No. 42, on the second floor, that was converted to a church, and was named "Annunciation." In the following years not only was the church used as a religious and educational place, but military training also took place there. Greeks that wanted to go back and fight for Greece against Turkey in the war in 1912 formed a group called "Ieros Lohos" (Holy Body), who named themselves after the best body of the Revolutionary Greek army that fought the Turks in 1821. Subsequently, the group consisting of 280 young soldiers went to Greece to fight.[14]

Later the community bought a place next to the original one and constructed a church and a daily Greek school which operated until 1931, when it was forced to close because of the depression and the economic difficulties that were brought about in the community. In the years that followed the depression, the school started operating again but only as an afternoon school.

It is important to mention that the Greeks could not keep politics away from the church. The progress of the church and the community in general was interrupted in 1914 by the political situation in Greece. A feud had developed between the King of Greece, who maintained that the nation should remain neutral (he was personally related to the King of Germany), while his prime minister, Venizelos, sided with the allies. The Greek nation as a result was divided into two antagonistic segments. The situation was reflected in the minds and emotions of Greeks throughout the United States as well as in the Detroit community which separated into two factions, and consequently resulted in the break up of the congregation of the church. As a result, the people siding with venizelos remained in the old church, while the Royalists created new churches with priests not recognized by the church. These disputes lasted between 1910 and 1929, at which time the problem was settled, the community was reunited, and the old members returned to the church. Since that time the church owes allegiance to the Ecumenical Patriarchate of the Orthodox Church in Istanbul, Turkey.[i]

In regard to residence, the Greeks in Detroit at the beginning of their immigration lived in the vicinity of what came to be called Greek Town, a neighborhood of Greek shops and businesses located on Monroe Street between Beaubien and St. Antoine, in downtown Detroit. Early in 1910 they settled on Macomb Street near Randolf and from there the colony gradually spread to

[h]Statistics show that in 1969 there were two million Greeks in this country. See Greek Orthodox of North and South America, Yearbook, 1969, p. 98.

[i]Currently the church has been demolished, and a new one is being erected behind the old one. The new church is being planned and will be the Cathedral of the Seventh Diocese District of the Greek Archdiocese.

include parallel streets on South Monroe, Lafayette, East Congress, and East Jefferson, north to Clinton Street, and east from Randolf to Russell Street.[15] By 1969 all that remained of the old colony was one block of Greek establishments on Monroe Street between Beaubien and St. Antoine, which served only as a business and entertainment place.

The early residential Greek colony dissolved when the Greeks became financially capable and followed the general American pattern by leaving for a more attractive residential area; the results were that they gained symbolic status, and managed to avoid the problems brought about by the new American immigrants from the South. They were also able to live closer to their businesses. Generally, the majority of the Greeks in Detroit became prosperous by the 1960s and could afford housing in the suburbs, which generally was more expensive than in the city.[j]

The scattering of Greeks throughout the city and suburbs may be seen from the locations of the Greek Orthodox churches that are usually located in the vicinity of the Greek Orthodox population. The churches are located on the east and west side of Detroit and the Detroit area, Lincoln Park (south-west), Palmer Park (north-west); a central church located close to Greek Town, and the old Calendar church, which is found on the east side.

Greek Family Traditions

The Greek family traditionally has been patriarchal.[16] The husband as the head of the family makes the decisions, which are binding upon the rest of the family members.[k] Women are not supposed to work outside of the home.[l] In fulfilling their cultural role, the women are expected to clean house, cook, raise children, and take care of their husbands.[m] The Greeks also believe that women should not become involved in other areas of social life, such as politics, which is strictly considered to be an area reserved for men. Greeks tend to overprotect

---

[j]According to the results of the Master's Thesis study conducted by the writer, more repondents answered that they preferred to live in the suburbs (94%) rather than the city (6%).

[k]According to Rothchild, the more educated the husband, the less he is domineering. Moreover, the authority of the Greek husband is maximum among those with the lowest social status and minimum among those with the highest status. See *Journal of Marriage and the Family*, vol. 29, (May, 1967).

[l]In the writer's Master's Thesis study, 71.8% of the women were not employed.

[m]According to the U.S. Census of 1960, even the education of Greek women in the U.S. was lower than that of men. The median average for women was 6.8 and for men 8.0. U.S. Census of Population 1960: Subject Reports: Nativity and Parentage. Mother Tongue of the Foreign-born. Final Report P.C. (2)-1 A. Washington, D.C.: U.S. Printing Office.

their children, even to the extent of wanting to find marriage partners for them.[n]

However, this is only the "idealistic cultural" description and very often it is not found as it is described. By the 1960s, for example, the small Greek businessmen in Detroit allowed their wives to work in their restaurants and often the very poor Greeks followed the same pattern, as well as the second generation Greeks. Questionnaires in 1969 showed that the majority of the first generation Greeks did not let their wives work outside in someone else's business.

Furthermore, the decision making in the family is made on a somewhat more democratic basis, with the husbands frequently allowing ample time for their wives to express an opinion. However, the fact that the wives generally remain at home and do not get the change to intermingle with the American community, and learn the language, places them at a disadvantage, since they do not have the social awareness for decision making. Moreover, the parent-child relationships are anything but democratic, especially in the case of the girls. The writer has rarely spoken with a Greek-American girl who did not express dispair over her parents' refusal to allow her to date and intermingle with boys. In regard to marriage, the Greeks prefer to marry among their own nationality. Parents prefer infrequent dating and only with certain people and under the condition that there are intentions for serious purposes, that is marriage.

Generally, the Greek family is very strong. There is a clear-cut differentiation of the roles of the members of the family, a high emphasis on status, economic and educational achievement, and as a result, a little family disorganization as evidenced by lack of divorce and crime.[o] From all the interviews conducted personally, and the great number of Greek people known to the writer, who are in excess of 1,000 persons, only one or two cases of divorce or involvement in serious crimes were known. These cases show that first generation Greeks mainly engage in crimes of illegal gambling in the Greek Town area, while the second generation adopt more liberal attitudes towards divorce, dating, and marriage. Thus, the divorce cases known to the writer mainly involved second generation Greeks. In relationship to crime, the Cypriot community, which in 1969 consisted of over 200 people, had a history of only one serious crime. This crime

---

[n]In Greece, the girl must have a dowry. Lambiri reports in a study about the effects of industrialization on the family that the family was a guiding, constraining influence on factory work. Specifically, women were attracted to industrial employment mainly to indirectly improve their social status through contracting a socially successful marriage. Thus, they used the new financial opportunities to enhance the dowry system. For further information see Dr. Lambiri, Athens Center of Planning and Economic Research, 1965, Research Monograph Series 13.

[o]According to statistics from the Greek community, the rates for 1968 per 1,000 population of marriage were approximately 2 and divorces numbered .16. In contrast, the rates for Americans as given by the U.S. Statistical Abstract of 1969 in which the rates for 1968 per 1,000 population were 10.3 for marriage and 2.9 for divorce. Thus, if we account for the fact that marriage rates are five times smaller in the Greek community, even still we have a smaller rate of divorce in the Greek community. For further details see the Greek Orthodox Archdiocese Yearbook, 1969, p. 98.

involved illegal gambling, and violations by business establishments of serving liquor after legal hours. In the Greek Orthodox Church it is very difficult to get a divorce, and as a result this may tend to be another factor in the low divorce rate. Furthermore, a divorced woman was disadvantaged socially because she was a threat to the sex taboos and morals of the community.

The Greeks in Detroit exhibited socializing patterns similar to those of other Greeks in the U.S. Their main social life consisted of visiting friends and relatives. They preferred to meet other people rather than the American pastime of attending a movie, perhaps because many of them could not understand the English in the movies. The Greeks greatly valued "kouventa" (talking) and socializing. Besides visiting, there was also the male habit of going to a coffee shop. Even in Detroit the males had the chance to practice one of their cultural privileges of spending time in the coffee shops, in the companionship of males, at the Greek Town area at Monroe Avenue. The habit was more exhibited by the younger Greeks who were not married, and who wanted to show their dates the Greek Town area, or much older Greeks who wanted to spend time with their fellow compatriots.

Another form of enjoyment for the Greeks in Detroit was dancing and picnicking. These events were organized by church and regional Greek organizations. At dances, one could meet old friends, make new ones, and moreover, the young people could meet and perhaps marry someone from their own community. The dancing was mostly Greek, but in order to please the second generation, they also had American dancing occasionally. The younger Greeks from the city, who found folk dancing less appealing, enjoyed this diversion. Girls danced under the careful watch of their mothers; the same procedure was usually followed at picnics.

Social Classes

The question of whether the Greek community in Detroit was divided into social classes or not is impossible to answer by statistical data at this point. Using the participant observation approach, the writer found three groups of people in the community, in addition to the natural clannishness that appeared in the whole Greek nation, leading people of the same region to stay together. Logically, it seems that the community in 1969 may be broken down into three classes of people, each possessing special characteristics, and allowing little interaction between each other. These groups were the old versus the new Greek immigrant, and these two versus the second generation Greeks.

A similar study conducted in Detroit in the Iraqui community of Chaldeans by Sengstock also showed the existence of three community sub-groups.[17] The three sub-groups were: the older immigrant group, who came to the U.S. prior to 1948, were ten years of age or older at the time of their immigration, or came after 1948 but were over fifty years old; the recent immigrant group which immigrated after 1948, but were not over fifty at the time of their arrival; and the American-reared or second generation Chaldeans. Thus, the community was broken down according to age and sex distribution, the relative numbers of foreign and native born; it is obvious that all of these factors had a significant effect upon the structure of the Chaldeans community.[18]

Additionally, among these Chaldean groups Sengstock found that there were differences in the life styles, cultures, and especially their pattern of social interaction. Attempting further to explain the differences among the three groups of Chaldeans, the older immigrant groups exhibited a high degree of ethnic identification; however, more recent immigrants tended to identify with their ethnic background, but dropped many aspects of their ethnic social interaction patterns; and thirdly, the second generation exhibited neither ethnic identification, nor a participation in the ethnic social interaction pattern.[19]

In this author's Greek sample, the three groups could not possibly be classified in a line of stratification (as upper or lower), but rather were groups of people who possessed different characteristics. The most important variables for classification seemed to be the time of arrival in the U.S., age, place of birth (Greece or America), and place of birth in Greece.

Specifically, the first group consisted of the old Greeks that came to Detroit prior to 1948. This group was composed mostly of people of older age, who were the pioneers of the community in Detroit. In 1960, for example, the average age of Greeks in the N. Central states was 57.7.[20] This older type of Greek has been described by writers like Fairchild and Saloutos.[21] Repeating some of their descriptions, verified from personal observation, this group was generally uneducated, extremely conservative, and had little interaction with the American community. It was mostly self-employed, came from a village,[P] was motivated by economic necessity, and became fairly successful economically.[22]

In their attitudes and outlook toward life, they approached the pattern of the working class American. They tended to stereotype people into categories, to speak in definitive terms, and mistrusted everything that was not Greek. They despised people who did not agree with their own ideology, and their attitude seemed to be that of intolerance. They did not favor customs such as dating, unconditional race equality, or absolute democracy, and generally seemed to fit the image of a very conservative person. Members of this older group were overrepresented among the patrons found at the Greek Town coffee houses on Monroe Avenue. In terms of the above characteristics described, the immigrants that came to Detroit before 1948 also seemed to fit within this group, because they were rural people immigrating as a result of the Greek Civil War.

The second group consisted of the younger Greeks, who came from Greece in the last ten or fifteen years. Among this group there were a greater number of people from urban environments, better educated and trained, having a better understanding of people, and seeming to be more liberal toward issue such as

---

PStatistics show that in 1910, out of 584 Greeks in Detroit, only 19 were married to a Greek wife. The remaining either were not married at all or married to an American woman. See U.S. Census 1910.

intermarriage among other nationalities, race relations, and religion. This group was not as successful economically as the older group in terms of private ownership of businesses, because the younger Greeks had formal education which helped them to learn English faster, adjust better to the American community, and therefore find jobs with American owned establishments. Thus, formal education destroyed the need for young Greeks to go into private business.

According to the results of one of the studies done in the Detroit area, one of the most significant differences between the first and second generation Greeks was in occupational patterns.[23] The first generation Greeks despised working for somebody else. Statistically, only 38 per cent were in blue collar jobs, and 17 per cent were in white collar jobs in contrast to 45 per cent who were self-employed and owned their business. However, the second generation showed a majority concentration on white collar jobs (56%), while 13 per cent were in blue collar jobs and only 31 per cent were self-employed. Thus, the rate of self-employed between the first and the second generation Greeks declined by 14 per cent. As one person confided, "I make a lot more money working for myself and also I don't have anybody on my head, why give it up?"

The younger Greeks seem to have entered the United States at a time when the country is more prosperous than at the time the old Greeks arrived. Therefore, they have faced less of the difficulties which the old Greeks faced. Additionally, they found the Greek community fairly well-established, the churches already constructed, and the afternoon Greek School ready for their children. As a result they have had to spend less time organizing, and have found more time for enjoyment. This is one of the prime reasons that the old Greeks have looked down upon them. There were also the differences in the ideology of the two groups, which rarely led to social contacts and communication.

The third group were Greek-Americans, the second generation Greeks, or as they liked to be called, "American-Greeks." This group, mostly the children of first-generation old Greeks, seemed to be the most educated group of the three.[q] They were mostly Americanized and did not intermingle with the Greek community as frequently. During their child and teenage years most of them faced tremendous problems in communicating with their parents as a result of their different ideology. This ideological difference was manifested even between second and third generation Greeks as shown by their attitudes towards Greek Town. Maroudas and Tassis[24] have contended that the third generation resembled the first generation in their patterns and perceptions of Greek Town more than the second generation. They have theorized that Greek Town served as a focus for identification for the first and third generation, while for the second generation it only served as a commercial place.

Summarizing, sub-groups in the Detroit community did not seem to be based upon income or any type of occupation. The community was divided according to the place of birth in Greece. Income itself was not a factor for drawing lines

---

[q]Numerically, this group in 1960 was larger than the other two groups of Greeks together.

for social association. Out of all the organizations present in the Greek community in 1969, none was based on income or education, but rather on regional, fraternal, national, or benevolent criteria. Generally, people tended to interact with each other on the basis of kinship, locality of birth in Greece, church affiliation and other possible relationships. Region of orgin in Greece seemed to be the most important factor for the group of older Greeks, but was not highly valued by the younger Greeks, who did not share much with the older. The alienation between the three groups of older, younger, and the Greek-Americans was continually widening and contact between them was very limited because of differences in income and occupational patterns.

Kimball Young's definition of assimilation states that "assimilation means the common blending and showing of folkways, mores, laws, and ways of life of generally two or more groups or societies or peoples that formerly had distinctive patterns."[25] Using this definition one can assert that the first generation Greeks were not assimilated to the American community but the second generation Greeks were, judging by the criteria of ability to speak English, the presence of a foreign language press, intermarriage, and social life.

First generation Greeks have not changed their values or norms even though they have at times conflicted with American norms and values. They learned English just well enough to get along in their work, but they did not use it in their homes.[26] The Greek language was learned and everyone was expected to speak it in the home. Greek children often could speak no English upon entering kindergarten, and many had to learn it once they began school.

Among the second generation Greeks, however, this pattern changed. According to a study by two Greek students, 91 percent of the first generation Greeks in 1969 spoke Greek at home, in contrast to 2 percent of the second generation.

Secondly, using the foreign language press as a criterion, the Greeks had local papers in addition to the national Greek daily papers of "Atlantis," and "National Herald," and a number of monthly magazines. By 1969 weekly local papers of the "Greek Tribune" and the "Detroit Athens" enriched the social life of the Greek people. These papers reported mainly local news and to an extent national news. In addition, there were three Greek radio programs in Detroit.

Thirdly, using intermarriage as a criterion, the first generation Greeks generally married within the ethnic group. Those interviewed felt this was done mainly for reasons of better understanding and common ideology. In a sample of one hundred and three Greeks interviewed, 82 percent of the couples were both Greek;[27] furthermore, they also felt that they would like their children to marry among their own group. In addition, from a sample of sixty names collected from St. Constantine Greek Orthodox Church, only three people were married to members of outgroups.[r]

Using social sociations and life style in general as a criterion, the first

---

[r]According to reports attributed to the St. Nicholas Church priest, the rate of intermarriage for the second generation is 70-80%.

generation Greeks seemed to spend most of their time among members of their own community. Since they gathered at Greek Town, went to dances and Greek picnics, where they spoke their own language, they felt little need to change or adjust to American society.

In contrast, the second generation Greeks had a completely different outlook since they attended American schools, joined the American army, and had American friends. The Greek-Americans, although they attended Greek events like dances and went to afternoon Greek School as well as church and affiliated organizations, incorporated more of the American culture and little of the Greek.

Conclusions

By 1969, the Greek community was fairly large, consisting of 30,000-35,000 people. The Greeks were fairly prosperous, mostly in the restaurant business, working for themselves with a reputation of being very hard-working people. The Greek community was organized religiously with the churches serving as a headquarters for group organizations, and as a place to sponsor dances and social activities. Greek Town served as the symbol of the community, reflecting an ability to maintain an ethnic identity even to the present. The community was breaking away and being assimilated into American society as the older Greeks were dying. Furthermore, the younger Greek-Americans did not seem to participate in the maintaining of a separate cultural community other than the church.

Bibliography

Adams, T.W. Department of the Army Pamphlet, No. 550.22, *U.S. Army Area Handbook,* Washington, D.C.: Government Printing Office, 1962.

Annunication Greek Orthodox Church. *Golden Anniversary Booklet,* Detroit, Michigan: Eagle Printing Company, 1908.

Bardis, Panos. "The Changing Family in Modern Greece," *Sociology and Social Research,* Vol. 40, No. 1, (1955-56), pp. 19-23.

Detroit Area Study. *A Review of Some Recent Research,* Project 870, Survey Research Center, University of Michigan, October, 1960, #1704.

Fairchild, Henry. *Greek Immigration to the United States,* New Haven: Yale University Press, 1911.

Friedl, Ernestine. *Vasilika: A Village in Modern Greece,* New York: Holt, Rinehart & Winston, 1962.

Greek Orthodox Church of North and South America, Yearbook, 1969.

Lambiri, Athens Center of Planning and Economic Research, 1965, Research Monograph, Series 13.

Markides, Kyriakos. "Assimilation of Greeks in Youngston," Master's Thesis, Bowling Greene State University, 1966.

Mayer. "Ethnic Groups in Detroit," Wayne State University, Department of Sociology and Anthropology, 1951, p. 23. (Paper written in celebration of the First International Festival in Detroit.)

Maroudas, Tom, and Jim Tassis. "A Study of Intergenerational Greek Patterns Toward Greek Town," Paper written for Dr. Thompson, Geology Department, Wayne State University, June, 1969.

Rankin, Lois. "Detroit Nationality Groups," *Michigan History Magazine*, XXIII, (1939), pp. 129-211, Burton Historical Collection of the Detroit Public Library.

Pereida, Andreas. "Sources of Dispersal of Michigan's Population," *Michigan History Magazine*, Vol. 32, p. 384.

Politis, Fizazi Stella. "Cretan Community in Detroit," Master's Thesis, Wayne State University, Detroit, 1967.

Pollis, Adamantia. "Political Implications of the Modern Greek Self," *British Journal of Sociology*, Vol. 16. 1965, pp. 29-47.

Rothchild, D. "A Comparison of Power Structure & Martial Satisfaction in Urban Greece & French Families," *Journal of Marriage and the Family*, Vol. 29, (May, 1967).

Saloutos, Theodore. *The Greeks in the United States*, Cambridge, Mass.: Harvard University Press, 1964.

Sengstock, Mary C. "Maintenance of Social Interaction Patterns in an Ethnic Group," Washington University, Unpublished Ph.D. dissertation, 1967.

Stephanides, Marios. "Methodological and Sociological Investigation of the Greek Community," Master's Thesis Study, Wayne State University, Department of Sociology, 1969.

U.S. Census of Population, 1960, Part 24, Mich. U.S. Dept. of Commerce, Bureau of the Census.

Thirteenth and Fourteenth Census of the United States, 1910, Vol. 11.

U.S. Census of Population, 1960: Subject Reports: Nativity and Parentage. Mother Tongue of the Foreign-born. Final Report P.C. (2)-1A. Washington, U.S. Printing Office.

Vlachos, Evangelos. *The Assimilation of Greeks in the United States*, National Center for Social Research, Athens, 1968, Greece.

Young, Kimball. *Sociology*, New York: American Book Company, 1949.

Notes

1. See Mayer, *Ethnic Groups in Detroit* (Wayne State University, Dept. of Sociology and Anthropology, 1951), p. 23.

2. Theodore Saloutos, *The Greeks in the United States* (Cambridge: Harvard University Press, 1964), p. 1; also see Andreas D. Pereida, "Sources of Dispersal of Michigan's Population," *Michigan History Magazine*, Vol. 32, p. 384.

3. Ibid., p. 22.

4. As quoted by Evangelos Vlachos, *The Assimilation of Greeks in the*

128

United States, National Center for Social Research, Athens, Greece, 1968, p. 64; quoted from U.S. Dept. of Justice, Annual Report of Immigration and Naturalization Service, Washington, D.C., U.S. Government Printing Office, '65, pp. 47-49; also see discussion concerning discrepancy of rates between census figures and community figures.

5. Henry P. Fairchild, *Greek Immigration to the United States* (New Haven: Yale University, 1911) pp. 10-11.

6. Theodore Saloutos, *The Greeks in the United States*, p. 75.

7. Stella Politis, *Cretan Community of Detroit*, Masters Thesis, 1967, Wayne State University, p. 30. Venizelos was the prime minister of Greece at that time.

8. See A. Pereida, *Michigan History Magazine*. Figure does not include Greeks from Cyprus, Turkey and Epirus.

9. See Mayer, *Ethnic Groups in Detroit*, 1951, Wayne State University, Department of Sociology and Anthropology, p. 23.

10. See Thirteenth Census of the United States, 1910, vol. 11, p. 946. Also Fourteenth, 1920, vol. 111, p. 477.

11. "Why Greece's Colonels Are That Way," *Time*, April 18, 1969, p. 32.

12. Maroudas and Tassis, "An Intergenerational Study of the Greek Community's Attitude Toward Greek Town," paper submitted to Dr. Thompson, Geography Dept. of Wayne State University, June, 1969.

13. *Golden Anniversary Booklet*, Special Edition.

14. Ibid.

15. Lois Rankin, "Detroit Nationality Groups", *Michigan History Magazine*, XXIII, (1939), pp. 129-211, Burton Historical Collection of the Detroit Public Library.

16. Panos D. Bardis, "The Changing Family in Modern Greece," *Sociology and Social Research*, vol. 40, no. I., (1955-56), p. 23.

17. Mary C. Sengstock, "Maintenance of Social Inter-action Patterns in an Ethnic Group", Washington University, 1967. (Unpublished PhD. dissertation.)

18. Ibid., p. 30.

19. Ibid., p. 395.

20. U.S. Census of Population 1960, p. 14.

21. See Fairchild, *Greek Immigration to the United States*.

22. Maroudas and Tassis, "An Intergenerational Study"; see also Marios Stephanides "Greek Studies" papers, Wayne State University, Department of Sociology.

23. Ibid.; see also Stella Politis, *Cretan Community of Detroit*.

24. Maroudas and Tassis, Ibid.

25. Kimball Young, *Sociology*, (New York: American Book Company, 1949), p. 77.

26. Maroudas and Tassis, "An Intergenerational Study."

27. See Marios Stephanides, Master's Thesis.

An Italo-American Voluntary Association in Detroit

Leonard W. Moss and Julie S. Flowerday

"Cortina" (a pseudonym for a small village in South Italy) has furnished many hundreds of her sons to the labor forces of the United States, Canada, Australia, and other parts of the world. The village was studied *in situ* by Cappannari and Moss (1954-55; 1955-56; 1961-62; 1963; and 1969). The village was selected because it was relatively isolated; not in a land reform area; had a high incidence of individual land ownership by the *contadini*; and, exhibited a high out-migration to and return from America. Out-migration had served as a safety valve for the overpopulation of the *paese* (village). The years following World War II reflected a worsened condition of life since the population, by force of circumstance, had been thrust inward upon its own resources.[1]

The original study showed a relatively stable economic pattern with most *contadini* existing at the subsistence level through self-sustaining agriculture. What marketing was done was more often on a barter rather than cash basis. Small, fragmented plots of land had been owned by the peasantry since at least 1806. The typical inheritance pattern split land-holdings to the point where the *contadino* described his piece of terrain as: *come un fazzoletto* ("as small as a handkerchief").[2] Little mechanization could be used under the circumstances. The life of the village was dominated by a "death orientation" in which the future held little hope.[3] There was both a poverty of economics and a poverty of spirit.

Rivalries between the parishes of the commune split the population. "Differences" in dialect prevented communication, or so argued the inhabitants of the two parishes. Within each of the parishes, rivalries between families stifled any development of a sense of cooperation.[4] There was a studied inability to find mutual solutions to mutual problems. One's own nuclear family came above all else; and, one's kinfolk came before those who were neighboring dwellers.[5]

Traditional distrust of those outside the family was a guide line to social conduct. Those outside the village were viewed with even greater distrust: "The unknown evil . . . ," those "in authority"—even when resident in the village—were to be feared as representatives of a distant and unfeeling government. The political apathy and lack of political skills made the villager feel powerless in the arena of self-government. He felt removed from politics and lacked knowledge and comprehension to participate in the political process. When it rained, he muttered, *"E' piove, governo ladro!"* ("It rains, thief of a government!") These were the boundary conditions which seemed to mark the village as it existed over the years. Basic concepts, central to American society—in the ideal—were alien to the vocabulary of the Cortinese. The essential elements of urban social and political participation—*community, neighborhood, cooperation, voluntary association*—were all conspicuously absent from the thoughtways of the residents of Cortina.[6]

This is the cultural background from which thousands of Cortinese journeyed forth to seek their fortunes. We have no accurate estimate of the numbers who left. Suffice to say, the resident population of Cortina in 1901 was 4,779; today, it numbers approximately 2,000.

Although the earliest emigration to America is unrecorded, many Cortinese men had journeyed forth to America in the late 1890s and the early years of the present century. This migration—more properly termed—tended to be a temporary sojourn. The young men had come to seek their fortune in the land where the "streets were paved with gold." Working as a section hand on the Delaware-Lackawanna Railroad together with other southern Italians, under the supervision of an Italian foreman (known to the Italians as *"Il Bosso"*; known to management as the "Guinea Pusher"), the men had scant opportunity to learn English or the lifeways of the strange country in which they worked. They longed for the day when their carefully husbanded funds derived from a substandard salary would be sufficient to permit them to return to their village and buy a patch of land.

Few of the early migrants established roots in the United States. Many were unable to cut the umbilical cord to the family; yet, lacked the economic ability to bring their kin to America. For some this meant spending a year or two in squalid rooming houses, pinching pennies, returning to the village and then back to America for another round of backbreaking toil.

Following World War I, a larger number of Cortinese left for the New World. They had heard the stories of the old-timers about the opportunities and the tribulations. The younger emigrees heard the curses of the returned *Americani*: *Ammazza Colombo or Managia Colombo*! ("a curse on Columbus [for discovering this crazy country]"). Determined not to make the same mistakes as the earlier migrants, they set forth on a more or less permanent emigration. These groups settled in Fairmount, West Virginia, and Lancaster, Pennsylvania. They secured employment with the Owens Illinois Glass Company, with lumbering firms, on the railroads, and in the mills and mines. A third center of Cortinese settlement developed in Youngstown, Ohio, where the men found work in the steel mills and factories. The last and largest center began to develop in Detroit in the early 1920s.

Prior to 1920 there were only five Cortinese in Detroit. The burgeoning automobile industry made Detroit a hungry labor market which gobbled up skilled and unskilled workers alike. One Cortinese began a chain of migration which first brought kinfolk, then others from within the parish, and, finally, those from the other parish. During these periods many of the men were able to establish themselves on a sound economic basis, sending for their families, obtaining United States citizenship, and purchasing homes. Though there may have been a nostalgia for the village, it was clear that America was the new home, the place where one would rear his children.

Though life in the village had been hard and often filled with bitter factionalism, one does not turn his back on his mother. The Cortinese kept in touch with family and kin even though he had made the unalterable decision to take up life abroad. *Campanilismo* sets limits to the horizons of the villager but does not necessarily imbue him with a sense of community. So it was in Cortina, but there existed two campanile, one for each parish! Geographic identification did not make for feelings of communality. To an American, he was Italian; to an Italian, he was Molisano; to a Molisano, he was Cortinese; to a Cortinese he was from one parish or the other; to a fellow parishioner, he was a member of a specific family. It was this latter identification which was, in fact, his community. That is, until he came to America. Thrown together with fellow villagers in that strange land, he began to feel bonds of mutuality which transcended the rivalries so important in the life of the village.

The Neopolitan foreman of the Hannah Furnace Company had been instrumental in bringing the first Cortinese immigrants to Detroit. He organized an Italo-American Mutual Benefit Society and urged the workers at the plant to join. Earliest known participation by Cortinese was in 1923. The association functioned primarily as an illness and death benefit society, guaranteeing a modicum of dignity to its members in distress. Many factors determined the demise of the organization, not the least of which was its strong support of Mussolini. By the early 1930s the society was disbanded. Evidently, several Cortinese felt that such an organization would meet certain needs of their growing community. Having profited from the lessons learned as members of this earlier association, they founded the Cortina Club of Detroit in 1934.[7]

The fragmented Cortinese population, living in a predominantly Hungarian section of Detroit, found themselves beset by many problems in the new land. The economic depression unleashed forces totally alien to the newcomers. Urban problems, welfare programs, the growth of militant industrial unionism, and a host of other factors which had never been faced in the village were threatening to the immigrants. Past rivalries, so meaningful in the village, now seemed to be submerged, to be dwarfed by the mere problem of existence. Forced inward on their own resources, the Cortinese created a constitution to insure the survival of their club.

In a real sense, the club seemed to serve as a foster family by providing for the needs of all Cortinese, not simply those who were related by kin ties. Emphasis was placed on village identity rather than on the parish moieties which divided the village. There were few formalized positions in the organization. The focus of the club was on personalized interests and personal behavior of the individual members. The constitution was written in the simple, direct language of the peasant, often incorporating dialect and ungrammatical expressions. It established a simple structure, sufficient to permit legal incorporation of the organization.

Over the years the club grew and began to feel the growing pains and strictures of its now archaic constitution. A new constitution was drafted to reflect the changes which had taken place. A highly segmented division of labor occurred in which a number of status positions became recognized as the working structure of the club. Indeed, one might even speak of growing bureaucratization, for that is the most applicable term. The club had shifted away from the highly personal and informal behavior of the past toward an impersonalized, businesslike approach which placed emphasis on parliamentary procedure. No longer were the meetings punctuated by small groups drifting off on their own; catcalls and verbal derision were no longer accepted behavior. Meetings were scheduled and strong attention was paid to the formalities of organizational existence. The Business Meeting followed the strictures laid down by Robert's Rules; reports from the officers proceeded before the reports from the committees; all of this before the club members could enter into their social functions. The serving of beer and wine, soft drinks for the young, were all delayed until the sober business had been handled. Then, and only then, were the members permitted to drift off into their social groups. Men in one corner of the hall, women in another, and the youngsters still elsewhere. The serving of snacks went hand in hand with the card games of the men. When all were dutifully tired, as after the old walks in the piazza, the families would drift off to their cars in the parking lot.

In its formal structure and in its format of meetings, the organization is today—in every way—American. Though some of the old dialects persist and punctuate the floor discussions, the business of the organization is undifferentiated from the hundreds of thousands of voluntary associations which dot the American landscape. The serious business of managing its funds is handled along with the equally serious business of planning the annual Christmas Party, New Year's Eve dinner-dance, and the summer picnics.

Over the years there have been changes in more than the structure of the organization. The alterations in values and practices are a reflection in the microcosm of the club of the many events and changes in the broader socio-cultural context of American society. In the sequential analysis of the constitutions of the club (1934, 1938, 1959, and 1964) are revealed the changing practices and purposes of the association.

As originally conceived, membership in the organization was open to any "Cortinese" over the age of two living in either the United States or Italy. The membership was expected to exhibit good moral character, to refrain from the use of offensive language, and to be loyal to the club. Though an initiation fee was collected ($1.25), there were no formal dues. Each member was expected to contribute to the ad hoc funds created at the time of need for sick benefits, death benefits, and funeral flowers. The male dominated organization prohibited political involvement by the club and forbade both the discussion of politics and religion during the meetings. Members were free, however, to discuss the economic and social conditions of the working class.

The second constitution, as in the first case written in Italian, moved the organization toward exclusiveness and formality. Membership was restricted to

"Cortinese" adult males (18-55) resident in Detroit. Formal applications were required, regular monthly dues were assessed, and meetings were scheduled on a monthly basis. Though the sick benefit was dropped, each member was assured that this family would receive $150 at the time of his death. English became a permissible language for use during the business meeting.

By 1959, the constitution underwent other changes. In its third rewriting, this time in English, the club liberalized its membership to include male and female "Cortinese" over the age of 18, resident in the general Detroit area. The death benefit was dropped and a retirement fund was created. At age 65, each member would receive one-half of the amount of dues he had paid over the years. After the exclusion of women from membership (1938), a women's club had been formed. Obviously, this demonstrated the social needs of at least this segment of the population. A second women's club was formed by those "Cortinese" who had moved to the suburbs on the southwest fringe of Detroit. The 1959 constitution attempted to re-enlist in the ranks of the club all the members of the community.

A fourth constitution made its appearance in 1964. Written in English, the document acknowledged that Italian may be spoken during the business meetings. The dues structure was regulated on an annual basis and all of the earlier benefits were eliminated. The association had evolved from an ethnic mutual benefit society to a formalized organization, still ethnically based but placing its emphasis on social activities exclusively for its own members. As the German sociologist Tonnies noted: a movement from *gemeinschaft* to *gesselschaft*.

In 1966, the club had a total of 70 female and 68 male members. Overwhelmingly (70 percent), the members represented one of the two parishes in the village of origin. What is significant, however, is that the association includes members from both parts of the village. The population is aging, some 70 percent being over the age of 40. Sixty-six percent were born in the village, 19 percent are descendants of village-born "Cortines," and 15 percent are non-"Cortinese" who have married in. Two large kinship nuclei account for 69 percent of the total membership. Ten additional families account for 29 percent of the group.

Though thousands of similar ethnic associations in America have gone out of existence, the "Cortina" Club continues. Its major service to its membership has been an expression of ethnic identity in an exclusive setting. As recently as 1966, the organization revealed little social differentiation among its members. Some 94 percent of those employed were skilled industrial workers or were self-employed. Given the high degree of similarity in educational background, socioeconomic status, and ethnic identity, there was a high degree of social cohesion within the group. Sixty-six percent of the married members were endogamous within the village group. Hence, the association continuation can be explained by its relatively late beginning, the stability of its population, and the strong bonds of familism and ethnicity. Its perpetuation, however, is dependent upon a continued source of recruitment which is diminishing.

134

From a village in which voluntary associations were unknown, the immigrants created an ethnic association to promote their own welfare and to prevent the pervasive anonymity of the strange, urban culture. Their association through the process of acculturation became more and more like voluntary associations found throughout America. The club functioned primarily as an adaptive mechanism, cushioning the impact of changing events in an impersonal environment. The association aided its members and their children in becoming part of the new cultural milieu and, thus, the club has paved the road to its further alteration or, perhaps, to its demise.

Notes

1. L.W. Moss, "Ricerche socio-culturali di studiosi americani," *Bollettino delle Ricerche Sociali*, Anno I, No. 6, Dic., 1961, pp. 502-17. L.W. Moss, "Il metodo dell 'anthropologia culturale," *Il Pensiero Critico*, Anno IV, No. 3-4, Dic., 1962, pp. 29-39.

2. L.W. Moss and S.C. Cappannari, "Estate and Class in a South Italian Hill Village," *American Anthropologist*, Vol. 64, No. 2, April, 1962, pp. 287-300.

3. L.W. Moss and S.C. Cappannari, "Folklore and Medicine in an Italian Village," *Journal of American Folklore*, Vol. 73, No. 288, April-June, 1960, pp. 95-102.

4. L.W. Moss and S.C. Cappannari, "Patterns of Kinship, Comparaggio, and Community in a South Italian Village," *Anthropological Quarterly*, Vol. 33, No. 1, January, 1960, pp. 24-32.

5. L.W. Moss and W.H. Thomson, "The South Italian Family: Literature and Observation," *Human Organization*, Vol. 18, No. 1, Summer, 1959, pp. 35-41.

6. See, for example, E.C. Banfield, *The Moral Basis of a Backward Society*. Glencoe: The Free Press, 1958. Banfield unfortunately failed to take into account the patron-client system of the village. This complex of reciprocal obligation forms the normative basis of the social system. Unfortunately, too, Banfield used the pejorative "backward" to describe the lifeways of the villagers. See also, the critique of Banfield by F. Cancian, "Il contadino meridionale: comportamento politico e visione del mondo," *Bollettino delle Ricerche Sociali*, Anno I, No. 3-4, 1961, pp. 258-77.

7. The club was studied by Julie Smith Flowerday, See: J. Smith, *An Italo-American Voluntary Association: a Study of Acculturation*. Detroit, Mich.: Wayne State University, Unpublished Master's Thesis, 1967.

8. F. Tonnies, *Community and Association* (London: Routledge & Kegan Paul, 1955).

Part III
Some National Cases

10 The Russian Minority in America

Helen Kovach and Djuro J. Vrga

Racial relations, ethno-cultural minorities, cultural pluralism, religious relations, and majority-minority relations represent a set of complex and interrelated problems of serious public and political concern in America. All these questions are treated publicly as issues of paramount importance for the normal, effective, and functionally positive operation of American institutions and for prospects of American society in the future.

Many ethnic and religious minority groups are mentioned very rarely or never in the most extensive studies of ethno-cultural minorities. Most neglected are the ethnic minority groups with origin or background from Central and Eastern Europe, perhaps because they are small numerically and are therefore weak politically.

The Russian ethnic minority deserves special attention. Russian contributions to American society should be appraised objectively as we are finally trying to reappraise the role of Negroes in the history of the United States.

The Study Approach

In major studies of ethnic and cultural minorities today the assimilationists approach is commonly used.[1] Instead of the assimilation approach from the perspectives of the dominant group, the attention of an ethnic minority study should be focused on the structure and functions of the minority group as a social system through which its members satisfy many of their psychosocial needs or express frustrations resulting from their unsatisfied expectations and basic aspirations in the larger society. When the question of adjustment of immigrants and their American-born children is raised, it does not imply that assimilation and acculturation are neglected. For understanding their life and reactions to stresses, it seems more fruitful and promising to explore the nature of a series of their adjustments.

Adjustment is a process by which the individual solves the problems of tension and frustration and achieves satisfaction and a pleasant feeling of acceptance. According to Sheldon Stryker's definition, "the adjustment of the individual is a function of the accuracy with which he can take the role of the other(s) implicated with him in some social situation."[2] Whether an individual is effectively adjusted or maladjusted depends upon the degree of coordination of "his previous habits, perceptions, motives, and emotions."[3] Therefore, maladjustment is always, Parsons suggests, "an adequate response to present difficulties."[4] Accordingly, persons who feel comfortable in their positions and roles assigned to them by the society would be adjusted.

By taking adjustment as the frame of reference in the study of ethno-cultural minority groups composed of more successive immigrations and their American-born descendants, it is possible to establish a relationship between the successive immigrations' adjustment to the larger American society and to each other. It is suggested that, in the study of ethnic minorities with a sizable number of immigrants, attention be focused on what may be called the dual adjustment, i.e., first, the adjustment of successive immigrations to each other and to their American-born descendants, and second, the adjustment of each immigration to the larger society. The successive emigrations may be leaving the native country under different conditions and motives, and the social conditions under which they are accepted by the host society are never the same.

The Identity and Composition of the Russian Minority Group

Identity. The first question to be faced in the study of minority groups is to establish the main criteria of identification. In the main, cultural and linguistic characteristics are most usually considered the main criteria of a group's identity. For certain group's, cultural inheritance and historical background are taken together as the source of ethnic distinctness and originality.[5] Certain groups may consider their religion as the major indicators of their ethnic identity, as the Poles recognize the Catholic religion, the Arabs their Islam, and the Serbs the Orthodox religion.

There is a widespread controversy concerning the Russian identity in general. Russians are considered by many as those people who are Great Russians by provincial origin. We think that the recognition of the provincial origin of certain people is not the most reliable criterion for determining their ethnicity. In some instances neither racial nor geographic origin of people are indicators of their ethnicity. For instance, the Bulgarians are not Slavs nor Caucasians by origin but feel that they are the most prominent and best representative Slavic nation. Therefore, it is suggested that the emotional feeling of ethnic identity is of primary importance for distinguishing ethnic groups. It is not our purpose to deny Russian identity to those people who consider themselves Russians although some would insist they are White Russians, Ukrainians, or Carpatians because of the place or province of their origin.[6] If the state or the place of origin of Jews were taken as the principle indicators of their identity, there would then be no Jews in the United States.

There is also a tendency not to consider as Russians some of those immigrants or their descendants who were converted from the Uniate to the Orthodox religion. In our opinion, if they continue calling themselves Russians, their feeling of identity is the basic criterion of their ethnic identity.[7]

For the above reasons the Russian minority group in America is composed of those immigrants who consider themselves Russians regardless of the place, province, and state of their origin.[8] The descendants of immigrants who recognize their Russian background and continue sharing a certain Russian cultural heritage are also considered members of that minority group. In addition, it is suggested that belonging to the Russian Orthodox Church is the main indicator of one's feeling of Russian identity.

Composition. The Russian minority group is composed of two major immigrations and American-born Russians. The old immigration includes all immigrants who came before World War II, while the new immigrants are Russians who entered the States after the Second World War. Each of these two major immigrations represents two or more distinctive categories of Russians (Table 10-1).

First, the old immigration includes those Russians who came before World War I and those who came between the two wars. For intragroup adjustment and, consequently, for Russian community life in America, the fact that the two

Table 10-1
Composition of the Russian Minority Group

| Period | Composition and Origin | | Occupation Before |
	Immigrations and American-born	Categories	Immigration and Occupation of American-born
Before World War II	Old Immigration	Before World War I	
		Between the two world wars	professionals military laborers
Post-World War II	New Immigration	Escapees and refugees from Soviet Union	professionals laborers
		Russian post-World War I immigrants from European and Far Eastern countries	military professionals
	America-born Russians	Second Generation	laborers skilled workers
			enterpreneurs
		Third Generation	professionals enterpreneurs skilled workers

categories of immigrants had different motives for emigration and also differences in their background social experiences and their aspirations was especially important. Those who came before World War I left their country of origin in search of a better life including more political freedom. The great majority of them were also from the peasantry stratum of their native society.

The second category of immigrants of the old immigration represented refugees after the Bolshevik seizure of power in the former Russian Empire. Beside the exiled Russian scientists, the majority of this relatively small category of Russian immigrants were fighters against the communist revolutionaries. Because of quota restrictions, the number of Russian immigrants to America between the wars was relatively small.

Second, the composition of new immigrants deserves special attention. The first category of new Russian immigrants includes those who escaped from the Soviet Union during the war or refused to return home after release from German war prisoners' camps as well as from concentration and enforced labor camps.[9] The second category represents former Russian immigrants to various European countries and their children. Russians who came to the States from the Far Eastern countries, China mainly, represent a special category of Russian new immigrants. However, many anti-Bolshevik fighters came to the States through the Far Eastern countries between the wars.

Discriminatory attitudes of Americans toward Russians were best demonstrated immediately after the war when the Soviet refugees from displaced persons camps in Germany were handed over and repatriated to the Soviet Union. Those people spent years in Soviet concentration camps in Siberia if they were lucky enough to escape punishment by death before reaching their native country. Therefore, many Russians and members of other ethnic groups from the Soviet Union were afraid to disclose the name of their province of origin and even more their ethnic identity due to fear of repatriation from their camps in Germany by Americans. Many Russians who escaped the forced repatriation identified themselves to representatives of the American government either as Poles or members of some other ethnic group in order to be granted an immigration visa. This problem of mispresentation of new immigrants from the Soviet Union came to public attention in America when Rodion M. Akul'shin admitted that his immigrating name Rodion Berezov was a pseudonym used in order to escape repatriation to the Soviet Union and to be granted the immigration visa.[a]

Intragroup adjustment. To understand the Russian pattern of social behavior and attitudes in emigration the behavior of Russian immigrants and their

---

[a]When Akul'shin admitted that while applying for an immigration visa his statement about the province and state of origin was not correct because he was afraid of deportation to the Soviet Union, the immigration authorities were ready to deny him the right to citizenship and to deport him as well. Finally, the so-called Berezov case came to the attention of the President and the Congress, which passed a law concerning similar cases. Consequently, Berezov was granted the right to become a citizen of the United States.

children from European countries and the Far East should be recognized. First, those Russian immigrants were not expected to renounce their ethnic identity although most of them have become citizens of European countries which accepted them. In most of those countries the children of Russian immigrants attended Russian elementary schools and gymnasiums (high school).

The different social backgrounds and socioeconomic and political experiences of Russian immigrants in their native country or the countries of their previous immigration had had differential affects on their expectations, ambitions, opportunities, and achievements in America. Also, the differential psycosocial experiences of different immigrant categories strongly reflected on their intra-ethnic group adjustment as well as on their adjustment to the larger American society.

Although the former anti-Bolshevik fighters and the post-World War II escapees or refugees from the Soviet Union had significant differences in their life experiences and motives for exile, they adjusted to one another relatively fast and with mutual satisfaction. In his treatment of their adjustment in the literary field, Gleb Struve, a well known professor of literature at the University of California, Berkeley, admitted that the two groups found many grounds for mutual understanding and cooperation.[10] He also recognized that the acceptance of the new immigrants from the Soviet Union by the American Society was more favorable than its acceptance of the former "White Army" fighters.

Size of the Russian Minority Group

As stressed in other studies, Chyz and Roucek's especially, census data are not very reliable for determining the size of the Russian minority group as they are not reliable for the estimate of the size of many other groups, especially those from multi-ethnic countries and that part of Europe where state boundaries changed often during the last century.[11]

The coming of Russians to the new world is different than that of other European ethnic groups because the first Russian appearance on the continent of North America happened from the north-west, i.e., in Alaska from which the Russians moved down to California at the very beginning of the last century.[12] The immigration of Russians on the Atlantic side of the United States became well noticed only by the end of the last century, although in 1850 there were 1,414 reported immigrants from the Russian Empire.

According to the census data of 1960 there were 276,834 foreign-born who reported the Russian language as their "mother tongue."[13] We suppose that the census reported Russian loss from 356,940 in 1940 to 276,834 in 1960 is much larger than reflecting the mortality rate for twenty years. In addition, although the number of displaced persons and refugees from the Soviet Union is relatively small, it should be admitted that there were Russians among 42,231 Soviet displaced persons and refugees beside those Russians who came from various European countries and the Far East.

The Membership of the Russian Orthodox Church. Who are the members of the Russian Orthodox Church? Are the majority of them Russians or not? We visited many Russian Orthodox parishes in various American cities and talked with several prominant Russian Orthodox clergymen and did not ascertain that there were many church members who could identify themselves as Ukrainians, although there are members who were Russians born in Ukraina. It is true, however, that there are inter-ethnic Orthodox parishes under Russian jurisdiction. At the same time, in the majority of parishes there are members who are not Russians either by origin or by ethnic identity. Therefore, it can be said that not all reported membership of all Russian parishes is Russian.

According to the reports of the Russian Orthodox Church outside Russia and the Russian Orthodox Greek Catholic Church in America their membership is 810,000.[14] It is presumed that about 75,000 of this reported membership are not Russians by birth or descent. If it is accepted that there are about 300,000 foreign-born Russians in the United States, (this number is obtained by adding conservatively 25,000 of Russian new immigrants from the Soviet Union and the whole of Europe and the Far East to the reported 276,834 in 1960, less mortality between 1940 and 1960), the church membership of 735,000 of foreign and American-born Russians is not exaggerated. In 1920, there were 392,049 foreign-born Russian who constituted with their American-born descendants a group of 731,949. When we deduct from this number those who returned to the native land and those who died, but add the number of immigrants who came after World War I to the present and their American-born children, and the third generation of ethnicly conscious Russians, our number of 735,000 members of the Russian Orthodox churches is not exaggerated.[15]

It should be recognized that many third generation Russians are members of the Russian Orthodox Church for many reasons, the first of which would be recognition of the Orthodox religion by over thirty states as a religion of social importance, which is a strong factor affecting the religious orientation of Orthodox descendants.

While the children of old immigrants who were on the bottom of the American social structure could have felt shame at being members of a "non-American" church, the Russian descendants today feel proud to be members of the Orthodox Church.

The loyalty of Russian immigrants and their descendants to the United States is unquestionable. The recognition of Russian contributions to the United States seems to be especially important for the Russian acceptance of the United States.

The Acceptance and Adjustment of Russian Immigrants

Immigration Before World War I. With a small number of exceptions, the Russian immigrants to the United States before World War I were peasants by social and occupational background. While a relatively small number of those peasant immigrants became farmers the majority of them became miners and industrial workers. The majority of Russians live in the north-east region of the United States, mainly the state of New York. Pennsylvania has the second largest number of Russians. By metropolitan area, the largest number of Russians live in New York City, then the Los Angeles-Long Beach area, Philadelphia, and Chicago.[16]

The acceptance of a great number of Russian immigrants from the end of the last century to World War I was not much different than that of immigrants of other nationalities from central and eastern Europe. After their initial settlement, the Russian peasant immigrants were usually subjected to much different treatment than other immigrants. The treatment of Russians was reflective of the international policy of America. The anti-Russian attitudes of the American government during the Russo-Japanese War strongly reflected on the treatment of Russian workers in the American mines and factories.

On the other hand, the United States was giving cordial treatment to the political ideologists and agitators against the government and political order in Russia regardless of their ethnic origin.[17] When the Bolsheviks succeeded in the revolution of 1917, American disagreement with the communist ideology and opposition to the Bolshevik determination to cause a world revolution showed itself clearly in the treatment of Russian workers. As Jerome Davis reported, the Russian immigrant workers understood their position as slavery because of their twelve-hour day, seven-day week on the lowest paying but most dangerous and least protected assignments, which they had never experienced in their native land.[18] The capitalist employers in America considered their Russian workers as Bolsheviks and by treating them with discrimination they made Bolsheviks of many of them.[19]

The Russian workers received the lowest possible wages and were to be laid off or refused admission after strikes.[20] The identification of Russian immigrants with the Bolsheviks had effects on the treatment, poor housing, health, and social isolation of immigrants whose image of America before their emigration was most favorable.[21]

The Russian second generation faced more serious problems than the second generation of many other nationalities. A certain percentage tried to receive more favorable treatment from their American countrymen by denouncing their ethnic background and by joining some Protestant denominations and even by Americanizing their names. However, the great majority remained loyal to their parents and contributed to their families.

Immigration Between the Two Wars. Although Russian immigrants between the two wars were escapees, refugees, and expellees from the Soviet Union, they all were not accepted equally in America. The Russian scientists continued to pursue their scientific endeavor, and their rise in prestige was very fast.

The occupational background and social experiences of another category of immigrants were quite different. While the military education and training of many of them served as a "social stairway" in their native country, they served as an obstacle to regaining their social standing and even more as an obstacle to upward mobility in America. Like many other professionals, former military officers accepted employment of the lowest occupational level.

The occupational discrepancy of many immigrants between the wars affected their adjustment to the old Russian immigrants with whom they shared low social standing. In addition, the earlier immigrants were in commanding positions of the Russian community and Russian parishes. Therefore, they were not ready to entrust leadership to the newcomers. Adjustment between these two groups of Russian immigrants passed through several stages of tension. As a consequence, the newcomers resorted to the organization of associations which became best expressions of their life experiences and anti-communist aspirations. Numerous publications of the new group of immigrants served as a means of re-enforcing their convictions and maintaining communication among them. The newcomers also began organizing parishes which recognized the canonical and hierarchical leadership of the Russian Orthodox Church Outside Russia[b] while the old peasant-immigrants remained under the jurisdiction of the Russian Orthodox Greek Catholic Church of North America. However, the two groups of immigrants were not engaged in a struggle between themselves, and their churches were trying to reduce differences between them.

The New Russian Immigrants. The new Russian immigrants from the Soviet Union are represented least by the military. Although there are professionals among them, the majority came from the labor class. Of those from the European countries, the majority were born or brought up in those countries and almost all of them came as professionals in different fields mainly engineers, teachers, administrators, jurists, and physicians.

Russian new immigrants, with certain exceptions, began their life in America on the lowest occupational level. In the course of time, however, the great percentage of professionals succeeded in regaining their social status by achieving employment in the field of their specialization.

Therefore, it can be said that Russian new immigrants began adjusting to American society under less tension and with less frustration than all previous Russian immigrants, except the recognized scientists from the previous immigration. As far as intra-ethnic Russian adjustment, the new immigrants easily established friendly relations with the previous immigration between the wars. Interestingly, the immigrants from the Soviet Union share their identity and interests with the Russian immigrants from the European countries. At the same time, they establish social relations easily with the immigrants between the wars and the earlier immigrants.

It should be admitted that Russian immigrants in America have different inter-ethnic experiences than many other ethnic minority groups. The Russians

---

[b]The synod of this church has been in America since 1950. Before the war, it was in Yugoslavia. For treatment of the problem "The Orthodox Church in America: Past and Future" see a special issue of *The St. Vladimir's Seminary Quarterly*, Vol. 5, No. 1-2, 1961.

have very tolerant and cooperative attitudes toward other ethnic groups simply because of their inter-ethnic experiences in the native country.

One particular case is of special interest for the understanding of Russian ethnicity and the Orthodox ethos. In 1963, when the various denominations were forbiding Negroes to enter their churches, we saw a Negro monk in the Russian monastery in Jordanville. The Negro and other visiting students of Russian languages from Vermont were surprised but also very impressed when they saw the Negro monk in an ethnic Orthodox Church.

The social relations of Russians are best secured and emotionally expressed through friendly visits and celebrations. In this respect, the Russians are known for their hospitality, friendly and respectable treatment of their guests. Russian hospitality is not restricted to having good time with other people but by their readiness to help them in need.

The Russian immigrants are very loyal American citizens. Their contribution to America make them feel as proud citizens. The educational attainment of Russian children is an evidence of their feeling equal and humanitarian treatment.

The Russian Press in America

The number, linguistic quality, purpose, and orientation of ethnic publications of a minority group with a large number of immigrants reflect the educational attainment of immigrants, and their occupational achievements before emigration. At the same time, ethnic publications disclose the immigrants' attitudes toward the host society.

Although the number of reported Russian immigrants in 1920 was much higher than ever before or later—392,049 (in 1910—57,926; in 1960—276,834), the Hoover Institution reports 18 Russian publications up to 1920.[22] Of those 18 publications, only 6 survived up to 1940. However, from 1920 to 1966, there appeared, according to the report of the Hoover Institution, 26 Russian publications, monthlies, weeklies, or dailies, although the number of foreign-born Russians supposedly declined from 392,049 to 276,834. The publications which appeared before 1920 were evidences of problems and interests of Russian workers like *Golos Truzhenika*, a Weekly of the Industrial Workers of the World; *Khleb i Volia*, a Weekly of Russian Workers; *Narodnaia Gazeta*, A Weekly Socialist Gazeta; *Novyi Mir*, a Weekly Workers' Gazette: Russian Organ of the Communist Party of the United States; *Rassvet*, a Daily Gazett of Organizations of Russian workers; *Znamia*, a Daily workers' Gazette. The publications which appeared in the 1930s were mainly expressions of expectations, aspirations, and adjustment of immigrants who had escaped from Russia after the Bolshevik seizure of power. It suffices to mention just a few of those other publications: *Amerikanskie Izvestia*, a Weekly of Russian Cultural educational Organizations; *Nashi Vesti* ("Our News") issued by the associations of Former officers of the Russian Corpus; *Russkii Natzionalyni Komitet G. Niu Yorka*; and *Vera v*

Pobedu, an Organ of New York's part of the Russian Imperial unit and of the 2nd part of the association of His Highness Prince Nikita Alexksandrovich.

In his index of Russian publications, P. Goy[23] gives the titles of exactly 33 publications, but he does not mention a few important Russian publications including *St. Vladimir's Seminary Quarterly,* which is published in the English language, as well as *Russian-American Orthodox Messenger, Our Way, Russian Orthodox Journal,* and *Orthodox Life,* all of which are religious periodicals, and the daily *Russkaya Zhizn'* published in San Francisco. Because of space we cannot give the titles of many publications which deserve attention because of diversity of their publishers, content, and objectives. It should be mentioned, however, that *Novyi Zhurnal* (New Review) is a quarterly with over 300 pages per single issue with content from different disciplines. Its appearance, stages of development, publicity, and effects are of special interest.[c] The daily *Novoye Russkoye Slovo,* which also deserves special attention, began appearing in 1911 and now has a circulation of over 22,500 copies.[24]

It should also be mentioned that almost all Russian Orthodox parishes publish their local bulletins regularly and report social changes among their membership. In the ethnically mixed parishes, bulletins are published mainly in the English language.

In general, the reported incomplete number of Russian publications in America is relatively great and is also sufficient evidence of different backgrounds, experiences, and interests of Russian immigrants. The Russian publications are indicators of a relatively large proportion of well-educated immigrants, and of Russian tendencies for self-expression, and readiness to discuss their beliefs and values publicly.

The Associational Involvement of Russians

There was an opinion that "The Russian immigrants have shown very little inclination for organized social life on a large scale."[25] The above opinion was suggested in 1939 when the great majority of Russian immigrants belonged to

---

[c]*Novyi Zhurnal* began appearing in 1942 under the editorship of M.A. Aldanov, a well-known author whose twenty-four books were translated into other languages. This journal has three stages of development: (1) 1942 to 1945, (2) 1945 to 1954, (3) 1955 to the present. During the second period, most prominent were contributions from the philosophers Berdyaev, Losski, and Shestov. The next important contributors were escapees from the Soviet Union and Russian immigrants from European countries. Alexander Kerensky was one of the important contributors during the second period, mainly in the politico-cultural area.

Interestingly, since 1958 this journal receives contributions from the Soviet Union. That the journal is now read in the Soviet Union can be concluded from the fact that references to it are made very often. See Siberstein's article about M. Gorky in *Literaturnaya Gazeta,* April 19, 1966.

See Roman Gul', "Dvadtsat Piat Let," a lecture presented at the University of New York, *Novyi Zhurnal,* Kn. 87, 1967, pp. 6-28.

the pre-war Russian immigrant category with predominantly peasant background and lower educational attainment. Some associations of post-World War I immigrants represented status groups of people with a special social background and standing in the Russian society; while the old Russian immigrants with lower class background were inclined to belong to mutual assistance associations, workers' organizations, and political associations whose members shared background and occupational similarities and emotional identification.

It seems that the influence of a relatively great number of Russian immigrant-scientists between the wars on the pattern of associational involvement of Russians was not as strong as of immigrants from the same old-immigration category who had been military, professionals, and laborers in the native country and who were degraded occupationally in America. It is certain that the scientists who retained their pre-emigration status in America concentrated on scientific work. The scientists did not feel a great need for recognition and emotional acceptance from the Russian ethnic community as the status skidders did. However, as members of Russian voluntary associations, many of them such as Professors Timasheff and Schmemann, were very active. The pattern of associational life of Russians today is much different than before World War II and even more than before World War I.[d]

It has been noticed through contacts with many Russians in the Detroit area that those immigrants who became status skidders in America tend to belong to a greater number of voluntary associations than their upwardly mobile nationals. As the names of Russian associations indicate, those immigrants who share the same background and life experiences tend to organize special associations, as for instance the organizations of cadets who attended gymnasium (high school) in Yugoslavia under the guidance of the former Russian military officers. Or, there is an association of women who attended a Russian institute which was on the level of gymnasium or girls high school in Yugoslavia.

The Russian new immigrants from the Soviet Union have organized many associations with two principal objectives in all their variations: first, the overthrow of communism in the Soviet Union and, second, the organization of a federation of free nations on the territory of the Soviet Union. For that reason those associations are supported by other Russian immigrants and other nationalities. Therefore, the SBONR *(Souz Bor'by za Osvobozhdenie Narodov Rossii (Union for the Struggle for Liberation of Nations of Russia)* is today one of Russian active voluntary association which publishes its propaganda material and sends it to the Soviet Union. Almost equally popular is the NTS *(Narodno Trudovoy Souz)* which has more specified social objectives. These two organizations are functioning in all other countries with Russian immigrants.

It seems that best known and most popular among Russians are organizations with charitable and humanitarian objectives and functions. Such an organization

---

[d]Regarding the adjustment of immigrants, Oscar Handlin suggests, "In understanding the character of that adjustment, it is essential to know about the circumstances under which the newcomers departed from the lands of their birth." *Immigration as a Factor in American History* (Englewood Cliffs, New Jersey: Prentice-Hall, Inc., 1959), p. 20.

is the Tolstoy Foundation, which provided guarantees for new immigrants and presently provides care for the aged and helps the unemployed. In addition, it sends help to the indigious Russians in Europe. The Tolstoy Foundation has a relatively larger membership and also receives many contributions from almost all Russians. Similar to the Tolstoy Foundation is the *Fond Srochnoi Pomoshchi* (The Foundation for the Fast Help). Very popular and much praised by the old immigrants especially is the ROOVA, which provides assistance to the old immigration primarily, and to the second and the third generation of Russians. It also helps the indigent Russians. It has over 100 local branches in America and provides educational facilities for youth.

Especially association prone are the immigrants from the time between the two wars and the post-World War II new immigrants. It suffices to mention just a few of their associations which serve as status groups on the local level and for mutual assistance as well as the propagation of their ideas and objectives:

Souz Voennykh Invalidov (Association of Military Invalids);

Souz Chlenov Russkogo Korpusa (Association of Member of the Russian Corpus);

Ob'edinenie Oficerov Imperatorskoi Konnitsi i Konnoi Artilerii (Association of Imperial Cavalry and Artillery);

Ob'edininee Byvshikh Yunkerov Nikolaievskogo Kavaleriskogo Uchilishcha (Association of Former Cadets of the Nikolaiev's Cavalry School);

Socially significant functions are performed by certain occupational associations or those which indicate the former social role of members:

Russko-Amerikanskoye Medicinskoye Obshchestove (Medical Association of American Russians);

Russko-Amerikanskoye Obshchestvo Inzhenerov (Russian-American Association of Engineers);

Obshchestvo Pensionerov (Association of Retirees);

Litfund (Association for the Relief of Russian Writers and Scientists) is an association with the most effective fulfillment of its functions. It seems that it mainly helps the Russian writers and scientists outside America.

Russkaya Akademicheskaya Grupa v S.SH.A. (Russian Academic Group in the United States of America) deserves special attention because of the composition of its membership and its high scholastic standards.[e]

Many Russian associations are of local character, especially in communities with a large number of Russians. Such an organization is *Beseda* ("Conversation" in Philadelphia) or *Russko-Amerikanskoye Obshchestvo* (in many cities), as well as the *Russian Club* and *Novaya Zhizn'*.

---

[e]Before 1948, Russian scholars in America belonged to the Association of American Foreign Scholars. In 1948 new immigrant-scholars and the Russian-American scholars organized *Ruskaya Akademicheskaya Grupa* in America. One of the main objectives of the group is publishing scientific works of Russian scholars in the Russian language. Two large volumes of studies were published in 1967 and 1968.

Especially important for the Russian intragroup adjustment and ethnic consciousness are organizations which have double objectives: first, the protection of the Russian youth from alienation and deviation and, second, the development of the youths' consciousness of Russian ethnic origin and their attachment to the Russian Orthodox Church. *Russkie Razvetchiki*, which is similar to the boy scout clubs, is becoming very popular and widely supported by Russians. The Tolstoy Foundation is very popular because of its well-organized summer camps. *Obshchestvo Pomoshchi Russkim Detiam Za Rubezhom* (The Association for Assisting Russian Children Abroad) should also be mentioned because of its great help to Russian children in South America.

It is worth mentioning that St. Sergius High School in New York is a fully accredited high school which is also attended by children of non-Russian origin. In that school teaching is conducted in the Russian language.

A very great and nationwide support is received by the *Fund for Assistance of the Russian Orthodox Church Outside of Russia*.

Very well-known to the American and Canadian public are certain Russian choirs like *Donskoi Kazachii Khor Zharova, Kazachii Khor Generala Platova*, and *Metropolichii Khor Afonskogo*.

Regarding the associational involvement of Americans, we can say that the degree of Russian associational involvement is much higher. The low social status of many Russian immigrants who have experienced a drastic status degradation in America, is positively related to their higher membership in voluntary association, which serves as means for the relief from frustration and disappointments caused by their status degradation in emigration.

Russian Contributions to the American Society

The Russian immigrations have made many different contributions to American society. As Chyz and Rouchek say, "Together with American and immigrant workers of other nationalities they (Russian immigrants) have helped to build up this country to what it is today."[26] The immigrants from the Russian Empire brought "numerous varieties of seed" which enriched American agriculture. The acceptance of Russian music and the great popularity of Russian literature, art, and ballet are reflective of international recognition of their significance.

Valuable Russian contributions to American Society are apparent in almost all fields of knowledge. The most distinguished Russian contributors belong to the immigration between the wars and the new immigration.

In order to show that the Russian scientists made contributions in many different fields of all sciences, their names will be given in reference to the field of their specialization:[27]

Astronomy—Otto L. Struve, a professor at the University of California, has become an internationally recognized authority in the field of astronomy. Equally recognized is Ivan I. Kovalevsky, who worked at Yale University.

Aerodynamics—A recognized authority in the field of aerodynamics, D.P.

Riabushinsky, a member of the French Academy of Science, used to visit America to deliver lectures in the physical-mathematical science.

Zoology and Botany—Internationally known scientists in this field are N.A. Borodin, a Harvard University professor, and Mihailo M. Petrunkevich, a professor at Yale. Also living in America is Mihail M. Novikov, who was the rector of the University of Moscow.

Biology—As a recognized scientist in biology, A.A. Maksimov, a professor of the University of Chicago also became widely known because of his methodology in research. Professor V.N. Boldirev established the Pavlov's Institute in Michigan. Other well-known professors of biology in America are A.I. Konev, A. Romanov, and V.I. Okulich.

Chemistry—Vladimar N. Ipatiev, an internationally known academic, was in America from 1930s and also served as a scientific consultant abroad. As a pioneer in the advancement of chemistry, Professor V.N. Ipatiev established a special laboratory in Chicago. Professor A.V. Tolstouhov became known in a special field of chemistry. Significantly. G. Kistyanovsky served as the President's advisor in the area of science and technology.

Mathematics and Technical Sciences—It suffices to mention just a few names of Russian scientists in these two disciplines. V. Zvornikin is considered the originator of theoretical explanations and foundations of television. Well known among many mathematical theoreticians are Professor I. Uspensky, S.P. Timoshenko, and M.E. Kovalevsky, Professor Yadov made special contributions in the field of electrotechnics.

Jurisprudence and Economics—Of specialists in these fields best known are Professors B.S. Izboldin and E.V. Spektorsky.

Sociology—Professor Pitirim A. Sorokin was not only a great American sociologist but an internationally recognized great sociological theorist. Professor Nickolas S. Timasheff is another Russian immigrant whose sociological contributions will remain most valuable.

History and History of Literature—Especially great contributions in the field of history were made by Professors G.V. Vernadsky, Mihail M. Karpovich, who also was a dean of Harvard University, and G.V. Lantzev. A well-known literary critic is Professor Gleb Struve, whose twenty-some books were translated into English. L. Rzhevsky, a new immigrant from the Soviet Union, is a writer and literary critic and a professor at the New York University.

Philosophy and Theology—Especially prominent in the field of philosophy was Professor Nikolay O. Lossky. Professor Georgii Florovsky is one ofthe best known Orthodox theologians in America. Also well known in the inter-denominational theological circles are Professors Ivan Meyerdorff and Alexander Schmemann, who represented the American Orthodox as an observer at the last Vatican Council.

There are also many more Russian names in the same fields and especially in the fields of *art and music*. World recognized composers are Sergei Rachmaninoff who also was an excellent pianist, and Igor Stravinsky also a recognized conductor.

Literature–Vladimar Nabokov is the author of several world renowned novels, which qualify him as one of the greatest American writers. Many writers and critics are already known, some are escapees from the Soviet Union. The poet Ivan Elagin is a university professor now. Much translated is Igor Chinnov, a poet, and a professor at the University of Pittsburgh. Especially well known as a literary critic is the poet Yurii Ivask, a professor at Seattle.

Aviation–Igor Sikorsky's contribution to aviation, especially to the development and improvements of helicopters is worth great recognition and appreciation. He was the son of Professor Ivan A. Sikorsky, one of the best known Russian psychiatrists.

It should be stressed that the mentioned Russian scientists are not simply professionals in certain natural and social sciences but theoreticians and originators of new ideas.

The Influence of Russian Scientists on the Russian Minority Group. The dedication of scientists to their disciplines and their rapidly recognized prominence attracted the earlier immigrants and their children. American-born Russians were impressed by the scientists' feeling of Russian origin and by their recognition of many humanitarian aspects of Russian culture, and by their Russian contribution to the advancement of many sciences. At the same time, the Russian minority group became more aware and gradually proud of its origin. The scientists' avoidance of any attempt to influence the Russian minority group politically was a factor of special significance for the increase of their prestige and admiration by Russians. Many Russians believe that the publicity and contributions of Russian scientists strongly affected the educational aspirations of many American-born Russians.

Conclusions

The Russian minority group is composed of successive immigrations and American-born descendants of Russian immigrants. The adjustment of the main immigrations and their segments to each other and to the larger American society was affected by socioeconomic conditions in America, by American attitudes and objectives in foreign policy, and by the American ideological orientation. At the same time, the social background, achievements, experiences, and aspirations of immigrants from different segments of the two main immigrations reflected on their mutual adjustment as well as on their adjustment to the American-born Russians and to the American host society. Secondly, the prevailing American concepts about the nature of expected and desired responses of minority groups—Americanization, melting pot, and cultural pluralism—reflected on the acceptance and treatment of Russian immigrants and their descendants.

It is suggested by our adjustment approach in the study of minority groups that the greater the satisfaction of their needs and expectations and the greater the recognition of their ability to perform certain socially functional roles, the greater the probability for their greater contributions to the American society and their feeling of receiving the undiscriminatory and humanitarian treatment from Americans. The intellectual competence of Russian immigrant-scientists was demonstrated in their scientific achievement, in Russian contributions to the advancement of science in America, and in their contributions to the progress of American society.

The pattern of associational involvement of Russian immigrants is affected, first, by their social standing in their native country and, second, by their status discrepancy—negative or positive—in America. Therefore, we have indicated that the negatively status discrepant Russian immigrants, i.e., those who have experienced a drastic status degradation in America, tend to belong to a greater number of voluntary associations, many of which are manifestations of their socio-political experiences, shared expectations, and background. In this sense, their associations represent a kind of status group whose members, according to Weber, share the same or a very similar style of life.

Especially functional are Russian associations of mutual assistance and care for the indigent and for the Russian youth. It was found that one of the main characteristics of the Russian Orthodox Church is, besides its purely religious role, the multi-functional social role. The main role of the Russian Orthodox Church is communal in character; it shows great concern about its individual members.

It is believed that the reported membership of the Russian Orthodox Church is not exaggerated because of the impact of the new immigrants, especially those from the Soviet Union, or the American-born Russians, and because of the present religious trend in America. For these reasons it is justifiable to consider the Russian Orthodox Church as one of basic criteria of Russian ethnic identification. The Russian Orthodox Church contributes to the inter-ethnic adjustment of Russian younger generation, which now synthesizes its Americanism with its awareness of Russian background.

Numerous Russian publications of various kinds are the indicator of the complexity of the Russian ethnic minority group, and of psychosocial needs of the sponsoring segments of the Russian minority groups. By referring to the events in America, those ethnic publications perform the role of Americanizing their readers.

The contributions of Russian scientists and professionals to the American society are great and worth recognition. However, also praiseworthy are the social life, mutual assistance, and the very close relations of old immigrants of peasant background with the American-born Russians, because these relations are expressions of Russian cultural values concerning morality, the role of family, and mutual obligations in the community life.

Our main objective was the recommendation of the adjustment approach in the study of minority groups whose segments and individual members have special psychosocial needs because of their background, pre-emigration social standing, experiences, and aspirations. We believe that the more humanizing and responsive acceptance of members of a minority group the greater their contributions to American society and the more sincere their loyalty to American society.

Notes

1. See Milton M. Gordon, *Assimilation in American Life* (New York: Oxford University Press, 1964); and Milton L. Barron, *American Minorities* (New York: Alfred A. Knopf, 1957), Ch. "Minority Group Reactions and Adjustment, pp. 411-458.

2. "Role-Taking Accuracy and Adjustment," *Sociometry*, XX (December, 1957), pp. 286-296, reprinted in *Symbolic Interaction*, Jerome G. Manis and Bernard N. Meltzer (eds.) (Boston: Allyn and Bacon, 1967), p. 482.

3. Lawrence Frederic Shaffer, *The Psychology of Adjustment* (New York: Houghton Mifflin Co., 1936), p. 382.

4. Talcott Parsons, *The Social System* (New York: The Free Press of Glencoe, 1964), p. 203.

5. For the definition see Bernard Joseph, "Nationality: Definition of Terms," in M.L. Barron, *American Minorities*, pp. 69-73.

6. See Dr. Ivan Shlepecky, "Pryashevskaya Rus'," *Slobodnoye Slovo Karpatskoi Russi*, Free World Carpatho Russian Monthly, Newark, N.J., Issue XI, No. 11-12 (131-132), pp. 14-15.

7. See Alex Simirenko, *Pilgrims, Colonists and Frontiersmen* (New York: The Free Press of Glencoe, A Division of the MacMillan Co., 1964). See also Jerome David, *The Russians and Ruthenians in America* (New York: George H. Doran Co., 1922).

8. Ibid., and *Svobodnoye Slovo*, Issue XI.

9. See Richard Feree Smith, "Refugees," *The Annals*, Vol. 367, September, 1966, pp. 43-52.

10. Gleb Struve, *Russkaya Literatura V. Izganii*, (Russian Literature in Exile) (New York: Chekhov Publishing House, 1956), pp. 385-390.

11. "The Russians in the United States," *Slavonic Review*, 17, April, 1939, pp. 638-58.

12. Ibid., pp. 638-641; see also R.A. Thompson, *The Russian Settlement in California Known as Fort Rosa* (Santa Rose, Cal.: Sonoma Democrat Publishing Co., 1896), Lillian Sokaloff, *Russians in Los Angeles* (University Withdrawal from California), reprinted from the *Quarterly of the California Historical Society*, Vol. XII, No. 3, September, 1933.

13. Bureau of the Census, *1960 Census of Population*, Vol. 1, Characteristics of the Population, Part 1, U.S. Summary, Table 70, pp. 1-203.

14. National Council of Churches of Christ in the U.S.A., *Yearbook of American Churches*, 1969, p. 270.

15. Will Herberg, *Protestant-Catholic-Jew* (Garden City, New York: Anchor Books, Doubleday & Co., Inc., 1960), Chapters 1, 2, 3, and 4.

16. See Bureau of the Census, *U.S. Census of Population* 1960. Subject Reports Mother Tongue of the Foreign Born, Table 2.

17. For a review, see Arthur W. Thompson, "The Reception of Russian Revolutionary Leaders in America, 1904-1906," *American Quarterly*, 18. Fall, 1966, pp. 452-476.

18. Jerome Davis, *The Russian Immigrant* (New York: The MacMillan Co., 1922), pp. 16-20.

19. Ibid., p. 25.

20. Ibid., p. 35.

21. Ibid., pp. 42-44. Davis says that the Russians have suffered discrimination in all respects because "the public has associated them with the Bolsheviks in Russia," Ibid., p. 109.

22. *Soviet and Russian Newspapers at the Hoover Institution*: A catalog, compiled by Karol Maichel (Stanford University, 1966).

23. *Bibliography of References of Materials for Russian Area Studies*, issued by The City College Library, The City University of New York, 1962, mimeographed, pp. 45-55. See also *Directory of Newspapers and Periodicals*, 1969, pp. 14-32.

24. About the importance, informative objectives, and orientation of *Novoye Russkoye Slovo* see Alexandra Tolstoya, "Obrashchenie K Ruskoi Obshchestvenosii," *Novoye Russkoye Slovo*, December 20, 1969, p. 3.

25. Chyz and Roucek, "The Russians in the United States," p. 650.

26. Chyz and Roucek, "The Russians in the United States," p. 655.

27. The identification of most of the scientists is found in Prof. P. Kovalevsky "Nashi Dostizheniya;" *Rol' Russkoy Emigratzii V Mirovoy Nauke* (Muenich: Izdatelstov COPE, 1960).

11

The Frontiersman as Ethnic: A Brief History of the Scotch-Irish

Frank Barna

Why is it social scientists allow themselves to speak of "southern whites" while they would never dream of speaking about "northern whites"? A common sense reply to this question may suggest that "northern white" would be a social science conception too broad in its boundaries to be of any use, while "southern white" is a conception assumed to have distinct boundaries, and, therefore, is useful. But what evidence supports this assumption? Clearly the North is made up of so many different ethnic groups that on the face of it "northern white" is an absurd category. So now the question is whether or not "southern white" is an absurd category—a question no one has apparently bothered to ask. Thus, one may ask if the South has been populated by one ethnic group and culture. The answer is definitely no. Then, have different ethnic groups and their cultures merged to form something called "southern whites"? Apparently no one is sure because so little attention has been paid to ethnic groups and their histories in the South. Then, why have social scientists used "southern white" as though it were a generic body in the real world?

I bother the reader with this first paragraph of questions and answers because this paper concerns itself with the possibility of an old stock American group, the Scotch-Irish, continuing as an ethnic group with much of its population and identity existing in the South. For more than ten months, by no means an exhaustive period, I have surveyed the literature on the Scotch-Irish. Nearly all of the literature was written before or just after the turn of the century. Because of their settlement in the South, I have also involved myself in some of the current literature on the South. Of late there has been only one study of the Scotch-Irish and its chief contribution was essentially a coordination of the older literature.[1] Other southern old stock literature is also unfortunately lacking. Apparently, nothing substantial has been written about the South in terms of old stock ethnic immigration, settlement, population, and culture for nearly sixty years.

Sometime between 1915 and 1930 "southern white" began to be used as a social science conception. Why ethnic distinctions were dropped in favor of a "southern white" conception is, as I mentioned earlier, uncertain. A number of possible explanations immediately surface: (a) it could be that social scientists are unaware of the history of the South and therefore ignorant of the different national groups who settled there; or because (b) they have assumed that these different ethnic groups have merged to form the "southern whites"; or because

155

(c) the social scientist's liberal bias has precluded such a detailed study of the South; or because (d) the Scotch-Irish, unknown to the social scientists, have stamped most of the South with their culture and, therefore, they *are* the "southern whites." If the last possible explanation is, indeed, correct, then it would make about as much sense to call Scotch-Irish Americans "southern whites" as it would to call Polish-Americans "northern whites."

At the present time the literature "carves up" the South only along regional lines. Thus, it concerns the border states, the deep South, the Appalachian Mountains, and other geographical sections. While useful, such distinctions are often too local in character and devoid of a historical context to explain much of southern history, or southern people. Perhaps this is what is so disappointing in the use of the "southern white" category. It is empty. It tells nothing about the history or culture of the people while allowing for out of context explanations and moral judgments, rather than serious scientific investigation. In any case, such a "categorical house cleaning" is for the future, for my intention is to simply outline the history of the Scotch-Irish.

The history of the Scotch-Irish, like the history of any people, is detailed and complicated, and cannot be fully covered within a few pages. Furthermore, while there has been some research on the Scotch-Irish, much of the history is not known, and perhaps never will be. So this paper offers only a thumbnail sketch of presently limited information. Therefore, its conclusions and to some extent its data should be tentatively held.

Because this paper is dealing with the history and transformation of a certain kind of folk people it will tend to focus on their religious experiences and institutions when it considers change.[2] I place the emphasis there for two reasons: (a) because the folk world is a sacred world it is, perhaps, easier to view change in that world by looking at religious beliefs over time; and (b) because this kind of focus helps frame an otherwise ambiguous paper. The reader, however, will note that not all of my attention—nor enough of it, for that matter—is placed on religious activity.

Although research is scarce, confusion about the Scotch-Irish is not. Part of the confusion about the Scotch-Irish stems from their name. Contrary to what the name implies, the Scotch-Irish are not a blend of Scot and Irish people. Rather, they are descendants of Lowland Scot Presbyterians who emigrated to North Ireland during the early 1600s as part of a plan by the English Crown to control the "heathen Irish." There was apparently little intermarriage with the Catholic Irish during their century stay in Ireland, perhaps for religious reasons, perhaps because the Irish hated them as invaders, perhaps both. Thus the name Scotch-Irish came to refer to people who lived in North Ireland (Ulster), but were of Lowland Scot stock. In America, at least, their ethnic identity is sometimes difficult to detect. One reason they are somewhat invisible is because they have so many different labels applied to them. For example, those who have migrated to the larger cities like Detroit are called hillbillies, southern whites, working class, stump jumpers, ridge runners, or sometimes just "bums." More recently they have been included in that global term "Applachian," which was coined by the federal poverty bureaucracies and popularized by the news media. Another reason they have not been widely recognized as a culturally distinct group, even among themselves, is that they consider themselves to have already "blended" with many other groups in the country and thereby to have become "true" Americans. However, a brief glance at the literature concerning the surnames of those groups whom I suspect to be Scotch-Irish leads me to think this self-image is largely myth, and that there may be much more cultural homogeniety than they realize. Any group that imagines it has already been "assimilated" into another could hardly feel much threat to its existence or identity. Indeed, this frame of mind might well operate to preserve the culture almost intact. My guess is that the Scotch-Irish may be the least assimilated sub-culture in America for precisely this reason. But for now this remains only a guess.[a]

It should be noted that Lowland Scots are culturally distinct from Highland Scots. At the time of emigration from Lowland Scotland to Ulster most of the Highland Scots were living in relatively isolated tribal societies. The Lowland Scots, however, had a much closer relationship with the English, and to some extent had undergone feudalization. By 1600 the Lowland Scots had experienced about 400 years of relationships that were not exclusively tribal. However, they did not live in a distinct feudal system. Vertically arranged kin relationships, rather than lord-peasant relationships, predominated the Lowlands throughout its "feudal" history. A ranked, hierarchical order common in most of Europe did not exist in the Lowlands. A kind of "egalitarian" spirit flowing perhaps from this kind of kin relationship was a marked quality of the Lowland Scot.[3]

Scotland has had a long military tradition going even further back than the early Norse integration and settlement, which, of course, encouraged that warrior spirit. Centuries of war with the English and among each other made the warrior the culture hero and tempered his prowess and skill at combat. In the Lowlands military commanders were often made Lords. Bastards and those of unroyal birth often became chiefs as the Lowland Scots prized a man more by leadership and military capabilities than by his birthright.[4] Although it might be stretching the cultural dimensions a little, it could be argued that the Lowland society was a warrior society. This military tradition and skill continued in Ulster and America as they became expert at beating tribal natives into submission.

Although essentially engaged in cattle raising and agriculture, the Lowlanders were also excellent sailors and roamed throughout much of the known world. An early English saying which testifies to the Scot's wanderlust claimed "in every port one might find a Scot, a rat, and a Newcastle grindstone."[5] Throughout Europe there were Lowland settlements which perpetuated Scottish

---

[a]Most of this paragraph appeared in a grant-in-aid request written by Rolland H. Wright and Frank Barna. It has been slightly rephrased for this paper. My thanks to Dr. Wright for allowing it to appear here.

customs and law. For example, in the 17th century 30,000 Scot families were living autonomously in Poland.[6] To a man who was a farmer, a warrior, and wanderer the Ulster plantation of 1600 must have been appealing indeed.

Ulster: The First Frontier

The Scotch-Irish experience since 1600 has been a frontier experience. There have been four Scotch-Irish frontiers with Ulster being the first, while America provided the latter three. Although each frontier was different and changed the Scotch Irish, there are some striking continuities. From Ulster to the American Far West they have raised cattle and farmed. Their most important activity, however, was the continued subjugation of tribal people in front of an onrushing Western civilization.

Each frontier was also a "freeing" experience. Every move west further released a man from his previous traditions and social order. Although relatively close to Scotland, Ulster was not an exception to this rule. What feudal relationships that did exist in the Lowlands ended for the Lowlanders when they arrived in Ulster. A man's birth no longer influenced his place in the community. Many who were lowly tenant farmers in Scotland became prosperous cattle men, or linen manufacturers. The "egalitarianism" of the Lowlands became even more pronounced in Ulster. The position and even the word "laird" vanished from both the Ulsterman's social order and vocabulary.[7] And although they did not own their land in Ulster, the contractual nature of their relationship with the English landlord made for a kind of "market" relationship, rather than a peasant-lord one.[8]

The Presbyterian Church, the church of the Scotch-Irish, however, did not change much during its century stay in Ulster. The re-ordering of the Ulsterman's social world with the termination of feudal relationships did not call for a major upheaval within the Church. As we have mentioned, Lowland society was not really feudal, and the Presbyterian Church with its traditional stand against church and state affiliation was in the vanguard of the reformation. The Ulster Presbyterian was also conscious and perhaps threatened by the knowledge that he shared Ulster with the Irish Catholics and to a lesser extent the English Puritans. Furthermore, the presbyterians were subject to some religious persecution from the Puritan Roundheads, and later from the Anglican Church of England. All of these factors probably contributed to the continuance of the Presbyterian Church in Ulster much the same as it was in Scotland. It also should be noted that intermarriage with the English in Ulster was limited, while intermarriage with the Irish Catholic was virtually nonexistant.

Although religious persecution is often suggested as the chief reason for the Scotch-Irish migration to America, economic hardship appears to have been more the cause. The harsh "rack-renting" practices of the absentee English landlords reduced the once prosperous Ulsterman to utter poverty. Drought and crop failures accompanied the rack-renting as the Scotch-Irish faced nearly six continuous years (1714-1719) of insufficient rainfall. Thus, although the English Test Act brought severe religious discrimination and persecution on the Ulster Presbyterian, the very immediate poverty and dislocation overshadowed all other concerns. All of these factors played a part in the cause of the Scotch-Irish migration to America, and influenced his expectations of the New World.

The American Northeast: The Second Frontier

Some 200,000 Scotch-Irish came to America between 1717 and 1776. While their migration was nearly continuous some scholars view it as a series of waves.[9] Nearly half of the immigrants came as indentured servants contracted for four years to work for predominantly English East Coast land owners. However, as soon as their contracts expired they went directly on the frontier. They settled first in southeastern Pennsylvania and on the outskirts of the New England states to serve as an Indian buffer zone for the Quakers and the Puritans, respectively. In fact, many Puritans openly encouraged Scotch-Irish settlements on their northern and western frontiers in order to protect themselves from the "Indian menace." Cotton Mather, the famous Puritan minister, for example, was greatly interested and involved in placing Ulstermen on the New England frontier. Despite the image painted by American myth, the Puritans of New England were not genuine frontier people. They were reluctant to face the perils of the frontier. Perhaps it would serve our interest to dwell on the differences that exist between the Puritans and the Scotch-Irish in order to better understand what kind of man would go out on the frontier.

One difference is that Puritans are more institutional than the Scotch-Irish. One Scotch-Irishman described his people as dedicated to "individualism" and "familism" while Puritans were pledged to the "community" or the "state." (This appreciation of independence (individualism) and kin ties (familism) is, to say the least, a curious mixture of qualities that are antithetical.) Puritans, he felt, thought people should surrender themselves to the "community" and work for the betterment of it, while the Scotch-Irish felt the state or community should work for the people.[10] The Scotch-Irish also appear to be a people who "pack" their institutions around within themselves which might have afforded them the ability to be so mobile.[b] The Puritans, however, were not a constantly moving people, although they were among the first to arrive in America. As the Scotch-Irish pushed west their insistence on freedom from external institutional control increased.

In any case, the Scotch-Irish were not reluctant to be on the frontier, perhaps

---

[b] By stating that they " 'pack' their institutions around within themselves," I do not mean to imply that they internalize abstract institutional ways of behaving. Rather, it implies that they are able to take key personal relationships, such as kin ties, and in a sense 'swallow' them. This ability to internalize personal relationships in such a manner may have been what allowed the essentially folk-like Scotch-Irish to wander far and permanently, yet have their kin relationships remain important and definitive.

because of their long military tradition, their desire for land, or their recent successful handling of the tribal Irish.[11] Although they suffered numerous setbacks with both the Indians and the land, they were generally successful. In western Pennsylvania they were perhaps too successful as the moralistic Quakers were appalled by their treatment of the Indians. Besides breaking the trust the Quakers felt they had established with the Indians, the Scotch-Irish destroyed the Indian trade which was a substantial part of the Quaker's economy. Later the Scotch-Irish in southeastern Pennsylvania began their trek down the Shenandoah Valley to be joined by immigrants from Ulster. They soon filled the valley from the Carolinas to Pennsylvania.

But what was the immediate effect of the frontier on the Scotch-Irish in Pennsylvania and east of the Blue Ridge? If we look at the changes in the Presbyterian Church we can begin to see some patterns developing. First of all, the stern, dour, and somewhat "puritanical" European Presbyterian died out, and the church took on a distinct American flavor. This Americanization included a lessening of the church's constitutional rigidity, the establishment of Princeton University, revivals, and camp ground meetings. These changes allowed Presbyterians to remain the frontier religion during the first half of the 18th century. However, its strict theological stance was not completely adaptive and as the frontier progressed with an ever-increasing influence on the people, Presbyterianism lost much of its appeal. To understand why this was so, we must remember some of the general life conditions of the early American frontier. Four general conditions were: (a) the local nature of the settlements; (b) the very tenuous existence on the frontier; (c) the leveling of all men to an egalitarian status; and (d) the close contact with the Indians.

The Presbyterian Church gave way to sects such as the Baptist and Methodist which were institutionally flexible and more "democratic" in design. Ministers no longer needed a Princeton education to preach. Any man who felt "the call" could come forward and offer himself as a preacher, and could become a minister provided his congregation *elected* him. This activity towards local organizational sects occurred principally in the Cumberland Valley of the South. The Americanized version of Presbyterianism survived quite well in Pennsylvania as that Frontier closed and became less intense.

The South: The Third Frontier

By 1740 the Scotch-Irish were pouring into the Cumberland Valley. They shortly filled the valley from Tennessee to northern Virginia. They were also massed in western North and South Carolina and some were as far west as Kentucky before the revolution. The frontier experience continued for those who migrated south. Those patterns we saw developing in Ulster and later in the American Northeast were pushed just a little farther and became more pronounced in the South.

It was this area which gave rise to men like Davy Crockett, Andrew Jackson, and Daniel Boone. The first two are of Scotch-Irish descent and the latter was socialized by Scotch-Irish people. In many respects they are typical of the southern Scotch-Irish. They were independent men, yet they were tied to kin by obligation and identity. Although they fought and killed Indians and saw their families killed by Indians, their relationships with them were often close. Many "civilized" easterners were fearful that the frontiersmen would revert to "savagery" because of their involved contact with the native population. They were emotional and egalitarian men and their religion—principally Baptist—reflected those qualities.

Many easterners also feared the egalitarian spirit of the Scotch-Irish. That spirit and their low status in the social order may have contributed to their early stand against slavery. Both the Baptist and the Methodist churches adopted antislavery measures late in the 18th century. Unfortunately, when slavery later became the backbone of the southern economy, Scotch-Irish institutions, such as the southern Baptists and Methodists churches, withdrew their opposition and suspended their protest.

Perhaps their "democratic fervor" spurred them to fight in the Revolutionary War, though it appears that their hatred of the English had more to do with their taking up of arms. In any case, almost to a man the Scotch-Irish from New England to the South fought on the American side. It is also interesting to note that in nearly every major American victory there were large numbers of Scotch-Irish troops. Shortly after the war the push for western territory began, principally in the South.

The West: The Fourth Frontier

Though some Scotch-Irish families came west from New England and Pennsylvania the most dynamic migration came from out of the South. Arkansas, Kansas, western Kentucky, Missouri, and Texas were the first territories to feel the influence of Scotch-Irish populations. Later they inhabited the southwest and northwest Rocky Mountain area.

Perhaps the first and most extreme versions of the Scotch-Irish in the West were the Mountain Men of the 1820s, '30s, and '40s. Perhaps here the fears of "civilized" members of American society that the frontiersmen would "revert to savagery" came close to becoming realized. The Mountain Men were the early trappers of the Rocky Mountains. Having little technological hardware they were forced to pay very close attention to the environment they plundered. Though some "educated" men continued to live among them, many took on an appearance and behavior as rough and wild as the Rockies.[12] The ethnic make-up of the Mountain Men was not entirely Scotch-Irish. It appears that French trappers were in the Rockies before the 19th century and were still there when the Scotch-Irish arrived. Without having done much research on this particular area I would guess that there were two migrations into the Rockies. The first people to come in were mostly French, while the second group was composed mostly of Scotch-Irish.

Another social type of the West who is immediately recognizable and who in most instances was Scotch-Irish is the cowboy. Travel was his constant companion, and although kin and friendship relations were important, the cowboy resented being tied down by them. His love to fight, travel, and his egalitarian spirit, though exaggerated by a romantic America, were nothing really new to the Scotch-Irish.[13]

Baptist and Methodist churches continued to find support as the frontier moved west. The Disciples of Christ, however, was the most successful of the churches genuinely created in the West. Another church of the West was titled simply the Christian Church. Of all these, Methodism enjoyed the greatest popularity. As Niebuhr writes of Methodism in the early West:

With its fervent piety, its lay preaching, its early sectarian polity, it accorded well with the spirit of the West while the itinerancy and the curcuit system were admirably devices for the evangelization of the frontier.[14]

Having finished my thumbnail sketch of the Scotch-Irish, perhaps I should add that the Scotch-Irish were usually not alone in their occupation of the frontier. Anglo-Saxon, German, and French settlers were often on the frontier with them. Their contributions were considerable, and it is not the purpose of this paper to discredit them. However, it is my opinion that the Scotch-Irish as a community stamped the frontier settlements with their culture and life style. The mere size of the ever-expanding Scotch-Irish population, their continued presence on the frontier, and the quality of frontier life suggest that they were the major frontier influence. They appear to be the people most responsible for the clearing and settling of the United States within 200 years. As one member of the Scotch-Irish Congress of 1889 stated:

New England Puritans have in large part written the history of the United States. They did not act the principal history of the United States. Although in the popular histories of the United States, individuals of the Scotch-Irish race have received due notice and full praise, yet the influence of the Scotch-Irish as a people in obtaining our independence, forming our independence, forming our institutions, and maintaining them, have never been properly recognized in written American history.[c]

Hopefully, the reader of this brief sketch will begin to see some of the qualities of the Scotch-Irish. Their overriding experience for the last 300 years has been the frontier. That experience became increasingly intense and recent as

[c]McDowell, *First Congress of the Scotch-Irish Society of America*, Columbia, Tennessee, 1898. Statements such as this should serve as reminders to social scientists that the term "white" is a culturally meaningless term. It points out that even among old-stock American ethnic groups great cultural diversity exists. The Scotch-Irish, as this quote indicates, are not the same people as the English Puritans, who in turn are not the same people as the tidewater plantation owners of the South. Distinctions such as this should also be used as boundaries for limiting that all to often "catch all" Protestant terms, WASP.

one follows them west. Their love of farming, fighting, and traveling have long marked them as a people. Now that they have reached the Pacific, and the frontier experience has been closed, where are the Scotch-Irish to go? From the South many rural people are coming north to the industrial cities. Their culture, experience, and life style are new to the industrial area, and the nature of their relationship with it is uncertain. The Scotch-Irish in the West are also beginning to taste a life heavily flavored by a technological order. Though it is too early to make a definite statement, neither seems to be enjoying the closing of the frontier.

Two possible post-frontier social types which might give us some insight into what future patterns the Scotch-Irish might follow are the hobo as described by Nels Anderson and a more recent possibility, the Hell's Angels.[15] Early in the 20th century Anderson described the aimless hobos of the West as frontiersmen without a frontier. Although some of the men he writes of are immigrants from Scandanavia and Germany, many of them appear to be old stock Scotch-Irish caught by the closing of the last frontier. My impression that the Hell's Angels are Scotch-Irish is just that, an impression. A friend of mine tells me that most of the Angels are descendants of the "Okies" who migrated to California from Oklahoma during the Great Depression. Many of the original Oklahomans appear to be of Scotch-Irish ancestry. So it is possible—though at this time quite impressionistic—that the Angels are men who were raised by people whose life expectations were based partly on a frontier existence. If this is so, then in a sense the Hell's Angels are frontiersmen without a frontier. Given that understanding one might well imagine that the highly technological life of California, say, may indeed "rub" them the wrong way, and produce a man who in much of his behavior appears pathological. In any case, I am at the present intrigued by the many descriptions of them which indicate that they are frontiersmen caught in a modern world.[16]

Finally, it seems to me that the key to understanding any people is the knowledge of who they are. That understanding must, therefore, include an accurate history of their relationships, culture, and experience. Without such an understanding those in power, well-intentioned or not, will make urban life that much more difficult for the Scotch-Irish.

Notes

1. James G. Leyburn, *The Scotch Irish* (Chapel Hill: University of North Carolina Press, 1962).

2. Rolland H. Wright, "The Stranger Mentality and the Culture of Poverty," *New University Thought*, Fall, 1969.

3. G.W.S. Barrow, *Robert Bruce* (Berkeley: University of California Press, 1965) p. 26.

4. Ibid.

5. Leyburn, *The Scotch-Irish*, p. 34.

6. Henry J. Ford, *The Scotch-Irish in America* (Princeton: Princeton University Press, 1915) p. 33.

7. Leyburn, *The Scotch-Irish,* p. 97.

8. Ibid., p. 162.

9. Ibid., p. 169.

10. E.C. McDowell, *First Congress of the Scotch-Irish Society of America,* Columbia, Tennessee, 1898.

11. William Christie MacLeod, "Celt and Indian: Britain's Old World Frontier in Relation to the New," in *Beyond the Frontier,* ed. by Paul Bohannan and Fred Plog (Garden City: Natural History Press, 1967), p. 33.

12. Ray A. Billington, *The Far Western Frontier* (New York: Harper and Row, 1956) p. 41.

13. Andy Adams, *The Log of a Cowboy* (Garden City: Doubleday and Company, 1902).

14. H. Richard Niebuhr, *The Social Sources of Denominationalism* (Cleveland: The World Publishing Company, 1957) p. 171.

15. Nels Anderson, *The Hobo* (Chicago: University of Chicago Press, 1932).

16. Hunter S. Thompson, *Hell's Angels* (New York: Random House, 1967).

12 The Changing Role of the Polish-American Congress

Joseph A. Wytrwal

This paper is neither indictment nor apology, neither celebration of the Polish-American Congress nor a lament about it. My emphasis is primarily on the meaning of the Polish-American Congress and its relation to the cultural, intellectual, and spiritual development of the American of Polish descent.

As one reads the editorials and articles in the publications of the ethnic press, or listens to the lectures of the various scholars and leaders of the ethnic communities in our country, one has the feeling that we are living in an age in which we do not know what the objectives of the ethnic communities in America should be. Yet we know that the members of our ethnic communities, young and old, immigrant or native born, want not only security, comfort, and luxury, but they also want meaning in their private as well as collective living if they are to attain fulfillment. And if our age, our culture, our civilization, and our leaders do not or cannot offer great meanings, great objectives, great convictions, then our ethnic communities will settle for shallow and trivial substitutes.

The objectives by which we might have defined the culture and civilization of the American Polish community eighty, forty, or even thirty years ago are gone. At the turn of the century the objectives were clear, simple, and clean cut. However, in our own generation, in this age of complexities, hard realities, and many anxieties the old pattern is gone. If I may use the American Polish organizations from 1880 to the end of World War I, as an example, they had one all-absorbing motive that is best expressed in the word POLSKA.

To arouse the Polish national spirit among the Polish immigrants, to foster it, and to direct it towards the liberation of Poland was the goal set by these organizations. The life insurance established by the organizations served two purposes: it gave economic security to the Polish immigrants, and it was the means through which the leaders of the organizations inculcated in the masses of Polish immigrants the spirit of Polish nationalism and patriotism. Having sold the masses of Polish immigrants on the idea of life insurance, the American Polish organizations proceeded systematically to sell them the ideal of working toward the liberation of partitioned Poland.

Taking this objective into consideration, it would logically follow that the American Polish organizations would strive to prevent the Americanization of the Polish immigrants. This was not true. On the contrary, the objective facilitated the acculturation of the Polish immigrant in America, for the leaders

165

of the American Polish organizations realized that only as American citizens would they be taken into account—only as Americans would they be able to advance Poland's cause.

To be successful Americans they had to be active in the cultural, educational, religious, social, economic, and political life of the United States. And what did they do? To raise the prestige of the American Polish group, the American Polish organizations were instrumental in erecting monuments to two Polish American heroes, Pulaski and Kosciusko, in Washington, D.C. and other American cities. To make the American Polish group more articulate, they were the first to encourage Polish immigrants to attend evening schools in order to learn the language of the United States. To be more effective in their demands for justice for partitioned Poland, they organized naturalization classes. Through these classes hundreds of thousands of Polish immigrants traveled on their way to citizenship over the strong bridge constructed by the American Polish organizations which utilized the Polish language as the indispensable means of communication until the English language was mastered. To provide opportunity for American Polish youth, to enable them to become leaders in America, they provided scholarships.

To raise the cultural level of the American Polish group, annual calendars were as vital to the Polish immigrants of the twentieth century as were the early almanacs to the American pioneers. They explained the immigration rights, citizenship requirements, bankruptcy laws, etc., of the United States. And the calendars were also the first publications to rectify the gaps in Polish culture, for they introduced to the barely literate immigrants such great writers as Slowacki, Kochanowski, Mickiewicz, and others. American Polish groups also initiated circulation libraries and encouraged attendance at various musicals and concerts. Celebrations to honor historic events in American and Polish history were also planned. Their interest were not only local and Polish; they also participated in many national American projects. For example, they were instrumental in the restoration and the preservation of Liberty Bell, and as a result of their contribution, the Liberty Bell was sounded in memory of many historical Polish observations. To improve the economic status of the new arrivals the American Polish organizations maintained immigration homes in New York, Boston, Baltimore, and San Francisco, starting in 1910. Here temporary shelter and proper guidance was provided.

Because these early immigrants had a definite ideal, life had meaning; everything they did was necessary if the liberation of Poland was to become a reality. Because the ideal had meaning, they were able to reach their destiny. As someone once stated: "Ideals are like stars. You cannot touch them with your hands, but like the seafaring man on the desert of waters, you choose them as your guides and following them you reach your destiny." And what was their destiny? Explicitly to liberate Poland. Implicitly to provide a foundation upon which to build an ideal American society—economically, socially, politically, and culturally.

And this foundation, so necessary for an ideal American community, the established. To provide for a richer cultural life, they built large and imposing national homes. Here plays, dances, and lectures were given. To provide leaders and give educational opportunities, they established Alliance College in Cambridge Springs, Pennsylvania. To be effective in voicing their opinion and desires, they learned the English language and they became citizens. To have the opportunity to practice charity, they improved themselves in the economic activities; they advanced steadily from unskilled to skilled work, and from the skilled to the professional ranks.

From the beginning of the Polish economic immigration to the end of World War I, the American Polish ethnic community was punctuated with successes in its political, social, and economic endeavors. One of the factors that made for success of the American Polish community was its emphasis upon things Polish. The leaders were wise enough to realize that the emphasis on Polish blood, Polish origin, Polish culture, and Polish ties was the secret to the growth of the National American Polish organizations, the Catholic Parochial school system, and the various social organizations in the community. But after the establishment of the Polish ideal—a free and independent Polish Republic—the primary objective that had conditioned the culture of American Poles was gone. Now it became necessary for all American Poles to find a new orientation for their aspirations.

With two political realities: America the land of opportunity, and a free Poland, the period from 1919 to the present was one of changing moods and of mixed patriotic emotions for the American Polish community. It was a period of transition for the entire ethnic group. The old pattern was gone; what was the new one to be? A new ideal had to be found, and it was. The leaders of the community now directed their activities toward maintaining the Polish language. They believed that if the Polish-Americans maintained their ability to speak Polish, Polish culture and civilization would be preserved on American soil. Before long, the Polish language and the Polish culture were made synonymous, and everything that could contribute to a knowledge or understanding of the Polish language was encouraged.

Polka programs featuring loud music with announcers peddling beer or meat were enthusiastically accepted, because they were vaguely Polish. Paintings representing Polish themes were awarded prizes, not because they were works of art, but because they had Polish themes. Concerts and programs of various organizations were encouraged, not because they had something to offer, but because they made an attempt to present something with a Polish flavor. Scholarships were provided to students who elected courses in Polish history. Discounts in tuition and maintenance were allowed if students maintained a "C" grade in Polish subjects.

Entrusting the preservation of the Polish language and culture to the Polish Felicians and other Polish religious orders, the American Polish community naïvely assumed that the Polish language and culture would be preserved and perpetuated in the United States. But in fact, an era of indifference to Polish language and culture developed; the years from 1918 to 1970 could well be called years of *retrogression* in the American Polish communities. Because of the shallowness of its ideals, the American Polish community lost its sense of the past—the remembered record of what happened, the force of collective experience. Because of these shallow ideals, the closely integrated organizations, which had perpetuated the best in skills, information, and traditions declined, and the deep seated belief in the dignity of work and the joy of achievement disappeared. There was no longer a universal acceptance of the responsibility for service to their ethnic group among Polish-Americans. The profound sense of responsibility to posterity diminished; members of the community no longer believed that they must leave their community better than they found it. No longer did they believe that unless man enriched the community through his life in it, he should never have been born, and that any generation which did not enrich the life of succeeding generations had lived in vain.

Had it not been for the heroic resistance of the Poles in World War II, the gross discrimination against Poles in the American Catholic Church, the anti-Polishness in the Polish sisterhoods, the rise of the "Polish joke," discrimination in employment, the Negro Revolt, the Potsdam and Yalta agreements—it is quite possible that the Polish ethnic community would now be on its way to extinction.

The events just enumerated brought about the establishment and stimulated the continued existence of the Polish-American Congress to assert the coincidence of American, Polish, and Polish-American interests. The Polish-American Congress is in position to enrich American culture and civilization as Joseph Conrad enriched the English culture, as Madam Sklodowska Curie enriched the French culture, and as General Kosciusko enriched the American culture. This challenge which confronts the Polish-American Congress in a time of social and intellectual ferment that threatens to shatter the traditional structure of the American Polish community and that is eroding the identity of the individual American of Polish descent is attainable. The many obstacles that confront the Polish-American Congress in an era of indifference can be eliminated if the Polish-American Congress strives for a more penetrating and effective awareness of the Polish heritage by learning its culture and civilization, and by developing ideas.

Language is the last resource of cultural survival. If the language is eliminated, the culture goes with it. It has happened in Ireland. Most of the priests and sisters in the Polish parishes pay only lip-service to their Polish heritage. They emphasize it only when fund drives are underway; few of them deliver in the parish or classroom. There is no interest in the Polish language, history, or culture among the American Poles in their parishes. More often than not the priests and nuns see no practical purpose in studying one's ethnic heritage. They firmly believe that the sooner the community becomes "American" the better. Somehow, these "rootless" priests and nuns have failed to recognize the possibilities of motivation in stimulating interest of the parishioners in the parish through their Polish heritage.

The Polish-American Congress will command the attention and respect of every American if it openly denounces in the front pages of every newspaper the anti-Polishness which exists in the American-Polish sisterhoods. The Polish-American Congress should be wise enough to realize that the Catholic schools established by Polish immigrants and entrusted to the Felician and other Polish orders have been the most effective instruments in the destruction of Polish culture and language in the United States. It is in these Catholic schools that ideals of lasting value are submerged and de-emphasized. Students in these schools are robbed of their identity, cultural traits, and history. The American of Polish descent, though removed by generations from Poland, has never been, and cannot be expected to be, indifferent to the land of his forebears. This remote heritage is part and parcel of his being. This inheritance, like his Americanism, should be understood by the Felician sisters. The Felician sentimentality toward assimilation or toward chauvinistic nationalism (to be more American than the Americans) is blatantly wishful, unrealistic, and contrary to the fact, insofar as the masses of Americans of Polish descent are concerned. The renaissance of the Polish-American culture has to begin again where it ended: in the Catholic schools established by the Polish immigrants.

Americans of Polish descent have contributed to American culture not by denying their identity but by asserting it through music, folklore, drama, poetry, novels, essays, paintings, etc., in spite of the harsh circumstances in which they found themselves. Indeed, they stand to contribute more to the culture and welfare of American society by recognizing and appreciating their own identity rather than by denying their ethnic descent. Even if the Americans of Polish descent are completely assimilated, the desire for ethnic self-assertion will continue to manifest itself in their social and cultural life, in private as well as in public matters, though it may take various forms.

De-education is a difficult process. The Polish heritage has been in existence a thousand years. It is not easy to uproot. Thus, for every generation, the attempt at de-education has to begin anew—since each generation considers their heritage a special gift, an inheritance. Out of this inheritance each generation shapes uniquely for itself their own quest, which they consider a special good for them. What each generation values indicates what they are.

The conflict of cultures continues in the schools. A child of Polish descent goes to school to wonder. The school is where he enters the American world with shy curiosity. The sister is his sorcerer, knowing all sorts of facts and magic. The child is proud of his grandfather, he boasts of his Polish heritage. He does not know that he is supposed to be culturally deprived. In school, he is told he must choose between being American or Polish; it is an impossible choice for him, for he is neither, but both. He will not argue, he will grow silent. Because of this type of encounter with the sister, his idealization of education is ended, and by the time the child reaches high school, he feels cheated, betrayed, and frustrated.

Today, nowhere in the curriculum is there a word on the Polish culture. In all the classes, the emphasis is upon the de-education of the child of Polish descent. He has to be *de*-educated before he can be *re*-educated as American. The language and culture of Poland are seen by the sisters as a prime hindrance to his progress, not only in learning English, but in "becoming an American." In the non-ethnic parishes the conflict may be subtle, but in the American Polish schools staffed by the Felician sisters it is vulgar and cruel. The sisters desperately try to make the students forget their history, to be ashamed of being Polish, and of speaking Polish. And they succeed in making them feel empty, and angry, inside.

The Polish-American Congress should have the temerity to suggest that Polish-American history be a required course, especially in schools which were built and supported by Americans of Polish descent. The Polish-American Congress should remind the pastors that parents send their children to Catholic schools not only to preserve their religion but also their culture.

The American-Polish community has to rediscover itself. What is Polish history in the United States? There are no textbooks of the history of the Poles. Yet the history of the Poles in this country is more than 350 years old. We know the Poles pre-date the landing of the Pilgrims and the American Revolution. What has happened since then? The Polish American history has been lost. It has to be rediscovered. Just as a tree without roots is dead, a people without history or cultural roots also becomes a dead people. And when you look at those who we call "rootless" Americans, we call them rootless because they are like dead people. They have nothing to identify themselves as part of a culture and civilization. We know what a tree is by looking at the leaves. If the leaves are gone, the bark will reveal what kind it is. But when you find a tree with the leaves gone and the bark gone, with everything gone, you call that a stump. And you cannot identify a stump as easily as you can identify a tree.

Many are in this position in America today. They are rootless Americans. Formerly they could be identified by the names they inherited. When they first arrived, they had different names. They had a different language. And these names and this language identified the culture and the land they came from. But once their names were changed and the language obscured, their identity was destroyed and their roots were cut off with no history. They became like a stump; something dead. They became rootless Americans.

The Polish-American Congress must also remember that the Catholic Church, the institution into which the American Poles poured their limited funds by the billions of dollars and to which they gave their greatest loyalty and support, is also guilty of gross discrimination and grave injustice in the appointment of bishops in the United States. In city after city across the nation, we have outstanding churchmen who are continually ignored when appointments to positions of leadership are made, thus eliminating for them the opportunity for elevating their intelligence, talent, and dignity. Young American priests of Polish descent look upon their cultural inheritance, and their religious ritual and practice as a handicap that destines them to minor roles in the Catholic Church in America. The Polish-American Congress must look at the statistics to learn of the flagrant discrimination which the "One, Holy, *Irish*, and Apostolic Church," directs against the Polish-American community. Even though the priests of

Polish descent suffer in silence, there is no reason for complacency. We should realize that when the rights of one minority are threatened by prejudice and discrimination, the rights of all are endangered.

Also, the Polish American Congress must eliminate situations where the priests and nuns must make a choice between religion and culture. We must remember that it was the Catholic Church which succeeded in Poland in identifying Poles as one and inseparable from Catholicism. The same situation occurred in Ireland, where religion was also equated with nationality. Because the Irish arrived in America earlier, they exploited the situation to benefit Irish nationalism. Poles trying to emulate the Irish were faced with a problem; they could not attain a similar end. The Poles had to make a choice between their culture and their religion. Many of the Polish religious leaders were forced to make a choice between Catholicism in Irish form with the rejection of their Polish heritage, and the rejection of Catholicism with the preservation of the Polish language and culture outside the Catholic Church. Thus, Bishop Hodur emerges as a great religious hero in American history. At the expense of sacrificing total loyalty to the Catholic Church, he preserved successfully the Polish heritage and the Catholic religion in the Polish form. He yielded to no one. Others, like Father Dabrowski, suffered for their culture and civilization in silence, while Father Kruszka openly chastised the existing American Catholic hierarchy.

On the occasion of the Polish Millenium, President Johnson stated that: "Our National Heritage is rich with the gifts of the Polish people." However, little is known of the contribution of the Poles to American culture and civilization. At present, no concentrated effort is being exerted to enlarge the very limited collections of material in our public libraries. No effort is being made to assemble books of historical significance relating to Americans of Polish descent or their communities. The Polish-American Congress will render great service if it provides the stimulus and the standards by which the social, cultural, and educational life of the American Polish community can be raised to a meaningful community force.

Thomas Carlyle thought that history was the biography of great men, and so it is. We study the lives of those who have left footprints on the sands of time to determine what qualities made for greatness; and in reading biography, we note that love of God, love of country, and love of one's fellow man are not just catch phrases, but that they really lead to personal greatness. We should select heroes from our Polish heritage and study them. Americans of Polish descent should be proud of their contribution; and in this pride, they should remember that the most remarkable fact about America is its diversity, which reaches every corner of the earth, crossing national and ideological boundaries. If America was dominated by a single nationality or race it would be culturally a poor country. However, that composite of cultures that has become the real America is increasingly richer, more exciting, and more alive, since each expands and enriches the other. It is from this diversity that the greatness of America springs, and it is the triumph of America that in the midst of such diversity there is also unity—the mingling of traditions, temperaments, and cultures.

Assimilation is not synonymous with elimination in the evolution of a cosmopolitan nation, for much of the foreign flavor introduced by the thousands of immigrants is fortunately of a lasting nature. The people from the faraway lands change a nation, even as the nation changes them. Once the two elements are joined, nothing is ever the same again—neither the people nor the nation. It is part of the mystery and wonder of America that there still is no such person as "the typical American," nor is there a "typical American city." This metamorphosis continues with fickle disregard for the calculations and predictions of the experts!

If the Polish-American Congress accepts the challenges of today, it will enrich the forming pattern of America's great culture by bringing into it the best from Polish sources of inspiration and accomplishment. The potential exists. It should be brought out and made to bloom with the fullness of achievement.

Wiser and more sophisticated Americans now have abandoned the old concept of a national melting pot in which all elements must lose their identity, and have adopted instead the idea of an All-American stew, in which each of the ingredients remains identifiable. Under this concept, no minority need be considered an unassimilable clot. Retaining its identity, it nonetheless contributes its particular flavor to the enriching of a more desirable society in America. Only in this context will the genius of the American people be released to attain its fullest potential.

13 Serbians in America: The Effect of Status Discrepancy on Ethno-Religious Factionalism

Djuro J. Vrga

Introduction

This report presents partial findings of a survey concerning factionalism in the Serbian ethnic group whose size in America is approximately 150,000 members. As a religious division, this factionalism appears in the form of a conflict between Serbs who recognize the authority of the Serbian Eastern Orthodox Church in Yugoslavia, and Serbs who reject it because they insist that the Mother Church acts in accord with the Yugoslav Communist regime.

This schism occurred in 1963 over the question of whether the Mother Church acted in *good faith* when it suspended and divested Bishop Dionysius, and divided the single Serbian Diocese of the United States and Canada into three new dioceses. Immediately after the bishop, whose removal was supposedly requested by American Serbs, denounced the Mother Church the Serbian ethno-religious community began splitting into two factions.[a] Finally, the bishop won a majority vote in 20 of 59 parishes in the United States. The schism received wide publicity, especially because of allegation of a communist conspiracy against America and because of disorders at membership meetings in many parishes.[1]

This schism represents the first break in the unity of the Serbian Orthodox Church, which, with the *Svetosavlje*, its ethnic brand of Eastern Orthodoxy, had always served as the primary source of Serbian historical identification, and a means by which the descendants of Serbian immigrants could trace their ethnic ancestry. Since the schism was charged with a very high emotional tension, it deeply affected intragroup relations of Serbs on all levels; the followers of the two factions no longer cooperate in any common endeavor, nor do they attend religious services together. In addition, many old friendships turned into hostilities and members of many families turned against each other.

The Serbian ethnic minority group in America consists of two successive immigrations (1. the old immigrants who had immigrated before World War II,

---

[a]The bishop declared, "I do not recognize this communist decision from Belgrade." *Srbobran*, a Serbian daily newspaper (Pittsburgh, Pa.) May 25, 1963. In his *Epistle* of May 25, 1963, the bishop argued that the formation of new dioceses "was demanded and desired by Tito's regime, which hinders the work of this Diocese, and which desires to subjugate also this part of the free Serbs through bishops loyal to it," although all three bishops were his candidates for the posts of his auxiliary bishops.

173

and 2. the new immigrants who came after World War II, mainly as refugees or escapees) and American-born Serbs. The factional cleavage among Serbs occurred along some lines of internal group differentiation; mainly, recency of immigration, educational and occupational background of immigrants, and also the Yugoslav province of origin of immigrants or of ancestry of American-born Serbs.[2]

The Serbian ethnic group, which is still predominantly immigrant in its composition, represents a social system through which its members satisfy most of their social needs and express frustration resulting from their unsatisfied expectations and blocked aspirations in the larger society. Therefore, any study of social processes in predominantly immigrant minority groups should take into account the major background factors which affect most the immigrant's self-perception, expectations, and aspirations, as well as the direction of his emotional reactions to his position in the ethnic group and also in the larger society.[3] From this it follows that immigrants, especially those whose cultural background is significantly different from the culture of the new society, have to make two different kinds of adjustments: (1) to their own ethnic group, and (2) to the larger society. An immigrant finds himself in an ambiguous position if he is faced with confusing role expectations in his ethnic group and in the larger society. But his status becomes inconsistent, especially when the ethnic group treats him in one situation according to his pre-emigration status and in the other according to his different social standing in the adopted society.[4] When he becomes convinced, however, that his opportunities in the larger society are limited either because of his minority status or because of some of his pre-emigration attributes he may turn against his own ethnic group.[5] On the latent level of reaction, this hostility may be directed against both the larger society and his own ethnic group.

Method

This report is based on data which were obtained from a double stratified random sample of 84 male members of a Serbian Eastern Orthodox parish in Chicago. The sample was drawn from the list of over 700 adult parish members as of February 2, 1964, when the final voting on the issue of controversy between Bishop Dionysius and the Mother Church took place. An interview schedule consisting of 127 structured and open-ended questions was divided into several parts, each of which covered a special topic of relevance for the structure of the parish, and also the beliefs, attitudes, and aspirations of parish members.

Interviewing began by the end of 1966 and was completed in February, 1967. Interviewing was conducted in English and Serbian but mostly in Serbian because the great majority of respondents were immigrants.

Hypothesis

The purpose of this study is to test the hypothesis: *the maladjustment of immigrants is directly related to their occupational dislocation and to the degree of their frustrated status aspirations in both the larger society and the ethnic group.* In other words, strains and conflicts in a predominantly immigrant ethnic group would develop if a significant number of immigrants experienced a drastic status discrepancy, which represents the difference between their social standing in the native country and their achieved status in their adopted society.[b]

The type of education received by immigrants was of crucial importance for their occupational achievements both in their native country and in the American society. In addition, the same occupational background and similar occupational opportunities of immigrants in the new society result in their sharing of similar values, "life style," and aspirations as well as an inclination to react to the same social stimuli in a similar manner. Therefore, the segments of the same immigrant ethnic group tend to develop, each for itself, a strong sense of identification and belongingness, if the differences in their educational and occupational backgrounds from the time before emigration are significant. This generalization leads to the proposition that factionalism in the Serbian ethnic group has resulted from the differential adjustment of various segments of the group to one another and to the larger society.

In this report, the attention is focused on the relationship between the immigrants' educational and social background in their native country and their occupational achievements in America on the one hand, and on the impact of that relationship on the immigrants' preference in the church controversy on the other.

The followers of Bishop Dionysius are identified as the autonomy faction while those Serbs who stand for unity with the Mother Church constitute the unity faction.[c] The term faction is used for two reasons. First, it is used by the American legislative and legal authorities and by the spokesmen of the two feuding sides in the church controversy. Second, since the break in the unity of the Serbian Orthodox Church did not result in the appearance of a new sect with different religious beliefs and practices, the term schism can be used rarely and only in reference to the religious leadership and authority.

---

[b]Joseph Lopreato uses "status discrepancy" in terms of differential vertical mobility in his analysis of political orientation of mobile people in Italy. "Upward Social Mobility and Political Orientation," *American Sociological Review*, 32 (1967), pp. 586-592. However, the most frustrating consequences of downward mobility or social degradation are expressed in status inconsistency which results in serious strains, as Gerhard Lenski says, when "The individual prefers to think of himself in terms of his higher status or statuses while others have a tendency to treat him in terms of the lower." "Status Inconsistency and the Vote: A Four Nation Test," *American Sociological Review*, 32 (1967), p. 298. See also Djuro Vrga, "Status Discrepancy as a Source of Ethnic Factionalism," *Research Reports in the Social Sciences*, Vol. II. Spring, 1968, pp. 45-62.

[c]It seems that the term *faction* was used first by Senator Dodd in his making distinction between the feuding sides in the church controversy. Senator Dodd's identification of what we call the unity faction as a "pro-Belgrade faction" was later accepted by the opposing faction. *Congressional Record, Senate*, Proceedings and Debates of the 88th Congress, First Session, December 20, 1963, No. 211, p. 24114. See the autonomy faction's *The Diocesan Observer*, II (January 10, 1967), p. 3, and (February 28, 1967), p. 1. In the unity faction's magazine *Glasnik-Herald*, III (July-August, 1967), p. 4, the autonomy faction is called the "schismatic faction." Aldo J. Simpson, Judge of the Elkhart Circuit Court, Indiana, called the feuding sides in the church controversy "factions." See *Parish Bulletin*, Sts. Peter and Paul Serbian Orthodox Church, South Bend, Indiana, (June, 1967), p. 4.

Findings

Nativity, Recency of Immigration, and Factional Preference. The recency of immigration was an especially important factor affecting the preference of immigrant parish members in the church controversy.[6] The unity faction has attracted 73.1 percent of all old immigrants, while 66.8 percent of new immigrants identify themselves with the opposing faction. In this church controversy, however, 70.3 percent of American-born parish members favor the unity faction over the autonomy faction.

The province of origin of immigrants and of ancestry of the American-born Serbs was another significant factor affecting the choice of parish membership in the church controversy. Of all members with origin or ancestry from the province of Serbia, 79 percent are for autonomy. The same faction also received the majority (58 percent) of those from Montenegro. On the other hand, the unity faction received 66 percent of those members who are by birth or ancestry from other Yugoslav provinces whose population is more or less mixed ethnicly and religiously.

When the variables, the recency of immigration and the province of birth, are considered together, the recency of immigration appears far more important because the majority of old immigrants from all Yugoslav provinces, including Serbia and Montenegro, with their predominantly Serbian ethnic population, are for unity in the church controversy. This fact supports the suggested proposition that successive immigrations which differ in background characteristics tend to develop the feeling of identity just as the old immigrants did through decades of living a very intimate communal life with commonly shared interests and common perspectives in America.

The Literacy Level of the Immigrants. The educational profile of Serbian immigrants in America reveals a great difference in educational attainment between the two major successive immigrations and between the immigrants and the native population in Yugoslavia. While 26.0 percent of the total Yugoslav population were illiterate in 1948, no illiterate respondent was found in the sample.[7]

Of all immigrants, 27.0 percent had attended or completed only elementary school while in 1948, 52.4 percent of the total Yugoslav population 10 years old and over, had received no more than elementary school education.[8] The difference between the numbers of university educated immigrants and the Yugoslav population with a university education is surprisingly great. Only five persons out of 1,000 of the total Yugoslav population, 15 years of age and over, had completed university education in 1948, whereas 95 out of 1,000 immigrants had completed university or some equivalent school of higher education.[9]

That the Serbian immigrants are far better educated than the native Yugoslav population may best be concluded from the fact that the educational attainment of the Yugoslav population, 10 years old and over, was approximately 1.9 school years completed in 1948, while the mean number of school years completed by immigrants was 8.0.[10] The average number of school years completed by the new immigrants from the unity faction is 9.7, compared to 8.5 years for the autonomy faction. This may be explained on the basis of difference between the factions in their median age.[d] The old immigrants, the majority of whom are on the unity side, had not received any education beyond the elementary school; at best they had completed a lower trade education during craft apprenticeship.

The Pattern of Education of Immigrants. A relatively high ratio of military educated immigrants is the most significant characteristic of the educational profile of immigrants (Table 13-1). Of all immigrant respondents, 36.6 percent had received lower or higher military education in their native country. Noticeably, more than one-half of this percentage, or 20.3 percent, had completed the school for noncommissioned officers. After the completion of this school and subsequent training and additional education, the noncommissioned officers could advance as officers.

All military educated immigrants with a background in military training belong to the category of new or post-World War II immigrants.[e] However, their percentage of new immigrants in the autonomy faction is disproportionally higher than in the unity faction: 54.4 percent and 30.0 percent respectively (Table 13-1). It is worth noticing that one-third of new immigrants from the autonomy faction completed the school for noncommissioned officers, compared to 13.3 percent from the unity faction.

There is yet another difference between the two antagonistic factions in the

Table 13-1
Factional Distribution of New Immigrants by Completed Military and Nonmilitary Education in the Native Country (in Percentages)

	Education	
Faction	Military	Nonmilitary
Autonomy(N 33)	54.5	45.5
Unity (N 30)	30.0	70.0

[d] It was found that at the time of their immigration, the median age of those for the autonomy faction was 40.0 years, compared to 34.0 years for the unity faction. Djvro J. Vrga and Frank J. Fahey, "Structural Sources of Ethnic Factionalism," *Social Science*, Vol. 44, No. 1, Winter Issue, January, 1969, p. 15.

[e] It should be stressed that majority of them were war prisoners in Germany and were admitted to the U.S.A. as displaced persons. In reference to the adjustment of immigrants, Oscar Handlin strongly emphasizes the importance of background factors by saying, "In understanding the character of that adjustment, it is essential to know about the circumstances under which the newcomers departed from the lands of their birth." *Immigration as a Factor in American History*, ed. Oscar Handlin (Englewood Cliffs, New Jersey: Prentice-Hall, Inc., 1959), Introduction to Chapter Two, p. 20.

type of education received in the native country. A larger percentage of new immigrants with some university education is found in the unity than the autonomy faction: 23.4 percent and 12.2 percent respectively. The survey data show that the majority of immigrants with university education had peasant background and that their fathers were not rich peasants or the so-called "kulakhs."

The Education of Immigrants in America. Of all immigrant respondents 74.3 percent did not receive any education in America. Although the immigrants' educational attainment in America is low (educational scores of all immigrants on 600.0 points basis is: the autonomy faction—91.0 pts; the unity faction—132.5 pts), it is still commendable in view of the fact that 66.2 percent of all immigrants respondents were over thirty years old at the time of immigration.

The Education of American-born Serbs. The Serbian appreciation of education is best reflected in the educational attainment of American-born Serbs. The average number of school years completed by the American-born respondents, the youngest of whom was thirty-five years old at the time of interviewing, is 13.5 compared to the average 11.3 school years completed by Americans of twenty-five years of age and over, in 1960.[11] Five of the ten American-born respondents have college education, three are high school graduates, and two completed ninth to eleventh grade. Besides their formal education, the majority of American-born respondents have acquired additional education in certain fields of specialization. Significantly, the educational attainment of American-born Serbs is 1.5 years higher than that of white natives of native parentage whose average number of school years completed, in 1960, was 12.0.[12]

The Intergenerational Mobility of Immigrants in Their Native Country. By occupational background, the old immigrants were mainly peasants while the new immigrants, even though more than one-half of them originally came from the lower strata, experienced a high degree of upward occupational mobility in their native country (Table 13-2). The fathers of 51.4 percent of all immigrants were peasants while the percentage of the Yugoslav population engaged in agriculture and forestry was 78.5 in 1931, and 78.3 in 1948.[13]

In comparison with the 61.8 percent of the fathers of immigrants for autonomy who were peasants, 42.5 percent of the fathers of immigrants who are on the unity side were peasants. Of the fathers of immigrants for autonomy, 8.8 percent were professionals compared to 15.0 percent of the fathers of those for unity.

While 52.9 percent of immigrants on the autonomy side were professionals in _ative country, as against 8.8 percent of their fathers who had been _ionals, only 20 percent of immigrants for unity were professionals _d to 15.0 percent of their father-professionals. It was found that exactly _f immigrant professionals on the autonomy side were peasants by _nparison with one-fourth of the professionals from the unity faction.

Table 13-2
Percentage Distribution of Occupations of the Fathers of Immigrants and of Immigrants in the Native Country, by Factions

Faction	Occupation Fathers and Their Emigrant Sons	Professionals	Proprietors, Managers, & Officials	Clerical Workers & Skilled Craftsmen	Semiskilled Laborers	Unskilled Laborers	Peasants	Students	Children	Total
Autonomy (N 34)	Fathers	8.8	17.6	2.9	5.9	2.9	61.8	–	–	99.9
	Sons	52.9	5.9	14.7	2.9	2.9	11.8	8.8	–	99.9
Unity (N 40)	Fathers	15.0	22.5	20.0	–	–	42.5	–	–	100.0
	Sons	20.0	5.0	27.5	–	–	20.0	12.5	15.0	100.0
Both Factions (N 74)	Fathers	12.2	20.3	12.2	2.7	1.4	51.4	–	–	100.2
	Sons	35.1	5.4	21.6	1.4	1.4	16.2	10.8	8.1	100.2

The survey data show that 31.7 percent of the sons of semiskilled and unskilled laborers and peasants remained in the occupational category of their fathers, while 41.4 percent became professionals, and the rest became clerical workers and skilled craftsmen. On the other hand, 33.3 percent of the sons of clerical workers and skilled craftsmen became professionals and, interestingly enough, 44.4 percent pursued the occupation of their fathers, while the remaining 22.2 percent became either semiskilled laborers or peasants. However, of all those whose fathers were professionals or managers or officials, 91.0 percent remained in the same category, while the others skidded to lower occupations.

The above findings indicate that the intergenerational mobility of immigrants from the autonomy faction was far greater than that of their counterparts on the unity side. This points to the fact that the immigrants from the unity faction have experienced less drastic changes in reference to group identification in the native country than have these for autonomy.

Discrepancies between the occupations of fathers and their emigrant sons, and between the immigrants' occupations in the native country and in America are shown in percentages in Table 13-3. In comparison with one-third of the immigrants from the unity faction, 73.5 percent of those from the autonomy faction achieved in their native country occupational positions that were above the positions of their fathers. It should be mentioned that of all occupational climbers from the autonomy faction, one-third made the jump from the bottom to the top of the Yugoslav occupational ladder. The occupational discrepancy

Table 13-3

Discrepancy Between the Occupation of the Fathers of Immigrants and of Immigrants in Their Native Country, and Between the Immigrants' Occupations in the Native Country and in the U.S.A. (in Percentages)

	Discrepancy Between			
	The occupation of the immigrants' fathers and of the immigrants' in the native country		The immigrants' occupation in the native country and in the U.S.A.	
	Faction		Faction	
Type of occupational Mobility	Autonomy (N 34)	Unity (N 40)	Autonomy (N 34)	Unity (N 40)
ʼd	73.5	32.5	8.8	27.5
ɪge	26.5	37.5	26.5	32.5
ɪ	–	15.0	64.7	25.0
	–	15.0	–	15.0
	100.0	100.0	100.0	100.0

scores[f] show that the immigrants from the autonomy faction were, on four points occupational prestige scale,[g] upward mobile intergenerationally for exactly two occupational categories, while their counterparts on the unity side moved upward for three-fourths of the distance between the bottom and the top of one single occupational category.

The Intergenerational Mobility of American-born Serbs. Intergenerationally, the American-born Serbs, who are not shown in tables, were even more upwardly mobile than the immigrants from the autonomy faction in their native country Yugoslavia. While the occupational score of the fathers of American-born Serbs measured on the four points basis was only 0.70 point in America, the occupational score of their American-born sons reached 3.10 points, which represents an upward mobility of almost two and one-half occupational categories.

Occupational Achievements of Immigrants in America. Table 13-3 shows that the immigrants from the autonomy faction have experienced a status degradation upon entry to America almost as striking as their rise above the occupational level of their fathers in the native country. The immigrants from the unity faction, however, have succeeded in maintaining their pre-emigration occupational level. While 64.7 percent of immigrants from the autonomy faction moved downward in America, only 25.0 percent of immigrants for unity experienced occupational degradation. On the other side, 27.5 percent of those for unity moved upward, compared to only 8.8 percent of those from the autonomy faction.

The former peasants were the most upwardly mobile category of Serbian immigrants in America. While immigrants from other occupational categories are found among the occupational climbers in the unity faction, none are found in the autonomy faction.

Educational Background and Mobility of Immigrants in America. The factional preference of immigrants in the church controversy is patterned after their occupational mobility which, in turn, was conditioned by their educational attainment in the native country. Although the same table shows that there are immigrants with the same type of education among the downwardly mobile immigrants on both sides of the church controversy, the autonomy faction has, however, attracted more immigrants with a greater degree of occupational degradation. It was found, for instance, that more than one-half of those on the

---

[f]The occupational score of a group is one hundredth of the sum of scores of various occupational categories which are obtained by multiplying the percent of subjects in each category by the number of points assigned to corresponding categories.

[g]In this study, occupations are grouped in categories according to occupational prestige scores: 4. professionals; 3. proprietors, managers, and officials; 2. clerical workers and skilled craftsmen; 1. semiskilled laborers; and O. unskilled workers and peasants.

autonomy side who had climbed from the bottom to the top of the Yugoslav occupational structure have skidded to the bottom of the American occupational structure. On the other side, no single immigrant from the unity faction experienced such a drastic occupational degradation in America.

And again, of those on the autonomy side who skidded for three occupational categories (17.6 percent), one-half had completed lower or higher military academy. No respondent on the unity side who had completed the lower or higher military academy, however, skidded for three occupational-training categories. In general, the percentage of immigrants with military training in the autonomy faction who were downgraded in America (44.1 percent of the faction's total) is five times larger than the percentage of those who managed to acquire positions in the same occupational category (8.8 percent).

Collected information about immigrants with military background indicates that the majority of those for unity served in the branches which required more technical skills or received additional education in some applied fields.

Not less surprising is the fact that university educated immigrants from the unity faction achieved far greater occupational success in America than their counterparts on the autonomy side. While the majority of those for autonomy were occupational skidders, the majority from the unity faction were either climbers or in the same occupational category.

Immigrants with elementary and trade school education from the autonomy faction reflected the same overall occupational trend as their counterparts from the unity faction.

Conclusion

The presented findings show that the controversy in the Serbian Eastern Orthodox Church in America resulted in the factional division of the whole Serbian ethnic minority group along certain lines of internal differentiation. The most important finding of this study indicates that the kind and level of education of immigrants are the major factors conditioning their social mobility and status in both the native country and America. It is presumed, therefore, that the failure of immigrants to transfer their occupational skills from the native country to America, and to regain their former social prestige, can obstruct their adjustment in the new social environment, and become the major cause of their frustration.

The intergenerational mobility of Serbian immigrants, especially of new or post-World War II immigrants, represents reliable grounds for an understanding of socio-cultural conditions and the degree of flexibility of the system of social stratification in their predominantly agricultural native country before World War II. At the same time that mobility serves as a sufficient indicator of their psychological and ideological reactions caused by their kind of achievements and expectations.

Table 13-4

Educational Background of Immigrants and Changes in Their Occupational Status from Occupation in the Native Country to Occupation in U.S.A. (in Percentages)

Faction	The Type of Social Mobility	The Type of School Completed						
		Elementary & Trade School	Lower & Upper Gymnasium	School for Noncommissioned Officers	Lower & Higher Military Academy	University (some) & University Diploma	Unclassified	Total
Autonomy (N 34)	Upward	8.8	–	–	–	–	–	8.8
	No change	11.8	–	5.9	2.9	5.9	–	26.5
	Downward	8.8	2.9	26.5	17.6	8.8	–	64.7
	Total	29.5	2.9	32.4	20.5	14.7	–	100.0
Unity (N 40)	Upward	12.5	7.5	–	–	7.5	–	27.5
	No change	15.0	–	2.5	7.5	7.5	–	32.5
	Downward	5.0	5.0	7.5	5.0	2.5	–	25.0
	Unclassified	–	–	–	–	–	15.0	15.0
	Total	32.5	12.5	10.0	12.5	17.5	15.0	100.0

The fact that the educational attainment of immigrants was far above the average educational attainment of the total Yugoslav population might lead us to the conclusion that the opposition to communism was concentrated in the privileged social class. When the educational attainment of immigrants is evaluated in terms of their social background, however, it becomes evident that the access to education in the pre-World War II Yugoslavia was not conditioned by the system of social stratification in the sense that education for different callings was restricted, like in England, to children from different social strata. It should be stressed, however, that the fact that the student's fees and tuitions were determined on the basis of his father's income taxation or earnings was of crucial importance for the prolonged education of peasants. Since education was the main avenue for social advancement in Yugoslavia, it can then be concluded that the pre-war Yugoslav society was an open society in the sense that occupational opportunities were not dictated by class origin exclusively. As the presented data show, immigrants from different social strata have experienced different degrees of mobility. Interestingly enough, the immigrants of peasant origin experienced much more upward mobility than those whose fathers were clerical workers and skilled craftsmen. On the other hand, a greater percentage of immigrant clerical workers and craftsmen than of immigrant peasants were in the occupation of their fathers.

Information about the occupational achievements of immigrants in America indicate that the new immigrants have experienced a very drastic occupational and status degradation from their position in the native country. It is especially significant, however, that the autonomy faction has attracted many more downgraded immigrants than the unity faction (Table 13-3). On the other hand, three times more immigrants from the unity faction than the autonomy faction experienced upward mobility in America (27.5 percent and 8.8 percent respectively). The great majority of immigrants from the autonomy faction with military training and university education are occupational skidders in America.

Even when taken as a single independent variable for determining the factional preference in the church controversy, education sufficiently supports the proposition that the background differences among the segments of the same immigration, not the successive ones only, can become causes of conflict and strains in an immigrant ethnic group. In this respect, education can be considered in terms of its two functions. First, education as a socializing process affects one's cognition, self-perception, and group identification.[14] Second, the differential education of members of a group differently affects their occupational opportunities, and consequently, their position in the social structure. While military education and training often serves, in Sorokin's words, as a "social stairway," in the native society they may become an obstacle to upward mobility in emigration.[15] Adjustment difficulties and confusion as the "normal consequence" of status transition of those who change their military status for civilian status in their native society can be noticed very easily.[16] If these psychological and behavioral effects of occupational changes can be noticed in cases when the accepted civilian occupation provides them with the degree of social prestige equally high as the prestige of their former military rank, one can imagine reactions of a former Yugoslav army general or colonel with the highest possible military education when he becomes a laborer after years of sufferings in the nazi POW camps, or after fighting nazis and communists for years.

A great discrepancy between the occupational status of immigrants from the autonomy faction in the native country and their achieved status in America was a factor affecting their attitudes toward both their ethnic group and the larger American society. While the old immigrants had sympathies for the displaced persons from their native country, they also thought that the newcomers could replace them on their own low social position, as it had been happening throughout the history of successive immigrations in America.[h] As a consequence, the old immigrants who felt well adjusted to the way of life in America, expected to monopolize the leading positions in their ethnic community with support of their American-born children. Treatment received by a great number of new immigrants from the American society and their ethnic group resulted in their feeling of frustration. In fact, their occupational degradation and loss of social prestige resulted in their social ambiguity and their feelings of powerlessness and isolation, which, in turn, reinforced them in reflection of adjustment. For that reason the great majority of immigrants on the autonomy side of the church controversy became doubly uprooted. Unlike the refugee of other ethnic origin whose initial adjustment only "was greatly influenced by the degree to which his preconceived hopes coincided with reality" mainly because of "difficulty in finding suitable employment," a great number of Serbian post-war immigrants became even more frustrated later.[17] The adjustment of many Serbian immigrants was more difficult than President Kennedy estimated when he said that "each new group was met by the groups already in America, and adjustments were often difficult and painful."[18]

Religious strains and social conflicts in a predominantly immigrant ethnic group are likely to develop when the successive immigrations or parts thereof, as in the case of Serbian post-war immigrants, significantly differ in social occupational, and educational motives or reasons for emigrations, and in contact situations with the host society. The presented findings show that education and pre-emigration occupation as the most important background factors are strongly associated with the immigrants' occupational achievements in America. Furthermore, these two major factors strongly influence their occupational expertations and aspirations in America. Data presented and analyzed in this study strongly support the suggested hypotheses: *the maladjustment of immigrants is directly related to their occupational dislocation and to the degree of their frustrated status aspirations in both the larger society and the ethnic group.*

[h]In his analysis of achievements and adjustment of immigrants, Will Herberg emphasizes the opportunities for mobility in America but also recognizes that "Each new group, as it came, pushed upward the level of its predecessors, and was in turn pushed upward by its successors." He also admits that "this process of upward movement took place not without painful friction, not without conflict even . . . " *Protestant-Catholic-Jew*, rev. ed. (Garden City, New York: Anchor Books-Doubleday & Co., Inc., 1960), p. 8.

It is apparent that the Serbian Orthodox Church in America was not able to integrate many different primary groups and special segments of the Serbian ethnic group. Therefore, the autonomy faction attracted the great majority of Serbs who felt unadjusted to their ethnic group and to the American society because of a very drastic occupational degradation and loss of status.

The purpose of this study is to identify some social sources of schism in the Serbian Orthodox Church in America because it is proved that religiosity and religiousness of the feuding factions are the same,[19] while the desired socio-ethnic functions of the church are different for the followers of the opposing factions.[20] Data presented in this study indicate that schism in the Serbian Orthodox Church has a multifactorial causality which reflects the differential social backgrounds and the differential social achievements of members of the feuding factions.[21] At the same time, the presented data call special attention to social change and social mobility as well as to the immigrants' motives for emigration.[22] It is also thought that this schism was an expression of frustration of many members of the autonomy faction. This means that personality characteristics of members of feuding factions or sects of a religious body should not be neglected in scientific studies of religious divisions.

Notes

1. See *Congressional Record, Senate*, Proceedings and Debates of the 88th Congress, First Session, December 20, 1963, No. 211, pp. 24114-24115.

2. For differences concerning recency of immigration, the province or origin and ancestry, the age of immigrants at the time of leaving their native country and of immigration to the U.S.A., and reasons for leaving the native country, see Djuro J. Vrga and Frank J. Fahey, "Structural Sources of Ethnic Factionalism," *Social Science*, Vol. 44, No. 1, Winter Issue, January, 1969, pp. 12-19.

3. See Anne Anastasi and John P. Foley, Jr., *Differential Psychology* (New York: The Macmillan Company, 1956), pp. 704-705.

4. For a typology of contact situations between the indigeneous population and migrants, see Stanley Lieberson, "A Societal Theory of Race and Ethnic Relations," *American Sociological Review*, 26 (1961), pp. 902-910; and R.A. Schermerhorn, "Polarity in the Approach to Comparative Research in Ethnic Relations," *Sociology and Social Research*, 51 (January, 1967), pp. 235-240.

5. About one's hostility against his own group as a source of factionalism, see Harold Lasswell, "Faction," *Encyclopedia of Social Sciences*, VI (1931), p. 50. About conditions producing the Jewish self-hatred, see K. Lewin, *Resolving Social Conflicts*, ed. Gertrude Weiss Lewin (New York: Harper and Brothers, Publishers, 1948), Chapter 12.

6. See Vrga and Fahey, "Structural Sources of Ethnic Factionalism," pp. 14-15.

7. *The Population of Yugoslavia* (Washington: Government Printing Office, 1954), (Table VI-L), p. 68.

8. Ibid., Table VI-G, p. 65.

9. Ibid., p. 63. In 1937, 44 persons out of 1,000 in the same group in America had completed four years or more of college education.

10. Ibid., Table VI-H, p. 66.

11. U.S. Bureau of the Census, *Census Population: 1960*, Subject Reports—Educational Attainment, Final Report, PC (2)-58, Table I, and II, pp. Iff.

12. Ibid.

13. *The Population of Yugoslavia*, p. 73.

14. See *On Education—Sociological Perspectives*, ed. Donald A. Hansen and Joel E. Gerstl (New York: John Wiley & Sons, Inc., 1967), Essays 2, 3, 4, and 5, pp. 36-223. For the impact of military education on the formation of group identification, see C. Wright Mills, *The Power Elite* (New York: Oxford University Press, 1959), pp. 192-194.

15. Pitirim A. Sorokin, *Social and Cultural Mobility* (New York: Free Press, 1959), p. 165.

16. Robert Bierstedt, *The Social Order* (New York: McGraw-Hill Book Co., 1957), pp. 225-228.

17. Richard Ferree Smith, "Refugees," *The Annals*, Vol. 367 (September, 1966), pp. 50-52.

18. John F. Kennedy, *A Nation of Immigrants* (New York: Harper and Row, 1964), p. 63. Oscar Handlin thinks that "the nature of the opportunities open to the immigrant and the length of time afforded him for adjustment" are more important for his adjustment than his cultural heritage. *Race and Nationality in American Life* (Boston: Little, Brown and Company, 1957), p. 194.

19. Djuro J. Vrga and Frank J. Fahey, "The Relationship of Religious Practices and Beliefs to Schism," *Sociological Analysis*, Vol. 31, No. 1, Spring, 1970.

20. Djuro J. Vrga, "Participants' Identification and Subjective Interpretation of Causes of Their Religious Division," forthcoming in *Social Compass*.

21. J. Milton Yinger, *Religion, Society and the Individual* (New York: The Macmillan Co., 1967), pp. 131-142.

22. Ibid., p. 139.

Part IV
Detroit Institutions and Ethnicity

14 Henry Ford's Melting Pot

Jonathan Schwartz

In his characteristic gift for self-advertisement, Henry Ford once remarked: "I am more a manufacturer of men than of automobiles." This paper is a study of the Ford Motor Company's efforts at remaking the immigrants who came to Highland Park in the 1910s to work on the world's largest and (I am told) fastest assembly line. I shall examine the Company's Americanization programs and I shall also describe how these programs were experienced by one of the many ethnic groups that found its way to Highland Park during this period: the Armenian refugees. This paper, then, is a study of the theory and practice of the melting pot in its hottest and most active phase, the period of the First World War.

The idea for this paper first occurred to me when I visited a retired UAW members' picnic at Belle Isle in September, 1963. I went to the picnic with my father-in-law, a retired Armenian Ford worker, and was introduced to a community with a distinct history that reached back to the early days of the assembly line—retired rank and file members of Local 600, and proud of their union. But these men had worked at Ford twenty and thirty years before they had a union, and it was their initial contact with Detroit and the Ford Motor Company that drew my attention. The only way to discover this history was to talk with the members of the community, and since that afternoon at Belle Isle I have visited several coffee houses and other picnic tables at Palmer Park. Always I was able to gain entry to the groups of Armenian men through a member of my wife's family, either my father-in-law or my grandfather-in-law. I found very soon that while almost every Armenian man who came to Detroit had worked at Ford, not all of them remained Ford workers to the time of the UAW. Some had escaped, some were laid off. Those who were able to stick it out at Ford up to the days of the UAW organizing drive, tended to continue at Ford until retirement, with a UAW pension. Occupational differentiation did not result in any discernible contrasts of attitude or values among the Armenian men. The men who left the assembly line to start a shoe repair business or a grocery store did not consider their new trade in the terms of upward mobility and the fulfillment of the American dream. Establishing a business in Highland Park was a means, perhaps the only means, of establishing a permanent Armenian community. It was also a way of acknowledging the permanence of the Armenian community. Rather than being assimilated and "Americanized," the Armenians who came to Detroit, and worked at Ford's at least for a time, built a

191

rather stable and autonomous ethnic community. The surviving founders of the early Armenian community in Detroit still meet regularly and informally in the coffee houses and clubs and, when weather permits, at the picnic tables of Palmer Park. The categories in which much sociological phenomena are cast simply do not fit the experience of the men I met and spoke with. Henry Ford's dream of the great melting pot never happened, fortunately, and the sociological constructs which are derived from the melting pot image—assimilation, acculturation, upward mobility—do not fully describe what did occur among ethnic groups.

In January, 1914, came the announcement of the $5.00 a day wage from the Ford Motor Company in Highland Park. Thousands of men appeared at the factory gates seeking a daily wage that in many cases doubled what was the standard rate for assembly line workers. So turbulent was the scene outside the Ford Company that the Highland Park fire department turned hoses on the men to dampen and freeze their enthusiasm. Behind the dramatic episode at the plant gates was a systematic program of the Ford Motor Company to Americanize the foreign workers. The Ford Profit-Sharing Plan was the theory which "justified" the $5.00 a day wage, and the Company created two agencies to implement the plan. First was the Ford English School and second was the Ford Sociological Department. In no other large American manufacturing firm was the "melting pot" idea so completely institutionalized.

The Ford English School sought to instruct the foreign born in basic English speech and writing. But like most of Ford's actions, a moral and even a religious impulse seemed to be at work. To teach English also meant to discourage the use of native languages. To teach English meant also to Americanize, and the Ford Company pursued its aim with missionary zeal. A contemporary spokesman for the company described and explained the functioning of the Ford English School.

For their (i.e., the workers') intellectual improvement we have provided, among other things, the Ford English School. This is a school for foreigners in our employ, the enrollment averages about 2,000. The pupils are grouped in classes of about 25 to a class. The teachers are volunteers from the office and factory. There are over one hundred and sixty of them. Each class meets twice a week, and the session lasts about one hour and a half. Attendance is virtually compulsory. If a man declines to go to school, the advantages of the training are carefully explained to him. If he still hesitates, he is laid off and given a chance for uninterrupted meditation and reconsideration. He seldom fails to change his mind.

There are over 50 nationalities in the factory and there may be as many nationalities in each class as there are men present, for we make no attempt to group them according to language and race. The fact is we prefer that classes be mixed as to race and country, *for our one great aim is to impress these men that they are, or should be, Americans, and that former racial, national, and linguistic differences are to be forgotten. (My emphasis.)*[1]

To further impress upon the students in the Ford English School the fact that they were being remade into Americans, the administration of the school designed a unique graduation ceremony. Again I quote from the text in the archives of the Ford Motor Company:

Not long ago this school graduated over 500 men. Commencement exercises were held in the largest hall in the city. On the stage was represented an immigrant ship. In front of it was a huge melting pot. Down the gang plank came the members of the class dressed in their national garbs and carrying luggage such as they carried when they landed in this country. Down they poured into the Ford melting pot and disappeared. Then the teachers began to stir the contents of the pot with long ladles. Presently the pot began to boil over and out came the men dressed in their best American clothes and waving American flags.[2]

The melting pot doctrine found a perfect ritual in this graduation ceremony, but if that ritual meant one thing to the ministers, it probably had different meanings to the members of the flock. The symbolic transformation of the foreigner inside the melting pot into a flag waving American, may have been convincing to the teacher of the school, but it hardly touched the students. Ethnic communities survived the melting pot to the point where one can ask: *was* there in fact a melting pot? save in the minds of its creators? Changing clothes does not remake the man. Acquiring the basic skills in English, moreover, does not transform the immigrant worker into an American.

We may now ask how the other agency of the Ford Motor Company's "melting pot," the Sociological Department, attempted to reshape the men who worked in the plant. The $5.00 a day was to be paid only to those Ford workers who were deserving of it. The Ford Sociological Department sent investigators to visit the workers' homes, and if an employee met certain standards of behavior and habits, he would receive the $5.00 wage. Otherwise he would have to wait until he passed. Alan Nevins, in his monumental history of the Ford Motor Company gives a compact description of the Sociological Department's method:

Each investigator, equipped with a car, a driver, and an interpreter, was assigned a district in Detroit, mapped to contain a due proportion of Ford workers and if possible, a limited number of language groups. The subjects for inquiry made up a formidable list. Naturally, each worker was expected to furnish information on his marital status, the number of dependents and their ages, and his nationality, religion, and (if alien) prospects of citizenship. In addition, light was sought on his economic position. Did he own his home? If so, how large was the mortgage? If he rented a domicile, what did he pay? Was he in debt, and to whom? How much money had he saved, and where did he keep it? Did he carry life insurance, and at what premiums? His social outlook and mode of living also came under scrutiny. His health? His doctor? His recreations? The investigator meanwhile looked about sharply, if unobtrusively, so that he could report on 'habits,' 'home condition,' and 'neighborhood.' Before he left a given family, he knew whether its diet was adequate; whether it took in boarders—an evil practice which he was to discourage; and whether money was being sent abroad. All this information and more was placed on blue and white forms. The Sociological Department was nothing if not thorough.[3]

Unfortunately, for my research, the written reports of the investigators are not preserved in the archives of the Ford Motor Company. I would have liked to make these descriptions as concrete as that of the Ford English School's graduation ritual. I have spoken with several Armenian men who remember the investigators. One recalls having photographs taken of his living room and bedroom. Several Armenians mentioned one of their brothers who failed to pass the inspection. He was living at the time in a rooming house in Delray. He didn't receive the $5.00 a day. Eventually this man quit Ford and started a grocery store in Highland Park.

The investigators from the Ford Sociology Department cooperated on occasion with the Police Department, helping to correct their employees' bad habits. S.S. Marquis cited a letter from Detroit Police Commissioner:

The Commissioner of police declared that the work done by the Company had 'decreased in number the cases against your employees,' and that the work done by the Sociological Department 'very materially improved the housing conditions in this community, resulting in many thousands of men becoming better and more dependable citizens.'[4]

One of the ways in which the Ford Sociological Department justified its moral and financial supervision of the workers was its claim to protect the employees against ethnic swindlers, who, the company said, frequently cheated their own people. John R. Lee, the first director of the Sociological Department, described how the Ford Company helped to "liberate" the foreign workers from ethnic exploitation:

We have actually found in Detroit petty empires existing. For instance, we know it to be true that when a group of Rumanians, we will say, arrive in New York, in some way or other they are shipped to Detroit and the knowledge of their coming imparted to someone in our city, who meets them at the station and who confiscates the party, so to speak, persuades them to live in quarters selected for them, to buy their merchandise in markets other than their own choosing and to live unto themselves and apart from the wholesome environment of the city, so that the instigators of all this may benefit through rentals and large profits on food, wearing apparel, etc.
    Of course, it is to the interest of such men that these foreigners shall know nothing of the English language, of American ways and customs, or of local values, as these are the things which would liberate them from the bondage (and it is nothing more or less) under which they have unconsciously been placed.[5]

Though the actual reports of the Ford Sociological Department investigators are not contained in the archives of the Henry Ford Museum, there is a printed statistical analysis of the findings of the investigators for the year 1916. It is interesting that the classification of employees is by ethnic origin. Thus we have a way of comparing the different ethnic groups' behavior in Detroit, but only from the criteria used by the Ford Sociological Department. Of its 40,903 employees, 16,457 were native Americans, though separate categories are given for "Negroes" (106) and American Indians (33). The Ford Company lists 58 different nationalities in its employ. There are twenty-four nationalities with at least 100 employees. They are as follows:

1.	American	16,457	13.	Lithuanian	541
2.	Polish	7,525	14.	Scottish	480
3.	Italian	1,954	15.	Serbian	456
4.	Canadian	1,819	16.	Armenian	437
5.	Rumanian	1,750	17.	Irish	399
6.	Jewish	1,437	18.	Ruthenian	368
7.	German	1,360	19.	Greek	281
8.	Russian	1,160	20.	Bohemian	240
9.	English	1,159	21.	Swedish	166
10.	Hungarian	690	22.	Croatian	159
11.	Austrian	573	23.	Finnish	106
12.	Syrian	555	24.	Negro	106

The method in which the Ford Sociological Department represented "nationality" is, of course, highly misleading. This method reflects the mechanistic views of the department towards ethnicity. The category of "American" which heads the list tells only that this group is white and native. It says little or nothing of its ethnic or regional background. One can assume that this group of "Americans" included a fairly large proportion of second and third generation immigrants. When we examine the behavior of this group of Americans by the investigators from the Sociological Department, it does not appear that the Americans were particularly good in their behavior or prudent in their habits. In other words, the Americans in this employ of the Ford Motor Company are not to be taken as examples to be followed by the foreign born. The ideal of American in the Americanization program is not, therefore, a folk or ethnic pattern. The idea of American is a norm, a moral standard, which was set and enforced as much as possible by the administration of the Ford Motor Company. If we were stunned at the concreteness of the Ford English School's graduation ceremony of the melting pot, we ought to be stunned also at the abstractness of the Ford Sociological Department's standards of behavior. The investigators judged the employees "habits" as "good," "fair," and "poor," and statistics in these terms were compiled for each of the fifty-eight ethnic groups. No explanation of what constitutes good, fair, and poor habits is given. However, by talking with at least one ethnic group, we can gather what type of thing the Sociology Department had in mind. Gambling apparently was a "poor" habit—almost universal, but definitely to be discouraged. Saving in a bank was a "good" habit. The investigators urged the worker to start a savings account with the wages that he might otherwise have gambled. Living in a rooming house was not as "good" as buying a home. Living in an ethnic community was not as "good" as living in the wholesome environment of nondescript Detroit. It seems on reflection that the ideal of the Ford Sociological Department was a purely impersonal world, a world of interchangeable men who would operate like interchangeable parts of a machine. The "melting pot" at Ford's was an assembly line.

If we now turn to the Sociological Department's statistical summary of the 437 Armenian Ford workers in 1916, we would see that at least from the standpoint of the Ford Motor Company, this relatively small nationality was well on its way to being melted down into the American society. By nearly all of its standards of behavior and good habits, the Armenians were being assimilated and Americanized. Only four Armenians of the entire number were found unable to speak English. Those Armenian workers who have savings accounts in Detroit banks held savings that were more than double those of the average employee. Armenians, moreover, were taking out life insurance policies at about the average rate. A smaller number of the Armenians than the average were married and had families, but this fact only testifies to the circumstances of the Armenian immigration to the United States. Armenian men immigrated, without families, and generally preceded by five or ten years the immigration of women. Young Armenian women often lived in orphanages in Armenia, for the earlier Turkish massacres were aimed at the male population. The women remained in orphanages until they received the money for passage to America. In Detroit the Armenian workers lived in rooming houses and shared the cooking and housework. They spent their leisure hours in the coffee houses and parks, as they do to this day. According to the Ford investigators the habits of the Armenian workers were "good" or "fair." They had the mode of behavior which marked them as dependable. Thus, the Armenians resembled in several respects the "norms" established by the Sociological Department.

The statistical portrait of the Armenian Ford workers hardly tells the real history of this group. The early immigrants were saving their wages at a higher rate in order to buy passage back to their native land. These men had left Armenia to avoid being drafted into the Turkish army. The World War and the subsequent massacres by the Turks in a sense sealed the fate of the Armenians who had already come to America. After 1915 there was no going back to Armenia. Rather, it became imperative to bring the survivors to the United States. Hence the powerful motive for saving among Armenian Ford workers. While the Ford Sociological Department viewed saving as "good" because it showed the character of restraint in an individual, we can see that the act of saving money can also represent a collective and not merely an individual will. The Armenian Ford workers saved money in order to create an *Armenian* community, not to individuate themselves in the American society. Similarly, as I mentioned at the opening of this paper, the reasons for starting a business in Highland Park were primarily those of building a solid economic base for the growing Armenian community. If an Armenian Ford worker quit Ford to start a business, it was not to separate himself from his fellow Armenians but to better cement his bonds with them. The business often served the Armenian neighborhood. We ought not to mistake these ethnic aspirations as attempts to realize the "American dream." For these several hundred Armenian men at Ford, the awesome consciousness of the survivor was far more persuasive and real than the American fantasy of the self-made man.

We must move ever closer to particular cases, away from the abstract profiles of the Ford Sociological Department. The historian who does research through conversations—oral history—has to develop a different temperament from that of the researcher in archives. In the archives one does a rapid interrogation of the materials at his desk, sorting through and discarding an immense number of documents. We usually know what we are after; and when we find it, there is the joy of discovery, a drink at the fountain, and the copying of the text in the notebook. While listening to old workers telling about the early days on the assembly line, the historian cannot be in a hurry, nor can he pounce upon the evidence when he hears it coming from the lips of his informers. The Armenian men I spoke with, or listened to, could not quite figure out why I was asking them all those questions. Sometimes they referred me to authorities or to experts on Armenian history. I never took their advice. I considered the men in the coffee houses the best experts on their own history, although they did not regard what they had done as historically significant. I rather think otherwise.

The men did not arrive in America as whole communities with a definite social organization. It took nearly two decades to establish Armenian organizations, like the Church, in Detroit. The men arrived in this city after spending about two or three years moving from job to job in the United States. These wanderings are remarkable. One man recalls arriving in New York in 1907, making his way to Providence, Rhode Island, then and now an Armenian center in the U.S., and then up to Island Falls, Maine, where he worked in a shoe factory. Laid off from this job, he lived alone in the Maine woods for several months, hunting deer. Hearing of other Armenians in Pennsylvania and Missouri, he made his way to both places always asking for other Armenians en route—not simply using a grape vine, but *making* a grape vine. Harry M. came to Detroit three years after landing in New York. He lived and worked briefly in Delray, and then got a job at Ford's in Highland Park in the gear cutting department. In 1910, he was the third Armenian to be hired at Ford. He recalls how Ford used to take walks through the plant, something like a general reviewing his troops. He came up to Harry at the lathe and pulled his long dark hair, smiling and saying, "I wish my hair were like that." None of the later Armenian workers remembers such a bouyant Henry Ford. Harry recalls the passionate feelings pro and con toward Henry Ford among both immigrants and natives. One worker who called his dog "Ford," was attacked in a restaurant by a Ford loyalist. When a fight broke out, the man with the dog was arrested and fined for creating a disturbance. The loyalist was released.

Episodes such as these reveal better than any statistics the character of the factory city in those days; this character combined the explosiveness of frontier

America and the harsh discipline of the assembly line. Ford himself personified these traits, but they were traits which could not be transmitted to all who came to work at Ford's factory. My informants in the Armenian community tell me that when an Armenian arrived in Detroit needing work, one of the Armenian Ford workers would give that man's name to his foreman, and the foreman would pass the name to the employment officers, who might then call the name in the waiting room, ask the man a few questions, and assign him to a department where he was needed. In this way, the Ford Company managed, informally, to keep some distribution of ethnic groups. Favoritism, and sometimes bribery, could also get a man a job. No Armenian man from these early days ever remembers being promoted into a high post in the company. Nor did other ethnic groups rise in the ranks of the Ford management.

From what I can gather from the small number of former Ford workers I spoke with, the very early days at Ford in Highland Park were quite different from the late nineteen-tens, and particularly the twenties after the Rouge Plant was built.

Ethnicity is very much a part of the industrial and labor history of Detroit. Too often historians like to keep their categories separated from one another. The economic historian looks at the manufacturing firm; the labor historian looks at the local union; the ethnic historian looks at a particular nationality. But history does not live in the categories of scholarship. The social history of modern times cannot be placed in neat compartments. Rather, we can discover our history at those junctions or intersections where we, as people with distinct history, meet head on with institutions like schools and factories.

I hope that my little research into the Armenian workers who worked at Ford's in Highland Park can be seen as an example of the kind of historiography which reveals the character of our society.

Notes

1. Henry Ford Museum, Archives. Accession 293, Marquis Papers, "The Ford Profit-Sharing Plan," pp. 11-12.

2. Ibid.

3. Alan Nevins, *Ford: The Times, The Man, The Company,* 3 Volumes. (New York, 1954) Vol. 1, p. 554.

4. S.S. Marquis, *Henry Ford: An Interpretation,* (1923).

5. John R. Lee, "The So-Called Profit-Sharing System in the Ford Plant," *The Annals of the American Academy of Political and Social Science,* 65, May, 1916, pp. 305-6.

15 The Schools and Ethnicity in Detroit

Christopher H. Johnson

This paper is drawn in part from a project which I have been directing on the teaching of history in the public secondary schools of Detroit. As a teacher of history at Wayne State I am committed to the concept that the university must develop a major effort to render more than specifically academic service,—that is, to relate more concretely—to the community around it. The secondary school history project, (sponsored jointly by the Wayne State Council on Urban Affairs and a federally funded program of the Board of Education, the Teaching of Teacher Trainers,) and the Conference on Ethnic Communities of Greater Detroit are good examples of Wayne's growing concern to fulfill this obligation.

Throughout our history project, my fellow researchers and I have given special attention to the treatment of the various major ethnic groups of this nation—and especially those of Detroit—in the adopted textbooks, teacher manuals, and in the classroom. Also, by means of a questionnaire and interviews, we have attempted to determine teacher and student attitudes toward the problem of ethnicity as a factor in the educational process. While our main emphasis has naturally been on history we have taken a look at other subjects as well.

What I would like to do is to give a brief report on our findings, assess the problems and pressures within the Detroit educational system as they relate to ethnicity, and to present a proposal for a new approach to the teaching of American history on the secondary level which may serve the triple function of enhancing the student's sense of identity, decreasing racial and ethnic polarization within American society, and—a little self-interest is never out of order—increase the student's interest in history (which at present, according to our findings, is very low indeed: "who wants to learn about dead people").

First of all, let me clarify a key matter. Ethnic consciousness is currently most prevalent among black people, American Indians, Mexican-Americans, and Puerto-Rican Americans. It is natural therefore that secondary school teachers and administrators should conceive of ethnic history and ethnicity in general largely in terms of these groups. Our investigation of textbook criteria, the examination of texts themselves, our teacher questionnaire and interviews all bear this out. Personally, I would say that such a focus seems legitimate given the social context of America today. Clearly, every effort to show the real role of these groups in American history, to demonstrate the injustices perpetrated against them, and to adjust curriculum and teaching methods to a framework appropriate to their cultural background should be applauded.

199

Yet such a focus—if limited exclusively to these groups—fails to take into account the reality of ethnicity as a factor in the lives of many other national, racial or religious minorities in this country and the stigma of prejudice which many of them still suffer. The Polish joke is, after all, a degrading, racist slur. The term "hillbilly" creates a stereotypical image of oafishness and stupidity which television continues to perpetrate. Synagogues are still bombed and Jews often remain stigmatized as the *only* slum-lords, the *only* pawnbrokers, or inner-city grocers. The Oriental, especially on the west coast, has not been freed from the paranoic stereotyping which, thirty years ago, caused Earl Warren to defend and Franklin Roosevelt to sanction the imprisonment of California Japanese-Americans in concentration camps. Even more assimilated groups such as the Italians, face popular imagry which mocks their accent, expects arm-waving volatility, and suspects all of them of Mafia connections.

So, in defining "ethnic groups" and "ethnic history" I am talking about any element which identifies itself or is identified by the larger society (or both) on the basis of characteristics rooted in race, religion, or national origin. I also see a legitimacy in paying more attention to some groups than others, because of their sheer numbers, because of their relatively higher degree of ethnic consciousness, or because of their oppressed condition within American society, currently or historically.

This said, let me first report the major findings of our secondary school history project. The most important data for this discussion derived from question #22 on a questionnaire distributed to all history teachers in the secondary school system of Detroit. It reads: "Do you feel that a greater emphasis on ethnic history is desirable? Please comment." On a simple raw score basis, city-wide, the answer was overwhelmingly "yes." Out of 185 specific answers (a minority either did not answer or equivocated) there were 135 yesses and 50 noes. This in and of itself is not very helpful because both positive and negative responses were usually qualified. No question evoked more comment and it is through the comments that we can get a fairly clear idea of the attitude of teachers toward ethnic history. Although it is difficult to make a statistical assessment of subject comment without using content analysis methods I would say that possibly two-thirds of the affirmative respondents (and probably a fair number of those who gave qualified noes) would agree with this remark by an American history teacher at MacKenzie High School (which is currently about 90 percent black).

Yes. Black students whom I teach are interested in knowing more about what blacks have done in American history. Many resent the paucity of attention their textbook gives to this matter. I feel that there should be an effort to teach integrated history in which activities of *all* racial and ethnic groups are given proper credit. I do not wish to teach American history as exclusively black or white oriented—nor do I wish to sacrifice objectivity toward these goals. Yet, more black awareness should be incorporated to maximize the effectiveness of teaching in situations similar to mine.

There are five basic elements in this statement which must be stressed: (1) The institutional neglect of black people in American history; (2) The need to recognize that black people as an ethnic group are not, however, alone in this neglect; (3) The need to maintain objectivity in incorporating more ethnic emphasis; (4) The importance of nevertheless giving greater stress to the history of the group or groups which constitute sizable portions of a particular student body; and (5) The preference for *integrating* ethnic history into general history presumably rather than putting such stress on separate ethnic courses. Currently, only the first of these points is beyond controversy although school boards are, as we shall see, making efforts to rectify this neglect of the black man in American history. The problems and differences of opinion raised by the other four points are quite serious and were reflected in the questionnaires.

Number 2 is perhaps of the greatest interest. The question is this: To what extent is it desirable to give attention to the history and accomplishments of ethnic groups other than blacks: Among our negative answers, their dominant reasons for *de*-emphasizing ethnic history (presumably of others as well as black) was the divisiveness of an ethnic orientation. Typical answers were these: "No. It tends to point up differences rather than unifying people. History should not be separated into fragments." or "No. Emphasis on ethnicity is as bad as emphasis on nationalism" (both from Redford High School). Thus these people would not only reduce the current focus on Afro-American history, but avoid the history of other ethnic groups as well. But there were also serious objections from the other side of the coin. Said one teacher at Jefferson Junior High School: "This depends on whose 'eth' you're talking about. The 'melting pot' theory should be taught but I would not like to see special emphasis given any specific ethnic groups except Blacks. Only Black people, *because of their Blackness*, have been of monumental significance in the formation of American (Western) society. If Poles or Italians or Jews (etc.) want to train their children in their own history, that is a matter of parochial interest. None of them, *because of their ethnic identity only*, has so shaped history as the Black man." Another point of view does not recognize the historical slighting of other groups (this from Cooley): "Yes. Only black history—and that because of immediate circumstances and to correct past omissions."

These points of view represent the extremes. The usual positive response on this issue was in fairly close agreement with the teacher from MacKenzie. It is true that the first extreme was more likely to be found in all-white schools—especially those, like Redford, where the school population is heavily middle-class—while the second normally came from inner-city schools. There were also some differences within the majority view on including other ethnic groups. Many teachers from largely white schools made their positive answers *contingent* upon the inclusion of white ethnic elements along with blacks, Spanish-Americans, etc., while on the other hand responses from black schools, if they raised the issue, merely *recommended* the broader ethnic scope. Perhaps the most interesting responses on this score were those of the teachers of

Afro-American history. Possibly because they are deeply immersed in the concept of identity-building through an ethnic emphasis, they often raised the question of other ethnic groups. Thus a teacher of Afro-American history at Pershing remarked:

Right now we are concentrating on one ethnic group—the black. Greater emphasis could be given to the American Indian, the immigrants from Southern and Eastern Europe, and the Asiatic American. This would promote greater toleration and understanding.

Or the Afro-American teacher at Central: "Yes. Emphasis on ethnic contributions foster a greater understanding among all students with varied backgrounds." Perhaps the best brief statement on this question came from an inner-city Junior High teacher of world history: "I think the students should know about the contributions of various ethnic groups. Then maybe they will understand that this country belongs to all of us."

A final interesting note. Several teachers in largely white schools stressed the need for ethnic history in order to enlighten their students on the cultural variants which go into the making of America. A Denby response: "This is an important subject. It may help the ignorant student to know other people—background, history, customs, traditions, and morality." From Redford, a school without a significant "ethnic" student population: "Yes. Too many of our students are unfamiliar with the history of various minorities and their problems."

In summary, it would seem that a majority of the secondary school teachers surveyed welcome not only a greater emphasis on black history, but an expansion of programs to focus on the history of other prominent ethnic minorities as well. This is clearly the most significant finding of our project as it relates to the issue of ethnicity.

The other three points raised by our "typical" response from MacKenzie can be dealt with more rapidly—in part, because they are all interconnected. The question of objectivity is clearly an important one. The goal of education is the discovery of truths, no matter how painful they might be. It is evident that history—and most other subjects as well—has been taught in the past with a white, Anglo-Saxon, middle class bias and therefore was *un*-truthful as regards the culturally different (not "disadvantaged"!) ethnic minorities of this nation. The balance must be redressed. But there is the danger, especially in history, of emphasizing the role of various groups to such an extent that the students' vision of the past is greatly distorted. This potentiality was raised by several teachers in our questionnaire, especially those with longer experience teaching in predominantly white schools. *On the other hand*, many teachers thought it necessary to give greater attention to the history of particular groups which predominated in the student population.

Is it really possible to maintain objectivity if one is "playing to" a particular audience? Many of those involved with the history profession, especially on the college level, would say no. They regard Afro-American history, for instance, as a kind of betrayal of objectivity or at best a "fad" which has developed only because of popular pressure without any real historical justification. This view was reflected by a few teachers in their questionnaires and by a couple of those whom we have interviewed. Yet perhaps there is a way out of this apparent dilemma and this is where our fourth controversial point enters the scene: this is the question of an "integrated" American history course versus separate ethnic history courses.

We have already noted that a majority of the teachers in the schools would wish to include study of other important ethnic groups in the school curriculum. There also exists the overwhelming sentiment for developing an approach which incorporates the ethnic emphasis *within* the regular required American history sequence. Afro-American history teachers, if they mentioned this issue, gave full sanction to this idea. One, teaching at an inner-city high school, even went so far as to say:

[Separate] ethnic history is needed *for the moment*. In the long run—hopefully—the contributions and role of minority groups will be incorporated into high school survey courses in American and World history.

This might be done on a fully objective basis in which various groups are represented in relationship to their true role in American history. Yet what about the other desire: to give *more* attention than might actually be warranted on the basis of objectivity to a dominant ethnic group (or groups) within a particular school? It would seem to be the case that the only solution to this is to offer (and continue to offer) separate ethnic history and culture courses *in addition to* the "integrated" survey courses. One teacher at Southeastern put the matter well in responding to the desirability of greater ethnic emphasis:

This depends upon the student body. Where there appears to be a desire on the part of the student body and the community for in-depth studies of ethnic history, it should be provided. Staff members should be alert to the needs.

Thus it would appear that: (1) a greater emphasis on ethnic history in general is deemed desirable by a majority of the history teachers responding to our survey; (2) this should definitely be incorporated into the secondary school survey courses on the basis of thoughtful objectivity; (3) in order to satisfy community and individual need, separate ethnic history courses should be offered for purposes of enhancing pride and identity and to make the student enthusiastic about the importance of the study of the past—indeed about the social sciences and humanities in general.

But what are the secondary students in Detroit presently learning? As we will note in a minute, the School Board is currently trying to meet some of the desires outlined above. We all know that black history courses, since the Rebellion of 1967, have been developed in a majority of the public schools of Detroit, and that Latin American history has been introduced in schools where it is relevant. Much supplemental reading in minority history is supplied for the survey courses. Yet only next year will the 1964 Teacher Manual for eleventh grade American history be thrown out and a revised edition supplied. Thus, in this required survey course, teachers have been presented a list of 68 "Personalities to stress" in American History II. Of these, three are black (Booker T. Washington, W.E.B. DuBois, and Martin Luther King, Jr.), two are Jewish (Samuel Gompers and Albert Einstein), two are either immigrants or second generation (Gompers again and Walter Reuther), and four—all Irish—are of recognizable "ethnic" stock (John and Robert Kennedy, Joe McCarthy, and Robert McNamara). Besides the gross under-representation these figures represent for the groups involved, there is not a single Mexican-American, not a single Oriental, not a single person of Southern- or East-European extraction! The revised edition has expanded the list—but only to include many more blacks.

The general textbooks have not been much better. A majority of teachers in our survey did not feel that the texts in world and American history related to their students' backgrounds sufficiently. And these are the *revised* editions. A recent detailed article by a California historian, Mark Krug, appearing in the *School Review*, underlined the fact that the major American history texts (including those adopted for use in Detroit) remain woefully inadequate with regard to minority history. My own team corroborates this view. For instance, Todd and Curti, one of the two adopted eleventh grade texts, after noting the 1619 arrival of some black indentured servants and then Crispus Attacks, does not mention black people again until page 302 in the discussion of the background to the Civil War. According to this book, therefore, the slave trade and its evils as well the fantastically important role of African labor in creating agricultural and commercial profits in the eighteenth century are figments of someone's imagination. It is better in the post-Civil War period, but the focus plays down conflict and stresses the "Negroes' progress" toward integration. The removal and veritable extermination of large groups of Indians receives little mention. Other ethnic minorities and the problems and consequences of immigration receive scant treatment, although a certain moral outrage is manifested against the discriminatory quota systa established by 1924 (p. 637). Wade, Wilder, and Wade does a somewhat better job but still fails to do justice to any important ethnic group.

A new ninth grade world history text recently adopted makes a remarkably better effort than the older one to view world history as something more than the history of Western civilization. The African section—though last in the book—is long and well done, as is that on Latin America. Lacking significantly, however, is much attention to the history of Eastern and Southern Europe, although Russia gets a section by itself. Whatever its merits, this book, called *Man's Cultural Heritage*, has one grave shortcoming: its reading level is geared to middle class standards and thus the wonderful coverage may well be lost on many of Detroit's students from ethnic groups whose family and educational background have not provided the bases to read it fruitfully. As a reviewer on our team noted, this is a rather clear form of "institutional racism."

There are two rays of light in the current approach to ethnic history in the schools, however. The first is a new textbook which will be adopted next year for the seventh grade U.S. history course called *American History for Today*, written by the Oakland (California) Social Studies Supervisor and a college Afro-American history professor. It is oriented toward current problems, attempting to trace their historical roots. The treatment of the role of the Indian, black man, and Spanish-American in American history is full and accurate. The cruelty suffered by these groups at the hand of the dominant majority is not minimized; in general, struggle and conflict are seen as a part of American life. There is none of the amoral, "concensus" orientation which marks almost all other texts. The adolescent who will read this book will therefore not be so inclined to think that the problems and conflicts in American society today began only the day before yesterday. Or what is worse, think, because of his own daily experience, that history is largely irrelevant to life—or simply one big lie. Immigration and the problems of immigrants are treated realistically, and one section compares the transatlantic movement of black slaves and European immigrants, noting the great suffering for each, while at the same time, of course, the involuntary nature of the transportation of the former. The only shortcoming, perhaps, is the fairly brief treatment of immigrant European ethnic groups after they arrived and the failure to emphasize fully important leaders from these groups.

The second ray of light is a one-semester course developed at Chadsey High School called "Our American Heritage" taught by Land Moore. Not specifically a history course, this elective, which drew nearly 100 students in three sections the first time it was taught this past semester, examines the cultures of the main ethnic groups of Detroit; because Chadsey is largely made up of blacks and students of Polish and Ukrainian working class background, *these* inheritances received the most attention. Mr. Moore was not entirely pleased with the way the course went this semester, but upon interviewing him it became clear that he was being a bit hard on himself. The major focus was to compare cultures, and he found that discussions and presentations of music and food were among the best vehicles to stimulate interest. The students also seemed fascinated by the comparison of the problems of black people today (most of the black children are second generation migrants from the South) and those of the East European immigrants fifty years ago, as well as more recently. One possibly negative finding, however: the Polish children by and large seemed uninterested in their own cultural heritage—indeed a bit ashamed of it. They appeared to be more interested in black culture than their own. Overall, this course, while one should not over-romanticize it, would appear to be a vital first step toward the creative use of ethnic history as a means of decreasing polarization and establishing a more certain self-identity among our high school students.

To sum up: what our children have actually learned up to this point in time is largely that American history is *white, Anglo-Saxon* American history. Black studies are making their way, but the required survey courses, especially given the texts and the current teacher manuals, maintain the myth of the melting pot, the image of peaceful, homogeneous progress, and do not adequately recognize the diversity of American pluralist society. Yet the will to develop greater realism appears to be growing in the Social Studies Department of the Detroit Board. Teachers seem to be still more advanced in their thinking and their pressure, along with that of the communities of Detroit, should assure the resolution of many of the institutional inadequacies which presently exist.

A final note on this subject: social studies naturally deal more directly with the problems of ethnic underrepresentation. The required literature materials used in the schools, which I have examined in a rather cursory fashion, seem to be further behind. Except for one optional general text, all the major literature books are almost entirely limited to the presentation of Western literature (in the narrowest sense) and emphasize unstintingly Anglo-Saxon, middle class values.

In conclusion, I would like to leave you with some suggestions for a reformed program—which means, of course, new textbooks—for the teaching of American history survey courses in the secondary schools. What I say here appears to be in line with the desires of a majority of the teachers of history in Detroit. It is also very much in accord with a recent paper presented by our superintendent, Dr. Norman Drachler, on the "Shortcomings of American Textbooks." Emphasizing the cultural diversity of America and giving attention not only to the black man but also all our principal ethnic groups, he summarized his position as follows:

My plea is that we re-examine our texts and our history—not to distort the truth or to conceal shortcomings—but to re-evaluate the question, 'Who is an American—and what is an American deed?' If we do that, then I am certain that more children in our urban schools will achieve, through the texts, a sense of identity with our nation—and a feeling or worthiness and dignity so essential to learning.

My proposal is simple enough and runs as follows:

1. That the general approach in the survey course be such that it might be entitled: "The Peoples of America: the Making of a Nation." This means a much greater stress on the role of ethnic groups in American history and a recognition of the obvious fact of ethnicity in American life. The myth of the melting pot is just that, and kids know it because of their day-to-day experience. What should be stressed instead are the common problems and the common goals which various ethnic groups have shared historically, even though these problems and goals may have emerged at different times. Thus, for example, the initial struggle with the realities of urban life in America and the cultural exclusivism which grew out of it among Polish immigrants in the teens, twenties, and thirties, should be compared with the same process developing among black people today. This would obviously help in the growth of intergroup toleration and understanding. Another example: it should also be known that there were lots of Irish, Polish, and Italian "radicals" in earlier years of American history.

2. To understand the "peoples of America" special emphasis should be given to the common folk among them—these are the *real* people after all. Leaders and important contributors to American development should of course be mentioned, but real history is in the work-a-day world, the styles of life, and the cultural framework of the entire group. Thus the ideal textbook would have a social and cultural history orientation.

3. The course should not minimize conflict. It is simply a part of the American reality. But it should try to explain the roots of conflict, and how it has been, and can be, resolved. In discussing inter-*ethnic* groups conflict it seems mandatory to demonstrate the real social, economic, and chronological bases of such conflict and above all, show how the very ethnic groups which have had so much intergroup strife are the very ones who have been mutually the most oppressed by the larger society.

4. Another key point: the most successful secondary school teachers at the present time seem to be those who have a good grasp of local Detroit history. This brings history home to the students—they often already know the names, the organizations, the streets. It seems to me that one of the major tasks of the school board is to provide plenty of supplementary material on local history. And here Wayne State University can help immensely, for we have two of the most knowledgeable historians in the country on the history of Detroit, and the Labor History Archives has a vast amount of material—including films and recordings—which could go into making an excellent package for the schools. The history of the peoples of America as illustrated through local history ought to have a great appeal.

5. This raises a final point. Detroit, besides being an "ethnic" city, is also a working class city. It would appear that, in line with the earlier suggestions, a greater focus on labor history—national and local—is highly desirable. And this hardly violates the canons of objectivity, given the immense role of the laboring man in American history. Such an emphasis would also provide the average Detroit student with *another* source of identity beyond the ethnic and give him a sense of the *mutual* relationship which he has with members of other ethnic groups.

This program is obviously only a rough and sketchy outline. But it seems to me that it would perform the role—if well conceived and carefully articulated—of serving the three functions outlined earlier; the enhancement of identity; the reduction, of polarization through a realistic understanding of the nature of ethnic pluralism in America as modified by stress on those *common* elements which cross ethnic lines; and finally a greater appreciation of the past which will assist the student to place himself firmly in the present.

16 Church History and Ethnicity in Detroit

Dan Finley

On Saint Anne's Day, July 24, 1701, Cadillac's arrival at what is now downtown Detroit marked the beginning of the history of the white settlers in Detroit. Heading a predominantly French Catholic expedition (one Italian captain is mentioned), one of his first acts was the establishment of the St. Anne's Church. During the French domination, at least four church buildings for use by the Church of St. Anne's were erected to replace previous buildings, which were either too small or burned down.

1701 erected
1703 burned & replaced
1709 replaced
1712 burned—1723 erected
1755 replaced because of smallness
1805 fire—1818 cornerstone laid—
1828 completed and first used

For over a hundred years, no other parish of any denomination was established. Although the English gained possession of Detroit in 1760, the area remained predominantly French much after that. Cadillac had come to establish a fort for two reasons: (1) to advance the lucrative fur trade, and (2) to establish a rudimentary military post out of respect for the English activity on the Atlantic coast. Neither of these purposes necessitated the growth or establishment of a city. The area was permeated with farmers and trappers with the barest of town-life adornments for the entire 18th century. The fact that in 1770 there was a Canadian population of 150,000 adult male Catholics and only 360 adult male Protestants (less than 2%) presents strong and uncontradicted evidence of the Catholic-Protestant ratio and reflects the Detroit ratio at that time.[1] During the political shuffling between Britain and the United States from 1760 to 1813, when Detroit became an American possession permanently, Detroit retained this ratio. In 1820, the population of Detroit was only 2,222.[2] In 1805 a fire leveled Detroit. The difficulty encountered by Father Richard when he petitioned the governor and judges for a grant of land for a place to rebuild the Church of St. Anne's is the first manifestation of the diminishing homogeneity of Detroit and the resulting ethnic tensions. Jefferson Avenue was laid through the cemetery ground, and the church was somewhat uncooperative

209

in the rebuilding and expanding of Detroit. But finally the church moved their dead, and a cornerstone for a new church was laid in 1818. Places of worship in the surrounding farmland, a tent and later a warehouse, variously served in the interim. An advertisement in the Gazette in 1820 reflected the Church of St. Anne's desire to remain the sole religious pillar of the community in what were then changing times.

A short address, explanatory of the ceremony, will be delivered at half-past four. Christians of all denominations are welcome. It is expected, however, that they will conform to all rules observed by Catholics on such occasions by standing, walking and kneeling. The military on duty only may remain covered.

The general reverence afforded to men of the church was not in great strength. Father Richard excommunicated a member for marrying a second time. The member sued for $1,116 injuries. Father Richard ended up in jail and was bailed out by three well-to-do Frenchmen.

In 1827, Detroit was still principally French, with only one German in all of Michigan.[3] But changes had already begun. In 1820, a meeting was held to determine a site and to receive subscriptions for a Methodist Episcopal Church, and in 1821, a society was organized.

The articles of incorporation bear the signatures and approval of A.B. Woodward and James Witherell, judges; Charles Larned, Attorney General; and Lewis Cass, Governor of the Territory. The society was thus doubly legalized, for it was not only duly organized under the Act, but the articles received the specific and written endorsement of the governor and two of the three judges; and as the governor and judges then possessed legislative powers, the articles had almost the force of a special enactment.[4]

The governor and judges also were quick in granting land. Earlier, in 1816, a Protestant minister, John Monteith, came to Detroit and "preached regularly every Sabbath in the Council House, except that on every third Sabbath in the evening the services were conducted by a Methodist minister." In 1817, "the First Evangelistic Society of Detroit was organized with the object of sustaining the services."

Excerpt from an address to the above Society, Published in the Gazette.

First Evangelic Church of Detroit—On the morning of the 23rd inst. an assembly was held at the Council House in this city for the purpose of establishing a Protestant religious society there being no Protestant Church yet established in this Territory. One of the judges of the Territory addressed the assembly and deduced the origin of the word Protestant from the publication on the Church door of Wittemberg, on the 31st day of October, 1517, of the theses of Luther, containing ninety-five propositions against indulgences; and the subsequent protest and union of certain potentates of Germany, published on the 10th day of April, 1529. He then stated the events connected with the Centennial anniversary of October the 31st, 1817, and the resolutions to reduce the

Protestant sects into one general denomination under the name Evangelic. He read parts of the decree signed by the Minister of the Interior at Berlin on the 3rd day of June, 1817; reducing the Protestant sects into one denomination; and assigning the reasons for abolishing the term Protestant and substituting the term Evangelic. After some further explanations it was successively resolved to adopt the term Evangelic in lieu of the term Protestant or any less general Sectarian denomination, to designate the first religious society established within the Territory of Michigan, of a persuasion different from that of the Roman Catholic.

The following edition contained these two articles:

The notice contained in our last number respecting the establishment of a Church we found to be incorrect. We published it only according to the information we received, supposing that although there had been for a long time regular worship in this city, there probably was nothing before that could be called a church. In this, however, our informant was mistaken. No organization of the Society took place on the specified day.

The First Protestant Church in the Territory of Michigan was erected at the River Rouge on the 31st ultimo by a society of Methodists, a body corporate belonging to the Episcopal Church in the United States. The said society was established at the River Rouge in the year 1810, and, through the storms of war and various other trials and by the Divine blessing is still in a prosperous way.

The above items taken from Silas Farmer illustrate the apparent rivalry between the church supported by the First Evangelistic Society of Detroit (which took the name First Presbyterian Church in 1825) and the Methodist Church.

The First Evangelistic Society of Detroit first wanted to replace St. Anne's as the central church of the community as especially indicated by the choice of the word Evangelistic. In 1820:

The society was still composed of Episcopalians, Presbyterians, Methodists, Congregationalists, and persons holding no particular creed; and it was perhaps in deference to the Episcopalians or Methodists that Mr. Monteith received the appellation of 'Bishop' in the notice. The Presbyterians were conciliated by the ordaining of three elders, Messrs. J.J. Deming, Levi Brown, and Lemuel Shattuck; and as all pew-holders, or those who paid $5.00 a year, had a right to vote on questions connected with the society, the Congregationalists must have been satisfied.[5]

Neither church retained central control. St. Paul's Episcopal Church was established in 1824, claiming 300 members. Bishop Monteith's church, which had started with 400 members in 1818, apparently almost all of them non-catholics, had only 39 members in 1825. The Methodist Episcopal Church claimed the rest of the non-Catholics. In 1812 it had 175 members; in 1829, only 78 members. According to Silas Farmer, St. Paul's was the "Fashionable church of the palace . . . favored by the city government."

In 1833, the population had reached 3,000.[6] St. Anne's was giving mass in French, English, and German. These German Catholics became the parish for St. Mary's, which was consecrated in 1843. The early German Protestants formed the parish for St. John's German Evangelical Church.

By 1837, all but 125 names in the city directory of 1,355 adult males (6,775 population) were non-Gallic. These 125 French names represented 625 people. Somewhere in the diocese were 20,000-24,000 Catholics, among them 3,000 Indian, 8,000 English, Irish, American, and German.[7] The remaining 9,000-13,000 French were scattered away from the cities and towns. The English, Irish, and American Catholic population in Detroit was large enough to warrant the purchase of Holy Trinity Church from the First Protestant Society in 1834. It was later moved to its present site on Sixth and Porter, and a brick building was erected in 1856.[8] The list of churches in 1837 reads as follows:

> German Lutheran (first service in 1837)
> St. Anne's Roman Catholic
> Holy Trinity Roman Catholic
> Methodist Episcopal
> St. Paul's Episcopal
> Baptist
> 1st Presbyterian (1st Protestant Society)
> An "African" Methodist

In 1840, despite national financial chaos resulting from the suspension of specie payment by President Jackson, the population had grown to 9,114.[9] The Irish began immigrating heavily in this "Black Decade." Some had already come indirectly from France and Canada. As early as 1808, St. Patrick's Day was celebrated. In 1813 a religious document written in ancient Gaelic was found in Detroit. But no church central to the Irish community was built. In 1844, well over half of the 10,948 population was Catholic. There were eleven church organizations, plus a colored Methodist and a colored Baptist.[10] The new churches were Saints Peter and Paul (Roman Catholic), St. Mary's (German Roman Catholic), St. John's (German Evangelic), and the First Congregation, newly established that year. An address to the First Congregational Quarter Centennial celebration referred to the "aristocratic proprietors of the Episcopal and Presbyterian Churches" in 1844 and to the earlier establishment of Protestant religious societies as such.

At this time (1844) a majority of the population of Detroit was Catholic, numbering probably from 6,000 to 7,000. The oldest, most numerous, and wealthy, Protestant organization was the First Presbyterian Church, or as its corporate name was, the First Protestant Society. This society was informally organized in August, 1816, and the Rev. John Monteith, who reached here the June preceding became its minister. In 1818, a church was organized Presbyterial in its character, but not Presbyterian and nearly the entire Protestant population for a time joined its support . . . membership about 400.[11]

Thus the many Protestant religions started in Detroit simultaneously with the beginning of rapid population growth and large scale ethnic immigration. The Germans were the first minority group to immigrate. The Irish came too, but melded into the general population. The Germans preserved themselves in communities, especially on the near east side, along Gratiot and Monroe Avenues. Detroit was becoming a city. Fourth, Dequindre, the river, and a French farm three miles from the river formed the city limits. Within these limits, there were only 65 streets, none paved, with Woodbridge being the longest. The French moved up and down the river, away from the city. Symbolically, Detroit, was bordered on two of her three sides by French farms.

The Poles began their immigration in the 1860s. By 1870, the Polish community was large enough to establish a church, St. Albertus, on land donated by the French St. Aubin family. The Germans were twice as many as the Irish. The Poles, Hungarians, and Belgians were about equal in number, with the Norwegians being more numerous than any of these three, but not as numerous as the Irish.[12]

The figures for the population growth of Detroit are as follows:

```
1876— 79,577
1891—205,000
1900—285,704
1910—475,766 (33.6% foreign born; booming Stove, Drug, and Auto
                industries supporting the immigration)
1914—526,000
```

The percentage of foreign born had fallen from 33.6 percent in 1910 to 25 percent in 1930. The tremendous expansion of the three industries mentioned above attracted most of the immigrants, the majority of whom were Polish.

This excerpt from an editorial in the August 25, 1910, Free Press describes a prevalent sentiment towards this immigration.

The Extinction of a Race
According to a recent dispatch from Washington, census officials say the rate of increase of the native born people of this country has fallen in 10 years from 21 to 6 percent. They prophesy that by the time another national census is taken, this native population will probably show an actual falling off. In other words, we must depend upon immigration for future numerical growth.

If the report is correct, the condition is a grave one, more grave than the problem that confronts France. France must maintain itself against armed forces; but we must maintain ourselves and our traditions against immigrating hordes that come to steal away our very national individuality. The reasons for the existing state of things are too obvious to need discussion. Irrational growth of cities, increasing love of luxury, increasing wealth, increasing frivolity, are some of the principle ones.

If our immigrants were still coming largely from Great Britain, Germany, France, Norway, Sweden, or even from Poland, the situation would be less threatening, for in that case we would be welcoming the blood kin of the founders of the nation, people who hold essentially the same ideals with them and with us. But as everyone knows, our new immigrants are not of this character. Even today the process of digestion and assimilation is becoming increasingly difficult. If that portion of the population upon which depends the important work of instruction, actually shrinks, what will be the end?

How soon will the immigrant begin to force his ideals on us? There is apparently some reason in the voice of the alarmist who says that the American people of the future will not be as the American people of the present.

The prospect is not a bright one for those who love American ideals and American institutions. There are two ways in which to change conditions. One is to conserve and increase the native population. The other is to let it die out and allow the Asiatics and the people of Southern Europe to found their own empire here. The choice must be made very soon. It is a matter that concerns the welfare of the rising generation.

The two maps (in the Appendix) showing ethnic distribution in 1900 and 1927 reflect two basic trends in immigration to Detroit. From 1830 to 1900, Germans immigrated steady and established themselves in communities, especially along Gratiot Avenue. They retained many of their old customs and established a multitude of churches. One early newspaper even described this part of Gratiot Avenue as more German than any avenue in Berlin. The Irish came too but did not establish such strong communities. Perhaps their similarities with the English-American residents provided for their easy assimilation into the general population. Whatever the case may be, the Germans built many churches to function in their various communities, while the Irish did not. No other group immigrated in such a way as to establish such integral communities until the Polish began immigrating in 1860. The organization and erection of St. Albertus Church manifests the establishment of such a community. Subsequent Polish immigration warranted the erection of several large churches, among them Sweetest Heart, St. Josaphats, St. Catherine, St. John's, St. Stanislaus, plus the churches needed to serve the Polish communities located near Michigan and Junction. The second trend in immigration was precipitated by the rapid growth of demand for unskilled and semiskilled. Such demand did not attract integral communities, accounting for the resulting paucity of church buildings.

With this in mind, I limit my architectural concern to the following churches:

St. Anne's Roman Catholic Church	French
St. Paul's Episcopal Church	Protestant
First Presbyterian Church	Protestant
First Central Methodist Episcopal Church	Protestant
St. Mary's Roman Catholic Church	German
St. Joseph's Roman Catholic Church	German
St. Albertus Roman Catholic Church	Polish
St. John's Roman Catholic Church	Polish

First Congregational Church	Protestant
Christ Episcopal Church	Protestant
St. John's Episcopal Church	Protestant
Fort Street Presbyterian Church	Protestant
St. Josaphat's Roman Catholic Church	Polish

Notes

1. Silas Farmer, *History of Detroit*, Vol. 1, General.
2. Detroit Free Press, December 9, 1869.
3. Palmer Scrapbook, Volume 2, P. 176.
4. Farmer, *History of Detroit*.
5. Ibid.
6. Palmer Scrapbook.
7. Detroit Free Press, December 9, 1869.
8. "Detroit in 1837," series of articles in Detroit News-Tribune, September 15, 1895.
9. Detroit Free Press, December 9, 1869.
10. Ibid.
11. Ibid.
12. Detroit Saturday Night, August 7, 1926, P. 12.

Other Sources

Burton Scrapbook, Vol. 76, P. 161-2. Vol. 11, P. 194-5. Vol. 68, P. 152-3.
Detroit Saturday Night, April 3, 1926.
Detroit Post, February 25, 1877, P. 4.
Detroit Daily Advertiser, Monday, Oct. 8, 1855.
Detroit Free Press, May 27, 1850; Feb. 24, 1852; Feb. 2, 1859; Jan 22, 1860; Dec. 9, 1869; March 19, 1893; May 2, 1898; March 1, 1910; May 21, 1911.
Michigan Historical Magazine, Vol. 23, "Spring," 1937.
Palmer Scrapbook, Volume 2, P. 176-177.

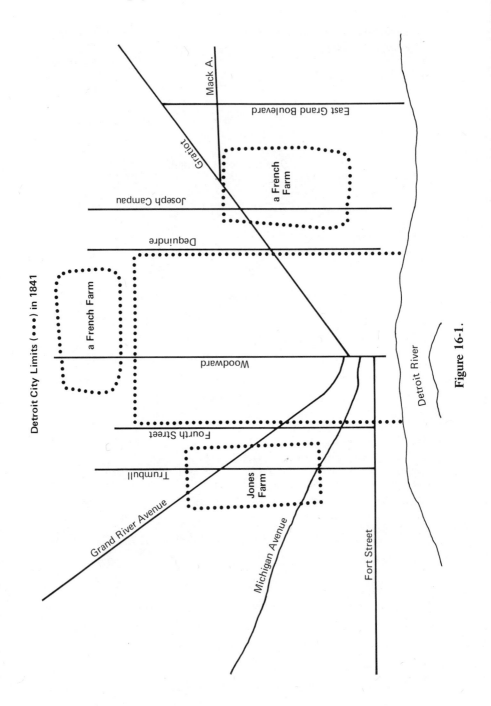

Figure 16-1.

217

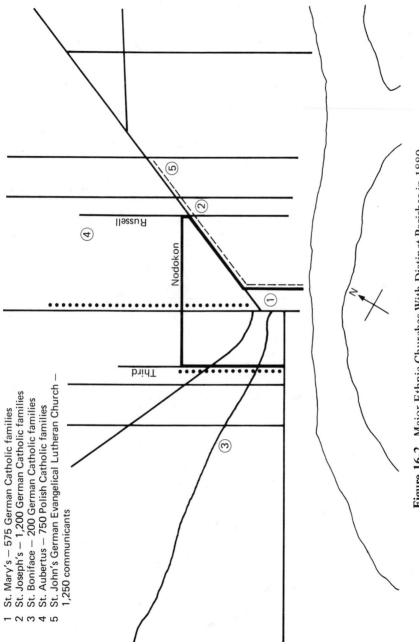

1 St. Mary's — 575 German Catholic families
2 St. Joseph's — 1,200 German Catholic families
3 St. Boniface — 200 German Catholic families
4 St. Aubertus — 750 Polish Catholic families
5 St. John's German Evangelical Lutheran Church — 1,250 communicants

Figure 16-2. Major Ethnic Churches With Distinct Parishes in 1880.

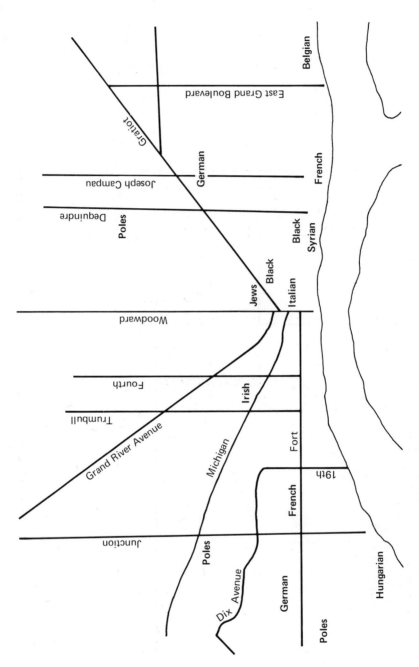

Figure 16-3. Ethnic Distribution in 1900. Source: *Burton Scrapbook.* Vol. 76, pp. 161–162.

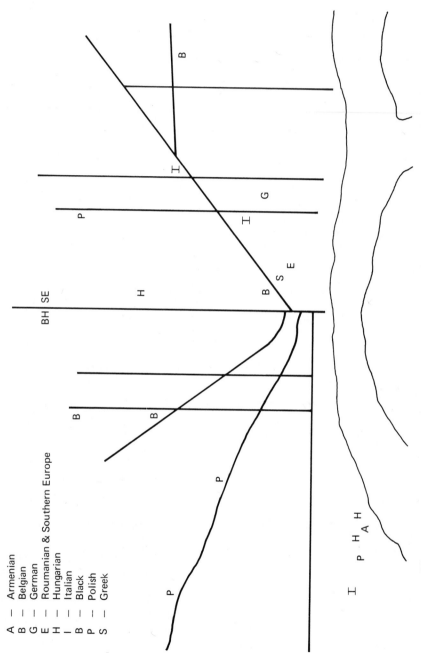

A — Armenian
B — Belgian
G — German
E — Roumanian & Southern Europe
H — Hungarian
I — Italian
B — Black
P — Polish
S — Greek

Figure 16-4. Ethnic Communities in 1927. Source: *The Detroit Night*, August 7, 1927.

Table 16-1
Early Protestant Churches—Membership

First Protestant Society
(First Presbyterian Church)

1825	39
1837	102
1844	400
1850	448
1860	300
1870	368
1880	753

St. Paul's

1824	300
1830	40
1840	291
1850	250
1860	265
1870	296
1880	448

Methodist Episcopal

1829	78
1844	280
1850	198
1860	270

Congress Street Methodist

1844	60
1850	150
1860	180

(Methodist Church & Congress
Street Methodist united in
1864 forming):

Central Methodist Episcopal

1870	600
1880	769

Baptist

1827	150

Scottish

1844	65
1850	300
1860	350
1870	350
1880	292

Fort Street Presbyterian

1849	26
1850	62
1860	196
1870	282
1880	686

First Congregational

1850	166
1860	355
1870	279
1880	516

Second Congregational

1863	110

Christ Protestant Episcopal

1850	14
1860	149
1870	399
1880	500

St. John's Episcopal

1880	700

St. John's German Lutheran

1844	200

Table 16-2
Number and Names of Churches Mid-19th Century

1832	1859
St. Anne's Roman Catholic	38 Churches (33 have buildings)
St. Paul's Episcopal	9 Scottish
First Presbyterian	7 aggregate Presbyterian
Methodist Episcopal	2 Kirk of Scotland, Associate
	8 Methodist Episcopal
1837	1 French
St. Anne's Roman Catholic	1 German
St. Paul's Episcopal	1 Black
First Presbyterian	1 was the Woodward
Methodist Episcopal	6 Protestant Episcopal
Holy Trinity Roman Catholic	St. Paul's (1824)
Baptists	Mariner's
German Lutheran	St. John's
Black Methodist	5 Catholic
	Sts. Peter and Paul
1846	St. Anne's (French)
16 Churches	St. Mary's (German)
4 Catholic	St. Joseph (German)
3 Methodist	Trinity (English, Irish &
2 Episcopal	American Catholic)
2 Baptist	4 Baptists
1 Presbyterian	3 Lutheran
1 Scotch Presbyterian	1 Congregationalist
1 Congregationalist	1 Union
1 German Lutheran	1 Unitarian
The Sailor's Bethels	(1 New Jerusalem)
	(1 Christian)
1850	
20 Church buildings	
10 places of worship	

Table 16-3
Early German Churches

St. John's German Evangelical Church—Monroe Avenue moved out Gratiot Avenue later		
services held in carpentry shop centrally located in 1833	1840 –	175 c
building built 1837	1850 –	375 c
	1860 –	638
	1872 –	1,550
	1880 –	1,250
St. Mary's Roman Catholic Church—Monroe Avenue		
service in St. Anne's 1833	1880 –	575 f
consecrated 1843		2,900
First German Church (Methodist Episcopal)—Monroe Avenue		
1847(org.)	1850 –	48 m
1851	1860 –	78
	1870 –	100
Second German Church (Methodist Episcopal)—16th & Michigan		
1857(org.)	1880 –	100 Av. Att.
1858		
St. Anthony's Roman Catholic Church—Gratiot outside city limits		
1857(org.)	1880 –	300 Av. Att.
St. Joseph's Roman Catholic Church—Gratiot		
1856(cons.)	1880 –	1,200 f
St. Boniface Roman Catholic Church—13th & Michigan		
1869(org.)	1880 –	200 f

Seventeen other German churches both east and west, all but one non-Catholic, built by 1880 (not including St. Vincent de Paul, which served 1,100 Catholic families west of 11th Street and South of Grand River, many of them being Germans).

Key
c – communicants   cons. – consecrated
m – members   f – families (5 persons)
org. – organized   Av. Att. – average attendance

Table 16-4
Distribution of Church Members in 1880

The following information was obtained from Silas Farmer's *Detroit—A General History*:

8,100 German Catholic Church Members
6,400 German Protestant Church Members
1,000 Polish Catholic Church Members
  500 Bohemian Catholic Church Members

Out of a total population of 85,000 –
  17–1/2% – German Church Members
  1.3% – Polish Church Members
  .7% – Bohemian Church Members

Table 16-5
Foreign Born in Detroit

	1900	1927	1930
British Empire	44,378	157,000	–
Canada	28,944	88,000	–
Ireland	6,412	12,800	–
England & Wales	6,447	36,200	–
Scotland	2,496	20,000	–
Germany	32,027	58,000	–
Poland	13,518	–	200,000
Russia	1,332	50,000	21,000
Austria	1,174	21,500	–
Italy	904	45,000	28,000
Hungary	–	–	22,000
Lithuania	–	–	4,800
Belgium	671	11,500	–
France	589	–	–
Switzerland	491	–	–
Holland	397	–	–
Norway & Sweden	347	–	–
Denmark	231	–	–
Bulgaria & Macedonia	–	–	5,000
Yugoslavia	–	7,500	23,000
Finland	–	–	2,800
Greece	–	–	6,300
Rumania	–	–	7,500
Syria	–	–	3,200

1900 Figures & map from Burton Scrapbook 76:161-162.

1927 Figures from August 7, 1927, Detroit Saturday Night.

1930 Figures from Michigan Hist. Magazine Vol. 23, "Spring," 1939.

17 Ethnic Issues in the Church

Kazimierz Olejarczyk

It would be an impossible undertaking to discuss all the ethnic issues in the Church within a brief article. Therefore the discussion will be within the context of this Conference on Ethnic Communities, that is as only those issues which will be facing the Polish-American Community in Detroit and Michigan in the present decade, and it will be further limited to the Roman Catholic Church and will not deal with any issues which may be affecting the quarter of a million Polish-Americans who belong to the independent Polish National Church in this country.

The fact of ethnicity is one of the fundamental characteristics of the world and it cannot be separated from the Christian Church. "Go, therefore, and teach ye all nations" was her divine mission from the outset. The first act of the Apostles after the Pentecost was to preach the great works of God in the language of every national and ethnic group present among the spectators.

This is not the occasion to trace the riches and complications which ethnicity brought to the Church through the ages. Let me only recall that already in the year 1215 the Fourth Lateran Council decreed that the Bishops should provide those of their flock who speak a different language with the pastoral care in their own rite and in their own language.

In this country the ethnic issues in the Churches arose with the mass immigration of the nineteenth century. The great differences in language, culture, traditions and mentality among the immigrants from so many nations created tensions with the earlier immigrants, particularly the Irish, who had established themselves as the "native" element in the hierarchial structure of the Catholic Church.

On the other hand, these same differences, of necessity, led to establishment of a special type of a parish, a national, or ethnic, parish whose specific purpose was to serve the religious, pastoral, and social needs of a particular group of people from the same nationality. As we know, one-third of them, over 900, were founded and maintained by the Polish immigrants.

The enmity of the Irish-American hierarchy towards other ethnic groups, which were bent upon the preservation of their language and traditions, is a well-established fact. It has lasted now for over a century and may be epitomized in the infamous saying of Cardinal James Gibbons, "To Catholicize America we must first Americanize the immigrants." I leave this topic to competent historians. It has been treated by Dr. Joseph A. Wytrwal in his latest book, "Poles in American History and Tradition."

225

The key to the ethnic issues in the Church in the present decade as well to their solutions can be found in the three preceding decades. It was Pius XII who, faced with the onslaught of Nazi racism, came to the defense of every nation's traditions during the 1940s. He stressed in his very first encyclical the understandable pride with which each nationality defends most fiercely its sacred cultural heritage.

At the basis of the deeper unity of the human family he placed the mutual interchange of goods, material as well as spiritual, which should lead to mutual respect and love. He warned of the grave consequences brought by the loss or abandonment of one's own religious and national traditions, which often leads to pusillanimity, apathy, inferiority complex, and even to the gradual loss of human dignity.

At the same time that World War II against the Nazis was being fought and won, and the influx of new immigrant-soldiers, refugees, and displaced persons was once again passing by the Statue of Liberty, another quiet battle was being lost on the ethnic home front. The national parishes, under the pressure from chanceries and boards of education, were losing one of their most essential characteristics: the thorough teaching of mother tongue, history, and culture in the grade and high schools. The objective was: unity through uniformity. The method: alienation of the children from their parents and grandparents. The result: the reinforcement of the inferiority complex and the proliferation of "rootless Americans." This policy has been maintained in force in the fifties and sixties, making the Roman Catholic Church in this country a regressive and reactionary force in this aspect of education.

While the existing ethnic parishes were thus to be deprived of new generations and their legal status was to be quietly changed, new ones were not to be erected. This policy, which must have been secretly agreed upon in the latter part of 1920s has been carried out with 100 percent thoroughness until this very day. In spite of millions of new immigrants from Catholic nations of Eastern and Southern Europe, from Puerto Rico, Cuba, Mexico, the Philippines—not a single national or ethnic parish has been established in this country, although the Canadian hierarchy has done so after the issuance of Exsul Familia.

Another policy adopted probably in the 1920s was to starve the Polish ethnic parishes by cutting off the supply of priests trained in the language, culture, psychology and theology at the St. S. Cyril and Methodius Seminary, now at Orchard Lake, Michigan, founded specifically for this purpose by Father Jozef Dabroski, who arrived in this country exactly one hundred years ago. It is a matter of public record that the dioceses with the largest Polish populations: Chicago, Detroit, Buffalo, Philadelphia, have not been sending any Polish-American candidates for priesthood to be trained in theology and to be ordained at Orchard Lake. The "youngest" priest alumnus in Chicago Archdiocese already has celebrated the 50th anniversary of his Ordination at Orchard Lake.

Finally, the very idea of an ethnic parish was being attacked and discredited and a power play for the ultimate and absolute authority to suppress them was underway, culminating in such an express petition by the American Bishops submitted directly to the Pope in the Spring of 1967.

Before the sixties, however, the fifties brought what Pope Paul VI has termed "the fundamental pontifical document of recent times on the problems of migration," namely the Apostolic Constitution Exsul Familia, which continues to be, now in an updated form, the law of the Church.

This "Magna Charta" of the rights of immigrants to proper pastoral care in their own language and traditions was for several years ignored by the Catholic press and religious periodicals in this country, save for the Orchard Lake Seminary which was the first to publish a thorough commentary on Exsul Familia.

The 1960s brought numerous magnificent pronouncements on the problems of ethnic and minority groups by Pope John XXIII. He did not hesitate to call the uprooting of national traditions of others an immoral act and to categorize the denationalizing fervor of some priests as, "false and certainly un-Christian." Paul VI, in a similar vein, while addressing Slovak pilgrims, stressed most strongly the importance of maintaining the link with own culture and tradition.

Then came Vatican II. The Fathers of the Council devoted a whole chapter of the Pastoral Constitution on the Church in the Modern World to the "Proper Development of Culture." In numerous other utterances throughout other documents the Council made explicit pronouncements on the proper pastoral care for immigrants, refugees, linguistic and ethnic minorities, and other migrants. In the wake of aggiornamento which followed the Council, the Vatican undertook the work of bringing up to date that fundamental pontifical document, the Apostolic Constitution Exsul Familia. Here two trends clashed. One was the serious intention of the Apostolic See of extending the rights of the members of ethnic groups, now called generally "migrants." The other was the demand of national hierarchies for more autonomy and decentralization.

The result was the Motu Proprio of Pope Paul VI of August 15, 1969, followed a week later by the Instruction issued by the Sacred Congregation for Bishops. It is a compromise. It stresses the rights of all migrants to a proper pastoral care and outlines the forms which this care should take but leaves the implementation of them to the good will of individual bishops while secretly hoping for a change of their hearts.

The Instruction states that it was composed after repeated consultation with the various episcopal conferences. It is unfortunate that the various immigrant and ethnic groups and layity were not given the same consideration. There is, however, hope in this regard as we shall see.

After reviewing the new forms of migration the Instruction stresses that migrations will promote the unity of the human family only when each party is at the same time a giver and a receiver. The many hazards and difficulties of migration present a threat to the faith if the human and cultural heritage is also put in danger. That is why the Church, whose pastoral concern encompasses the whole man and all his rights, stresses repeatedly the right of the migrants and ethnic groups to their own language and culture.

"Migrating people carry with them their own mentality, their own language, their own culture, and their own religion. All of these things are parts of a certain spiritual heritage of opinions, traditions, and culture which will perdure outside the homeland. Let it be prized highly everywhere.

"Not least in its rights to consideration is the mother tongue of emigrant people, by which they express their mentality, thoughts, culture and spiritual life."

That is why the pastoral care must be carried by priests of the same language and nationality, who know well their mentality and culture. For that they should be specially trained in educational institutions and seminaries which should be set up for that very purpose.

Out of the various means which the bishops should use according to the circumstances of place, customs, and needs of the faithful, the Instruction expressly states that:

Where there are great numbers of immigrants of the same language living either stably or in continuous movement, the erection of a personal parish can be advisable. It is to be appropriately set up by the ordinary of the place.

Let me point out that a footnote recalls a previously announced norm that the suppression is subject to the final authority of the Apostolic See if it involves the rights of moral persons, as it obviously would.

It is not possible to review all the provisions or ramifications of the new Instruction. It is not to be a final word. On the contrary, it specifically sets up institutions for periodic updating and refinement. For that purpose it calls for the establishment of a number of institutions on various levels.

It is most encouraging that the Instruction requires that among the members of those institutions there are to be lay people who are versed in the problems of migration (and this includes the well-established ethnic communities not only of first but also of following generations).

Thus lay people may be part of diocesan Office for Immigrants; they should be among the members of the national Episcopal Commission for Migration; lay people also are to be among the members of the Supreme Council for Migration in Rome and of the Study Commission which will study things of great importance or pressing need and propose suitable advice to the Sacred Congregation for Bishops.

Before leaving this overview of the Instruction let me mention that among other means it calls for the annual celebration in each diocese of the Immigrant Day.

A post-conciliar Synod was held last year in the Archdiocese of Detroit. Prepared through discussions in many speak-up groups in most parishes and in nine main pre-synodal commissions, it was finalized and promulgated by Cardinal Dearden on Palm Sunday. For the purpose of our discussion it is essential to note that in the chapter on the Laity the following paragraph has been incorporated:

All men are children of God but, as history provides and illustrates, they are also distinctive members of natural ethnic, national, and social communities. Differences must be admitted and even welcomed as instances of the rich creativity of God. Where differences matter at all it is only to our advantage and to the Church's. Thus, it goes without saying that since the people of God in this Archdiocese are a community standing as one in a 'Nation of Immigrants,' all are responsible for fostering means which are capable of promoting particular cultural expressions of the faith without discrimination of any sort. This is also a diocesan and parish responsibility.

Thus the teaching of the Church and its official laws on the world level and on our diocesan level set the framework within which the solutions to ethnic issues of this decade are to be found.

We, as members of the Polish-American community, stand of course ready to help the hierarchy put the teaching of the Church into practice. This, however, reminds me of the little boy, member of the cub scouts, who came home and proudly announced to his mother that his cub scout troop has done their good deed for the day. "And what did you do?" inquired the mother. "We have helped an old lady across the street." "Oh, that certainly was nice. But why it took all eight of you?" "Because she did not want to go."

Coming back to the ethnic issues which will face us in this decade I shall list some of the more important ones in the form of questions:

1. Will the "credibility gap" which exists between our community and the diocesan and archdiocesan administrations be filled through sincere and respectful dialog?
2. Will the glaring discrimination against the teaching of Polish language and heritage subjects be finally removed?
3. Will the "conspiracy of silence" in the diocesan press and mass media regarding the ethnic groups, particularly ours, be ended through regular reportage of all worthwhile events, activities, organizations and problems?
4. Will the Catholic Directory discontinue to misinform its users by hiding the fact of the existence of 32 Polish parishes, while designating only one as "Polish" and reporting only two as having Masses in the Polish language?
5. Will a Polish-American priest, who not only speaks both languages, but who knows and loves Polish culture and traditions and feels with the people, be nominated as bishop with the authority to care for the ethnic groups?
6. Will the People's Hymnal at last include religious songs in good English translation from the rich treasury of ethnic groups from old Catholic cultures, particularly Polish songs?
7. Will the Mass for Shut Ins be said also in other languages?
8. Will Polish-American priests and laity be again included in the appointments to decision-making posts in the Chancery and in the boards and commissions?
9. Will diocesan funds be channeled into specifically Polish and other ethnic needs in proportion to the contributions, present and past, of each group?
10. Will the respectful recognition be given to the legacy of Polish religious thought, philosophy, and culture, and to its unique values?
11. Will Catholic universities and colleges institute area and heritage studies of

230

Polish and other Catholic nations to at least parallel the Judaic and other non-Catholic institutes which they have set up?

12. Will teaching orders founded for particular ethnic groups be prevented from violating their original mission by not teaching the language and culture in parochial schools and own colleges?

13. Will the diocesan and national administrations cooperate with the Polish (and other) interdiocesan lay organizations, such as the Polish-American Congress and its Commission on Religious Affairs?

18 Southern Mountain Medical Beliefs in Detroit: Focus for Conflict[a]

Ellen J. Stekert

The current difficulties encountered by the Southern Appalachian family, newly arrived in a northern urban center, are hardly new. In her 1954 novel, *The Dollmaker*.[1] Harriette Arnow portrayed the agonies of such in-migrants; the Nevels' tragedy is described with an accuracy and eloquence uncommon in literature. Eight years later Rupert B. Vance suggested that the most promising solution to the social and economic plight of the Southern Appalachian region was to move the people to locations offering better economic opportunities. As he put it, "Since the mountains are not likely to be moved, we proceed on the assumption that men can be moved."[2] And, in fact, since 1950, shortly before Mrs. Arnow published her book, over a million persons have moved from the southern mountains to our northern industrial centers. However, as the old adage implies, it might be easy "to take the boy out of the mountains, but not the mountains out of the boy." While numerous studies have investigated the traumas suffered by immigrants moving to American cities from lands across the seas, far less has been done to document the situation of the native in-migrant who is moving with increasing rapidity from our rural regions to our urban centers.[3] His predicament is certainly as bad as that of the foreign immigrant of the late nineteenth and early twentieth centuries. One could say the in-migrant's situation is even worse: he is often thought of as "quaint" and "pure" while down on the farm or in the hills, but no more than a social problem in the cities. It is as though we feel that he should not *have* to make an adjustment, for he is supposed to be the embodiment of all we hold dear in our past American values; he should know better than to dwell in ghettos, have employment problems, and be ridden with illness. The grim fact is that he suffers from all of these plights, and more.

The in-migrant from the southern mountains comes from a culture as alien to that of our large urban metropolises as that of the fisherman from his fiord in

This chapter is based on "Focus for Conflict: Southern Mountain Medical Beliefs in Detroit," *Journal of American Folklore* (April-June, 1970), pp. 115-147. Used with permission.

[a]Throughout this paper the terms "southern mountain," and "mountain," or "mountaineer," are used when referring to those in-migrants from the Southern Appalachian region who are in low socioeconomic brackets. No attempt is made here to speak for the more fortunate in-migrant who escaped ghetto life. Also, it is recognized that many of the patterns of behavior described in this paper apply to other low socioeconomic groups as well. The attempt to relate them to the past traditions of the Southern Appalachian region is in no way meant either to claim them solely for the mountain in-migrant or to stereotype him.

Norway.[4] This has been pointed out many times in studies such as Marian Pearsall's *Little Smoky Ridge* and Elmora Messer Matthews' *Neighbor and Kin*.[5,6] However, it is also true that a transition *within* the southern mountain culture began over sixty years ago, when the introduction of lumbering and mining began to change the basic social structure.[7] Consequently, the southern mountain person has been caught for years in a situation where he was raised to believe in and live by certain traditional values, only to find the society around him in the mountains becoming just as alien as the society in the cities.[8] Informants interviewed for this study often strongly expressed the feeling that there was nothing to go back to in the South: they felt that the North and the cities were their only hope, although not without conflict. Like the foreign immigrant at the turn of the century, the southern mountain in-migrant has often chosen the conflict and hope of the city over the apparent certainty of failure back home.

The qualities of the differences between old southern mountain values and new urban values are presented sharply by Matthews in *Neighbor and Kin*.[9] She shows that southern mountain society traditionally regards the "community level" as the ideal goal: an individual does not want to be thought of as different or as better than the rest of the community. Ideally, one is an integral part of the community and does not compete with his neighbor for status. One's identity, and thereby one's value to the community, is determined by "ascriptive qualities" such as birth, sex, and age. Therefore, acute conflict confronts the southern mountain family when they move to a northern city such as Detroit and are faced with new, urban values. The concept of what constitutes a person's identity and value in urban society is quite different from that of the southern mountaineer. In the city one strives to be *anything but* "community level"; in the city one's goal must be to "achieve," to be "better than the next guy."[b] The southern mountaineer finds that his identity as defined in the mountains has little meaning in the city; who cares whose kin you are, or if you are the oldest son? The southern mountaineer finds that his identity in the city depends on behavior which he has not been taught to value; and he often ceases to care.

This conflict of values frequently becomes insurmountable, as Matthews points out, for "the intrusion of So-So families into a Go-Go society does not cause violence: it only leads to an enlarging of the lower strata of the Go-Go society."[10] The women, who have been taught to wait and suffer what comes to them, often continue to do so; and the men, robbed of their ascriptive patriachial status, simply give up. The southern mountain in-migrant travels from a culture which places a premium on being "average," to an urban culture where

---

[b]To those who might object to this view and point to the men in grey flannel suits and mass conformity in "other directed" urban America, I would suggest that his conformity is seldom thought of in such terms by the urban dweller himself. No matter how conformist he might be, he likes to view himself as different. Perhaps more important is the fact that one gains what is actually conformity in the urban center by achievement: one must "keep up" with the Joneses. In other words, conformity and ascriptive status are not necessarily the same thing.

he is automatically anything but "average" in status. The very ascriptive qualities which made him blend into his mountain society, make him stand out at the bottom of the class structure in urban society. Yet he still *feels* that he must blend, and in urban society to blend means to be middle class. He is forced to accept middle class status as his new norm; but not being used to a system where status is gained by achievement, he is soon lost in the dilemma of not being able to "drag himself up" to the "average" status which he has traditionally been taught to seek and value. He must use non-traditional means, that of "Go-Go" and "achievement," to attain an old and traditional value, the "community level." He is caught in a tearing, and often destructive, conflict.

The southern mountain white, because of his tradition of seeking and valuing "average" status, generally finds himself confused and leaderless in the new and tremendously complex structure of public services which he must use in order to survive. The main organizations which have shown concern for his welfare are church groups—and ironically, church groups which are far different from the fundamentalistic religious persuasion in which the southern mountain person was raised. The Catholics, Lutherans, and Methodists, for example, whose worship appears stiff and formal to the more evangelically-oriented person from the Southern Appalachians, are among the churches in Detroit most intimately concerned with his well being. The interviews conducted for this study revealed that none of the respondants regularly attended a church in Detroit, which corresponds with Griffin's findings in Cincinnati (and with the general decline in church attendance even in the mountains).[11] Yet, all respondents had belonged to some fundamentalist sect in the South; and although they did not participate formally in church services in Detroit, all regarded themselves as religious. All of the informants regarded faith as the most important factor in curing disease, and over three-quarters of them indicated a firm belief in faith healing. The persistence of these traditional religious attitudes, even in the absence of corresponding religious behavior, is characteristic of the general tendency of the southern mountain in-migrant to hold tenaciously to his beliefs even when circumstances favor a change in behavior.

When religious groups in Detroit succeed in attracting the Southern Appalachian person to their churches, it is usually for social rather than religious activities. The religious southern mountain person sees the church primarily as a place of worship; yet he rejects the type of worship he finds in the churches that do work for his well-being in the ghetto. This conflict is actually verbalized by many of the southern mountain people; for example, one respondent, who often goes to a nearby church with her children for community functions, remarked, "I don't see why they don't just open a social center."

However, these "alien" churches appear to be the only present rallying point and focus for leadership for the Southern Appalachian in-migrant in Detroit. The traditional social organization of the southern mountain does not stress community leadership, and therefore the Southern Appalachian people in the northern city are not well-organized. As a result, they often feel overlooked as a needy minority in social legislation. One Detroit religious leader who has been involved in attempts to organize the voice of white poverty in the city, bemoaned the fact that the southern mountain white population is too "timid" to organize and obtain funds from government agencies. Because they lacked strong leadership, he said, the ghetto Appalachian whites have to "sit back and let that money go to the Negroes ... They're growing Negro leaders while the poor whites go down, down, down."[12]

But lack of leadership is not a new phenomena for the traditionally individualistic mountaineer. Matthews has pointed out that "certainly the absence of recognized leadership is another important expression of the value the deme places on keeping status distinctions to a minimum."[13] This traditional value of non-achievement is the source of constant torment to the southern mountaineer in the city. The absence of an organized voice in the urban center results in his feeling slighted and bitter about welfare and poverty programs; among southern mountain people in Detroit one often hears the expression, "in this city poverty is black."

The black American is not alone in the impacted urban poverty areas of the United States. Often, as in Detroit, both Negro and white Americans live side by side in the city ghettos. Why, then, does the medically indigent Negro American utilize public health facilities in Detroit more frequently and effectively than his white neighbor in poverty?[c] This study was undertaken to answer part of that question: it was conceived as a preliminary investigation of one aspect of the Southern Appalachian in-migrant in Detroit. I chose the Southern Appalachian group because out-migration from that area has been both poor and "overwhelmingly white."[14]

My investigation focused on the fate of traditional medical attitudes and practices brought to Detroit by the southern mountain in-migrant, and sought to determine whether traditional behavior patterns and values have helped or hindered him in receiving adequate health care. In order to limit the study to a specific medical condition—one for which public services are available to the medically indigent in Detroit—the areas of health practices investigated were restricted to those concerning prenatal care, birth, and infant care.[15] However, no area of culture can be studied in and of itself; the behavior and attitudes of southern mountain women towards the specific practices focused on in the study cannot be separated from the greater fabric of the southern mountain culture and beliefs from which these women came, and often fled.

Toward the end of the first phase of this investigation, I sat in one of the large Detroit hospitals and listened to a pediatrician tell me that if she were to have her choice as to whom she should try to communicate her advice, it would easily be the medically indigent Negro mother rather than the southern mountain one. She had found in the past that Negro women listened more openly and seemed to benefit more fully from her advice. Sadly enough, my

---

cThe term "medically indigent" is used in this study to denote persons who are unable to afford medical expenses without financial deprivation resulting in an inability to pay for the basic resources needed for subsistence.

study substantiates her observation: that medically indigent southern mountain women in Detroit tend not to seek or to follow accurately the medical counsel available to them. Even when their judgments and behavior change in the urban environment, their attitudes remain those of past tradition.[d] The southern mountain mother rarely seems to internalize the advice offered her by the city physician.

While segments of the urban Negro population also retain some medical traditions and practices in the city, (for example, many Negro women in Detroit treat an umbilical hernia by taping a silver coin to the naval[e]), the important question is: how long are traditions which are *antithetical* to good health care retained? This study was not intended primarily as a comparison of the health practices and attitudes of the medically indigent urban white with those of the underpriviledged urban black population. However, it was begun shortly after the violence in Detroit during the summer of 1967, and under this shadow one could hardly avoid recognizing the fact that every single health service contacted reported that the overwhelming majority of the people who used their facilities, both before and after the riots, were black. Where was the black Detroiter's neighbor, the southern mountain white, when it came to utilizing medical aid from which he could clearly benefit? Educated estimates are that Detroit's southern mountain population is presently about thirty thousand and will be double that number in a few years.[16] This does not include the large numbers of people from the Southern Appalachians who have been able to enter a higher socioeconomic status and live outside the Detroit city limits in areas such as Hazel Park, Warren, and Wixom. Traditionally, the southern mountain person has placed a high premium on the welfare of his children; of all the areas of health care, he is most responsive to hospitalization for birth.[17] Why, then, do the women not appear more frequently at Detroit's prenatal and child care facilities? A significant part of the answer lies in traditional behavior patterns and attitudes.

The Problem

Poor health is intimately related to poverty, and poor health in the prenatal period is often linked with a high rate of perinatal and infant mortality.[18,19] Given these facts, it is especially important for an expectant mother who is living in poverty, or near poverty, to seek and continue care throughout the entire maternity period, both for her sake and for the sake of her child.[20] Yet southern mountain women in Detroit are not receiving this care, and there is no reason to believe the situation is different in other Northern urban centers. The

---

[d]Earl Lomon Koos, *The Health of Regionville: What the People Thought and Did About It* (New York: Columbia University Press, 1954), p. 166. Koos distinguishes a "judgment" as an opinion about something and an "attitude" as an internalized belief or disposition toward something; his distinction is used in this paper.

[e]Reported by a nurse from the Visiting Nurse Association in Detroit, February, 1968.

medically indigent Southern Appalachian woman is among those high risk cases who need the comprehensive services of such medical assistance programs as the Detroit Maternity and Infant Care Project most urgently.[f]

Although C. Horace Hamilton reports that the perinatal mortality rate in the entire Southern Appalachian region in 1954-1956 was only 1.3 deaths per 1,000 births higher than the national rate (35.4), the majority of counties with rates from 9.6 to 14.6 above the national norm of that time are within the geographic area from which the respondents for this investigation were drawn.[21] The women interviewed for this study, therefore, came originally from high risk areas in the South. Dr. Hamilton is of the opinion that a medical "revolution" occurred in the Southern Appalachians from 1940 to 1955. Unfortunately, the statistics which support this view most strongly are statistics which reflect behavior patterns rather than attitudes. The percentage of children born in hospitals in the Southern Appalachians rose from 17.9 percent in 1940 to 89.4 percent in 1955. At the same time, the percentage of infants delivered by midwives decreased during that period from 14.3 percent to 3.2 percent.[22] However, my information indicates that these statistics represent only a small victory, not a "revolution."

Both the contact and the depth interviews conducted during this study indicate that while the women are quite willing to enter the hospital to give birth (in contrast to a determined abhorrence of hospitalization for anything not considered as "natural" as childbirth), they are still extremely negative about prenatal and postnatal care.[23] For example, a mother of three whose interviews revealed that she had probably suffered from toxemia and other complications during her first two pregnancies still sought no prenatal care for her third pregnancy. She was admitted as an emergency case to one of Detroit's large hospitals several months before the birth of the third child, with severe complications, and her interview suggests that she might have suffered a third time from toxemia. During her earlier confinements for birth this woman had been informed of the value and purpose of prenatal and postnatal care.

It does not seem to follow, then, that the fact that it has become customary for high risk southern mountain women to seek hospitalization for the actual births of their children indicates that they or their children will also be completely healthy, or will seek other medical aid at the appropriate time. (Note the high number of handicapped and dead children, as well as the number of complications during pregnancies, reported in Appendix III.) The women interviewed often expressed a desire to have their children at home; and they probably would have done so, had it not been for the fact that the doctors they contacted refused to make home deliveries, and that without a doctor attending,

---

[f]The DMICP was begun in 1964 with the intention of reaching women from low-income groups. Its services include comprehensive care for the entire maternity cycle; hospital cost is determined by the financial situation of the mother. The DMIC is funded under a United States Children's Bureau grant, authorized by Public Law 88-156 to the Michigan Department of Public Health, for use with matching funds from the Detroit Department of Health.

birth certificates become a legal problem. Most of the women's interviews indicate that the advice given by doctors while the woman was in the hospital was often misunderstood, barely tolerated, or completely ignored after the mother and child were released. Time and again it was apparent that hospital confinement for a birth did not significantly change the general medical behavior or attitudes of the women involved. Thus, among the southern mountain women in Detroit, it appears that behavioral change—in this case hospital confinement for birth—does not change basic attitudes, nor lead to additional changes in medical behavior.

Infant mortality, as an index of general health, has long been of concern to this country. Since the President's State of the Union Message in January, 1968, it has become fashionable to lament the fact that the United States has fallen behind other "developed" countries to fifteenth place in infant mortality.[g] Our standing reflects a national problem. Prior to 1950, the trend in the United States infant mortality rate pointed to a decline that would have produced a rate of 15 per 1,000 births in 1964. However, after 1950, the decline leveled off, leaving the actual infant mortality rate at 24.8 in 1964, or 9.8 above the projections from the 1937-1950 trend.[24] The predicted rate of 15 per 1,000 by 1964 hardly seemed unreasonable, since both Sweden and the Netherlands had bettered that figure by 1964.[25] In addition, the statistics which show fourteen countries now superior to the United States in the area of infant mortality cannot be accounted for on the basis of discrepancies in definitions or the manner in which the statistics were gathered.[26]

One factor that makes it important to look specifically at the southern *mountain* woman is that she is usually lumped into a general category with all white southerners.[h] However, the patterns and values of the person from the Southern Appalachians—even from those areas affected by the mining and lumbering industries—are often different from the traditions of persons from southern urban centers and from other non-mountain areas of the South, such as the Tidewater or Bluegrass country.[i] The southern mountain woman, therefore, is a hidden statistic in the southern "white, non-white" category. It is important

---

[g]Helen C. Chase, "Prenatal and Infant Mortality in the United States and Six Western European Countries," *American Journal of Public Health*, LVII, No. 10 (October, 1967), p. 1737. The United States ranks (in order) behind Sweden, the Netherlands, Norway, Finland, Australia, Japan, Denmark, Switzerland, New Zealand, United Kingdom, France, Federal Republic of Germany, Belgium, East Germany, and ties with Canada for the honor of fifteenth position.

[h]This is not only a quirk of statisticians. See Lewis N. Killian, "The Adjustment of Southern White Migrants to Northern Urban Norms," *Social Forces*, XXXII (1953), p. 67. The author indicates that the general urban community does this, too. They tend to lump all southerners into one category and call them, disparagingly, "hillbillies."

[i]See Steven Polgar, "Health and Human Behavior: Areas of Interest Common to the Social and Medical Sciences," *Current Anthropology*, III, No. 2 (April, 1962), p. 168. "An individual in the Kentucky blue-grass community where sickness is almost 'enjoyed' (Birdwhistell, 1957) would presumably not wait as long as his cousin in the hills before signaling that he is sick." Informant LH, the only respondent from the Bluegrass area, showed this trait in contrast to the other informants who were from the mountain area.

to delineate her distinctive traditional patterns of behavior and attitude relating to prenatal care, hospital delivery, and postnatal care, for she is a member of an increasingly numerous high risk group in the poverty areas of our urban centers. If we understand her traditions, we can begin to reach her and to make available the care from which she and her family can benefit greatly, in a context in which she can accept and utilize that care.

Census tract "A" in Detroit, one of the several areas in the city where southern mountain people have moved alongside of poor blacks, and the area from which most of the informants for this study were drawn, shows an infant mortality rate of 36.8 per 1,000 live births in 1966, compared with an overall city average of approximately 28.1.[27] The woman from the Southern Appalachians in this census tract is certainly a high risk maternity patient. Although recent statistics point encouragingly to a drop in infant mortality in large American cities, according to Dr. Arthur Lesser, Deputy Chief of the U.S. Children's Bureau, this drop is largely the result of medical welfare programs; and if Detroit's negro/white clinic clientele is any indicator, it seems unlikely that there were many white mothers among the 700,000 to 800,000 women of low income families who were served by the maternity and infant care projects to which Dr. Lesser refers.[28,29,30]

It appears that one of the primary reasons why the southern mountain in-migrant does not take advantage of urban health facilities is that cultural factors affecting both the person from the Southern Appalachians and the urban health personnel cause a mutual deafness: neither really seems to hear what the other is trying to say. All interviews, both with contact people and with informants, indicate a serious communication problem. Much of the difficulty seems to lie in a basic conflict between the values and traditional practices of the "medically educated" urban professional (and the urban public), and those of the southern mountaineer. Clearly, what one does not understand, one cannot hear. This makes it important to understand some of the basic life patterns and values of the Southern Appalachian resident, and to attempt to relate these attitudes and modes of action to the in-migrant's medical situation in the city.

Medical Behavior in the City and Prior Tradition

It appears that the general pattern of maternity behavior among first generation southern mountain women in Detroit is to have little or no prenatal care, to be hospitalized for the birth, and to have little or no postnatal care. This also appears to be the current pattern in the South today. Most of the Southern Appalachian women interviewed for this study would rather have had their children in their homes. One woman even told of a couple who served the southern mountain population in Detroit by delivering children at home; the couple had no medical training, but their fee was cheaper than that of a private doctor. Most of the women interviewed preferred a private doctor to the series of unfamiliar doctors in a public clinic.[j] Although the women interviewed stressed their desire for personal attention and sought private physicians, they also indicated that they switched doctors frequently. Most of them retained the traditional basic distrust of all physicians. They also retained a strong traditional modesty; prenatal and postnatal examinations were regarded as inherently humiliating.

These attitudes, and others, are part of the tradition which the southern mountain in-migrant brings with her to the urban center. They are the area of Southern Appalachian folklore that falls under the category of "beliefs" or values—beliefs that often manifest themselves in structured behavior such as the practice of "folk medicine." My study is concerned with both aspects: that of the traditional attitudes and values, and that of folk, or traditional, practices (cures). The interviews revealed both the knowledge and application of a wealth of southern mountain folk remedies in Detroit. Understandably, these are apparently beginning to blend slowly with general urban folk medicine (which also exists, and ranges from chicken soup to aspirin). The widespread retention of southern mountain cures, or at least the knowledge of them, seems to be primarily a reflection of the persistence of basic traditional medical attitudes. A convenient metaphor would be to view the actual cures as entities which travel embedded in a traditional body of belief to which they owe their existence.[31] Without the attitudes the cures will not persist. The traditional southern mountain folk cures are still practiced in Detroit, although they are beginning to be modified or replaced by urban variants; but the traditional *values* regarding medical behavior are resisting change with a fantastic energy.

A. Glorification of the Past. Most medically indigent Southern Appalachian people who have come to the large urban centers in the North have done so to escape an agonizing existence in the South. One informant succinctly stated why she had come to Detroit: "There was nothing down there, and I mean nothing!" The South, too, has been going through many changes, and often life is not as romantic in the hills as northerners might think. The northern city often presents a dream of better things for the southern mountaineer, who is faced with the prospect of major adjustments and changes no matter where he chooses to live.[32] In fact, the southern mountaineer has usually moved from a situation in which he was having to cope with the influence of urbanization anyway.

The imperative quality of the move to the northern city is coupled with hope for a better life, which often turns to bitterness in the reality of urban ghettos that are hardly better than southern rural poverty. When the present offers excessive conflict and disappointment, it is understandable that a return

---

[j]Ann DeHuff Peters, "Patterns of Health Care in Infancy in a Rural Southern County," *American Journal of Public Health*, LVII, No. 3 (March, 1967), p. 412. Peters reports that the majority of Negroes in the study had help from non-private sources while the white mothers used private physicians in preference to public clinics.

to old attitudes and traditional behavior often results. This is true of the southern mountain person in the city ghetto. One of the outstanding themes in the interviews—an attitude present in even the most medically "sophisticated" respondents—was that the way in which things were done back home in the past was far superior to the present. I frequently received the impression that if the southern mountain woman with whom I spoke had sought medical advice during her maternity cycle it was mainly because it "was the thing to do," rather than out of any conviction that it would really help. Thus, she clung to the past in two ways: first, she did not completely accept professional medical care, since her traditional distrust remained; and, second, she was acting according to the dictates of her "So-So" culture by doing the "accepted" thing, in terms of her new, urban, middle class oriented environment.

The glorification of past medical practices showed up in several different ways. Often, after a large part of the Questionnaire was covered and the interviews turned to that section which deals with common childhood ailments, respondents displayed an intense respect for the home cure and a disdain for anyone—especially city people—who "gives in" and goes to doctors. The traditional dislike, or at best indifference toward, the medical doctor, and the common glorification of the skilled practitioner of home medicine (usually an older woman), which prevailed in the South, is reflected in this persistence of traditional attitudes. Often respondents spoke of the older woman who knew the folk cures as the embodiment of the perfect person—again a clear idolization of the past: "She was the greatest person in the world." Another evidence of the tenacity of the past is the tendency of most women to go back to the South for care when they are either severely ill or pregnant. When the dream of the city dies in the reality of the present, it is only natural that memory of the pain of the past fades and the past begins to be idealized and glorified.

One example of the persistence of past values can be seen in the person of DG, and the history of her pregnancies and her attitude toward them. She came to Detroit from Kentucky a few weeks before her first child was born because her mother was there; she had no prenatal care, and she delivered her child in a Detroit hospital. She lived in Kentucky during the entire second maternity cycle, had no prenatal care, and had the child at home. Although the local doctor, whom they had known for years, was attending at this second birth, DG suffered extensive injury to her reproductive organs. As she describes it:

She [the baby] came right away. Of course as big as she was I didn't know then that everything tore out and the doctor didn't tell me or make any examination. He took the afterbirth and had C [husband] go bury it someplace . . . that dogs or nothing, you know, they couldn't dig it up.[k]

---

[k]Wayland D. Hand, ed., *Popular Beliefs and Superstitions from North Carolina* in *The Frank C. Brown Collection of North Carolina Folklore*, ed., Newman I. White, VI (Durham, North Carolina: Duke University Press, 1961), p. 13, item #59: "If the afterbirth is gotten hold of by a dog, the woman will always have a weak back." It is also traditional in the Southern Appalachians to send the husband to bury the afterbirth. DG's doctor acted in accord with the local folk tradition.

However, DG still feels that this second birth was her easiest: "I had a real easy time." She remembers it as her most ideal delivery, even though when she went for an examination in Detroit during her following (third) pregnancy, the doctor expressed concern about her ability to carry the child, and she eventually had to have an operation to repair the injuries resulting from the second birth.

For her third pregnancy, DG had prenatal care and delivered in a hospital. After a year, then, she had her operation:

About a year afterwards I went in and they called it the suspension. They pulled everything up like it was supposed to be and put it back in place then stitched up down there where it was all ripped out and told me that I was just like a new woman.

Several years following the operation she had her fourth child, and again had prenatal care and delivered in a hospital.

The case of DG is interesting and typical: in the course of her four pregnancies she *has* altered her *pattern of behavior* to comply with what medical authorities feel is correct. However, her *attitude* has changed little. She still regards the second birth as the best—as she terms it, "natural"—even though she is quite aware, as indicated in the above quotations, that she was harmed during that delivery and almost lost her next child as a result of this poor medical attention.[1] Even though DG has altered her behavior pattern, she still clings to the old attitudes and values.

Although she has spent most of her adult life in Detroit, DG, like many others, thinks of herself as "in but not of" the urban community.[33] On the other hand, it appears that she idolizes the home community of the past, not the present: in Killian's words, "its norms [were] still praised as the best, even when they could not be followed."[34]

BR is another example of this tendency to hold to the past regardless of contradictory experience. She spent most of her interviews vociferously praising the good of doctors, but often slipped into such statements as "My mother didn't have all of this medication [and hospitalization] when I was born, so I don't think that I have to have it either." This is almost identical to Koos' New York State respondent who refused postnatal care in the name of tradition and mother by saying:

Nuts to him [the doctor], I said. I didn't see any reason to go—I felt fine, so I just didn't. I'm not going to do something like that when my mother didn't.[35]

In the case of BR, however, there is an additional factor which shows how she must forget important facts because of her need to glorify the past. As cited above, BR implied her mother had an easy time during her birth, but as the

---

[1]"Natural childbirth" to DG means that she had no medication; she was not referring to the voguish practice of "natural childbirth" followed by many urban women.

interview progressed, it became clear this was completely untrue: BR almost died at birth. It appears that she was born with an Rh factor complication, and would have not lived (as was the case with her two brothers) had she not been immediately rushed to a hospital for blood transfusions.

The persistence of traditions which sometimes, *though not always*, are at odds with rationality, is a formidable factor. It appears that the more stress the individual is placed under, the more likely he is to fall back upon past patterns of behavior and past attitudes. For example, in James Agee's *A Death in the Family*, the conflict between southern mountaineers is a central theme; in this case, the belief that the dead father returned to his home to say goodbye to his family is a very comforting idea and eases the grief of his kin. And birth, like death, is a time of adjustment and stress. It is easy to agree with Nancy Milio when she observes "that lower-class women are more likely to resort to their folklore for coping with crisis."[36] Living lives which are ridden with immediacies and emergencies in the urban ghetto, the southern mountain in-migrants understandably rely on the patterns learned in the past; they do not have the time for the luxury of learning new attitudes.

B. Patterns of Movement. In attempting to determine why southern mountain women do not use the facilities available to them in the Metropolitan Detroit area, it is necessary to consider factors which have to do with the city itself, as well as those resulting from the southern woman's traditional values and patterns. Although Detroit is an extension of their home communities, for many of these Southern Appalachian in-migrants the city is still not at their disposal.[37] The southern mountain person, especially the woman, is surrounded by invisible walls within which she moves. In this respect she is not unlike most urbanites. However, she has more severe limitations than most, for she is usually without transportation and money, and often has several small children to take with her wherever she goes. In addition, she is burdened with the traditional southern mountain assumption that she should stay home and not appear often in public. An extreme example of this value was related by BT, who told of a woman who was rendered entirely helpless when her husband died, for he had been the one who transacted all the business with the outside world—including grocery shopping.

In many ways, it is more difficult for an in-migrant to find his way around Detroit than many other cities. Detroit's public transportation system is insufficient, costly, and difficult for the new arrival to master. In addition, the hospitals where a medically indigent woman can receive the best care are often located far outside of her familiar neighborhood. Few women living in the area of the Riverside Church on the east side of Detroit, or south of Wayne State University in the central part of the city, can easily manage the six or ten mile trip to Mount Carmel Hospital in the city's northwest section, via a complex and often frustrating bus system. Few can even manage the shorter trips to Detroit Memorial or Hutzel Hospital in the center of the city. The southern mountain woman is often more familiar with the route, and more comfortable about returning to the mountains, than she is about traveling to the hospital in Detroit. The difficulty is compounded by the fact that she probably does not even believe in visiting the hospital in the first place.

Some strides toward breaking down this territorial handicap have been made in Detroit. The Detroit Maternity and Infant Care Project (DMIC) has made it possible for half of the medically indigent mothers in the city to have all of their prenatal, delivery, and postnatal care in the same hospital. Before this project was established, a mother often had to go to three different health facilities and bear the difficulty of adjustment three times over. In addition to the DMIC, the ECHO project, Evidence for Community Health Organization, is trying to pinpoint the health problem areas of Detroit, in hopes of placing health facilities in the areas rather than attempting to move the population to the hospitals.[38]

But even if one understands the problems of territorialism within the city, and possibly eliminates all the difficulties arising from that, there is still the problem of traditional attitudes to be dealt with. Even the most "urbanized" informants—those utilizing health facilities most frequently and most effectively—showed a decided resistance to accepting them as proper. As indicated in the previous section, the informants often accepted the doctors' advice only when it suited them, and tended to revere traditional medical practices.

C. The Role of Women. In the Southern Appalachian region, the woman traditionally was, and still is, the primary transmitter of medical lore.[39] All of the depth interviews revealed a past reliance on a mother or grandmother who "always knew" what to do for an ailment. It was also this woman's role to determine when to call the doctor. Such a determination was usually made only in the most pressing conditions, such as those under which Sue Annie counsels Gertie to get her child to a physician in *The Dollmaker*.[m] To the southern mountain person, the point at which one calls a doctor is far beyond that at which the urban, middle class "native" seeks help. This is not to say that the acculturated urban mother does not do her own "doctoring" before, or instead of, calling a physician. She may also have a long list of home remedies; however, she still calls for medical advice far earlier than the newly arrived southern mountain mother.

The southern mountain woman in the city is placed in a difficult situation: she is hampered from fulfilling her traditional role as healer because she realizes that her home cures are considered "backward," and therefore not "average"; and even if she wishes to use them, she finds that in the urban environment it is difficult to obtain the herbs and other ingredients for the traditional cures. Thus she is caught in the city, wanting to fill her traditional role, but without the means to do it. This could lead to the adoption of traditional urban cures, but it appeared in the interviews that instead it first leads to experimentation—an attempt to find substitutes for the traditional ingredients used back home. Thus,

---

[m]Harriette Arnow, *The Dollmaker* (New York: Macmillan Co., 1954). Sue Annie sends Gertie to the doctor with Amos only when "the croup" becomes so serious after several days that the child's life is clearly threatened. In this case the disease was diphtheria.

LH used nail polish to heal a burn suffered by one of her children; and a number of mothers reported trying various commercial teas, instead of the traditional catnip tea, to make their babys "break out with the little red hives."[40]

The southern mountain woman in the city retains her role of deciding when the doctor should be visited; following the traditional pattern, she takes her child to the doctor, as one informant put it, "only when it is absolutely necessary." This condition of absolute necessity seems to hold true for her own pregnancy as well as child care, and helps to explain why so many southern mountain women do not have prenatal care (see Appendix III) and often appear as "walk in" patients at hospitals.[n] If she waits until the last minute to seek treatment for illness, it is easy to understand that the southern mountain woman would have a tendency to wait until the last minute for something as "natural" as childbirth.

Another adjustment the southern mountain woman must make when she moves to the city, especially if she is from a rural area, is the acceptance of what might be called a different "cleanliness imperative." In the past, it has been her job to determine and maintain the cleanliness of her home and children. Urban Americans seem to have a predilection for attempting to wash away their sins with an excess of soap and water; all good acculturated city folk know, according to the Social Gospel from the turn of the century, that "cleanliness is next to Godliness." The southern mountain mother has come from a different tradition. However, while urban America might seem to wash excessively, there *is* a good reason for the Southern Appalachian in-migrant to be more careful about personal hygiene in the city than she was in the mountains: the dirt of the slum carries the diseases of many people, and is often more deadly than the dirt of the more isolated rural environment. Although diseases spread in rural areas through such means as contaminated wells, one must admit that personal cleanliness is far more imperative in the overcrowded ghetto; when a sink or toilet backs up regularly in an urban slum, it becomes imperative that a mother wash her hands before feeding her child. Thus to preserve the health of her family, the newly arrived mother must also alter her role as a housekeeper, and change from her traditional "cleanliness imperative" to a new one.

Although the southern mountain woman is traditionally the one who actively perpetuates the medical lore of her culture, it is traditionally the man who is responsible for transportation.[41] When the decision was made in the mountains to finally consult a doctor, the husband was generally responsible for getting the sick person to the doctor, or bringing the doctor to the house. In addition, women usually stayed at home and seldom traveled to unfamiliar places. In the urban environment, however, with her husband not within calling distance, it is the responsibility of the woman to transport herself and her children to the doctor when she decides that professional attention is necessary. Given the deterrents mentioned earlier, it is understandable that many illnesses go untreated; in fact, it is a wonder anyone is treated at all.

[n]"Walk in" maternity patients are those women who arrive at the hospital when birth is imminent, often having made no prior plans with the institution for confinement.

The traditional role of the woman in the southern mountains is obviously quite different from the role she is forced and expected to assume in the urban environment. Much of her effectiveness as traditional healer is hampered until she learns to substitute new ingredients for unavailable ones in her traditional cures, and she must learn new and different patent and propriatory medicines. Often these are introduced to her through mass media, and are accepted in the absence of an older woman figure (the mother or grandmother) to advise her about home remedies. Ironically, the in-migrant southern mountain mother seems to be more influenced by her television set in medical matters than by the abundant and inexpensive public health facilities. In addition, she is not used to the responsibility, formerly that her husband, of having to transport sick family members to the doctor. It is a great effort for her to thread her children through the red tape of public transportation and welfare procedures at urban health centers; thus, traditionally waiting until symptoms reach emergency proportions, and disliking anything that resembles "welfare" in the first place, she is consistently discouraged from taking her children for care.

D. Attitudes Toward Welfare. It would be an understatement to say that traditionally, the southern mountaineer has not looked upon welfare programs with favor. This attitude is an important negative factor standing between the in-migrant mountain woman and proper maternity care. Although the resistance to public welfare programs in the South seems to have diminished, there still appears to be a basic scorn of them among the Detroit in-migrants.[42] The women interviewed for this study cited "pride" as a primary reason for their absence from those public health programs which treat the maternity cycle. The following excerpt from an interview, expresses in content and syntax the typical confusion and disgrace felt by the in-migrant when seeking medical "welfare" assistance:

"Well, down there you never take them to a doctor unless they are real sick, you know . . . And I guess it would apply after you come here, too. And then a lot of them don't know what place maybe if they don't have no money and they would be in a city and everything strange and new to them, why they don't know that a there—ah, ah, not—nobody told them some of them that a you know there's ways of getting treated anyway whether you've got money or not. And a lot of southern people are, especially the people from Kentucky, they have this pride—it may be a stupid pride in some ways, but they have this pride that they don't want to beg and they would maybe wait until the last minute you know, to take the child."

Such statements indicate that it is a combination of elements which keep the southern mountain woman from utilizing the services which are at her disposal; and among these factors "pride" is quite important. Like most human beings, the southern mountain person does not want to be regarded negatively; to him it is a reprehensible characteristic "to beg." He also feels it a negative characteristic to be thought ignorant and clumsy—to be viewed as a "hillbilly." As one informant stated, "Most of the people [Southern Appalachian] are not as stupid as most city people think they are."

The humiliation of being treated badly because of what she feels is an unjust stereotype is probably an additional element which discourages the southern mountain woman from using welfare. Whether or not the woman from the Southern Appalachians is, in fact, treated worse then anyone else is irrelevant; the southern mountaineer has been hypersensitive for years to the persistent stereotype of him. Fear of this stereotype itself alters his behavior patterns; for if he feels threatened with possible insult each time he goes to a public health service, he will soon cease using such facilities. Watts points out the inherent offense of "time consuming travel and waiting for a cursory inspection or a single injection and a noncommunicative word or two from a physician," while Yerby acknowledges the reaction of the patient who is often treated as "an unfeeling lump of humanity [with] discourteousness or demeaning familiarity [by] the staff" of public health facilities.[43,44] The service provided for persons using the public health clinics is often far from ideal, even for a desensitized person; but when a group likely to over-react to impersonal treatment is involved, such service often discourages that group from using the health facility at all. Clearly, the patient's self-image and fear of being stereotyped is an extremely important element in determining how he behaves; and if he is from the southern mountains he especially does not want to be thought of or treated as stupid, or as a begger, or as a "hillbilly."

Often, in the interviews, the bureaucracy of medical welfare facilities was mentioned as confusing and discouraging. The prevalence of what they considered "red tape" hardly helped motivate the informants to use the clinics for preventative checkups, and discouraged even emergency use. Non-medical "doctors," often more accessible and friendly, were consulted by many informants in times of stress. Almost all respondents commented on the long hours of waiting, a complaint which has been reported in other studies.[45] One woman related to the story of how she was made to wait (in Chicago) from 11:00 A.M. until 12:00 midnight before she was given a maternity bed in the hospital. She promptly delivered her son half an hour after she was formally admitted.

Because of the treatment they received, these women felt they were being stereotyped and rejected. They often reported that the agencies and people they went to for help tried to "send me back home to have my baby," and acted as if the child were illegitimate. There are legal reasons for determining the residency and the status of a child, and often the medically indigent woman must be asked about such things; but legal necessities mean little to the in-migrant woman, and the impressions she receives are an important determinant of her future actions. When no explanation is given concerning why a question must be asked, and when the question is embarrassing in the first place, the result can be a humiliating implication. The interviews indicate a severe gap in communication between the southern mountain woman and public health personnel, which led to further embarrassment for the already self-conscious southern mountain woman. Welfare is difficult enough for her to accept; but when it is accompanied by humiliation and lack of communication, acceptance becomes even more painful.

Perhaps part of this lack of communication stems from the fact that many clinic doctors are foreign, and that many native American doctors do seem to have a distinct prejudice against "poor white trash." Often doctors, as well as other public health personnel, have little time, and less inclination, to explain what the treatment will entail in terms which the southern mountain mother can understand. One informant reported her horror after receiving a spinal anesthetic for her delivery; since no one had told her what the effects would be, she became terrified, certain that she had been paralyzed from the waist down.

It is not only the lack of communication, the waiting, and the impersonality of treatment that deters the southern mountain woman from using public health services; it is also sometimes the method of billing. During the weeks I was interviewing one informant, one of her sons received a large gash in the back of his head. She took him to the Emergency Room of one of Detroit's major hospitals. He was released and asked to return after a week to have the stitches taken out. This woman, her four children, her husband, and occasionally her husband's brother and his wife, live in a small three-room apartment. The family pays $100 a month for rent; and on good weeks, which are seldom, her husband brings home $95. One day when I returned to continue the interviews, I saw that the child had had the stitches removed, and I asked the woman how she had managed to get to the hospital (I had volunteered to drive them when she expressed anxiety about not knowing how to get there by public transportation.) She did not answer at first, and only said that a few days before they had received a twenty-two dollar bill from the hospital for the emergency treatment. Later, she told me that her husband had removed the stitches himself. He had used the family nail clippers, which were kept on a dusty ledge over the door. There was also another factor which related to this home-doctoring: the hospital had instructed the parents to take the child to the division called "surgery" for removal of the stitches.

There are two elements here which deterred the parents from taking the child to the hospital—and may have also discouraged the family from ever using that facility again. First, the billing procedure of the hospital dictates that bills be paid either by welfare agencies or by private individuals. There is no graduated scale for patients who are not totally covered by welfare or insurance. Perhaps ninety-five percent of that hospital's patients have their bills sent directly to their welfare agency. This informant and her husband were attempting to live without the help of welfare, although they had needed to depend upon it in the past, and they thus fell within that five percent of the hospital's patients who personally received bills for their treatment. The family's initial reaction to the bill was confusion and alarm; twenty-two dollars is a significant amount of money to a family of six whose monthly income after rent is at best $280. In the first place, they do not believe in owing money; and in the second place, they could not understand why no adjustment was made for their financial condition. Initially, they had stoically planned to pay the entire bill. However, one of the husband's co-workers told him that if he did not pay, the hospital would absorb the cost. To my knowledge, the bill has not yet been paid, and this family learned a bit more about "appropriate" patterns of behavior in the city. What conclusions could they have reached, except that one does not go to the hospital, one should try to rely on welfare, and one need not pay bills?

In addition, the fact that the child was asked to return to a section of the hospital called "surgery," was a horrifying prospect. Traditionally the person from the Southern Appalachians cites, as one of his basic distrusts of doctors, the idea that they will "cut on him" or perform "surgery."[o] While this dread was probably not the prime reason for the home operation with the nail clippers, it was definitely a contributing factor.

My interviews did not reveal the intense anti-Negro feeling reported by Killian among the general "southern white" population in Chicago.[46] Even after the riots the preceding summer, it appears that the southern mountain in-migrant has less anti-Negro feeling than other segments of the southern population. However, the women interviewed did express some uneasiness about the fact that the majority of patients and professional personnel in the public health services were Negro. This factor seems to have had some deterring effect upon the southern mountain woman's use of the facilities, although other influences appear to be much more important.

More significant than the racial factor was the repeated expression of humiliation and confusion at having to face a new doctor each visit to the clinic. The traditional modesty of the southern mountain woman is fierce: the necessity of having to undress is in itself painful, and it becomes even more so when one has to appear in such a condition before a stranger—and a different one each visit.[P] Most of the women expressed acute embarrassment about the pelvic examination; several felt they had been physically hurt by it, and one woman commented that it "somehow wasn't right" having a strange man "handle" and "see" her just as if he were her husband. The most humiliating aspect of these examinations was the fact that the strangers were usually men. The southern mountain woman is not especially predisposed toward doctors, in the first place; but she is even less enthusiastic about having to submit to what she considers a highly personal examination by a man. In her tradition, prenatal counsel is given by a woman. Thus, the usual clinic situation intensifies the discomfort of accepting what is viewed as "welfare," and a visit is hardly an attractive prospect for an expectant Southern Appalachian mother.

It appears that no matter how good the public health facilities are, they will do little good for this population unless some action is taken to provide solutions for: the way in which transportation to the facilities can be obtained;

---

[o]Such statements recur with such consistency that they have taken on the status of proverbial expressions.

[P]During my field trips to Kentucky in 1960 and 1961 I noticed that older women often changed clothes by simply putting on a dress over one already being worn. Also, I observed that it was unusual for persons to disrobe in front of others, even those of the same sex.

the manner in which patients are billed; the length of time one is forced to wait for treatment; the impersonal way the doctor's treatment is conducted; and the embarrassment suffered from being examined by a new, and usually male, doctor each visit. All of these problems reinforce the southern mountain in-migrant's feeling that "to beg"—to accept public health care—is degrading. That belief will not die until the behavior which the southern mountain person views as "begging" is given some dignity.

E. Attitudes Toward Doctors. During the interviews one informant explained that in the old days many people had already raised their families before they even saw a doctor; in fact, she said, "They didn't even know doctors was like normal people." The idea that physicians are not quite like everyone else still lingers in the mind of the southern mountain in-migrant in Detroit. Unlike many segments of the urban population, the southern mountaineer does not regard the physician as sacrosanct; rather, the doctor is viewed in terms of the community values and is judged by his ascriptive rather than his achieved status. The fact that a physician has successfully passed examinations and mastered his profession means less to the person from the southern mountains than whose son he might be and how he relates to others as a person. It appears that a general suspicion of doctors exists among those mountain people most removed from urban influences, while a highly limited acceptance exists among transition groups affected by urbanization, such as the mining communities.[47]

The characteristics for which a doctor may be valued and accepted by the southern mountain patient seem to have little to do with medical competence. The patient must be familiar with the physician and view him as a neighbor and a member of the community. The doctor must take time to listen and talk with his patient, and must explain things to him clearly. Matthews reports similar attitudes in the Tennessee community she studied:

Ridge residents have a strong feeling against outside professional help. They prefer to use home veterinarians, home doctors, home preachers, and home undertakers . . . Most residents are horrified by the idea of being taken to hospitals, many of them exacting promises from kin that they will be allowed to die at home. They want "Doc   " to treat them at home or in his county-seat office because they have "plowed many a day with him barefoot."[48]

One of the women interviewed in this study put it this way: "If they [southern mountain women] been to a doctor at all, they had a little coal camp doctor; somebody they'd known all their life."

The fact that the southern mountain woman prefers a doctor she has known for a long time might account in part for her persistent search for private physicians as an alternative to public clinic services in Detroit. Often, in her quest, she goes from one doctor to another.[49] Notice the use of the plural in the following quote from a Detroit respondent: "Some [doctors] is good and some's bad, but naturally the ones I would pick for myself would be the doctors that knowed me all my life." The search for a private doctor is partly the search for private attention. It is also partly an attempt to act like the "average," middle class, urban person. However, the attempt often fails because even the private doctor is not able to give the kind of personal attention the southern mountain in-migrant wishes, and the southern mountain patient often cannot pay the fees which are usually geared toward a middle class income. All of the women interviewed in Detroit had "shopped around" for a regular private doctor; het, at the time of the interview, only two had found doctors with whom they were satisfied.

The southern mountain women interviewed for this study pursued their search for a private physician with an almost frantic dedication. One woman had "gone through" more than five different private doctors in the course of a single pregnancy and finally gave up and went back to her home in Kentucky to have her child in a private clinic attended by a doctor with whom she had gone to high school. This preference among certain groups for treatment by private physicians rather than medical welfare clinics has been reported elsewhere.[50]

In going the rounds of different private medical doctors, the southern mountain woman often finds her way into the offices of non-medical "doctors," many of whom are outright quacks.[q] Because she does not like "welfare" medical care, and because she chooses a doctor for reasons that have little to do with his scientific competence, the southern mountain woman is likely to consult such non-medical "doctors."[51] To her, they appear to be private "doctors" and often give her the attention a medical doctor has failed to offer. The interviews showed that the respondents were unfamiliar with the qualification of medical doctors and did not feel their training was significantly different from that of osteopaths and chiropractors. Almost all of them believed that the three were similarily trained, but that a medical doctor tended to perform "surgery," an osteopath was either a bone or foot doctor, and a chiropractor was a back specialist.

Marion Pearsall has described medical care in the mountains with particular reference to the maternity cycle: "[It is] still almost entirely part of the family system . . . This is especially apparent in the area of maternal health and the rearing of children. Childbearing, for example, is believed to be such a natural function that it is not generally thought of as a matter for medical attention."[52] The southern mountain woman today brings to the city an indifference, if not disdain, toward doctors; and a feeling that since maternity is a natural condition rather than an illness, there is little reason to consult a physician about it. Since the one type of doctor she might have consulted is unavailable in the city—that doctor with whom her husband might have plowed—she often goes without medical care. The only chink in the wall of this traditional non-medical approach to maternity is the fact that most of the southern mountain women today are having their children in hospitals. However, although this particular behavior pattern has changed slightly, it does not appear that the basic medical attitudes

---

[q]I use the term to refer to individuals professing medical skills and knowledge which they do not have.

have also altered. Most of the women interviewed would have preferred having their children at home, and usually ignored advice given them during their hospital confinement. Often they returned to their home as the time for delivery approached, so that they could be both with the doctor they had known for years, and with their mother or another older woman adviser.

The southern mountain woman brings to the large city the traditional attitude that medical care is seldom necessary for maternity, and that if a medical doctor must be consulted, he should be more a friend than a removed scientist. Each women interviewed for this study had one or more stories to illustrate her feeling that she was treated badly by doctors. In one way or another, the doctors she visited did not meet her expectations of what a doctor should do for his patient. First, every woman indicated that most of the doctors she visited treated her as though she were on "an assembly line." The feeling generally expressed was, "He made me feel as if he was trying to rush me out in order to get another one in." The best that could be said for one of the doctors was, "He was brief, to the point, and professional—which is about all you can expect from a doctor." Such statements clearly show the disappointment experienced. Somehow they had expected, but not been allowed, to communicate with the doctor.[53]

Although others have pointed it out, it cannot be stressed too often that many of these women have much more to complain about than the actual physical problems for which they visit the physician; these other problems are part of what they feel the doctor is not allowing them to communicate.[54] By not acting the traditional and expected role of "friend," the urban doctor often loses his southern mountain patient. If the urban physician does not want these patients to leave him, he must somehow find a way to fulfill their need for personal, meaningful, communication. They have come from a tradition in which a mother, a friendly family doctor, or a faith healer has treated their illnesses. All of these traditions involved an intense and reinforcing personal relationship between the healer and the patient. The stresses of acculturation in the city intensity the need to seek aid; yet it is a sad irony that the traditional sources of physical and psychic counsel have often been left back in the southern mountains.

What exactly should the medical doctor's role be in treating those aspects of the patient's condition which are caused by the life situation and result in mental, rather than physical, anguish? If a physician does not satisfy her traditional expectations, and help relieve her of emotional as well as physical stress, the southern mountain woman will continue to perceive his treatment as less than satisfactory. She will continue to shop around for new doctors in the city, return to her home in the southern mountains for treatment of severe symptoms, or retreat into the traditional attitude that doctors are not much help. If she chooses the latter two patterns, as in Detroit, she will only ask for medical care at the last minute, and then with reluctance.

Whereas the early doctors in the South crossed the mountains and had to learn the traditional patterns there, today it is the southern mountain woman who must cross over into a new culture to find medical help. There were difficulties for the early doctors going into the mountains, and there are difficulties now for the mountain woman going from her ghetto culture of southern mountain poverty into the urban doctor's office. The situation is reversed, but there are once again misunderstandings and differing expectations. The major complaint of the respondents in this study was that the doctor did not seem to care for them or about them. As Koos states, certainly "some of these differences [are] unavoidable. It appear[s], however, that some of the 'scientific distance' between patient and physician was artificial, and could be reduced."[55]

It is paradoxical that most of the women interviewed showed some desire to learn accepted city ways, yet they were thwarted in many of their attempts. One middle class urban value is the belief in physicians; yet as an uninformed person, the southern mountain woman cannot make the distinctions between different types of "doctors." Thus, she easily finds herself in the hands of non-medical charlatans who listen to her and talk with her in terms she can understand.[r]

Another urban value which the southern mountain woman quickly learns about is the respect for, and the power of, money. She soon discovers that money bought more in the South, even though there may be more of it in the northern city. One of her major complaints about medical doctors is that their fees are too high, yet the southern mountain woman will often spend an exorbitant sum on a chiropractor and not regret one penny of it. The chiropractor has usually spent time with her, and consequently she feels satisfied with his care. However, when a medical doctor charges what the mountain woman considers a large sum of money for care which does not include the needed (and expected) personal attention, a complaint understandably follows. After all, in a culture which tells you that money is important, and when money will not buy what you deem valuable, what can one do but complain? None of the women interviewed recognized that their complaints were the result of accepting the value of money from the urban culture while retaining the value of personal medical attention from the southern culture. (The "recognition," however, would hardly have eased their distress.)

The charge against city doctors most frequently stated by the women interviewed for this study was that physicians are interested in money, not people or their health. It is an easy progression from feeling that you are not getting enough personal attention, to realizing that much money is going for a service with which you are not satisfied, to feeling that it is your money rather than your health which most interests the doctor. As one informant bitterly put it: "Doctors are pretty much the same everywhere; they [only] want to be paid." Significantly, many of the women interviewed expressed the belief that people in higher economic brackets were better treated by doctors than they were.

Koos indicates that this is one of the prime reasons people in Regionville went to chiropractors.

The idea that physicians are primarily interested in money has become a firm part of the southern mountain woman's belief. It was manifested in a number of different ways in the interviewing. One common complaint among the respondents was that doctors did not personally give them medicine, but rather gave them a prescription which had to be filled at a drug store. As Koos put it, "The idea of the family doctor as one who practices medicine in the home and is a walking drugstore has had to be revised sharply in recent years."[56] However, to the southern mountain woman under urban financial stress, a prescription means more than just going to the drug store; it means lack of personal attention, as well as a trip through confusing traffic, usually with several unattended small children at home (or dragging behind her), in order to spend additional money in an often overpriced local drug store. The anger at incurring this extra trouble and expense is contained in the belief of one respondent that city doctors get "a fifty-cent kickback" on each prescription, while in Kentucky, she said, the doctor will usually "give you his own medicine from his own supply instead of sending you for a prescription."

Another commonly held belief used by respondents to document doctors' greed for money is the idea that a physician will usually keep you returning, visit after visit, in order to earn more from your illness. The value of repeated visits is difficult for the Southern Appalachian person to accept.[57] Likewise, it is difficult for the southern mountaineer, who traditionally treats the symptom only when it is impossible to ignore, to comprehend the value of preventative checkups. He seems to perceive his physical well-being much as he perceives his spiritual well-being. However, he does not realize that if one "backslides" in matters of medical attention, one cannot always be "saved." The return or preventative visit, to the mountaineer, is regarded primarily as another way for the doctor to make additional money—but often, the doctor has not taken the time to explain the necessity of a return visit.[58] Ideally, he should be able to do it in terms that the mountaineer would understand.

The belief that the doctor wishes his client to make a return visit in order to make money is reflected in some of the ideas the informants held regarding vaccination. They indicated a feeling that vaccinations were given to make a person ill so he would need to see a doctor. The reason one got ill from the vaccination was that the doctors put "germs" in them or made them from snake venom, mold, or extract from the bones of dead horses. On the other hand, some informants indicated that doctors often gave injections that were "just water" so they could make an additional charge. Clearly, none of these ideas reflect the type of trust the physician hopes to elicit from his patients. Among the mountain in-migrant, the intricate belief network which supports the basic feeling of distrust in the physician seems endless. Another common idea held by the respondents was that doctors, in addition to wanting higher fees, have some sort of sinister desire to "cut on you." This fear of surgery is compounded by the fact that it is usually performed in a hospital; and hospital stays (other than for birth) are dreaded almost as much as the surgery itself.[59] One informant told proudly how her fater-in-law left the hospital after refusing surgery, saying that he would rather "die at home"—which he did. It is no wonder that southern mountain women dislike having episiotomies when they give birth.[s]

Several of the women interviewed voiced the complaint that doctors required payment in advance for maternity care. Most of these women resented being asked to pay for services before they were performed, and expressed the feeling that somehow if the doctor cannot produce the desired effect, he should not be paid. One woman remarked, concerning her pregnancy: "Why should I go pay him in advance when I don't know what shape the baby would be in." To these informants, advance payment seemed to reflect distrust, and once again suggested they were irresponsible "hillbillies." One woman indignantly expressed her opinion: "I trust him with my good health and he should trust me to pay my bill."

The medically indigent southern mountain family, like many families in the low socioeconomic group, has a set of priorities that places medical care well below the necessities of life. Even after the necessities have been taken care of, medical care is traditionally a "must" only when there is an immediate and unbearable symptom. In order to encourage the rearrangement of priorities in the lives of the in-migrant southern mountain family—giving medical care the high rank it requires—the urban physician must offer something which the mountaineer needs and wants. Although he is quick to point to it as a reason, it is not simply money that keeps the mountain in-migrant away from the physician. SG, who makes an annual income of about $3,000, spent hundreds of dollars on a chiropractor. She did not bemoan the cost at all, because the "doctor" spent a great deal of time with her, and even gave her eleven pills to take before every meal.

Most of the informants in this study indicated that they felt the advice given them by doctors was not very helpful. Many put more stock in their own self-diagnosis than in what the doctor said. Often the women indicated that they had listened politely, and then returned home to do what they thought best. After all, the traditional role of the woman in the southern mountain family is that of diagnostician and healer. It would be natural for her to resist incursions on the assumed province of that role. After her first (and only) visit, one woman described the prenatal clinic as a place where: "they talk to you, give you vitamin pills and stuff [which] you go home and lay up on the shelf." Thus, it appears that there is frequently no significant correlation between behavior and medical advice, and that until the traditional attitudes change, behavior will not alter.[t]

Distrust and confusion about medical doctors abounds among the southern mountain women in the North. The southern mountain woman and her doctor appear to have virtually no dialog. This is undoubtedly due to difficulties on the part of both physician and patient. The southern mountain woman can

---

[s]The episiotomy is an incision of the perineum made during the second stage of labor in order to prevent laceration, or tearing, such as DG experienced.

[t]Peters, "Patterns of Health Care," p. 420, reports, "There was obviously no correlation of such advice [given by medical doctors and nurses] with subsequent behavior."

complain, as one respondent did, that "you can't hardly understand what they [doctors] are talking about in the city," while the doctor can complain that the southern mountain woman needs a psychiatric social worker more than a medical doctor.

The physician who deals with southern mountain women in the city will have to take cognizance of the fact that he is performing a role which traditionally was that of an older woman in the family—the healer—and that this role traditionally demanded a personal commitment between patient and healer which is antithetical to the "detached" stance of the scientist. It would be good for him to recognize the traditional modesty of the woman from the mountains; and to remember that in matters of maternity an older woman was usually the advisor, and at delivery it was often traditional for a woman to handle the proceedings. If he understands the traditional patterns of behavior and traditional attitudes of his patients it will be much easier for him to reach them. He will be able to use those folk cures which are not harmful, such as placing a knife under the mattress to ease labor, to gain his patient's confidence, and he will consequently find it easier to replace harmful traditions with constructive practices.[u] It is important that he remember that traditional behavior and attitudes fill important needs or they would not have persisted, and that when attempting to alter them, he must do so with practices and ideas which serve the needs originally filled by the traditions.

Koos has pointed out that the physician is often more highly trained in the science of his profession than in the humanistic responsibilities of it.[60] It is true that the doctor often comes from a group that values success, and he finds it difficult, if not impossible, to communicate with the poor white. He might find it helpful to examine his assumptions about the southern mountain in-migrant for traces of stereotyping—for if the cycle of distrust is to be broken, the doctor will probably have to make the first move. It will be difficult, but essential, for him to attempt to prepare himself *personally*, as well as he is prepared professionally, to treat whatever group needs his service. Part of this "personal" preparation is the objective study of the traditional beliefs and attitudes held by his patients. He must also learn to speak their language so they can understand him—even if he has to talk about "opening the lungs" or "keeping the fever out of the brain." Once he understands the basic attitudes of his patients, it might be easier for him to realize, for example, that when a southern mountain woman submits to a pelvic examination, it is often humiliating to her, as well as a sign of intimacy which may lead her to expect more understanding and personal attention from the physician than is actually received. Learning people's traditions is time-consuming, but it would seem a necessity if the physician is to take the first step in breaking the traditional patterns of medical behavior among groups such as the southern mountain in-migrant. If the doctor learns how to communicate with and understand his patient, he will be better equipped to help ease the mental and physical anguish of the people who need his skills and time

---

[u]A cure reported by several Detroit respondents. See Hand, *Popular Beliefs*, item #48.

but cannot pay for them. Once he succeeds in doing this, he will begin to look more "like normal people" to those in-migrants who regard him negatively.

F. Self-Diagnosis and the Persistence of Folk Medicine. The southern mountain woman appears to retain most of her traditional role as diagnostician in the urban environment. By the time she has decided upon a visit to a physician, she has usually concluded what is wrong. Not only has she probably diagnosed her own or her child's case before she appears at the doctor's office, but she has often also determined what is necessary for a cure. One informant reported that she ceased going to one doctor because she felt he had failed to prescribe the "right" medicine for her.

The description of complaints which the in-migrant mountain mother gives the doctor is often difficult for the urban physician to comprehend, for the woman will often use traditional expressions based on traditional attitudes toward disease. Any difficulty with breathing can be described as "smothering"; rashes must always be "brought out"; all manner of respiratory ailments can be called "pneumonia"; and "hives" can be "bold" hives, "little red" hives, or "stretch" hives. In order to understand the past medical history as well as the present complaint of a southern mountain in-migrant, the doctor necessarily must take time to understand both the terms used and the patient's feelings about the particular illness. One informant in Detroit reported that what she called "quick T.B." was the most dreaded disease in her family. It was caused, she said, by a menstruating woman taking a shower or being caught in a rainstorm. The blood flow would stop and "back up," resulting in sudden hemorrhaging from the lungs and death. Several of the women in her family had died from it. Fears of such medically undefined diseases is real and intense, as is the woman's belief that she could correctly make the diagnosis.

The tradition of self-diagnosis, coupled with the communication problem resulting in part from the very words exchanged between patient and doctor, is yet an additional factor discouraging the southern mountain in-migrant's use of city physicians. It also appears to be a contributing factor in the patient's frequent switching from one private doctor to another. If the doctor cannot understand the patient's complaint and diagnosis, and the patient cannot understand the doctor, it is unlikely that the two will have a satisfactory relationship. In addition, the tradition of not seeing the physician until the last minute makes the patient even less receptive to medical terminology and logic, especially if it contradicts the patient's own diagnosis and expectations for treatment. How can a southern mountain mother listen objectively to her doctor when she makes the visit, as one respondent described, under the following conditions: "Because when they [her children] are sick and need medical attention they need it at that moment, not a day or two days later."[61] The doctor is usually the last resort, rarely the first; one only visits him when there is something wrong.

These attitudes are often coupled with a traditional fatalistic approach to life and death.[v] This fatalism is more pronounced among the older people from the southern mountains, but it could still be detected among the young mothers in this study. The differing degrees of fatalism between the generations is well described by the following account of when and why an informant finally took her son to the doctor:

A. In the winter time pneumonia is very common.
Q. What did they do for that?
A. Well if it gets bad enough you go to the doctor.
Q. When is bad enough?
A. Well when a child is laying there tossing and turning and can hardly breathe and you get scared or [it] turns purple and starts strangling or something serious . . . Joe, he's laying in the bed and he's turning purple you know, and, ah, my mother-in-law runs in [and] instead of saying "you'd better take him to the doctor," she says "that's a dead baby, [name of informant], mark my words," and I grabbed Joe . . . and I ran, or partly ran, all the way to Doc [name] . . . I just thought to get him out of there, you know, I think I said "no, he's not dead yet," [and] off I went like a big bird.

The mother-in-law in this case represents the older tradition of completely discounting the effect of the physician in the face of what appears to be fated. The mother of the child remains fatalistic by not taking her baby to the doctor until the last minute, yet she is not ready to accept death in the name of fate until she uses the doctor as a last resort. This "last resort" pattern can be seen as an improvement, although not an ideal behavior pattern; it is related to and resembles the pattern of the southern mountain mother going to the hospital for birth but not for prenatal or postnatal care.

A tradition of self-diagnosis is often accompanied by a tradition of self-medication, and it is therefore not surprising to find that all of the southern mountain women interviewed for this study had an extensive knowledge of folk medicine. Many of them openly acknowledged that they used the cures in the city, although they recognized the stigma attached to such actions. Generally, the effects of urbanization had begun to influence the folk medical practices and beliefs retained by these women, and it is probable that many of the changes have already begun before the move to the North. However, the number of cures and the incidence of their use as detected in this study, indicate a significant retention of tradition among the southern mountain in-migrant women. Some beliefs and practices were only vaguely remembered; while many were remembered and altered; and others remained intact and were practiced in the city. Given the persistence of traditional attitudes and other obstacles in the way of obtaining medical care reported in the earlier sections of this paper, it is not surprising that the cures have remained embedded in the body of beliefs surrounding doctoring and health.

[v]See also Peters, "Patterns of Health Care," p. 421. The author points out that no matter how satisfying the experience was with a physician, patients often would not return for treatment because they felt "fate" determined the outcome of the illness.

Some cures show the effects of urbanization more than others. For example, the use of non-prescription medication appeared frequently in many of the cures reported by the women interviewed. The ubiquitous "baby aspirin" seems to have replaced such unavailable items as asafetida and turpentine. Castor oil and paragoric, although apparently not popular ingredients in cures in the old southern mountains, were frequently cited for various maladies: drinking a few ounces of castor oil was recommended to induce labor, and rubbing paregoric on a baby's gums was recommended for teething.[w] With increasing urbanization in the South, and the growing number of commercial outlets available, such patent medicines probably began entering the realm of southern mountain folk medicine long before the mountaineers began moving to the cities. However, since the urban environment makes it easier to find such items, while also making it impossible to locate other cure ingredients, the use of patent medicines is further encouraged. In the "old days," informants reported, a woman would drink herb teas to induce labor (Hand #s 38-42)[x], while a teething child might have its gums rubbed with the brains of a rabbit (Hand # 365)[y]. Thus, the tendency to replace older ingredients with patent medicines is increased in the urban environment.

Another traditional medical practice altered by urbanization is the manner in which a woman is supposed to be able to induce an abortion. The very idea of abortion itself seems to have been encouraged by urbanization. Most of the informants considered a large family a burden and a sign of poverty. While most expressed the traditional belief that women should have many children, they also expressed their present ambivalence by saying that they wished they had fewer children themselves, or did not want more. When describing a family who had "made it" out of poverty, one informant repeatedly mentioned that the family had only two children. Abortion, as well as birth control, has become more accepted by the younger, urbanized generation of southern mountaineers. The informants generally believed that turpentine and quinine would induce abortion (Hand #s 22 and 23). Since quinine was more readily available in the city, it was reported as actually used more often. The ways of inducing abortion by mechanical means seem to have been altered slightly in the city, too. An older informant indicated that women in the mountains would attempt to abort by breaking the "bag" surrounding the unborn child with a splinter from an elm tree. Most of the women indicated that they had heard of the same practice of breaking the bag, but had been told that a pencil should be used to do it.

Some women appear to have completely abandoned specific cures because the ingredients were too difficult to find in the city, while traditional urban replacements were more accessible. Thus, one woman, when asked what she would use if her child had a cold, answered at once, "baby aspirin and cough medicine," but when asked about what she used down in the South replied "coal

---

[w]Hand, *Popular Beliefs*, cites castor oil five times, and does not list paregoric at all.

[x]In this section all cures found in the Frank C. Brown collection edited by Wayland Hand will be listed by number in parentheses following the item in the text.

[y]The cure of rabbit brains was not reported by any informant in this study, although a number of teething cures unlisted in Hand were given, such as rubbing catnip tea on the child's gums.

oil and turpentine rubbed on the chest" (Hand # 1130). Many herbs that were the basic ingredients in teas and poultices in the mountains are unavailable in the city. Occasionally informants reported that they were able to buy such items as catnip tea in the drug store, but generally these traditional herbs are difficult to come by and the "cures" for which they are used tend to die out. For example, informants reported that it was generally believed in the southern mountains that all infants should be induced to break out in "little red" hives. If the infant did not break out with these hives, the disease would "go in" and turn into the dreaded, and fatal, "bold" or "stretch" hives. In order to make the child break out, catnip tea was usually administered as a preventative measure (Hand #312). The informants believed that all rashes should be encouraged, and that the more the rash was "brought out" (Hand # 1803), the better the chances were for the patient's health. However, most of the women recognized that the children they had raised in the city and who had not had the benefits of catnip tea, had never had the "little red" or any other hives, and seemed none the worse for it. Actually, it appears that catnip tea *causes* the "little red" hives; this particular mountain preventative measure probably "prevented" the fatal types of hives just as much as it kept the houses safe from tigers! The "cure," however, seems to be dying in the city—not so much from logic as from the absence of the ingredient.

When ingredients for the "cures" are unavailable in the city, the cure will disappear, receive a substitute ingredient, or be replaced by another traditional cure not discouraged by the urban environment. The herbs for poultices, used for "risings" (pimples) by one informant when she lived in the mountains, were not available in the city. Thus, to bring the blemish "to a head," she substituted another traditional cure whose ingredients *were* available in the city: she spread the skin from the inside of an eggshell over it (Hand # 1931). Almost all diseases have such multiple cures. Some of these cures involve a person with particular healing "powers," who acts in a ritualized manner. Thus, in the city, the absence of the herb "yellow root," which is used to make into tea for "thrash" (Hand # 399), did not bother the southern mountain mother who reported it as a cure. This fungus irritation, called "thrush" by doctors, has many cures in the mountains. One such cure reported by most informants, involves a "thrash doctor," often a person who has never seen his father, or who is a seventh son (Hand #s 221ff). These people with special powers are said to be able to cure an afflicted child by blowing into its mouth (Hand # 413 ff.). However, one mother, perhaps because she knew few people in the city and could not find a "thrash doctor," used another traditional cure: washing out the child's mouth with urine (Hand # 394). Similarly, as the respondents reported, if one cannot find a person with the power to "stop blood" (Hand #s 879 ff.), one can always treat the wound with cobwebs (Hand # 861) or scrapings from a woolen blanket.

Changes are common in the folk cures, reflecting the general influence of urbanization. At times the change is more subtle than the outright search for different ingredients or other cures. One respondent reported that pregnant women should not have permanents since the curl would not "take." This may be a modernization of the older belief that pregnant women should not comb their hair ten days before delivery or it will either fall out or turn grey (Hand #15).

Urbanization definitely has had a repressive effect on some beliefs associated with childbirth and child rearing. All of the informants indicated that they felt breast feeding was best for a child; that was the traditional way of feeding a child in the South. However, few of them had breast fed their children in the city, although they expressed regret about not having done it. The major reason given for not breast feeding in the city was that it "was not done." Whereas the traditionally modest southern mountain woman did not hesitate to breast feed her child in public in the mountains, she found that it was an embarrassing thing to do in the city.

Hospital delivery of children has also made continuation of many traditional practices impossible. The practice of burying the afterbirth (Hand # 59), of putting fat meat down the newborn child's throat to clear out the phlegm (Hand # 271), of believing that the first born child will be lucky if born in the father's lap (Hand #33), and numerous beliefs regarding the special powers of the child born with a "veil" (Hand #s 244 ff.), all of which were reported by informants in this study, can hardly survive when births take place in the hospital.[62] The tension which results from thwarting these traditions in the hospital may well contribute to the informants' general preference for having their children at home.

There are some traditional cures and patterns of action which are not hampered by the urban environment and therefore will probably continue much as they were brought to the city, unless the basic attitudes of the in-migrants change. One informant indicated that the best cure for a child who has colic or who is "liver bound," is to hold the child upside down by the feet (Hand #s 287 and 319). A traditional cure still used for nosebleeds is to put a scissor down the back of the patient's neck (Hand # 1893). Most of the women interviewed indicated that it was extremely dangerous for a pregnant woman to reach high above her head, for such action would cause the cord to wrap about the unborn child's neck and strangle it (Hand # 34). A traditional dietary restriction reported by many of the women interviewed prohibited the eating of fresh fruit or vegetables when pregnant. This practice clearly does little to furnish vitamins to an undernourished woman, and an awareness of this tradition would certainly be of help to the public health nutritionist. These are examples of medical beliefs which are not significantly affected by the urban situation and therefore can persist in the city much as they did in the mountains.

Some traditional beliefs survive in the city because they have been rationalized into forms which are acceptable to the urban dweller. For example, one woman reported the old belief that it is bad to have teeth extracted during pregnancy (Hand # 14). She claimed that her dentist had told her not to have extraction done during menses because she would lose too much blood, and she therefore concluded that, for similar reasons, a pregnant woman should not have teeth removed before the birth of her child. Another woman explained that one should not cut an infant's fingernails (Hand #s 233 and 252 ff.), but rather "you bit the baby's fingernails off because you could cut his fingers, you know, they were real tender and delicate." In urban society this explanation is much more acceptable than the belief that if a child's fingernails are cut with a scissor before he is one year of age, he will grow up to be a thief (Hand # 233).

Traditional beliefs relating to the maternity cycle have persisted with vigor among the southern mountain women interviewed for this study. Often, as was the case with the informant who cited her dentist as the authority for not having her teeth pulled, women claimed "professional" opinion as their authority for certain traditional ideas they still held. The feeling that this was necessary might reflect a general uneasiness about the ideas, or the inevitable tension of the interview situation. For example, the belief that the sex of the child can be predicted by the manner in which the child is carried by the woman before birth, "high" or "low" (Hand # 147), was reported by almost all informants.[63] However, one woman made it a point to explain that the nurses in the hospital where she delivered agreed that she would have a boy since she was carrying the child "low and broad."

The traditional belief, that a child can be "marked" by what the mother does or sees during the prenatal period, (Hand #'s 83-120) was reported with rich elaborations by virtually every informant.[64] This belief, more than any other investigated in this study, was expressed most often in the form of short tales, or memorates. These stories told how the mothers' behavior during the prenatal period resulted in "marking," which ranged from innocuous birthmarks (Hand ∝'s 85ff.), to specific personality traits (Hand # 83f.), to actual deformities (Hand #'s 114ff). According to the informants, the child was often marked by the mother's cravings during her pregnancy. Thus, the mother's behavior during the prenatal period is traditionally considered important by the Southern Appalachian in-migrant.

The stories of "markings" gathered in this investigation were numerous. One woman told of a younger brother who, "well, he just wasn't right" when born and died shortly after birth. She blamed the deformity, and the death, on the fact that while her mother was carrying the child she had seen youngsters killing bullfrogs. "You know how their stomach looks," she said, and explained that her mother had vomited at the sight of the dead frogs. The result, according to the informant, was that "this baby's stomach wasn't even in the right place and his arms hung different." Another story related by one respondent told of how, when she was pregnant, she had seen a friend of hers lose a leg while trying to "hop a train." When she rushed to help him "he said 'Lord have mercy, [name of informant], you ['ll] ruin your baby!' "

Just as the belief in preventative medicine revealed in the use of catnip tea for "bold" hives has not been translated into the use of medical services, such as vaccination, for preventative means, neither has the considerable concern for the child's welfare reflected in the extensive body of lore about such "markings" been translated into prenatal care for the mother and child in the urban environment. Clearly such stories ease the guilt felt at the birth of a deformed or dead child, but the vast number of beliefs in the area of "marking" show more than an attempt to accommodate guilt; they show a genuine concern of the mother for the welfare of her child. This concern could be of help to public health personnel concerned with prenatal care.[z]

There are numerous folk cures from the southern mountains which are not harmful in and of themselves. The practice of measuring an asthmatic child against a stick, believing that when he grows past that mark his asthma will be cured (Hand # 829), does not harm the child as much as not taking him to a physician for treatment. Putting a red thread about a child's neck to prevent the mumps from "falling" (Hand # 1832) is not inherently dangerous, and neither is the recommended juice of a baked onion for pneumonia (Hand #'s 1936, 1111). Informants in this study reported all of these remedies. Such beliefs and "cures" that are not inherently harmful could be used by the physician to help introduce an unfamiliar medical practice to the southern mountain patient. Similarily, the use of folk medical terms, along with urban terminology, can be useful to the physician who is attempting to establish rapport and treat the southern mountain in-migrant. It would not hurt the urban physician to utilize knowledge of such traditions in his attempt to treat his patients.

If the traditional practices which *can* prove detrimental to health are to be altered, then it is imperative that the doctor show a respect for that part of the tradition which is not harmful, and use it to reach his patient. If he does reach the southern mountaineer, then the attitudes and subsequently the behavior may begin to change. Hopefully, the pattern of self-diagnosis and self-medication will be replaced by more frequent and preventative visits to physicians.

There *are* practices in the folk medicine of the southern mountain in-migrant which are seriously harmful. Giving a child turpentine for a cold (Hand #s 2204 and 1456), as recommended by several respondents, can produce chemical pneumonia if it is rejected by the stomach. The abortion practices already described are hardly healthful, and can lead to serious infection and the death of both mother and child. The respondents' traditional use of baking soda to treat the inevitable heartburn of pregnancy (Hand # 1614), is extremely dangerous in a high risk population where toxemia is a constant threat. The sodium intake involved in this cure causes the body to retain water. Water retention is one of the major problems in toxemia, which is why pregnant women are often advised not to eat much salt.

A complex assortment of attitudes and traditional patterns of behavior keep the southern mountain woman from the physician in the city. Consequently, self-diagnosis and self-medication continue. While the folk cures of the southern mountains show slight changes in the urban environment, the conditions under which they are applied have not changed. There is still a basic resistance to physicians which is complicated, but certainly not caused, by the use of traditional medical practices. The continuation of self-diagnosis and self-

[z]Nancy R. Milio, "Structuring the Setting for Health Action," *American Journal of Public Health*, LVII, No. 11 (November, 1967), p. 1988, points out that knowledge of a group's folk medicine can be of great value in working with members of that group; the professional using the lore, however, will not always use it to the same end as the group member.

medication is not surprising, given the obstacles in the way of the mountain woman's obtaining medical care, and her glorification of past values and behavior. As long as the traditional attitudes remain, and as long as there is so little communication between medical professionals and the southern mountain in-migrant in the city, the folk cures will travel along with the traditional values, secure from the effects of modern medical knowledge.

Conclusions and Suggestions

How much of the behavior of the recently arrived in-migrant from the Southern Appalachians can be accounted for by the fact that he almost automatically becomes a member of what we politely call a "culture of poverty"? Certainly a good deal of his behavior is similar to that of other groups, such as Koos' lowest socioeconomic group in Regionville, upstate New York. However, despite similar patterns of behavior among many impoverished groups, we cannot explain behavior away by classifying it. The causes of patterns of action are beliefs rather than statistics; and in the case of the southern mountain in-migrant in Detroit, the traditional attitudes and beliefs he brings with him to the city are a major part of the reasons for his actions. His problems cannot be fully understood by simply analyzing convenient statistical totals such as fetal deaths, and neonatal deaths. Similar patterns of action and attitudes can be caused by dissimilar beliefs; the fatalistic world view of the southern mountaineer and that of the Hindu might cause similar behavior, yet they stem from sets of beliefs which are philosophically far apart. In order to understand behavior we must understand what is behind it, and to do this it is necessary to investigate traditional assumptions. Assumptions may control actions; and until the assumptions change, the actions will alter only slightly. Thus, folk medicine, both helpful and harmful, will continue in the city as long as the traditional southern mountain attitudes toward health and healing remain.

The southern mountain in-migrant does not feel that he is a part of the city; he more often regards himself as a temporary urban resident, while he basically identifies with his region in the Southern Appalachians. It is natural that the feeling of not belonging in a new place will result in a continuation of past traditional practices and attitudes. The necessary consequence of this situation is conflict; it is not surprising that the building in which hepatitis broke out in Detroit in 1967, causing a public outcry, was an overcrowded ghetto dwelling for southern mountain in-migrants. Southern mountain medical traditions and patterns of action in modern urban ghettos can only lead to sickness and misery. With the southern mountain population increasing markedly in Detroit, the situation is not promising.

The general picture resulting from this pilot investigation shows a persistance of tradition among the southern mountain in-migrant women in Detroit, and a use of old patterns of behavior and traditional attitudes to cope with problems presented by the new urban environment. The study revealed a decided tendency to glorify the past, an accute difficulty in dealing with the urban environment even in basic areas such as transportation, a conflict in the demands of changing role requirements, an avoidance of medical "welfare" services, and an indifference or distinct dislike of medical doctors which is coupled with a strong preference for self-diagnosis and self-medication. In addition, there is some indication that in the northern city there is a tendency for the southern mountain woman to revert to the medical attitudes and patterns of her parents' generation. This pattern seems to be at least partly the result of a gap in communication between urban medical doctors and the in-migrants. (In order to pin-point and clarify the preliminary findings of this study, future interviews will be conducted with southern mountain women and with physicians who treat them.)

The tenacity of prior tradition is found in many areas of the southern mountain in-migrant's life, but certainly no aspect is more significant than that of maternal and infant health in a population so prone to disease. The conspicuous absence of the medically indigent southern mountain woman in Detroit from the public health facilities, which offer her care and instruction during the entire maternity cycle, can only be regarded as a serious social problem—and as the southern mountain population in the city grows, so will the problem. The southern mountain woman's traditional values and patterns of behavior appear to lead her to little constructive contact with physicians during the prenatal and postnatal periods. During her pregnancy she has most often sought the advice of an older woman or a non-medical physician. Frequently she will return to the Southern Appalachians shortly before giving birth. Future investigation will clarify these patterns, and hopefully lead to an understanding of why these traditions have not been altered in the northern cities.

It is possible to make some tentative suggestions about how to help the southern mountain woman alter her traditional patterns in the city. One of the best ways of reaching a group is by involving its members in what is being done. Nancy Milio has succeeded in doing this with medically indigent Negro women in her Moms and Tots program in Detroit.[65] Given the reluctance of southern mountain women to travel outside their neighborhoods in the city, and their desire not to be seen in public when pregnant, it seems that a local center, partially staffed by southern women working with professional medical personnel, would be a logical solution to the problem of prenatal and postnatal care. Such a center could also run its own transportation system both to and from the hospital with which it would be associated. In addition, ancillary facilities could be attached to this service, such as a day nursery to care for the children of mothers who are having checkups, a food and clothing distribution center, and a recreation facility. It would also be helpful to have a city information center and general personal counseling services within the center.

The southern mountain in-migrant is more responsive to verbal communication than to print. This is one reason the personal interaction with the physician is so important to him. Doctors who treat this segment of the population should make an attempt to learn and to understand the traditional medical terminology and concepts of their southern mountain patient, as well as the tensions which affect him in the urban center. Fliers, posters, and billboards will have little effect in communicating what public health services are available for the pregnant mountain woman. It would be better to use the omnipresent television and radio as a vehicle for transmitting information about maternity and infant care projects. After all, the Southern Appalachian region is well known for the fact that it has had a long and distinguished history of oral tradition, and it would do no harm to capitalize on the receptiveness of the southern mountain in-migrant to verbal communication. The use of public television and radio might also help those fortunate enough to belong to a higher socio-economic level to realize that there are others in the society who live lives of continual and not so quiet desperation.

The most constructive innovation that can be made to improve the health of both mothers and infants in the southern mountain in-migrant group would be the establishment of a nurse-midwife program in Detroit.[66] Not only would this permit the desired home visit and home delivery, it would also be in keeping with the tradition of counsel and attendance by a woman during pregnancy. The idea is not farfetched. Such a program has been successfully implemented in Leslie County, Kentucky by the Frontier Nursing Association, and at Kings County Hospital in Brooklyn, New York.[67,68] It is a well-known fact that "in the west European countries, a great deal of prenatal care is supervised by nurse-midwives, and sizable proportions of births are delivered by them."[69] England, Wales, Denmark, and the Netherlands have flourishing nurse-midwife programs; all complications are referred to physicians, and a great number of the infants are born at home. All of these countries have lower infant mortality rates than the United States, although 95 percent of our children are born in hospitals.[70] The nurse-midwife program seems to be the ideal way of coping with the traditional attitudes which prevent the southern mountain woman from obtaining needed care during the maternity cycle, and it would certainly not jeopardize the health of either mother or child. Eventually it might even ease the "crisis in maternity care" in this country and lower our infant mortality rate.[71]

Some people are pessimistic about the future of health practices in the Southern Appalachians. Marion Pearsall has succinctly indicated the obstacles:

A history of difficult and limited access to good health services, hence a tradition of doing without; failure to identify certain abnormal states as true illness; willingness to accept and endure numerous symptoms fatalistically; heavy reliance on prayer and home remedies; lack of any real understanding or faith in modern medicine or its practitioners; and a great tendency to live from day to day, putting off decisions requiring purposive action.[72]

As this study has shown, all of these obstacles do exist. However, some authorities have claimed significant results in changing medical and health patterns of the mountain people.[73] Nancy Milio's experience in Detroit, and the findings of persons who have worked in the mountains, indicate that it is possible for the southern mountain in-migrant to alter his general attitudes and patterns of medical behavior in the city.

In the extensive public health literature concerned with the medically indigent, there has been a repeated call for "communication."[74] Although it is clearly a good thing to say "communicate," few depth studies have shown *how* to accomplish this goal with specific groups. The "culture of poverty" is not one culture, but many; and similar behavior can easily be caused by totally different factors. Unless one goes beyond an outline of the symptoms, and attempts to understand the causes of behavior patterns within the different cultures of poverty, "communication" will be all but impossible. The employment problems of the southern mountain male in the urban ghettos look much like the problems of the urban ghetto Negro, but closer investigation of the traditional attitudes behind these two similar behavior patterns might well dictate totally different methods of solving this problem in the two groups.

There are special problems involved in "communication" with the southern mountain in-migrant. As with most groups, one must learn not only how to speak their language, but also when *not* to speak. Communicating with the southern mountaineer is a special problem, for we tend to think we should have no difficulty with him. He seems deceptively to be the "basic American," the relished Anglo stock; but his values and folklore are antithetical to the tradition of achievement and Go-Go that now prevails in our urban centers. In the cities we have tended to overlook him because his skin color allows him to blend before he speaks. But when he does talk and act, he is as far from the American dream as the black American: he is the "hillbilly," the "poor white trash," who has somehow betrayed us all by not being the super frontiersman. Our cities no longer want the frontier or its values; but the southern mountaineer wants the city—more, he *needs* the city. The frontier has passed, even in the South. The city must learn to speak and respect the language of the southern mountaineer in order to help him adjust to a new way of life. The city must learn to speak with the Southern Appalachian in-migrant without thinking of him, or making him think of himself, as having betrayed his "pure stock" by being lazy and stupid. He has much that he can give urban America, and we should not be impatient with him by underestimating the pain of his adjustment. And, just as with the black American, if we fail to learn the language of the southern mountain in-migrant, we will reap a bitter harvest from our isolated certainties.

Appendix I

The Methodology

The purpose of this study is to report preliminary findings arrived at through an objective analysis of: depth interviews of southern mountain women in Detroit; field work done in 1960 and 1961 by myself in Clay and Harlan Counties, Kentucky; published materials; and interviews in Detroit with persons who have professional and non-professional contacts with the southern mountain population in the city.

Given only a three month period in which to contact informants and conduct interviews of a highly personal nature, the number of depth interviews presented here is understandably limited. Interviewing will be continued. At the present stage this study does not attempt statistical analysis. In the future, with a larger number of interviews, the data may be submitted for statistical digestion.

The interviews conducted for this study have been based on the Questionnaire which appears in Appendix II. The Questionnaire was not meant to be used as a rigid structure for the interview; rather it was conceived as a guide for material to be covered, and was intended to be applied with compassionate human flexibility.

It is my sincere hope that the lack of statistical analysis and the limited number of depth interviews will not detract from what I feel are valid observations. The preliminary findings in this study are drawn, in part, from data other than the interviews. Approximately forty hours of depth interviews can be found on tape recordings deposited in the Wayne State University Folklore Archive. They may be consulted for verification of the findings presented in this study. I might add that only responses which were those of more than two-thirds of the women interviewed are used in this report. Background data and identifying initials for these depth informants can be found in Appendix III.

In addition to library research, medical consultation for this study was obtained from medical doctors and public health nurses actively involved in public welfare medical services in Detroit. Most of these consultants were participants in projects involving maternity and infant care for the medically indigent.

Appendix II

The Questionnaire

Sample: Caucasian women who are in-migrants from the non-urban mountain areas of Kentucky, West Virginia, and Tennessee. Preferably ones who have had children in the south and children in a large Northern city. Preferably women who have had at least one child in Detroit. Preferably women whose income qualifies them as being able to benefit from the Detroit welfare services available for health care during the entire maternity cycle.

Background Information:
Name (in full):
Present address:
Maiden name:
Husband's name:

Husband's job(s):

Sources of income:

How much does your family earn during the year?

Mother's name and background: Is she alive? If not, when did she die? Of what?

Father's name and background: Is he alive? If not, when did he die? Of what?

Place and date of your birth: Were you born in a hospital? Did your mother have complications?

How many brothers and sisters did you have? Where are you in the order? Were they born in a hospital? Did your mother have complications?

Where did you go to school? Give dates and places:

What kind of jobs have you had?

Have you any special hobbies or do you like certain types of skilled activity?

Are you active in any religious group in Detroit? Give name(s), address(es), dates, and type of activity:

> Were you active in a religious group in the South? Give name(s), addresses, dates, and type of activity:

Are you active in any community group(s) in Detroit? Give name(s), address(es), dates, and type of activity:

> Were you active in any community group(s) in the South? Give name(s), address(es), and dates and type of activity:

When were you first married? Where? [If discomfort appears, do not press these questions] How many times have you been married? Give names, places, and dates:

When did you move to Detroit?

From where did you come to Detroit? What was the path, dates, places? Why did you decide to come North?

Why did you decide to come to Detroit?

What was your source of income before you came to Detroit? How much did you live on per year?

Tell me your general ideas of the city in contrast with the places you lived in the south:

History of Child Care:

How many children have you had?

> Please give name, date of birth, place of birth of each: [Interviewer should write this down for further questions later in the interview.]

> For each child: when did you first see a doctor? Give name and address. What type of care did you have, and how often during the pregnancy did you receive this care? Where was the child born? How often did you return to the doctor for checkups for you and/or the child during the first year following the birth? Which were welfare medical agency doctors and which were private? Who paid for each pregnancy? How much?

Have any of your children been born dead? Why do you think it was that way?

Have any of your children died before their first birthday? Of what? What did you do to try to cure it?

Have any of your children died (any age)? Of what? What did you do to try to cure it?

Have you ever taken any of your children to a doctor before their first birthday? Name and Address. Why? What did you do to help cure it? When? Where? Who paid? How did you follow doctor's advice?

What health services are there in Detroit for a woman going to have a child and who cannot afford to pay much for care?

Pregnancy:

What is the Southern way of calling a woman pregnant ("big," "in a family way")?

How soon after a woman knew she was pregnant, in the South, did she consult a doctor? What is the difference between generations in the South on this matter? Between the South and the North?

How often do women in the South visit a doctor during pregnancy? Was this different in the old days? Is this different in the Southern city?

Did you ask advice from anyone during your pregnancy (relative, midwife, nurse)? Who? Why? When? Whom did you most rely on during your pregnancy, in the South? In the North? What were you told by this person? Was the advice helpful?

Was the doctor's advice helpful?

What are the common disturbances during pregnancy? What did you do for them in the South? Here? What was done in the old days?

In the South was there anything a pregnant woman was not allowed to do? Do people feel the same way in the North? (eating habits, actions, etc.)

How is a pregnant woman regarded in the South? In the North? In the old days in the South?

Were there any particular rules governing a pregnant woman's husband?

Were there any ways of determining the sex of the child before birth?

What observances and beliefs were there concerning childbirth in the South? Here?

Were there any beliefs regarding when a child would be born? In the South? Here?

Are male or female children more welcome? In the South? Here?

Are any special beliefs held about: the first born, the seventh son, a child who has not seen its father, twins, a child born with a veil, others? In the South? Here?

Are there any particular attitudes toward children born out of wedlock and their mothers? In the South? Here?

Are there any traditional ways of preventing conception? In the South? Here? Attitudes about this?

Are there any traditional ways of getting rid of unwanted children before the birth? In the South? Here? Attitudes about this?

Delivery:

What steps were taken to insure a safe delivery? Did the husband have anything to do? What was done to ease the pain?

Who helped you at the birth? Midwife? Describe the birth you remember best in the South. Here.

What is a midwife like? What does she do? Are mem ever midwives?

Do women in the South prefer men or women to help at birth? Here?

What is done with the afterbirth in the South? Here? In the old days?

Infant Care:

Were there any precautions taken to protect the newborn baby from harm in the South? Here? In the old days? (Navel cord, washing, weighing, phlegm, etc.)

How was the infant cared for during the first year in the South? Here? In the old days? (Fingernail cutting, hair cutting, clothing, etc.)

How did you feed your new child in the South? Here? How was it done in the old days?

When were your children weaned? When were children weaned in the old days?

Did you eat or avoid any particular foods when nursing? Here? In the South? Did people in the old days? [check for cravings]

Were your children vaccinated in the South? Here? For what? How old? Why?

What was the popular attitude toward vaccination in the South?

What were the common infant complaints: symptoms, name, cures? In the South? Here? In the old days? (Hives, bold hives, croup, colic, boils, bleeding of any sort, thrush, colds, teething, coughs, earaches, etc.) Which of these did your children have? When? How did you treat it?

What were some of the serious childhood diseases in the South? Here? In the old day?s What were the symptoms and what were they commonly called? How were they treated?

Who was the person you most respected for knowledge of home cures in the South?

Do you feel home cures can be helpful? Why?

Attitudes Toward Doctors:

Under what conditions did you generally visit a doctor in the South? Here? What did people do in the old days?

Do you prefer a private doctor, a docto associated with a private clinic, or a public health clinic? Please rank in order: in the South, in the North?

Do you prefer home calls to office calls? Why? For pregnancy? Has your preference changed since you came North?

How do you pay for a private doctor? Insurance? How did you get insurance? Are you billed? Is cash demanded?

Do you feel that private doctors treat you differently in the North than they treated you in the South? Explain and indicate why this might be: Do you feel that your being from the South affects the way you are treated? Do you feel Northern doctors treat you differently from other patients? Explain.

What is your general feeling about doctors?

What is the general feeling about doctors in the South? In the past? Do people distinguish between city doctors and other doctors?

Have you ever gone to a public health clinic or a place where doctors treated people who could not afford medical care? Here? In the South? Please give name of clinic, doctors who treated you, place, dates, complaint. Were these public or private clinics? [write on pad for reference]

Describe what it was like visiting these clinics? [check for awareness of and attitude toward Negro patients and professionals]

Who else was there at the clinic to be treated?

Who paid for clinic treatment?

What is the general attitude of city people toward doctors? Do you feel they visit doctors too seldom, often enough, too often? Do you feel city women when pregnant visit doctors too seldom, often enough, too much?

What should a doctor do to be of the most help to his patient? During pregnancy?

Have you ever been dissatisfied with a doctor? Who, where, when, why?

Would you prefer a man or woman doctor?

Is there a difference between clinic doctors and private doctors here? In the South? What? Why?

What is the difference between osteopaths, chiropractors, M.D.'s and others? Have you ever visited any other than an M.D.? Identify. What complaint? Treatment? Were you satisfied? Why? Charge? How did you pay? Receipt?

Faith Healing:

Do you, or did you, belong to a religious group which used faith healing? Please name church, pastor, address, and give dates.

If yes — Have you ever been healed by it? From what complaint? Place, date.
         Have you ever seen a cure? What complaint? Place, date, etc.
         Why and when does it work?
         Did this group allow the use of other cures: doctor, home?

If no — Did you know of such groups: names, dates, etc.
         What did they do to heal?
         Did they allow any other type of cures? Doctor? Home cure?

Do you still belong or know of such sects in the city? Name, address, preacher?

How important do you feel faith is in being cured of an illness? What order would you rank in terms of effectiveness: doctor, faith, home cures?

Appendix III

Data on Informants Contributing Depth Interviews

Name	Age in 1968	Place of Origin	No. Children	No. Children Born in South	No. Children Born in North	Regular Prenatal Care	Complications During Preg.
BR	31h	Pike Co., Ky.	3 (1hc)	2	1	1	yes
BT	33	Knox Co., Tenn.	5 (1hc)	2	3	–	?
DG	36h	Harlan Co., Ky.	4 (1d)	1h	3	2	yes
JB	27h	Mingo Co., W. Va.	2 (1hc)	1	1	–	yes
JR	30h	Claiborne Co., Tenn.	4	1	3	1 (husb. in Army)	yes
LH	25h	Henry Co., Tenn. (Bluegrass area)	3 (1hc)	2	1	–	yes
RL	55h	Carter Co., Tenn.	1	1	–	1	?
SG	58h	Bell Co., Ky.	4 (2d)	4h	–	–	yes

Note: h = born at home
d = dead
hc = handicapped

Notes

1. Harriette Arnow, *The Dollmaker* (New York: Macmillan Co., 1954).

2. Rupert B. Vance, "The Region: A New Survey," in *The Southern Appalachian Region; A Survey*, ed. T.R. Ford (Lexington: University of Kentucky Press, 1962), p. 8.

3. See, for example, Paul J. Campisi, "Ethnic Family Patterns: The Italian Family in the United States," *American Journal of Sociology*, LIII (1947), 443-449. His tables comparing attitudes and behavior between generations reveal a great similarity between the acculturation process for the Italian migrants and the Southern Appalachian in-migrant.

4. Ralph Beals, "Urbanism, Urbanization, and Acculturation," *American Anthropologist*, LIII, No. 1 (January-March, 1951), 7: "rural-urban acculturation and cross-cultural acculturation differ only in degree and do not represent substantially different processes of change . ."

5. Marion Pearsall, *Little Smoky Ridge: The Natural History of a Southern Appalachian Neighborhood* (Birmingham, Alabama: University of Alabama Press, 1959), p. 174.

6. Elmora Messer Matthews, *Neighbor and Kin: Life in a Tennessee Ridge Community* (Nashville, Tennessee: Vanderbilt University Press, 1965).

7. Pearsall, *Little Smoky Ridge*, p. 77.

8. See Thomas R. Ford, "The Passing of Provincialism" in *The Southern Appalachian Region: A Survey*, ed. T.R. Ford (Lexington: University of Kentucky Press, 1962), pp. 9-34, and Rupert B. Vance and Nicholas J. Demerath, eds., *The Urban South* (Chapel Hill: University of North Carolina Press, 1954).

9. Matthews, *Neighbor and Kin*, p. 134.

10. Matthews, *Neighbor and Kin*, p. 145.

11. Roscoe Griffin, "Appalachian Newcomers in Cincinnati," in *The Southern Appalachian Region: A Survey*, ed. T.R. Ford (Lexington: University of Kentucky Press, 1962), p. 83.

12. Monroe W. Karmin, "Model City Muddle," *The Wall Street Journal*, XLVIII, No. 89 (February 20, 1968), 17.

13. Matthews, *Neighbor and Kin*, p. 78.

14. James S. Brown and George A. Hillery, Jr., "The Great Migration, 1940-1960," in *The Southern Appalachian Region: A Survey*, ed. T. R. Ford (Lexington: University of Kentucky Press, 1962), p. 67.

15. See Ann DeHuff Peters, "Patterns of Health Care in Infancy in a Rural Southern County," *American Journal of Public Health*, LVII, No. 3 (March, 1967), p. 412. For the accepted medical behavior during the maternity cycle, see: American College of Obstetrics and Gynecology, *Manual of Standards in Obstetric-Gynecologic Practice* (2nd ed., Chicago, 1965) and American Academy of Pediatrics, Committee of Fetus and Newborn, *Standards and Recommendations for Hospital Care of Newborn Infants*, Revised Edition (Evanston, 1964).

16. Martin Corcoran and others, "A Transcript of a Meeting Held at AYEP

on August 10, 1967 Between Dr. Martin Corcoran of the Appalachian Foundation and MCHRD Personnel," a mimeographed document prepared by the Area Training and Technical Assistance Center (Detroit, 1967), pp. 10 and 19. I personally disagree with Dr. Corcoran's estimate; in my opinion the southern mountain population in the city of Detroit is presently between fifty and sixty thousand.

17. C. Horace Hamilton, "Health and Health Services,'. in *The Southern Appalachian Region: A Survey*, ed. T.R. Ford (Lexington: University of Kentucky Press, 1962), pp. 219-244.

18. Howard L. Bost, "A New Outlook Upon the Problem of Poverty and Health in Eastern Kentucky," *American Journal of Public Health*, LVI, No. 4 (April, 1966), p. 590.

19. Steven Polgar, "Health and Human Behavior: Areas of Interest Common to the Social and Medical Sciences," *Current Anthropology*, III, No. 2 (April, 1962), p. 163.

20. Helen C. Chase, (Dr. P.H.) "Perinatal and Infant Mortality in the United States and Six West European Countries," *American Journal of Public Health*, LVII, No. 10 (October, 1967), p. 1743.

21. Hamilton, "Health and Health Services," pp. 221-222.

22. Ibid., p. 221.

23. This attitude is also reported by Marion Pearsall in her article "Some Behavioral Factors in the Control of Tuberculosis in a Rural County," *American Review of Respiratory Diseases*, LXXXV, No. 2 (February, 1962), p. 205.

24. Iwao M. Moriyama, "Present Status of Infant Mortality Problem in the United States," *American Journal of Public Health*, LVI, No. 4 (April, 1966), p. 623.

25. Chase, "Perinatal and Infant Mortality," p. 1737.

26. Moriyama, "Present Status of Infant Mortality," p. 624.

27. Detroit Department of Health, "Vital Events Which Occurred to Detroit in 1966," (Map) *Annual Report*, Section I (Detroit, 1967).

28. Physicians International Press, "Cities Report Drop in Infant Mortality," *Ob-Gyn* News (March 13, 1968), p. 6.

29. Ibid.

30. Ibid.

31. See Michael Owen Jones, "Folk Beliefs: Knowledge and Action," *Southern Folklore Quarterly*, XXXI, No. 4 (December, 1967), p. 306. Jones makes a similar distinction between action and belief. In his article "Toward an Understanding of Folk Medical Beliefs in North Carolina," *North Carolina Folklore* XV, No. 1 (May, 1967), p. 27, Jones indicates that the difficulty with existing collections of folk cures lies partly in the collectors' omission of the traditional value systems within which the cure travels.

32. See Rupert B. Vance and Nicholas J. Demerath, eds., *The Urban South* (Chapel Hill: University of North Carolina Press, 1954).

33. Lewis N. Killian, "The Adjustment of Southern White Migrants to Northern Urban Norms," *Social Forces*, XXXII (1953), p. 67.

34. Ibid., p. 68.

35. Earl Lomon Koos, *The Health of Regionville: What the People Thought and Did About It* (New York: Columbia University Press, 1954), p. 67.

36. Nancy R. Milio, "Structuring the Setting for Health Action," *American Journal of Public Health*, LVII, No. 11 (November, 1967), p. 1986.

37. Matthews, *Neighbor and Kin*, p. 59.

38. This has been suggested by Bost, "A New Outlook," p. 590, and has been successfully implemented by Milio, "Structuring the Setting," pp. 1985-1990.

39. Eugene J. Wilhelm, Jr., "Those Old Home Remedies," *Mountain Life and Work*, XLIV, No. 2 (March, 1968), p. 22.

40. Wayland D. Hand, ed., *Popular Beliefs and Superstitions from North Carolina* in *The Frank C. Brown Collection of North Carolina Folklore*, ed., Norman I. White, VI (Durham, North Carolina: Duke University Press, 1961), item #314.

41. See Pearsall, "Some Behavioral Factors," p. 203.

42. Ford, "The Passing of Provincialism," pp. 13-14.

43. Dorothy D. Watts, "Factors Related to the Acceptance of Modern Medicine," *American Journal of Public Health*, LVI, No. 8 (August, 1966), p. 1212.

44. Alonso S. Yerby, "The Problem of Medical Care for the Indigent Population," *American Journal of Public Health*, LV (August, 1965), p. 1215.

45. See, for example, Watts, "Factors Related to the Acceptance," p. 1212.

46. Killian, "The Adjustment of Southern White," p. 68.

47. Edward Suchman, "Social Factors in Medical Deprivation," *American Journal of Public Health*, LV, No. 11 (November, 1965), p. 1726.

48. Matthews, *Neighbor and Kin*, pp. 111-112.

49. Koos, *Health of Regionville*, pp. 59-60, shows this for his lowest socio-economic group in New York State.

50. Eugene B. Gallagher, "Prenatal and Infant Health Care in a Medium-Sized Community," *American Journal of Public Health*, LVII, No. 12 (December, 1967), p. 2134. Gallagher reporting on his work in a Midwestern community reports that the mothers in his lowest socioeconomic group preferred private physicians.

51. Koos, *Health of Regionville*, p. 63, and Peters, "Patterns of Health Care," p. 420, both point out that most people in the communities which they studied chose their doctors on non-medical bases.

52. Pearsall, "Some Behavioral Factors," p. 160.

53. Koos, *Health of Regionville*, p. 76 also indicates this. One of his respondents stated that doctors in the community were "not interested in us [the lowest class]."

54. Milio, "Structuring the Setting," p. 1986, and James A. Kent, and C. Harvey Smith, "Involving the Urban Poor in Health Services Through Accommodation—the Employment of Neighborhood Representatives," *American Journal of Public Health*, LVII, No. 6 (June, 1967), p. 997.

55. Koos, *Health of Regionville*, p. 77.

56. Ibid., p. 62.

57. See Yerby, "The Problem of Medical Care," p. 1215.

58. See Watts, "Factors Related to the Acceptance," p. 1212.

59. This is also reported by Koos, *Health of Regionville*, p. 35.

60. Koos, *Health of Regionville*, p. 146.

61. See also Gallagher, "Prenatal and Infant Health," p. 2134.

62. See also Thomas R. Forbes, *The Midwife and the Witch* (New Haven: Yale University Press, 1966), pp. 94-111.

63. Ibid., p. 54.

64. See also Charles H. Murphy, "A Collection of Birth Marking Beliefs from Eastern Kentucky," *Kentucky Folklore Record*, X, No. 2 (April-June, 1964), pp. 36-38.

65. Milio, "Structuring the Setting," p. 1985.

66. Alice M. Sundberg, "Influencing Prenatal Behavior," *American Journal of Public Health*, Vol. 56, No. 8 (August, 1966), pp. 1224-1225. Sundberg reports that such a program has been of great value in Baltimore.

67. This program is outlined in *Today, Yesterday, and Tomorrow* (Wendover, Leslie County, Kentucky: Frontier Nursing Service, Inc., 1963).

68. Richard R. Leger, "Modern-Day Midwives in Demand at Hospitals That are Short of MDs: Mothers-to-Be Prefer the Specially Trained Nurses," *The Wall Street Journal*, XLVIII, No. 131 (Friday, April 19, 1968), p. 1.

69. Chase, "Perinatal and Infant Mortality," p. 1745.

70. Ibid.

71. Leger, "Modern-Day Midwives," p. 1.

72. Pearsall, "Some Behavioral Factors," p. 205.

73. See *Today, Yesterday*; and Marilyn A. Jarvis, Mary Pullen, and Jane Downin, "Health Larnin' in Appalachia," *American Journal of Nursing*, LXVII, No. 11 (November, 1967), pp. 2345-2347.

74. See, for example, "Report of the Program Area Committee on Child Health, APHA, 'Requirements for Data on Infant and Perinatal Mortality,'" *American Journal of Public Health*, LVII, No. 10 (October, 1967), pp. 1848-1861; Yerby, "The Problem of Medical Care," p. 1215; Suchman, "Social Factors in Medical Deprivation," p. 1732; Watts, "Factors Related to the Acceptance," p. 1212; and Kent and Smith, "Involving the Urban Poor," pp. 997, 102. Also, Norman A. Polansky and Sara Q. Brown, "Verbal Accessibility and Fusion Fantasy in a Mountain County," *American Journal of Orthopsychiatry*, XXXVII, No. 4 (July, 1967), pp. 651-660: the authors indicate the mountain tendency not to express anguish openly.

19

Housing and Ethnicity: From Screening System, to Rule 9, to Fair Housing Laws

William E. Bufalino

I want it made clear from the very outset that I do not intend, by any of my remarks, to criticize any individual. I do, however, intend to criticize a *system*—a system which was widely used less than a decade ago by real estate brokers and others to screen out of neighborhoods persons of various races, creeds, color and national heritage; a system which aroused wide revulsion and public indignation. Neither is it my intention to make any particular suburb the target of my remarks, since the system which I am about to discuss was employed throughout the United States. It was operated on a hush-hush basis by scattered handfuls of selfish individuals who felt themselves far superior to those of ethnic backgrounds.

In one of our prominent suburbs, the job of deciding who would be desirable was delegated to property owners' associations or real estate brokerage groups. These agencies, in turn, made the ridiculous error of adopting a written slide rule point system for screening prospective purchasers. Their rules, among other things, set up a point handicap system for such things as "degrees of swarthiness"—as if swarthiness, in and of itself, would mean anything. Further, the point system was so rigged as to entirely exclude Negroes and Orientals; to make Jews barely acceptable; to make it a little easier (though not easy) for Italians to qualify; and for a Pole, a mite easier still. The varied scale of point requirements applied automatically to Italians, Poles, and Jews, causing one to assume that members of these groups are inherently inferior neighbors than others and must, therefore, be screened with more care than others, except, of course, for the totally excluded Negroes and Orientals. It was a clear policy of discrimination. It was a bold and brazen discriminatory practice.

The scoring system had a built-in handicap for Jewish applicants. The gauge used for scoring had two columns, one for Jewish applicants. The effect of the Jewish column was to establish a double handicap for a Jew who was a prospective purchaser of property. A Jewish person had to have more points to qualify for ownership of property than persons of most other ethnic nationalities, and he would score fewer points than others in similar circumstances.

Prospective purchasers of property in certain suburbs were required to pass a rigid test before they could become owners of property. Prospects were investigated by a private detective, and his findings were scored by a "Screening Committee" which consisted of a three-member panel. They were scored on name, race, degree to which they appeared to have absorbed local customs, and swarthiness.

Under ordinary circumstances, a person with a good Anglo-Saxon name would be entitled to seven points. But, if the name happened to be "Feingold," the prospect would receive no points. However, if the Feingolds had the courage, and cared to bring themselves into the good graces of the Anglo-Saxons by changing their name to Smith or Jones or any other Anglo-Saxon name, they could get four points. If, however, Mrs. Cohen, the mother-in-law of the former Feingolds, lived with them, they would reduce the property values; and they would be entitled to only three points.

Under the scoring system, one hundred points would be a perfect score. Jewish people would need eighty-five points; Italians would need seventy-five points, and Poles would need sixty-five points. The screening report contained the word "swarthy" followed by a question mark and four small squares indicating "very," "medium," "slight," or "not at all," and one would be checked.

I take particular pride in the fact that in 1959 I helped draw the battle lines in the Circuit Court and the Supreme Court of the State of Michigan. At that time, there were no fair housing laws. I had instituted a libel suit as the vehicle with which to expose the brokers and their screening system. There, the court said: "I do not condone the screening system. I do not condone any system of that nature that deliberately excludes people from minority groups from occupancy of property." The court's conclusion was that since this was a libel suit, the brokers had a qualified privilege to make a limited publication.

White the skirmishes in the courts lasted for over three years, from 1959 to 1962, the battle raged on another front activated by the Michigan Corporation and Securities Commission. After the conclusion of an extensive investigation, the Corporation and Securities Commission passed Rule 9.

In brief, Rule 9 prohibited real estate brokers and salesmen from discriminating because of race, color, religion, national origin, or ancestry. On August 14, 1961, Rule 9 barred real estate brokers and salesmen from individually or jointly refusing to sell, rent, or perform any other customary service because of race, color, religion, national origin, or ancestry "of any person or persons." Rule 9 had the effect of telling real estate brokers that they could not accept a listing where the owner specified that they must sell only to persons of certain color or ancestry. A broker accepting the listing of a piece of property whose owner put racial restrictions on it would subject his license to cancellation. The real estate brokers termed Rule 9 illegal and brought the issue to the Supreme Court of the State of Michigan. Three Lansing, Michigan, brokers immediately obtained a temporary injunction against the enforcement of Rule 9. Lawyers for the brokers argued that with the passage of Rule 9, the Corporation and Securities Commission had usurped a legislative function. The fight was far from easy. On Thursday, February 7, 1963, the Michigan Supreme Court decided against Rule 9, and real estate boards everywhere quickly hailed the court's decision as a victory over what they termed "political and ethnic pressures."

The real estate people felt they could continue to operate in their usual manner without being blocked by what they called "The administrative edict of a governmental bureaucrat." So you can see that by this time the proponents of the screening system had renewed hope.

The brokers viewed the entire matter through rose-colored glasses. They were heartened when Rule 9 was outlawed, but the proponents of the screening system failed to see the real significance of that decision. The court ruled, not against the merits of Rule 9, but against the action of the agency, the Michigan Corporation and Securities Commission, stating that an administrative commission should not legislate—that this was, in effect, a usurpation of a legislative function. Immediately thereafter, there was a public clamor for the adoption of legislation embodying the same principles as those contained in Rule 9. It was a matter that the Michigan Legislature could and did use its power to put the screening system to rest—once, and for all time.

I had insisted right along that Michigan should guarantee the equal rights of all citizens in the housing field, and I had repeatedly emphasized my personal belief in the principle of open occupancy. I worked on specific legislative proposals to eliminate discriminatory housing practices. Thereafter, they were submitted for legislative introduction. Much of this was taking place in February of 1963.

Now, bear in mind that, by this time, the real estate brokers seemed to be riding high. In quick succession, they seemed confident that they had won a libel suit—and they had nothing but praise for the Supreme Court's decision on Rule 9. They won the skirmishes—but lost the battle. The screening system had been thoroughly exposed for what it was. The eyes of the public had been opened to what had been a big secret for many years. And, once the public had become alerted, the ball game was over for the proponents of the screening system—for the opponents of Rule 9. The legislature—the voice of the people—enacted adequate and appropriate legislation embodying the principles of Rule 9 making it unlawful for any real estate agent or broker to discriminate in its dealings relating to property because of race, creed, color, national heritage, or ancestry. The legislature of Michigan moved with deliberate swiftness to rid the State of Michigan of those practices which were in violation of the very fundamental ethics and morality of any truly democratic society. Today, there is no place for a screening system. It is in violation of the laws of Michigan and of the United States.

Only by constant and persistent attacks on such a system—which has no place in a free America—were we able to strengthen our claim to our most cherished possession: human freedom and human rights. And, in this way, we have achieved freedom of opportunity in housing.

Part V
People vs. Institutions

20 The Cultural Impoverishment of Immigrants

Kazimierz J. Olejarczyk

Poverty is generally understood to mean economic destitution. Thus the four ugly faces of poverty appear linked together as on an Indian totem pole, with economic poverty at its base and the other three growing out of it in a nightmarish superstructure; or, again, like the four faces of the ancient god of the pagan Polish tribes, Swiatowid,: each face looking toward a different direction but all inseparably connected and all hiding the same fateful power.[1]

This paper is taking a somewhat different approach, namely that poverty as a dire lack of certain kind of essential human values, needs not always be equated with economic inadequacy. Not infrequently moral poverty manifests itself amidst economic opulence and intellectual poverty co-exists with a high standard of living.

The same may be applied to cultural poverty, or in this case to the cultural impoverishment of immigrants and their descendants through the loss of cultural values which they have brought with them to the new country.

I. Introduction: Migration—A Sign of Our Times

1. Migration—A Growing Phenomenon. Migration is as old as man. From the dawn of history individuals, tribes, and even whole peoples changed their place of abode in subconscious obedience to the command of the Creator to fill the earth. In our time, due to war dislocations, economic progress, and rapid growth in mass communications, it has assumed mass proportions and world-wide dimensions, as well as a degree of complexity which is peculiarly modern. As such migration is a subject of intense study and involvement by growing numbers of nongovernmental as well as governmental agencies, both national and international. It has formed the agenda of special international congresses organized by the UNESCO and by the Catholic Church.[a,b] Ecumenical Councils and Roman Pontiffs, particularly the last three, have been addressing themselves to the problem of migration and of the proper pastoral care for the migrants.[1] Pope Paul VI has been the co-founder of the Catholic Migration Commission,

---

[a]For instance, Conference in Geneva in 1949, another in 1950, and Conference in Havana in 1956. W.D. Borrie, *The Cultural Integration of Immigrants* (Paris: UNESCO, 1959), Preface.

[b]For instance, International Catholic Congress on the Pastoral Care for the Immigrants, Ottawa, 1960.

283

located in Geneva, Switzerland. From the times of Abraham the Church has been a migrant church and felt a particular compassion toward the migrants. It was this compassion as well as the understanding how pressing this problem has become in this century which prompted Pope Pius XII to issue the Apostolic Constitution "Exsul Familia" for the regulation and protection of the right of the immigrants to a proper pastoral care.[2] The problem of migration and of the immigrants has particularly preoccupied the great immigrant-receiving countries, and specifically the United States, which President John F. Kennedy has called "a Nation of Immigrants."[3] The problem is also vital to the progress of humanity, which has, generally speaking, profited in the long run from historical migrations, but not always without great pains and severe losses. In this time of an accelerated and accelerating trend toward more universal culture accompanied by cultural and spiritual upheavals and a state of flux, it is not insignificant to know which true values are preserved or engendered and which ones are prematurely lost or wasted.

2. The Immigrant and Poverty

The present paper deals with the immigrants, but it does not intend to construe their definition narrowly. It treats of any individual or group which changes the country of its residence and as a result of this faces significantly diverse cultural and ethnic surroundings. It thus covers both the voluntary immigrants—economic, political, or religious—and the involuntary immigrants—refugees, expellees, prisoners of war, and slaves. It also recognizes that the problem of the immigrant extends through several and sometimes even many generations.[4]

It is, of course, true that all the four facets of poverty affect the immigrant. He has to start usually at the lowest economic level and not infrequently has to live in dire need and destitution. He is socially uprooted, having lost his previous status which he may never equal in the first generation.[5] Often the language handicap and the lack of appropriate occupation dulls his intellectual and mental powers.[c] He faces increased dangers to his ethical standards and moral behavior particularly if he finds himself in isolation from his own ethnic group.

There is, however, another type of poverty which the immigrant and his descendants face. It is the spiritual impoverishment through the loss, erosion, or waste of cultural values which are a historical product of the genius of his ethnic or national group and tradition.

II. The Problem of Cultural Diversity

The immigrant has always been recognized as a carrier of culture understood not as a mere collection of unconnected traits but as an internally coordinated

---

[c]"Lack of opportunity is a more serious drawback than limited ability or education. . . A scholar who is forced to work as a day laborer soon feels that his mental powers become dulled and suffers, physically and psychologically, under his unsuitable employment." K.C. Cirtautas, The Refugee (New York: Citadell Press, 1963), p. 88.

integral whole.^{d} When he moves—or is moved—to a new country, to a new society with a prevalent different cultural make up, a difficult and complex problem of mutual attitudes and adjustment arises. This problem of cultural homogeneity versus cultural heterogenity gives rise to various reactions from both the immigrant, ethnic group and from the recipient, dominant society, reactions which have been well summed up by Pius XII in his 1953 address to the Italian Catholic Jurists:

The jurist, the statesman, the individual state, as well as the community of states should here take account of all the inborn inclinations of individuals and communities in their contracts and reciprocal relations: such as the tendency to adapt or to assimilate, often pushed even to an attempt to absorb; or contrariwise, the tendency ro exclude and to destroy anything that appears incapable of assimilation; the tendency to expand, to embrace what is new, as on the contrary, the tendency to retreat and to segregate oneself; the tendency to give oneself entirely, forgetful of self, and its opposite, attachment to oneself, excluding any service of others; the lust for power, the yearning to keep others in subjection, and so on.^{6}

The multifacet problems created by the meeting of two or more cultures, two sets of values, two modes of behavior initiate a search for a solution. As it so often happens when a human society is faced with a particularly difficult and complex problem, there is a temptation to simplify it, to find an easy way out, to give way to one of the inborn tendencies of which Pope Pius XII spoke. For, as Joseph B. Gittler succinctly put it, "The basic problem seems to be not diversity but the acceptance of diversity."^{7}

III. Devastating Solutions

1. Various Theories of Assimilation. Numerous theories which have appeared periodically, each offering "the final solution" to the problem of ethnic confrontation and of plurality of cultures, have been critically analyzed in the sociological literature.^{8} There is a certain lack of precision in the usage of terminology, with such terms as "assimilation," "absorption," "melting pot," "acculturation" meaning different things to different authors. Generally the theories gravitate toward one of the two extremes: either to destroy the diversity to save the unity, or to promote diversity even at the price of unity.

In order to understand the sources of cultural impoverishment and waste which befall immigrants and their descendants one must keep in mind the whole

---

^{d}"Groups as culture carriers have been recognized and described since the dawn of history... Any people is in a great measure a product of its cultural heritage. The configuration of its history, tradition, attitudes, beliefs, family patterns and institutions, symbols and values, tend to give the group its uniqueness." Joseph B. Gittler, *Understanding Minority Groups*, Wiley (New York: 1956), pp. 134-135. "Cultures, likewise, are more than the sum of their traits." Ruth Benedict, *Patterns of Culture*, (Boston: Houghton-Mifflin, 1961), p. 47.

gamut of assimilationist theories and of the attitudes and policies to which they have given rise. The enumeration which follows is taken, in abbreviated form, from the analysis of Msgr. Jasinski.[9]

1. Vandalistic theory and method which in its xenophobia blindly destroys all alien forms of culture, language, or tradition.
2. "Gradual strangulation theory and method which aims at suffocating the minority immigrant culture by hindering its exercise and growth with the goal of rapid "-ization" (Americanization) of the immigrant. (Unity through uniformity.)
3. Theory and method of toleration of other cultures and languages as a necessary evil and as useless for the dominant society with a fervent belief and hope that they will soon disappear.[10]
4. Paternalistic theory and method treating immigrant cultures as immature and underdeveloped with a benign hope that the immigrants will soon outgrow them. It is both irritating and quietly insulting to the immigrants.
5. "Melting pot" theory. A catchy name, used in 1909 with a somewhat romantic enthusiasm by Israel Zangwill for the title and theme of a play, became a most used (and abused) popular phrase in the U.S.[11] The theory proposes to solve the plurality of cultures by confusing all of them until they will all disappear in a new amalgamated common denominator; the policies and attitudes propagated under the banner of this theory brought great cultural losses for both the immigrants and the surrounding society.
6. Behavioristic theory claims that diverse traditions and cultures should be practiced privately without any public display. Externally all members of society should accept a uniform, standard mode of behavior, a prevailing "way of life."[e] It is, however, a fact of life that humanistic values which are denied the chance for external manifestation soon cease to exist.
7. Racist superiority theory maintains that only one culture and one language can exist in a particular state—the culture and language of the "superior" race.
8. "Struggle for power" theory and method would use the "Denationalization" of immigrants as a means of obtaining greater power or influence. Such was the theory formulated by Cardinal James Gibbons; "To Catholicise America we must first Americanize the immigrants."[12]
9. "Head in the sand" method hopes to solve the problem by ignoring it. This, of course, is no solution at all. Equally false are those solutions which tend toward the other extreme.
10. Atomization, cultural isolation, ethnic federation theories would propagate

---

[e]"It is not uncommon, for example, for those who have their nation's welfare at heart to speak of the national way of life—the American, the Canadian, the Australian, or the New Zealand way of life." Borrie, *Cultural Integration*, p. 46. "Whether the emphasis was on economic, political, or social matters, the common denominator in all policies was perhaps the concept that the immigrants should be capable of becoming *invisible*, that is, unidentifiable by the non-immigrants." *ibid.*, p. 91. Cf. also the whole problem of "passing" to which now the Afro-Americans so strongly object.

the diversity of cultures without any regard for others to the point of secession or disintegration.

11. "Country be damned" theory would not surrender any differences or would not contribute toward the Common Good.

12. "Co-existence" theory would refuse to share its cultural values showing no will toward a reciprocal exchange.

13. Disharmony theory would not attempt to harmonize various cultures thus creating a schizofrenic effect.

All these various assimilationist theories seem to have the same starting point: the concept of assimilation as the process of *assimilation of man* to surrounding society. This is diametrically opposed to the concept used by Pope John XXIII in "Pacem in Terris" as *assimilation of values* by man.[f]

2. Assimilationist Policies. The above mentioned theories of assimilation may have a variety of explicit motives and intentions, not necessarily bad or sinister in nature. Subconsciously, however, they are, quite plainly, rationalizations of those innate tendencies of which Pius XII had spoken. When strengthened by self-interest and coupled with power of decision they all too frequently lead to policies and practices which are as discriminatory as they are disastrous.

It is beyond the scope of this paper to examine or to document them. The literature on this subject, particularly in certain countries, is extensive and constantly growing. The main categories, however, should at least be mentioned by way of illustration.

In the field of primary legislation the most prevalent laws are those which restrict immigration or intentionally favor only certain groups, of similar "higher type" of culture and more "assimilable."[13] Establishment of "second class citizenship" by law would also fall in this class. There are also laws that hinder or forbid outright the teaching of languages and cultures of certain ethnic groups, even to the children of immigrants. Thus the dominant society in its hostility uses the younger generation against the older to undermine their most important cultural value: the language.[g]

---

[f]"Nor can one overlook the fact that, even though human beings differ from one another by virtue of their ethnic peculiarities, they all possess certain essential common elements and are inclined by nature to meet each other in the world of spiritual values, whose progressive assimilation opens to them the possibility of perfection without limits." *Pacem in Terris*, The America Press, p. 32f.

[g]". . . hostility displayed by various host societies towards foreign-language schools. . . By prohibiting such schools the host society is blocking one of the ways in which a migrant group settlement consolidates its position . . . Indeed, the host society is doing considerably more—it is carrying the fight into the enemy's lines, undermining, one might almost say, the central citadel: and it does so, very largely, by using the younger generation against the older. By this I mean that the history of numerous group settlements shows that the younger generations are relatively willing to accept whatever instruction they receive during school-hours—but, like most children, they are generally unwilling to spend much real energy in lessons out of school." Borrie, *Cultural Integration*, pp. 284-285. See also William R. Parker, *The National Interest and Foreign Languages*, Second Edition (Washington, D.C.: UNESCO 1957), for legislation in certain states forbidding the teaching of Spanish to Mexican children in the 1920's.

Even more important, because less publicized, is the secondary and regulatory legislation. As Milton L. Barron stated, "The social power enjoyed by majorities or dominant groups becomes embedded in the mores. Furthermore, their domination of minorities is supported by systems of enacted laws and status ascription . . . in addition to this official creed there is an unofficial creed implicit in secondary legislation and explicit in the remarks of the philosophers of racism and ancestor worship."[14]

Then, there is a vast domain of open or hidden decision-making—educational policies, employment policies, promotional policies—which, in effect, maintain "the establishment" and keep other ethnic groups "in their place."[15] In the field of public information, communication and entertainment there is a propagation of the myths of "the establishment" often through indirect or hidden persuasion.[16] The prevailing attitude of the dominant group or groups may come to reflect a firm assumption of their own superiority.[17]

3. Resulting Cultural Impoverishment of the Immigrants. The pressure of the assimilationist theories and practices upon the immigrant is often more than his psychic powers can withstand. When he loses his identity, his sense of belonging, his mental serenity, his family cohesiveness and even, at times, his moral fiber he loses spiritual and, therefore, cultural values of crucial importance to himself, to his own group, and to the society as a whole. How tragic is the loss of human lives through increased suicide rates, through mental disorders or through the disintegrating effects of deeply felt anomie of a lonely, despised, and forgotten "foreigner"! For, the word "culture" in its general sense indicates all those factors by which man refines and unfolds his manifold spiritual and bodily qualities."[18] When those qualities become warped or dwarfed there is definite cultural loss.

Samuel Tenenbaum, among others, has summarized well the abnormal adjustments that the hostility of the "in-group" generates in the members of minority groups.

"Members of minority groups seldom possess the wholesomeness and the integration of personality that comes from growing up in a friendly, helpful, secure world. Many of them grow up with damaged personalities. At times, this sense of inferiority makes them aggressive, ambitious, shoving. At times, the consciousness of enveloping hostility makes them neurotic, so that they are robbed of peace and are denied a feeling of being adequate and worthwhile; at times, this makes them oversensitive, so that they are ready to fight any slight, those that exist and those that are only imaginary."[19]

Culture conflict and the sense of not belonging are felt most painfully by the second generation, which Robert E. Park has defined as "marginal men."[20] Not being allowed to act as a natural bridge between two cultures and two social groupings, lacking often a deeper insight into their ancestral culture, they develop an inferiority complex which they display in various ways. This is a common and widespread phenomenon among all ethnic and immigrant groups and one of the best documented.[21]

Pope Pius XII, in whose allocutions every word was carefully weighed, used the strongest terms to describe "so many ship-wrecked souls" whom the loss of own traditions led to "pusillanimity and apathy" and to "gradual loss of their own human dignity."[22]

To prevent this alienation from their own culture all ethnic groups make great efforts to teach their children the language, culture, and traditions either in public and parochial schools or at least in their own Saturday or day school. This is true whether they are Polish, French, Latin, Hebrew, or Japanese. These efforts sometimes meet with marked success but more often with pathetic failure. And thus another natural resource, a marked cultural value and a key to other values, is lost to the second and third generation and to society as a whole.[23]

The break with parental tradition brings with it not only the traumatic crisis of identity but also the loss of accumulated wisdom of ages deposited in the particular culture.[24] It is a loss, though probably never realized, to the surrounding recipient society to which the descendants of immigrants have nothing to contribute, and a great blow to their own self-respect. Furthermore, by losing their own identity, dignity, culture, and distinctness they lose the ability to understand, appreciate, and respect those values in others, and they may develop more readily their own set of prejudices toward other groups.[25]

IV. Organic Integration–The Fully Human and Christian Solution

The importance of preventing cultural impoverishment will not be fully appreciated unless we, with Fathers of Vatican II, realize that,

Man, can come to an authentic and full humanity only through culture . . . [which] . . . indicates all those factors by which man refines and unfolds his manifold spiritual and bodily qualities . . . [and whicch] . . necessarily has a historical and social aspect and that the word "culture" often takes on a sociological and ethnological sense. It is in this sense that we speak of a plurality of cultures.[26]

The very plurality of cultures when brought together in a close contact creates one of the contradictions facing contemporary man; namely,

What must be done to prevent the increased exchanges between cultures, which ought to lead to a true and fruitful dialogue between groups and nations, from disturbing the life of communities, destroying ancestral wisdom, or jeopardizing the uniqueness of each people?. . . How can the vitality and growth of a new culture be fostered without the loss of living fidelity to the heritage of tradition?[27]

At the same time one needs also to see migration in a proper perspective. To quote Fr. Andrew Woznicki,

Contemporary historians and philosophers of culture stress the importance of migration movements in the process of the development of a civilization . . . The migration movement is but a form of a common rhythm of social life, a rhythm of a challenge and response, where flight leads to return, dispersion causes concentration, and rebellion issues in submission. This elementary rhythm is but a transition of a given society from the state of stagnation and peace to the state of movement and action. As a result of this stress and rhythm comes the process of spiritualization and the inner depth of given society that leads to the birth of a cultural life.[28]

Migrations give rise to pluralistic societies the advantages of which are being increasingly stressed. As Joseph Lichten pointed out, however,

Scholars from various walks of life presently devote a lot of time and space to discussions on the concept of the pluralistic society in which we live . . . These scholars tend, however, to underline racial and religious components with much less or no accent upon the ethnic aspects of a multifarious society.[29]

The social and political dominant groups, the so-called "establishments" in individual immigrant-receiving countries were even slower in accepting a correct view of their increasingly more pluralistic society described by Horace M. Kallen in 1915 as, ". . . . a multiplicity in a unity, an orchestration of mankind."[30] The great upheavals as a result of World War II and of its aftermath and the rapidly shrinking world brought into relief the importance of the interrelations of cultures and of their contributions to international understanding.[31]

Thus a new, world dimension has been added to the internal problem of cultural diversity. The advantages of cultural diversity in various fields, stressed by world-renown experts, when applied to a culturally pluralistic society point to the great cultural losses which an artificial elimination of diversity would entail. In the words of Edgar Sheffield Brightman, "Merely to state the conception of a uniform culture is to condemn it in the eyes of everyone who values freedom and creativity."[32]

Therefore, the proper solution to the problem of mutual adjustment between individual immigrant or ethnic groups and the dominant society has been defined as organic integration in contrast to assimilationist integration. The organic integration,

. . . could be described as a dynamic process, that strives to unify the various elements of a socio-cultural life into a harmonious whole maintaining at the same time the personal freedom of the immigrant and the preservation of the existing social order.[33]

This theory, which has also been called "sociological" theory by R.E. Park, understands integration of ethnic group as "a reciprocal process in which both native and alien participate and the result is a mutual enrichment."[34]

Here the sociological and the truly humanistic viewpoint is in full agreement with the Christian and Catholic answer to this problem. This answer is contained in the official teaching of the Church on the proper pastoral care for the immigrants and ethnic groups. Its beginning has been traced to the Fourth Lateran Council in 1215 but it has evolved in the nineteenth and twentieth century, particularly through the documents of the last three Pontiffs and of the Vatican II.[35]

Pope Pius XII, in the *Summi Pontificatus*, in an answer to totalitarian and atheistic racism, stressed that the object of international life is to enrich the unity of human race by the "reciprocal interchange of goods." He acknowledged that particular nations defend with pride and most fiercely, *(acerrime)*, their particular heritage. He also underlined that, although all cultures and traditions must be respected, the hierarchy of love demands a "place of honor in our affections and good works to those who are bound to us by special ties."[36]

Later, in his allocution to the College of Cardinals of 1946, as mentioned above, he stressed the importance of traditions to human personality. Earlier, he had described the interdependence between tradition and progress. He embodied his teaching in the Apostolic Constitution "Exsul Familia" of August 1, 1952, that *Magna Charta* of immigrants rights.

Pope John XXIII in his first encyclical "Ad Petri Cathedram" stressed the brotherhood of all nations and the need for cooperation for the Common Good of all humanity. In "Pacem in Terris" he devoted a whole sub-section to the treatment of minorities in which he denounced all efforts aimed at depression or extinction of minority peoples while praising,

... those civil authorities who promote the natural betterment of those citizens belonging to a minority ethnic group, particularly when that concerns their language, the development of their natural gifts, their ancestral customs, and their accomplishments and endeavors in the economic order.[37]

At the same time, he reminded members of minority groups to "act as a bridge, which facilitates the circulation of life in its various expressions among different traditions or civilizations," and pointed out that, "Through these dealings they can gradually enhance their own vigor and fiber with the good qualities of the others."[38]

Throughout this great document, as well as in the earlier "Mater and Magistra" and in his utterances on other occasions, there is a continuous exhortation for the great respect for the spiritual values which the genius of each people has incorporated in their individual culture and which should be guarded as a sacred heritage at all costs.[39]

Similarly, the present Holy Father, Pope Paul VI, on numerous occasions has shown the same grave concern for the preservation of value hidden in national traditions:

It is a characteristic mark of Catholic education to draw from history not only cultural material and memories of past events but also living traditions, which are the spiritual factor of moral formation and of consistent progress in the march of time. They offer guarantee of stability, which gives men their dignity, their right to life, their duty to act in concord and in harmony with other men.[40]

The Second Vatican Council also stressed the same teaching.[41] While specifically referring at one instance to cultural poverty, it devoted a whole chapter of the Pastoral Constitution on the Church in the Modern World, *Gaudium et Spes*, to the Proper Development of Culture.[42] In it the Council Fathers first noted that,

The growth of communication between the various nations and social groups opens more widely to all the treasures of different cultures. Thus, little by little, a more universal form of human culture is developing, one which will promote and express the unity of the human race to the degree that it preserves the particular features of the different cultures.[43]

After underlining again that for particular social group traditions form a heritage that is peculiarly its own, the Constitution warns against turning of culture into an instrument of political or economic power. All men have the same right to a humanistic culture and civilization free from any discrimination on account of race, sex, nationality, religion, or social conditions.

Thus, all the individuals and the social groups comprising a given people will be able to attain the full development of their culture, a development in accord with their qualities and traditions. Energetic efforts must also be expended to make everyone conscious of his right to culture and of the duty he has to develop himself culturally and to assist others.[44]

The great concern of the Church to prevent the loss of spiritual values and the cultural impoverishment is stressed in the Dogmatic Constitution on the Church, *Lumen Gentium*:

Through her work, whatever good is in the minds and hearts of men, whatever good lies latent in the religious practices and cultures of diverse peoples, is not only saved from destruction but is also healed, ennobled, and perfected unto the glory of God, the confusion of the devil, and the happiness of man.[45]

The same maternal care inspires numerous references in several other of the Council documents on the proper pastoral care for immigrants, refugees, linguistic and ethnic minorities and other migrants.[46]

V. Beneficial Results of Organic Cultural Integration

It would be belaboring the point to dwell at any length upon the cultural riches that accrue to pluralistic societies from accepting and practising the organic cultural integration, one which allows for mutual interchange of cultural goods on the basis of the mutual respect for individual distinct values and in the conditions of free and harmonious cooperation.

The host country, the United States, as one of the leading immigrant-receiving countries, has consciously grappled with this problem perhaps longer than others. Although it had to learn many aspects the hard way[47] and has not yet completed this education, at the same time it can proudly point to fine, extensive, and longstanding accomplishments in affording freedom and opportunity to its numerous ethnic and immigrant groups, thus allowing them to contribute to the common culture still evolving toward a more universal type.[48] Similar examples can be drawn from other pluralistic societies.

The Catholic Church is also here an outstanding example of mutual interchange of cultural values even though in its history it has suffered painful consequences when at certain periods men refused the cultural integration and tried to attain unity through uniformity.[49]

In our times, the cultural cooperation and interpenetration is now facilitated and accelerated by modern means of communication, by expanding tourism, by ever more complex economic, scientific, and health interdependence, by world-wide cultural and student exchanges. Even more, the cultural cooperation and international understanding have become now a matter of survival. Countries which previously indulged in a "splendid isolation" find that now their attitude and policies toward minorities and nondominant ethnic groups have unexpected importance for their international relations.

Even in the religious field, in the ecumenical movement, there is a growing recognition of benefits which may be derived from diverse religious views, traditions, and experiences.

For, as the committee of experts of UNESCO has once expressed it:

The problem of international understanding is a problem of the relations of cultures. From those relations must emerge a new world community of understanding and mutual respect. That community must take the form of a new humanism in which universality is achieved by the recognition of common values in the diversity of cultures... The achievement of international understanding and a new humanism is necessary for the success of the political adjustments of men; but understanding and humanism are important ingredients in the pursuit of knowledge, in the cultivation of values, and in the good life for which economic and political institutions are but preparations and foundations.[50]

VI. Some Suggestions for Practical Implementation

The beneficial results of organic integration, as just outlined, are not yet everywhere, or fully realized. The discrimination, the various forms of assimilation, the disregard or disdain for the values of diverse cultural heritage are still evident in various societies. The resulting cultural impoverishment of immigrants of first, second, or third generation is still occurring or may still occur. This is the thesis of this paper. What, then, should be done to prevent this cultural loss from occurring, to arrest the erosion of these natural resources? This is now the question for discussion.

Let me start with a few suggestions. First of all, in every country with immigrant or minority groups, however small, it must be honestly ascertained whether the policies, attitudes, and practices are such that an organic integration is facilitated and that cultural values of those groups are protected. The retention of those values, as we have seen, is primarily the function of the attitudes and policies of the dominant group.[51]

Based on the experience of other countries, I would be inclined to suspect that in a good number of countries the existence of this problem is not even realized by the dominant group.

Once it is realized, it should be thoroughly studied by sociologists and other social scientists and it should be fully explored through the mass media of communication.[52] Practical information on how to overcome it in individual areas should be dissiminated.[53] The proper solution, the theory of organic cultural integration should be taught in schools, public, private, and parochial. It should become a required subject in seminaries. The legislation, both primary and secondary, should be scrutinized for any discriminatory features.

Above all, the prevalent attitude should become one of deep reverence for the seeds of Truth, Goodness, and Beauty which the Divine Sower had planted in human hearts. Individual nations and ethnic groups, in patience and toil of ages, have produced an abundant harvest and from it have made their daily bread of culture and traditions.

In Poland, where I was raised, there is an ages-long custom, or more than a custom: a living, almost religious practice, that you never throw the bread on the ground. As the Polish poet Norwid once expressed it,

> Do kraju tego, gdzie kruszyne chleba
> Podnosza z ziemi przez uszanowanie
> Dla darow nieba —
> Teskno mi, Panie.

> For that land where people raise a crumb of bread from
> the ground out of respect for the gifts of Heaven,
> I yearn, O Lord.

And this, I feel, should be also our attitude toward the spiritual values ingrained in every culture. Let us not allow that any of them should get trampled underfoot but let us rather be ready to break the bread of culture with everyone.

Notes

1. Zbigniew Zysnarski, Kazimierz Olejarczyk, Janina Talik, i Adam Roba-kowski: "Papieze i Sobory o Duszpasterstwie Immigrantow," *Sodalis*, Listopad, 1967–Luty 1968.

2. Pius XII, *Konstytucja Apostolska 'Exsul Familia', Sodalis*, November, 1953.

3. John F. Kennedy, *A Nation of Immigrants* (New York: Harper & Row, 1964).

4. W. Lloyd Warner and Leo Srole, "Differential Assimilation of American Ethnic Groups," in Milton L. Barron (Ed.), *American Minorities: A Textbook of Readings in Intergroup Relations* (New York: Knopf 1957), pp. 434-445.

5. For a deep psychological insight into the heart and mind of the uprooted see K.C. Cirtautas, *The Refugee* (New York: Citadel Press 1963).

6. Pius XII, *The World Community* (Boston: The American Press, 1954), p. 8f.

7. Joseph B. Gittler, *Understanding Minority Groups* (New York: Wiley, 1956), p. 136.

8. W.D. Borrie, *The Cultural Integration of Immigrants*, (Paris: UNESCO, 1959), pp. 89-98.

9. Jasinski, Ks. Dr. Walery J., *Polonia Amerykanska: Okresy Dziejow-Asymilacja-Ideal* (Orchard Lake, 1951), pp. 21-24.

10. "Immigrant heritages are fading fast—not because they are inferior to American culture, but simply because they are irrelevant."—subtitle to Thomas F. Magner's article "Farewell to Pluralism," *America*, May 11, 1968. See also *America*, June 1, 1968 'Letters' for comment by the author of this paper.

11. Israel Zangwill, *The Melting Pot* (New York: Macmillan, 1909).

12. Cf. *The Contribution of the Poles to the Growth of Catholicism in the United States*. Sacrum Poloniae Millennium, vol VI, Rome, 1959, pp. 125-127.

13. Hubert H. Humphrey, Jr., "The Stranger at Our Gate," in Barron, *American Minorities*, pp. 240-260. See also Marion T. Bennett, *American Immigration Policies* (Washington, D.C.: Washington Public Affairs Press, 1963), *passim*.

14. Op. cit., p. 5.

15. Cf. A.C. Ivy and Irwin Ross, "Discrimination in College Admissions", in Barron, op. cit., pp. 133-144 also: Allison Davis, "Acculturation in Schools", ibid., pp. 446-449. "One of the chief methods used by the public schools to freeze the social status of pupils is, as Warner, Havighurst, and Loeb have shown, to assign them to curricula which lead to different levels of opportunity." p. 449.

16. Bernard Berelson and Patricia J. Salter, "Majority and Minority Ameri-cans. An Analysis of Magazine Fiction.", ibid., pp. 114-132. "Prejudice also finds its way into innocuous areas where people are exposed to them without consciousness that an ethnic problem is being raised at all." p. 114.

17. Gittler, op. cit., p. 128: "In intergroup relations the dominant group usually tends to have certain prevailing biases or prejudices toward the given minority. There always seems to be a strong in-group sense of superiority, and along with this feeling an implicit attitude that the dominant group has an inherent right to certain privileges, advantages, and opportunities."

18. *Pastoral Constitution on the Church in the Modern World*, Walter M. Abbott, *The Documents of Vatican II*, p. 259.

19. Barron, op.cit., p. 414-415. Tenenbaum is obviously referring to situations involving outright hatred for the minority groups when he claims that they "seldom" achieve integration of personality. In more "open" and less hostile conditions the attainment of successful integration is not as nearly infrequent.

20. Cf. also: Everett V. Stonequist, *The Marginal Man*, New York, 1961; Wallace E. Lambert, "Social Psychology of Bilingualism" in *Problems of Bilingualism*, John Macnamara (Ed.) The Journal of Social Issues, April, 1967, pp. 105-108.

21. "The basic conflict of the men of two cultures is that their two cultures have unequal prestige in the eyes of many. The Mexican, or Polish, or Italian American, as well as the lower-class white or Negro (often) comes to think of his original culture as inferior, and of the other culture as superior. This general characteristic of "second generation" groups is abundantly illustrated both in scientific studies and in autobiographical accounts." Allison Davies in Barron, op.cit. p. 447f.

22. Allocution to the College of Cardinals on the "complete man," February, 1946.

23. Cf. Toshio Yatsushiro, "The Japanese Americans," in Barron, op.cit., pp. 321-326. Cf. also: "Fishman's work *Language Loyalty in the United States* Hague-Mouton (1966), documents the struggle in one country. Aware principally of the disruptive power of language the United States set about making of its people drawn from all over the world, a monolingual nation. Now, at last, somewhat aghast at its success, the United States is becoming aware of the riches it has sacrificed to national unity and appreciative of the cultural groups that resisted its conscious, and unconscious, policies of homogenization." Macnamara, op.cit., p. 5.

24. "The men of any generation, as Bernard of Chartres puts it, are like dwarfs seated on the shoulders of giants. In developing knowledge men must collaborate with their ancestors. Otherwise they must begin, not where their ancestors arrived, but where their ancestors began." Walter Lippmann, from an address before the American Association for the Advancement of Science at the University of Pennsylvania, Dec. 29, 1940.

25. Cf. "The major psychological characteristic and problem of immigrants is a feeling of anxiety, of insecurity of their place in the community and in the society, of uprootedness, non-belonging and loss of personal and social status. . . . it gives rise to various psychological complications (defense mechanism, development of stereotypes and prejudices, etc.)" S.N. Eisenstadt, "Psychological Aspects of Integration of Immigrants", in Borrie, op.cit., p. 152.

26. Abbott, op. cit., p. 259.

27. Ibid., p. 261.

28. Andrew Woznicki, *Socio-Religious Principles of Migration Movements*, Toronto, 1968, p. 15.

29. Joseph A. Wytrwal, *America's Polish Heritage* (Detroit: Endurance Press, 1961). Foreword by Joseph L. Lichten, p. viii.

30. Horace M. Kallen, "Democracy Versus the Melting Pot", quoted in Oscar Handlin, *Immigration as a Factor in American History*, Prentice-Hall, 1959, p. 155. Englewood Cliffs, N.J.

31. Cf. UNESCO, *Interrelations of Cultures*, Switzerland, 1953.

32. Ibid., p. 221.

33. Woznicki, op.cit., p. 36.

34. William Carlson Smith, "The Process of Assimilation," in Barron, op.cit., p. 431f.

35. Cf. Zysnarski et al., op.cit.; Center for Migration Studies, *Migration in the Light of Vatican II*, New York, 1967.

36. Pius XII, *Summi Pontificatus*, The America Press, p. 15.

37. John XXIII, *Pacem in Terris*, #96-97.

38. Ibid.

39. *Mater et Magistra*, #181.

40. Zysnarski et al., op.cit.

41. Center for Migration studies, op.cit.

42. ". . . an ever clearer awareness of the responsibility of experts to aid men and even to protect them, the desire to make the conditions of life more favorable for all, especially for those who are deprived of the opportunity to exercise responsibility or who are culturally poor." *The Church in the Modern World*, #57, Abbott, op.cit., p. 264f.

43. Ibid., #54, p. 260.

44. Ibid., #60, p. 266f.

45. Abbott, op.cit., #17, p. 36.

46. Cf. Center for Migration Studies, op.cit., passim.

47. Cf. footnote 30.

48. There is a great abundance of sources on the history, sociology and cultural life of all these ethnic groups in the United States, including presently appearing works on the Afro-Americans and the American Indians. A fair insight can be obtained from such over-all surveys as one reported by Yaroslav J. Chyz and Read Lewis, "Agencies Organized by the Nationality Groups in the United States" (included in Barron, *American Minorities*, pp. 416-428.) grouping them as churches, secular organizations, and foreign-language press and radio. To quote: "The foregoing facts and figures are a convincing proof of the extent and vitality of religious life among nationality groups and of the importance and persistence of their churches. Those already referred to reach a total of some 15,000,000 members in more than 32,500 congregations: 5,092,000 members with 2,855 churches in the Catholic Church; 7,116,443 members with 24,998 churches in the Protestant denominations; 753,747 members in 929 churches in the Eastern Orthodox and other Eastern Churches; and some 2,000,000

members with 3,728 congregations in the different Jewish religious bodies." Contrast with this the request of the U.S. Bishops for authority to liquidate ethnic parishes since the rights of "few if any" physical or moral persons would thus be involved. For a good history of the life and contribution of one of these groups see Wytrwal, op.cit. Cf. also: "In the United States ... the rest of American culture is increasingly regarded, not as an amalgam, but as an orchestration, to use Kallen's happy word. Even ethnic groups that had lost their cultural roots have been reclaiming parts of their heritage. I refer to studies by Negro scholars, like Lorenzo Turner, identifying the African prototypes of the spirituals, the folk tales, and the vocabulary that Negroes can claim as their own contribution to the cultural wealth of America." Wayne A.R. Leys, "The Philosophical and Ethnical Aspects of Group Relations," in Gittler, *Understanding Minority Groups*, p. 7. For a look to the future cf. "It is in the second and third generations, and among the newer, younger, and more dynamic personality types emerging among minority groups in general that the minority group reactions and adjustments of the future must be sought." Barron, *American Minorities*, p. 412.

49. It is, for instance, revealing to imagine what would have been the history of Christianity were it not for the alienation of the greater part of Eastern Christians by the withdrawal by Rome of permission for the use of the Slavonic language in the liturgy obtained by S.S. Cyril and Methodius. A more recent example is the break with Rome of Polish, Lithuanian, and Slovak National Churches around the beginning of this century due to the "Americanization" policies of members of the U.S. Episcopate.

50. UNESCO, *Interrelations of Cultures*, p. 382.

51. Cf. "... it is becoming increasingly fashionable to speak of majority or dominant group problems rather than exclusively of minority group problems. Justification for this is found in the growing conviction that the former play a more strategic role than the latter in responsibility for either intergroup conflict or harmony." Barron, *American Minorities*, p. 4.

52. Here a special mention must be made of the most impressive strides made in this area in Canada in the last few years. One of proofs of the serious official approach was the formation of the Royal Commission on Bilingualism and Biculturalism. The extensive reports of its findings and recommendations in nine different areas of Canadian life are just beginning to be published by the Queen's Printer. (see *Book I: The Official Languages*, Ottawa, 1967).

53. A good illustration is the publication of the U.S. National Commission for the UNESCO, *The National Interest and Foreign Languages*, prepared as a discussion guide by William Riley Parker (1954, 1957, and 1961 editions). Another is the article by A. Bruce Gaarder, of the U.S. Office of Education (writing in his private capacity) "Organization of the Bilingual School" and his description of the successful experiment of such a school in the Coral Way Elementary School in Miami, Florida, since 1963, where a carefully planned strict adherence is applied to the principle of equal time and equal treatment given to both English and Spanish as languages of instruction for all pupils. Incidentally, such a system once prevailed in the parochial schools of ethnic parishes but had disappeared due to outside pressures.

21

Detroit: Discontents and Portents

B.J. Widick

New dimensions to Detroit's problems cast a heavy cloud of uncertainty over the city's destiny in the 1970s. Like the rest of the country, the city contains elements and options for social anarchy, social repression, and social viability. In this sense, the past has been a portent of the future. In time of acute crisis, neither the business and industrial interests, nor the trade unions or other social organizations evolved policies and processes which could restrain race and class conflicts by ameliorative action to a tolerable degree. Hence the labor conflicts of the 1930s and the race and class riots in recent decades.

The political process and structure worked at times, as Mayor Cavanagh's first victory testifies, to direct social protest in acceptable channels, but failed at other times, indicating the limited city power to prevent upheavals. The city of Detroit's problems are of a greater magnitude than any inherent or derived power on that limited basis can cope with. A similar judgment can be made of other forces in the local power structure.

Besides the "hopeless inadequacy" of the efforts by the New Detroit Committee, a new program initiated by the business community in February, 1970, suggests the inability of this segment of the community to face up to the issues confronting Detroit. The Central Business Association, supported by the newspapers, launched a "Talk Up Detroit" campaign with a plea to "Invest in Attitudes." Edwin O. George, president of the Detroit Edison Company, and leader of the newest attempt to revive the city, declared, "Idle chatter which downgrades Detroit hits us all in the pocketbook. The entire economy is sagging because the whole town has a chip on its shoulder." Any economist or reader of the daily press could inform the committee that the national administration's monetary and fiscal policies to curb inflation at the cost of some unemployment was largely responsible for auto cutbacks, layoffs, and a slowing down of the economy.

Furthermore, the optimism about Detroit's outlook in the statement of the new committee was based on metropolitan area statistics, which is a one-sided way of looking at the city of Detroit's economic woes. The white suburbs and metropolitan business and industrial areas have grown, while the city deteriorated. Any fruitful campaign to revive the city has to begin with a candid analysis of its economic inventory, rather than underestimating the depth of the problem.

The city of Detroit is a legal entity which has limited tax powers and has its
This chapter contains three short papers delivered at the conference.

299

own problems. We have a situation where metropolitan Detroit has by all accounts a lively future. It has an enormous future, even when the city of Detroit has been depressed, metropolitan Detroit has had successes, but we will deal primarily with the problems of the city of Detroit.

For examples: less than 30 percent of downtown Detroit is being used for active commercial and industrial purposes. Most is parking lots, highways, and vacant lands. For every new business moving into the city, two more move out. There are 7,000 vacant store fronts. About 20,000 white families have emigrated into the suburbs since July, 1967. The population has more than a normal share of old, and very young, and poor black and white. There is virtually no middle income or lower middle income housing in downtown Detroit. Upper income housing is at a premium. Walter Reuther's low-cost housing program, supported by some business interests, has failed to get off the ground after three years of valiant effort.

One of the problems of Detroit is that the city of Detroit is lost in the metropolitan area's statistics. Detroit used to have 6% unemployment, or 8% unemployment, and what was meant by that was taking this whole area of about 4 million people, the unemployment would be 6%; but if you look at it in terms of the city of Detroit, that in all probability meant 12% in the city and 3% outside the city. The classic example of this right now is that Detroit teenage black unemployment is 40%. A fantastic figure; a depression figure. But this is buried in the overall figures. "How's unemployment in Detroit?" "Oh, it's about 6%." Until the people of Detroit start seeing their city as it really is they can't begin to solve some of the problems.

The auto industry may pick up but it doesn't mean what it used to mean to Detroit. The auto industry picking up means metropolitan Detroit picks up; Michigan picks up. But look at Detroit. You see that the plants have left and will continue to leave. That implies an economic trend in the city of Detroit which results in a lower tax base.

Another aspect of Detroit city's problems: In the last two or three years since 1967, we have had a New Detroit Committee which, in theory, with a lot of good public relations and a lot of sincerity, tried to solve some problems. By their own estimate they are hopelessly inadequate. Without going into a long story, let me give you three little examples: If the auto industry, instead of having its high level executives meet with the committee and listen to people and say we want to do something, placed 100,000 unemployed young people into a crash educational program to make them auto mechanics (and the country needs a quarter of a million auto mechanics), they would have made a significant dent in teenage unemployment in Detroit and everywhere. That would have been facing up to the challenge. Another aspect, if the auto industry had given at least 1,000 full scholarships to black college graduates to give them MBA programs, send them to business schools to become executives in the auto industry, that would have been facing up to the challenge instead of pawning out a half a million dollars to help a handful of people set up small businesses, which are very tough to handle in a period of recession. If they would have done that instead of having the Chrysler program where you have 4,500 people training under government money and now they're all laid off because Chrysler's in trouble, the business community through the New Detroit Committee could have made a significant contribution; but they didn't, regretably.

Detroit lacks a rapid transit system to facilitate income-spending from potential suburbanite consumers, and the public sensitivity to race tension and well-publicized crime rates acts to keep potential buyers away. At night only a handful of whites can be seen in downtown theatres; restaurants and nightclubs do a minimum of business. Detroit's streets are so deserted at night the city appears to be a ghost town. Almost a state of de facto segregation exists. These signs forecast a lower economic base for the city when it needs greater income and tax funds.

The city's schools no longer attract since they are near a disaster stage of decline. "Our high schools are appallingly inadequate—a disgrace to the community and a tragedy to the thousands of young men and women whom we compel and cajole to sit in them," stated the Detroit High School Study Commission. Edward L. Cushman, Executive Vice President of Wayne State University, and Federal Judge Damon J. Keith, who co-chaired the study added: "This is not a hasty verdict. It is the conclusion of two years of work by some 350 dedicated citizens, professionals and laymen alike—who examined our high schools from every point of view."

The schools are "outmoded and overcrowded," and the "teachers over-burdened," and this explained, among other things, why 2,000 students at the all-black Northern High School called a strike to protest "inferior" education. No serious attention has been given to the sweeping and costly recommendations made by the Commission to stop the educational debacle.

The city police, supported by strong city and suburban white sentiment, remain a source of race irritation. They keep winning the "battles" with the black community. However, they will eventually lose the "war." For demographic trends assure the black population the decisive voting strength and political power in future elections. To facilitate the peaceful transformation of power, a crash program to reduce race tensions to a livable degree would include the immediate addition of 1,000 policemen, provided they were black. Then the foundations of law and order arising from mutual trust and respect would develop. Black Detroit deserves the kind of police protection its white counterparts in Grosse Pointe and other suburbs receive as a normal public service. Until then, the city remains a keg of social dynamite which may ignite by some incident, and more retrogression takes place.

Class differences in Detroit are now generally mitigated through the functioning of the collective bargaining process. Strikes are usually peaceful: neither the UAW nor the auto industry want class war. As a result, strikes act as a healthy social catharsis, a form of controllable unrest, with sufficient alleviation of divisive issues to make working conditions livable.

An immediate challenge to Detroit—and the nation—is to find a process or series of processes by which community unrest may gain a feeling of positive direction and redress sufficient to satisfy most participants. In part, the 1969 mayorality campaign—the political process—satisfied this need enough to curb the extremists of both right and left. A peaceful and meaningful struggle took place because black revolutionists and activist white racists felt community pressure they could not ignore. They were somewhat cowed and shunted aside.

Offsetting the negative tendencies in Detroit are two recent developments: (1) The political maturity of the black community and the rise of a new generation of leaders whose increasing experience in every phase of city work and life may furnish the city with the kind of political and executive talent its problems demand. It would be as misleading to underestimate this factor in the future of the city as it was for many blacks and whites to underestimate the candidacy of Richard Austin in 1969. They have a stake in the city, for it does offer a base for black power to dominate the direction of the city, and their own incessant struggle for full social, economic, and political equality.

(2) Concomitantly, the changing social composition of the city and metropolitan work force—the increasing proportion of black workers to white workers due to labor market shortages—indicates that after economic recovery the currently visible expansion of black power in local unions is bound to grow. The trend towards more and more local union election victories in auto, steel, and other unions has created a base of operations which may give unionism the kind of community role the CIO had in the 1930s. Black unionism will no longer be a paternalistic creation of some AFL-CIO unions, or UAW democracy and policy. It is increasingly standing on its own feet, and it does have an expanding mass base.

By supporting the regressive social and domestic policies of the Nixon administration, Detroit's business and industrial leaders assure themselves of failure to help revive and rebuild the city. The 1969-70 winter recession and Detroit's unemployment figures are reminders of their inconsistencies.

When Robert Knox, Detroit's housing and urban renewal director for seven years, resigned in 1969, he declared, "We've spent $44 billion on the interstate highway program, and we're spending $70 billion to put a man on the moon. But this country has spent only $2.6 billion on urban renewal." He might have added the $150 billion spent on the disaster in Vietnam.

Until national priorities are changed and resources are reallocated—an unlikely event in the near future—a city like Detroit remains a small island battered by a storm of economic and social upheavals. In 1970 Detroit was a city in which most blacks had separate and unequal status to whites. Perhaps on the way to an integrated society, the next step on the road is marked separate but equal status, at least in terms of its relation to to the growing white suburban areas. One thing seems certain, the black community will have more to say about this question than anytime in Detroit's past history.

Blacks in Detroit—Robert L. Green

Detroit, a large urban community, has experienced problems similar to those in New York, Philadelphia, and Los Angeles. The question of school desegregation and community control of the educational system by blacks in a city which is becoming increasingly black is only one of its major problems.

I was very impressed by B.J. Widick's comment that 40 percent of the teenage black male population in the city of Detroit today is unemployed. I see this as being related to two major factors: (1) racial practices as they have developed in the past and present, and (2) education, or I should say miseducation, in the field of public education. The two are linked together because individuals who are poorly trained from an educational standpoint have a difficult time entering the job market. On the other hand, I am critically aware of the data that strongly indicates that blacks in America, be it in Detroit, New York, Chicago, Philadelphia, Jackson, Mississippi, Atlanta, or Tampa, who have educations that are comparable to whites are also unemployed and under-employed. Black high school graduates in the country today earn about $2,000 less than the average white high school graduate. In fact, black college graduates nationally are not earning much more than white high school graduates.[1] Education is a critical factor because seldom do you find in any society a highly educated group of people who are basically poor or under-represented. However, a caste system exists in this country based on racial and class lines which makes it difficult for blacks with educational credentials to make progress commensurate with that of their white counterparts similarly trained.

Very briefly, I would like to discuss the role of education and how it specifically relates to the situation here in Detroit. I attended Northern High School and six of my brothers and sisters are Northern graduates. My oldest brother graduated from Northern in the mid-thirties and thereafter we have a series of Northern High School yearbooks ranging from about 1935 through 1956. A study of yearbooks and the yearbook content would make a major Ph.D. thesis in itself.

At Northern High there was a major change in racial composition during the period from 1935 through 1956. For many years Northern was considered academically strong; it was not known as an athletically oriented school. In the mid- to late 1940s, the racial composition of that school began to shift and it became known for its athletic achievements, rather than its academic programs. I would say that the racial composition was a determining factor in this change. It is interesting to note in the yearbooks that the French clubs, German clubs, Spanish clubs (there were no black study clubs at that time in the city schools) all began to disappear. The math club was discontinued. Taking their places were strong basketball teams, track teams, and football teams. Part of this may be due to what is sometimes referred to as student interest, but I believe that the expectations of teachers and administrators for the students were more responsible. Often administrators and teachers perceive black students as being more athletically rather than academically oriented. I am reminded of a study by Rosenthal and Jacobson in which they point out that the attitudes of teachers play a crucial role in academic achievement.[2] In their work, conducted in the South San Francisco Unified School District, they found that the actions of teachers in the classroom relate to the way in which youngsters are treated in learning situations, which in turn relates to their school achievement.

In the Detroit schools today, this is related to the question of decentralization. Classroom teachers and administrators often bring to the classroom the attitudes and views of the greater society. If teachers and administrators perceive the decentralization and community control as nor workable, its chances for succeeding are severely limited. We find this not only at the public school levels K through 12, but also in our major universities. There is a press for black students and Mexican-American students to become involved in higher educational programs, but resistance sometimes comes from faculty members who believe that education in America today is for the elite. Michigan State University and other land-grant institutions and schools like Wayne State University were set up in response to the elitism in higher education. State universities must become leaders in providing higher educational opportunities for the poor and establishing an academic and social climate related to their success.

In his paper, B.J. Widick mentioned the Detroit Study Commission report and summarized by indicating that many high school programs are unsuccessful and sometimes outdated. This we know. Most parents who live in urban communities today can witness and testify to the fact that the schools have not become or have not been the articulate spokesmen for those who are disadvantaged. Drake, in the *History of American Education*, points out that when large numbers of immigrants came to this country during the period from 1915 to about 1930, the schools were the spokesmen for those who were placed at a disadvantage because they did not speak the language and had difficulty adjusting to a rapidly changing nation. These immigrants did not have the educational skills that would allow them to flow out of the labor market into the career oriented market. This gave rise to adult education. Schools assumed the responsibility for representing, training, and educating a class in America who were considered to be at a disadvantage. In 1970 these same institutions must respond by meeting the needs of blacks, Chicanos, American Indians, and poor whites.

Decentralization, as I mentioned, is a critical question in this country from New York City to Los Angeles, and in Detroit. I see that the real resistance to decentralization in this community is simply based on the sharing of power. All residents of the community should have a voice in the management of the educational system, and they should have the power to make decisions about how their children are to be educated. This can be accomplished by supporting efforts related to decentralization and community control of schools.

Universities must also play a significant role in bringing about change, not only in Detroit, but in all major urban communities—Temple in Philadelphia, NYU and Columbia in New York City, San Francisco State College in the city of San Francisco, Los Angeles City College in Los Angeles, and Wayne State University in Detroit. These universities must share their resources and identify with goals that are commensurate with the progress of urban communities.

If one were to peruse the professional journals in education, sociology, psychology, political science, and the labor journals, reading articles written by men with Ph.D. degrees who are highly trained and highly articulate, one would find a series of studies over the past 25 years describing the plight of poor people and minority individuals in this country. Very seldom, though, do these studies articulate, advocate, or propose social programs for change. Even when one does find a study or series of studies that might advocate programs leading to social change, one does not witness university personnel moving out into the community and working with community people in a meaningful relationship that could assist them in bringing about change. Rather, successful university scholars often have used poor people to build university careers.

There is a tendency in this country to expect and look for the instant solutions. There are no instant solutions to the many critical social problems that we are confronted with and I would like to make a comparison between the way we view social problems and military problems in this country.

A short time ago the Westinghouse Report cited scholars who reported that certain programs had failed in some communities because youngsters in special programs for six months or a year were not reading at grade level after a year's experience in the program. Yet, should we expect young people who have been placed at a disadvantage for the first twelve years of their lives to reverse the disadvantaging effects of that background by simply putting them in an educational program for six months or a year, even if it is highly stimulating?

This is a social and an educational problem. Lack of educational achievement is related not only with what goes on in the school, but also with what goes on in the greater society. Young people who believe that even if they receive a well-structured, sound educational background, they will be unemployed anyway, do not feel the need to press for high academic performance.

But on the other hand, when I look at what has happened from a military standpoint (the race to the moon) I am reminded of the fact that we spend millions and billions of dollars for military weapons. Some weapons are dysfunctional before they are finally built; airplanes are a good example. We do not scrap our weaponry system. When America was attempting to get to the moon, the death of three astronauts did not lead to the scrapping of the moon program. We found two or three more astronauts whose lives we were willing to risk. We did not expect an instant solution there. We were willing to put money there; we were willing to lose billions of dollars to place three men on the moon.

In summary, it would seem that if we are willing to make those kinds of commitments and take these risks, then we need to re-examine our priorities from local and national standpoints. In respect to the priority of education, a new kind of tax base must be established in urban communities. Individuals who come to Detroit to earn their living must also help the urban residents who are here 24 hours a day to more effectively manage this major metropolitan city. Until we re-examine priorities and share our resources with urban communities such as Detroit, the urban crisis will only continue.

Notes

1. Daniel H. Kruger, *The Education and Employment Status of Blacks and Whites Since 1946; The Growing Disparity in Racial Crisis in American Education*, edited by Robert L. Green, (Chicago: Follett Educational Corporation, 1969).

2. R. Rosenthal and L. Jacobson, "Self-Fulfilling Prophecies in the Classroom: Teachers' Expectations as Unintended Determinants of Pupils' Intellectual Competence," *Social Class, Race, and Psychological Development*, edited by M. Deutsch, et al., (New York: Holt, Rinehart and Winston, 1967).

The Polish Person—Richard Kubinski

First of all, I would like to explain something; I am a Polish Person. This is a term which has been developed by myself and my friends as a derogatory reference to people of ethnic groups as, we feel, they are viewed by many other Americans. Categorizing is not just relegated to blacks and Mexicans and Puerto Ricans, but to such physically elusive people as Italian-Americans, Ukrainian-Americans, and German Americans. So I find that I am a Polish Person, who fits all the requirements.

The problem with being a Polish Person becomes most evident when I meet a fellow American and he is fooled by my appearance. You see, a Polish Person doesn't *look* different. If you are white and have the same features that most everyone else has, it is presumed that you belong, and that you are, indeed, like everyone else. But if you believe in the mosaic of America, you believe very strongly in people retaining their individual characteristics, their individual cultural ties. We are all Americans, but we all feel a certain identity which is our precious own. It never fails to make people nervous, however, when I answer their question, "And what do you teach?" with one simple, yet simultaneously terrifying and funny word. . . "Polish." They most always follow their tittering reaction with such profound questions as "Why?" or "Are you kidding?" or else they say, "Come now, tell us what you really teach," followed by "Funny, you don't look like a Polish teacher."

In all honesty, their reactions become more obviously chaotic, ranging somewhere between hostility and pandering, when they discover my unorthodox secrets: I am the director of a Polish dance ensemble; I have studied in Poland; I take part in Polish functions; I am vice president of a Polish cultural organization; I am a third generation American whose parents were born in the United States but raised in Poland.

I don't want people to become nervous or to feel threatened when they discover I am different after being fooled by my relatively normal face, speech, and mannerisms. I cannot help but think that, perhaps, most people want to be able to react to a person immediately, on the basis of physical appearances, instead of being misled into accepting a person before they know whether they want to or not.

I don't want to be a Polish Person, I want to be a Polish-American—hyphen and all—and there is a difference.

A lot of the things which I am going to say will probably remind you of the old things which it is now fasionable to reject. We have become afraid to repeat traditional cliches just because they are old. We think that their endurance has made them invalid. There are a lot of things which people from the past, accepted, which we, I think, can learn from. The fact, that sometimes, or even often, they did not live up to their own advice and wisdoms does not tarnish the validity of the concepts.

The first point which we should consider when discussing institutions is that we are they. . . we are the institutions. Where has the individual sense of obligation gone when we can either hide behind the massive institution or step out of it and call it wrong? We are that institution. I am a part of the establishment whether I like it or not.

When we discuss schools, we say that they are not teaching what they should or that our teachers are failing. Perhaps some of this is true, but it seems that we should also consider the much more influencial school from which students come, already fairly well molded into the adults they will become. Who are the real teachers if not the parents? And how many parents cover up a lot of moral failures with excuses, a method which their children learn and pass on as a conscience-salve to their children until the excuses multiply endlessly and the strivings for self-improvement dwindle away.

So what are the problems which we talk about here? They are human problems—human failures—and we might as well stop talking if we honestly believe the excuse that man is incapable of doing better.

We sit here as a group, but do we really feel our individual responsibilities to each other and to the group? Personal responsibility is something I try to teach my students to understand, and it should be easier for me since my students all come from, generally, the same backgrounds (in the Polish-American community) and the atmosphere in which they live at school, is either religious or specifically geared towards the priesthood, and yet, even with them, I am often disappointed in the lack of this sense of accepting responsibilities to one another, as a class or as a student body.

It is particularly frustrating to see students assume their legitimate right to question with bold fervor, yet without the intellectual or spiritual equipment to properly judge the answers, or sometimes even the desire to do so. A man I considered particularly wise in the field of education once addressed our faculty with these words: "We have taught our students to criticize but we haven't given them the values with which to do it." I tell my students that they are a class and that each student is responsible for the behavior, attitudes, and learning that go on in this class. One student who shirks his responsibility in his studies or in his behavior takes away from his fellow students in a very direct way.

We have failed in our striving to fabricate an American culture. In our great desire to level all peoples and groups to the same red-white-blue-hot-dog-Anglo-Saxon-blonde-and-beautiful norm, have fragmented our ethnic mosaic. What is a ghetto? It is where people go to find the freedom and acceptance to be and do what they cannot be or do somewhere else. Ghettos disappear as people give up their identities for suburbia. Neither extreme should have even happened in

America. Mutual respect and mutual responsibility from the very beginning could have saved us the chaos we have today.

I tell you these things in this rather disjointed way because I am still confused and scared. I don't know if I am overreaching, but I am truly physically scared and intellectually/spiritually confused. I know that in some ways I am part of what is happening in the United States today which a lot of people dislike, and yet I am definitely part of an establishment. I find myself wondering if this is right and which way to go. But I want to understand my responsibilities and the ramifications of my attitudes, words, and actions before I act, or judge or decide. I am constantly distracted by so many people, both the ill-educated and inexperiences as well as the well-educated and influential, making irresponsible judgments, statements, decision without qualm or question every day. That is frightening.

Perhaps in all of my fears and confusions I have contradicted myself a good many times today, but I speak with only one authority—as a young Polish-American. Perhaps I have also stepped beyond the limits of our discussion, but I really feel that much of what I have said, is what Robert L. Green suggested in his statement concerning "expectation." Do all parents and all teachers expect as much as they should from their children without the tranquilizer that is found in excuses? Will their children then expect as much as they should be expecting from themselves and from their institutions? All of our ancestors, whether black, yellow, Arian, or Slavic, felt a responsibility to meet certain self-imposed or socially imposed expectations. Some of these expectations, perhaps, were invalid, I agree, but they strove forward towards what they considered self-improvement. Today, we are afraid to expect anything from each other, whether it be a code of behavior or a kind deed, for fear that expectations just as binding and uncomfortable will be imposed upon us. "Do your own thing," is a cop-out. We must judge and expect to be judged accordingly. We must use our freedom to be responsible and obligated to one another individually and totally, or we must expect to lose this along with other freedoms. Isn't it true that in today's America we are expected to try our darndest to get away with as much irresponsibility as we can until we are stopped—by authority? Living in Poland for a year gave me a pretty good idea of what authority can become if given the chance to make moral decisions for its citizens who have relinquished that right. I don't want to see a government in the United States which forces the citizen to do things which he should have been responsible enough to do himself.

Our young people do have the right ideas on a lot of important things, and it is frustrating to see them misdirect themselves so often. But they have an openness in at least one area that counts, and that is personal interaction.

I hope, someday that I won't have to be a Polish Person anymore. I just want to be an American of Polish descent who likes to be. I don't want to have to make people nervous over this, because it is so unimportant. There are many more important things we have to do—together—like become a nation with a culture we can all identify with and with citizens who are willing to be responsible.

22

A Means of Change

Mediation of Community Disputes—Ronald W. Haughton

I would like to suggest that power has to be present to get any reals transfers of rights and ownerships. It does not have to be exercised in burning but there has to be real power before any group in our society gets noticed.

There is the story of the farmer who was a great man with balky mules and really understood them. One of his neighbors had a mule with its feet planted and it simply would not move that rig out of the barn. He called in the neighbor and the neighbor came over and picked up a 2 by 4 and gave the mule a resounding whack across the nose and the owner was a little distressed. He said, "I thought you were so persuasive with these mules and you understood their psychology". The expert answered, "Yes, but I have to get their attention first."

As a result of a lifetime of work with institutions and people, I recognize these institutional power structures. Their inertia is unbelievable. It takes pressure to move them.

In the mediation activities in community, ethnic, and racial disputes around the country, I noticed that if a group does not have power, it does not get noticed. In a voluntary negotiation situation, which is what we essentially have when a community is asking for something that it has not had before, there are not really any laws protecting or encouraging a "movement" such as the labor unions obtained to encourage collective bargaining 35 years ago.

A classic mediation situation developed in the California grape dispute in which I was involved as a fact finder-mediator several years ago. The agreement we worked out with the giant DiGiorgio Corporation and Ceasar Chavez' farm workers was accomplished because a balance of power was established, so that both sides recognized the great strength of the other side. It was apparent to both that neither could continue to live with this precarious balance any longer.

In ensuing years the growers of table grapes have had much greater power than Chavez, and they have not had to move until very recently, when they were beginning to hurt financially as a result of a nation-wide grape boycott. I was involved in the early stages when there were no contracts, no nothing, but the power of the boycott, for which I have come to have a healthy respect. In the DiGiorgio situation a boycott apparently broke the stalemate. Chavez, through his network around the country, was doing fairly well boycotting grapes, but the DiGiorgio Corporation owned a prestigious brand of food products which could be identified, the S&W brand. It is very well established on the west coast. Even on the east coast it is reasonably well established. In the West the S&W Tree

Sweet orange juice, for example, was outselling Minute Maid. As a result of the boycott, it was being taken off the retail shelves in California and even in Detroit. Apparently there is a maxim in the retail market that if a premium product is taken off the shelves, it is very hard to get it back on. This is because when the merchandiser takes it off the shelves, people buy a substitute. The producer of the substitute, wanting to get on the shelf, allows a higher profit margin, thus encouraging the retailer to live with his product. When customers get used to the product substitute it becomes questionable if they will return to the premium priced original product.

The DiGiorgio Corporation was bleeding to death on this one. It wasn't grapes; it was canned food. Chavez was bleeding to death because he was running thirty different strikes against thirty different growers and not doing very well. He needed a beach head. He needed a "book" (a collective bargaining agreement) that he could show, just like an auto workers' contract, around the industry. This could be used to convince the workers that here was a meaningful protective constitution or document, if you will, to govern work in the fields and on the property. The contract also had to be palatable to the other thirty growers. Thus even if DiGiorgio could be forced into a contractual relationship because of the boycott situation, it had to have some acceptability to the grower who wasn't being pushed quite as hard as was DiGiorgio.

Well there was enough of a balance of power so that both parties, after mediation and fact finding, in effect signed a blank check, and allowed another mediator and me to arbitrate the unsettled terms and conditions of employment on the properties. This was not done until after Chavez had demonstrated great power.

There has been a great training ground for community groups in the operation of poverty programs during the past few years. Through the required "community participation" the whole program developed community leaders. This may have been its most significant contribution.

The poverty program is virtually dead now but the people have been trained. In New York they learned how to function as leaders and are functioning aggressively. In Detroit I doubt if they have this same kind of strength and I don't understand why. Perhaps one of the reasons is that as tight as our institutions in Detroit are, they are a little more flexible. If one were a cynic, this circumstance could be regarded as, in effect co-opting community people. Another approach would be to say that there is a little more to go around here.

In Detroit, now, there is a need for the transfer of power. This kind of transfer is going on when community groups press for not only more participation but a bigger piece of the action. This calls for a rather different kind of mediation and negotiation by a third party than has been traditional in recent years in the labor-management situation where we have two powerful groups which can pretty well take care of themselves. Of course they do take care of themselves, frequently to an extent that other parts of the community will criticize. But in the transfer of power process where the community is very active, it takes a person to be an advocate.

I know from my own operations in New York that one must try to place one's relationship with the powers that be on a personal basis, and then use that relationship to the hilt. We have had to do this in one situation after another in New York City. This approach allows the person in the middle mediator advocate role to put tremendous pressure on the establishment when it is being hit with strength. If it is not being hit with strength, forget it.

Here is the establishment sitting on a pile of rights and the community down here is pushing really to get as many of those rights as it can; it wants in. If it is going to be effective it does not horse around with reasonableness. It just goes. I find I can push the establishment to an extent, if I have established the personal relationships. The establishment frequently is even willing to be pushed if it has a healthy respect for the strength down below.

As long as the mediator's suggestions do not look as unpleasant as the alternative of the community really wanting in, the establishment can respond to the mediators pressure. The mediator must not only find out what the community will settle for and wants, but he frequently has to make up his own mind in terms of equities. Sometimes he will push too hard to be effective. This happened recently with regard to our mediation of a dispute involving a community group and the Board of Education in New York. We progressed quite a bit, but we pushed the Board too hard to be effective, and now they do not care for mediation.

Recently I have been involved in another dispute in a large housing project apartment complex in the South Bronx. It is on the edge of a poor neighborhood, poor people, and poor housing. Organized blacks and Puerto Ricans took on this apartment house and sat-in. They took over the business office.

An associate of mine, a Puerto Rican, and I went out and met with the militants and the ownership. The latter was being hit so hard that it almost put itself in my associate's and my hands to see what could be worked out. We finally worked out a settlement in terms of more apartments for Puerto Ricans and blacks and more jobs for Puerto Ricans and blacks in the complex. This is the first settlement of this kind in the city or state of New York.

We were able to work out a mediated settlement because of the community threat of some political complications for the management. It was to the political advantage of the apartment house ownership to work something out in order not to be politically embarrassed. However, these community disputes hardly ever get completely settled. Now we have two subsidiary disputes. One is with the white apartment house tenants. Talk about the silent majority; well I have met them. There were some 400 people at a meeting the other night, mostly white. They were incensed because an agreement had been made which over a five year period will bring 178 Puerto Rican and black families into a 1,400 apartment complex. And then to show you that people are people wherever they are, the situation became more complicated because two Puerto Rican groups were at odds with each other.

It takes a long time to work out anything, but the name of the game of all of these community conflict situations in which I am involved is really the transfer of power and ownership. If a person, on whatever side, has any hang-up on traditional property rights, he is ineffective. Obviously the establishment owns the real property and the property rights in an institutional sense. When these rights are being challenged there is a real likelihood of a transfer of power and property. It is a very difficult process and it takes organization of a sort that poor people normally do not have. But because of a tremendous organizational network spawned by the poverty program in New York City, there was a development of secondary leadership which becomes active in new areas. Much remains to be done.

**Part VI
Who Makes It and Who
Doesn't**

23

Some Groups that Don't Make It

The Polish Community—Kazimierz J. Olejarczyk

While preparing this paper, I tried to obtain some material concerning discriminatory practices against Polish-Americans, East Europeans and Slavs. It turns out that there are no materials available. I tried the Library of Congress and have a copy of a letter which says, "Unfortunately we must report that there has been no research done in regard to discriminatory practices against East Europeans." I tried Wayne State University but apparently they do not have anything either; although Wayne State was awarded $165,000 in 1965 to study bias and discrimination in employment, apparently this did not cover Polish-Americans and East Europeans.

There are a number of policies in this society which contribute to the fact that some groups—ethnic groups, immigrant groups—do not make it. There was some legislation in this country, for instance, which forbade the teaching of the languages to the children of immigrant groups and this was even true in California as far as the native born Mexican-American children were concerned. State legislation forbade them to study Spanish, while the other children could study Spanish. It is this treatment that doesn't allow a group to make it. Certain legislation combined with the practices of society creates an unofficial creed as to the relative importance and value of different heritages. Furthermore there is the vast domain of open or hidden decision making on educational policies, employment policies, promotional policies, which in effect maintains the establishment and keeps ethnic groups in their place. In the field of public information, communication, and entertainment (the myths of the establishment) are propagated often through indirect or hidden persuasion.

One important factor is the general attitude and atmosphere regarding the particular group and the prevailing degree of esteem it carries with the others. The ridicule or the disdain of others works on the group and their young and undercuts their own self-esteem and self-respect by also cutting off their exterior chances of success. That is why the persistence and prevalance of so-called Polish jokes is not amusing; they are, in effect, vicious attempts at character assassination.

Now to come specifically to Polish-Americans, I here rely on the help of Mr. Radzialowski from the University of Michigan, who took great pains in obtaining this material. How are the Americans of Polish ancestry making it in politics? Of 12,500 entries in *Who's Who in American Politics*, there are only 82 Polish surnames, about 7/10 of one percent. In the Catholic Church they are not

This chapter is made up of two short papers delivered at the conference.

315

making it. You know that about 80 percent of all the bishops are Irish and there are only a few, six or seven Polish bishops (none in Detroit) at the present time. And in the American Catholics Who is Who, out of 4,500 entries, individuals with Polish names account for slightly less than two percent. Now as far as the students at the University of Michigan are concerned, we found that of 35,000 names, there are about 872 students that have Polish sounding surnames. In the Air Force Biographical Dictionary of 400 entries there are only four entries with Polish surnames, which is about one percent. In *Who's Who in Finance and Industry*, out of 27,000 entries, about 80 names sound Polish, some are quite doubtful, which is less than 3/10 of one percent. We don't have the material from the unions but who are the outstanding leaders in the unions except for the late Mr. Yablonski? In the Detroit schools, there are no Poles on the Board of Education itself at the present time. Out of key personnel listed, about 1,000 names, there are only 20 that sound Polish, which is 2/10 of one percent. Out of the principals of schools, there is none that is Polish. We see the same thing in the naming of schools; we don't find any names of Poles or Americans of Polish descent that are used for the naming of any schools. In a recent Detroit schools' bulletin there was a list of key personnel changes and out of all these names not a single one was Polish. And of course the same thing would probably be found in our university administrations, even though I have a roster of over 1,000 Polish-American scientists in this country. In the press and the media we are absent; we are often referred to, not us only but other ethnic groups, as the silent majority. Well it isn't of our choice that we are silent, but to be heard we need the voice, the attention of the media, and this is usually lacking or absent. So to conclude, one point I wish to make is our state universities should start serious studies to examine the apparent lack of opportunity for Americans of Polish descent.

The Spanish-Speaking Community—Gustavo Gaynett

The Spanish-speaking community of the United States comprises, on the basis of recent estimates, anywhere from 8 to 12 million people. Yet 90 percent are in unskilled jobs; 50 percent of that total earn under the poverty line set up by the federal government. The Mexican-American has the lowest educational achievement standards of any minority in this country with the exception of the American Indian. The Mexican-American owns less than one percent of the businesses of this country. We have the highest percentage of people in the military proportionately to our population in every state of the union, but only approximately 90 Mexican-Americans holding Ph.D. degrees.

Some terms are very difficult for Mexican-Americans to conceptualize. Power is one of these. The Mexican-American has been in this country from its conception. Yet the Mexican-Americans are those who don't make it. This would suggest a very serious problem since, for the first time in the history of the United States, the Mexican-American is no longer going to accept this role, the role of owning less than one percent of the businesses, of participating militarily at a higher proportionate ratio than anyone else in terms of population.

And better than 50 percent of the complaints filed by Mexican-Americans in this state have been ignored by the Commission.

It took us over five years before we were able to convince the Michigan Civil Rights Commission that it was a constitutional agency whose responsibility was to deal with minority problems before they conceded the fact that they should have a Spanish-speaking person as a commissioner. (Today out of a staff of over 128 people, they have only three Spanish-speaking persons on their staff.) If this condition continues to exist, the Mexican-American is going to demand equal participation in proportion to their numbers, and ask why it is that we do not possess either a legitimate, or an illegitimate way, if you will, to exercise some concern for our people. Being optimistic, I am inclined to think that this condition is a consequence of an unawareness on the part of our neighbors rather than by design. It would be a sorry state of affairs for the United States if that in fact were not the case.

24 Helping a Group to "Make It"

Chrysler, The U.A.W., and the Black Worker—
Anthony Connole

Even a casual reader of the daily press must come to the conclusion that the single largest group that hasn't made it in our country is the blacks. There is ample documentation; anyone who reads the releases of the United States Department of Labor and the Michigan Department of Labor, who reads the periodicals in our country, or the daily newspaper can see that blacks are the largest group of unemployed today. Even in happier economic times before this administered recession, there was an ample evidence that blacks didn't make it.

My personal experiences in the United Auto Workers Union, in the plants that we represent, and in my observations have caused me to conclude that blacks haven't made it primarily because of discrimination by non-blacks. They haven't made it in many many areas for that reason, but I would like to sort of focus my comments on to the industrial scene and more specifically the auto industry and, in particular, the Chrysler-UAW relationship. By virtue of discussing it from that perspective I don't want anyone to feel that discrimination is an economic problem only, obviously it is not; but just as obviously, economic want, economic poverty, economic adversity are some of the symptoms of discrimination in groups that have not made it. The societal success in this area—by success I mean eliminating that kind of a problem—depends greatly on what we do as individuals. It is too easy to say, "Well that belongs to the legislature," "that belongs to the school," "that belongs to the civic organizations or the unions or the companies," when in reality this is a dodge to avoid doing what each of us is obligated to do as a human being in relation to this problem.

A very recent study of progression upward in various industries devoted an entire chapter to the automobile industry. It was a study financed by the Ford Foundation and conducted by E. F. Shelley and Co. under contract with the American Foundation on Automation and Employment Incorporated. This study showed that in the automobile industry 69.6 percent of the total work force were operatives, laborers, or service workers. If you looked at the figures for blacks separately, to determine what percentage of them fell in that same category, the percentage rose to 94 percent. Likewise, the study showed that 15.9 percent of the total work force were craftsmen, but only 3 percent of the blacks were in the craftsmen category. Fourteen-and-a-half percent of the total work force was in sales, clerical, or technical occupations, but only 3 percent of the blacks. These statistics tell their own story. The same study found that the wage spread between the top and bottom rated jobs in the production areas of the plants below the level of skilled trades was so small that any upward movement within the production areas could not be considered upgrading in the normal sense of the word. The meaning of this is obvious: that the real upgrading within the shop in our automobile plants has to be from production to the craftsmen category, to tool makers, die makers, electricians, millrights, pipefitters, these sort of occupations—the skilled trades of the auto industry.

The UAW has no control over the creation of prosperity or recession. We can only blend in with a number of other forces which produce economic results in America, but we have some direct control on employment in the automobile industry. We have some direct influence, in other words, on who makes it. There has been a pathetic failure on the part of all of us who have any kind of an obligation, within the automobile industry and every other industry, to make sure that blacks have a share in the economic prosperity in the occupational status of our total industries. However, there is a determination to do something about this and it has been working for some time now in the Chrysler-UAW relationship.

We create skilled tradesmen by two routes: one we call the upgrader route which is used because there are insufficient journeymen and the facilities of the apprenticeship program will not manufacture sufficient journeymen to meet the needs of the automobile industry. Using the upgrader route means simply that we either hire someone from the street or transfer someone from the production areas of the plant and put them in a skilled trade hoping that by some mysterious process of osmosis or because we happen to select a rather brilliant guy, he'll somehow learn the trade by working in it, on the job, hoping that everybody who works with him will help him, give him the benefit of their knowledge and experiences of the past. This is not the most satisfactory way of creating a skilled tradesman. However, in 1967 when we wound up our contract negotiations with Chrysler, we decided that we ought to help that process, since we had to use it to make better skilled tradesmen, by providing for related classroom instruction in those subjects necessary to the particular trades. We also worked out an agreement that people in this category would no longer become specialists in some little segment of the trade but would be rotated across all segments of the trade, again depending upon exposure on the job to create the tradesman.

We found that one other thing is of great importance. During the period from September, 1967 to December, 1969, 19 percent of all new entrants into upgrader status were blacks. This was considerably higher than the percentage of blacks entering into apprenticeship programs, which meant that this was a more effective route to get blacks in the trade. We further found that by dividing that group a little further between those who were transferred from within the plant to upgrader status in a trade and those who were hired from the street, that the difference was astounding. About 22 percent of those transferred from the plant were black, whereas only 7 percent of those hired from the street were black.

Since transferring from the plant was a more successful way to integrate the skilled trade occupations, we immediately, as a union, started putting the pressure on all of the local plant managements in Chrysler (who control this hiring process into the upgrader status) to transfer from the plant rather than to hire from the street. We haven't completely solved that problem yet; some hiring from the street still does occur, although right now, because of the recession that we are in, no hiring is being done.

The second way to create a journeyman is through the apprenticeship program and this is the better trained journeyman because there is a planned effort to teach that apprentice to be a total well-rounded, well-educated tradesman. However, there were a great number of impediments to people, all people, not just blacks, entering into apprenticeship. One of them was the fact that the battery of tests that we have been using in the automobile industry contained a lot of unnecessary and duplicating nonsense. So in 1967 at Chrysler we just cut the tests in half, from eight tests down to four, and all we did was cut out duplication. But we are not altogether happy with the final results.

There was an economic barrier to entry into apprenticeship. It was caused by the fact that someone who transferred from a production job went to a rate which equaled 65 percent of the journeyman rate, a cut from most production jobs in the plant. Therefore, people who had family responsibilities, children to raise, to send to school and to clothe, mouths to feed, simply could not afford to take on an apprenticeship. So we worked out an agreement in the 1967 negotiations where a person transferring from a production job in the plant would go to a rate that was equal to 80 percent of the journeyman rate or his former production rate, whichever was the lower, and if he went to his former production rate the table for increases for apprentices would work up to him and then carry him along as it reached him. This took the economic barrier away. It meant that a young black, for instance, with a wife and two children, having a hard time making ends meet in the spending years of his career, could afford to enter into an apprenticeship program. As a result, many older people in the plants, older both in terms of years and in terms of seniority in the plant, are entering the apprenticeship programs and the community colleges where they take their classes. Their foremen indicate that they are more stable apprentices by virtue of being a little older and having more family responsibilities. In addition to that we said we could bring more blacks into the trade if we did more to confine our selections from among people in the plants. Now this is true of the Detroit area; it is not necessarily true when you get outside Detroit. But in the Detroit area, by virtue of the non-discriminatory policies of the Chrysler Corporation, there is a higher percentage of blacks in Chrysler employment than there is in the community and in many, many plants in this area. Which means that if we draw our apprentices from the plants, we draw from a higher proportion of blacks, and experience has proven this to be exactly what is happening. We worked out an agreement with Chrysler which said that while by law we had to open up the right to apply for apprenticeship to those who were outside Chrysler employment as well as those who were in, we would give absolute and deliberate priority to applicants who were presently Chrysler employees. And very frankly, when that list gets down low, we re-open again because we are getting more blacks in by using the seniority pool approach.

Another thing we did through a national training committee, which is a joint committee set up in the 1967 negotiations to create training programs; we worked out a remedial education program with the Highland Park Community College, and anyone who took the apprentice test battery and failed it was called in and offered the opportunity to enroll in Highland Park Community College in what is really a pre-apprentice training course, a course put together specifically to help a candidate double back, take the test again and pass it next time. This has been a highly successful technique in bringing more blacks into the skilled trades.

Again we noticed something that flows from the attitude of giving up on the part of those who for so many years thought that it was impossible to make it. Blacks were not responding by applying the way we wanted them to. So we called a meeting of all the black elected leadership of the Detroit area local unions and we said, "Look, this is your job; you have to turn out applicants; we'll help prepare them to pass the test; we'll change the tests any way we can to make them easier to pass without hurting the trade—but you've got to turn out the black applicants." We did this just before the last opening in December of 1969. These fellows went out and really turned out the applicants and the present list contains 449 seniority workers who were qualified and waiting for placement. The current recession is going to make it harder to place all of these people. One hundred and fourteen of these people, or over 25 percent, are black, and over one-third of those blacks were helped to pass this test by our pre-apprentice training program, both the joint one between Chrysler and UAW, and a "Project Outreach" program that we operate in UAW alone. We are proud of this, but this is not our ultimate goal, because the 25.38 percent is less than the percentage of blacks in the plant, less than the percentage of blacks in the community; so we've got a long way to go. However, this does represent progress over what has been and there is a very real determination to continue that progress until we bring real economic and social justice to blacks in the auto industry.

Part VII
Ethnic Power and the Vote

25 An Overview

Recent Detroit Elections and Ethnicity—
John P. Casey

The subject, ethnic voting power, is an important one to us because we do considerable work with practical politics, the winning of elections. Ethnic voting power and the fact that people do vote because of ethnic reasons is a fact of political life. My purpose is not to say what is good or bad about it. What is important is that ethnic voting does exist and has some possible weaknesses because it is open to manipulation, much more than individual voting would be. But voters are human beings. All of us have these same characteristics about what we like, where we feel threatened, where we feel the opportunity of accomplishment, and therefore we do have voting along ethnic lines.

The actual votes in the city of Detroit in the last few years follow certain neighborhood lines. The most current political map is that showing last November's mayoral election. Because of the ethnic and racial voting that occurred in that election, that map gives us the most up to date census of the black and white communities in the city of Detroit. It is based on precinct lines, precincts being typically five or six blocks; so it is broken down quite finely into small neighborhoods. Census tracts when reasonably current can be helpful in determining ethnic neighborhoods, but they are not as accurate really as this map, for political purposes. It shows clearly, by the way, that street lines still serve as racial boundaries. West of Livernois, between Seven and Eight Mile Roads, gave a vote of 90 percent or more for Richard Austin and 9 percent for Roman Gribbs. West of Livernois in this area is almost solidly black. East of Livernois is somewhat integrated, which is reflected by the actual vote in that area. Thus, if you didn't know the city of Detroit and you took the voting figures you would know where the black neighborhoods are and by checking some other votes, you can determine the Polish neighborhoods, or the ethnicity of any neighborhood where there has been an election, since, because of either the name or color or obvious ethnic background of the candidate, or because of certain issues, the vote divided along ethnic lines. Ethnic voting is a fact of life in America and I suppose any other place where democratic voting is allowed. This leads us to the reality of political power.

Currently we talk about Black Power but this is just the most recent in succession of what started in this country as WASP power—White Anglo-Saxon Power—and succeeded in certain areas, for example, Massachusetts, to Irish power. The Irish, as you know, took over the mayoralty of Boston with Mayor

325

Curley and others only to find later the Italians growing in political activity and numbers and electing governors of Massachusetts. When we reach the point where there are sufficient members of an ethnic strain or race we see that same phenomenon occur. We can trace this in Detroit where for years Irish names have been elected judges and to other offices; Polish judges have abounded. In multiple candidate fields, which usually is the case for councilmen and judgeships, the ethnic strain does not have to reach 50 percent to elect. This is called "plunking"; you don't vote for everybody when you can vote for five, you vote for one or two, which has a weighted effect for that candidate.

The state legislative races in Detroit are almost neighborhood contests, the typical state legislative district having 75,000 people. Some are Polish, some are black. Because of this we find that Detroit's legislative districts for years have been represented by a number of Poles, both in the Senate and in the House. In fact, because the Polish members all used to sit together, there was an area known as the Polish Corridor in the House of Representatives in Lansing. A Polish Corridor also exists on a map of Detroit. For similar reasons there were a number of black representatives in the House much sooner than in the Council Chambers. The reason once again is that the state representatives are from a smaller area, which represents more of a neighborhood. In the city as a whole, the black community contains about 42 percent of the registered vote, yet it was only very recently that there was any black representation in our City Council.

The first black representative was William Patrick in 1957. It was only in the fifties that Detroit elected its first black congressman, Charles Diggs, Jr., and in the 1960s a second congressman, John Conyers, Jr. In Council, just to show how things have been changing there, it was just a very few years ago—in the 1965 election—we had no black councilman; Bill Patrick having resigned in the interim. Nicholas Hood was elected in eighth position in 1965. He had finished eleventh in the primary. It was only through a great effort by a black/white liberal coalition that he barely managed to be elected although the black registered vote at that time was around 30 to 35 percent. Yet only one black was elected out of nine in a city-wide race and of the top eighteen candidates who made it past the primary, there were only two other black candidates, Mark Stepp and George Crockett. Of eighteen for Council in 1965, only three blacks made the top eighteen, only one got elected and there were no blacks nominated for mayor or for city clerk or city treasurer. However, just four years later, in 1969, there were six blacks nominated out of the eighteen and three of them were elected. Nicholas Hood, who was barely elected in 1965, finished second in 1969, and is now Council President pro tem. Also Robert Tindal, who had been elected in a special election, was re-elected, and Ernest Browne finished ninth.

Of six blacks who were nominated in 1969, compared with three in 1965, three were elected compared with one. In the mayor's race, Richard Austin received 49 percent of the vote. A black candidate was nominated for city treasurer. There were for all city offices last year, eight blacks compared with three just a few years before. If the black registered vote continues to climb and becomes a majority we can see how council could have six black and three white, or conceivably even seven, eight or nine blacks. There are some indications that this would not happen because the pattern of voting by blacks for council is not as racial as whites voting for council. When we had White Power, eight out of nine councilmen, even nine out of nine, there was no discussion about having a ward system for electing councilmen. But now we hear of plans to guarantee a racial representation on council, comparable to neighborhood representation.

In the voting for council last year, there was a myth that the three blacks were elected because white voters of Detroit were enlightened enough to give a lot of support to, say, Nicholas Hood, Robert Tindal, and Ernest Browne. In reality the typical white precinct, taken at random from those that used for analysis by WJR on election nights, tells a different story. In a key all-white precinct east of Woodward near the State Fair grounds, William Rogell finished first with 323 votes; in second place was Mel Ravitz; in third was Philip Van Antwerp; fourth Blanche Parentwise; Anthony Wierzbicki and Jack Kelley tied for fifth and sixth; Richard Carey finished eighth; James Fraser ninth; Carl Levin tenth; David Eberhard eleventh; and Norbert Wierziewski, a Polish candidate who was on the liberal-labor slate, finished twelfth. The first twelve were all white candidates, the last six were the six black candidates. Nicholas Hood, incidentally, finished thirteenth in that particular precinct, the front runner of the six black candidates. Another example is a precinct which is generally Polish and Eastern European near Michigan and Livernois. In that precinct the first twelve winners were white; the six black candidates trailed behind them.

In the solid white legislative districts of Detroit, the Northeast and Northwest, no black candidate finished in the top nine. The nine white candidates came in first. There were precincts where there were exceptions but the voting for council was very much on a racial basis in the white community. In the black community, and once again these are precincts taken at random, typically Nicholas Hood finished first; second was either Robert Tindal or Mel Ravitz; third would be either Ernest Browne or Carl Levin or David Eberhard. So of the top six (and don't forget, if there were black voting the same as white voting we would have had the six black candidates in the first six positions, and then the twelve white candidates), we had a mixture of known liberal white candidates running high up with the black candidates, being pretty much in order of how well they were known, with Nicholas Hood first, Robert Tindal second, and Ernest Browne third.

The school elections in Detroit also give a good indication of ethnic voting. In 1966 we had two millage elections in the city. The first one was in May for 2½ mills, and it was soundly defeated. The last millage campaign that was passed in the city of Detroit, perhaps the last one that will ever pass, was in November of that year. Typically in millage elections, the black community votes heavily for millage, the Jewish community traditionally has voted heavily for it—80 percent typically in many black precincts and in the Jewish precincts perhaps 75 percent yes. Where millage passed at all there were one of three things present: either a predominantly black neighborhood, or Jewish neighborhood, or an upper income neighborhood such as Rosedale Park. But less than 25 percent of the people in Northeast and Northwest Detroit voted for millage. The East side of Detroit because of ethnic background is a much more conservative part of our city. This is the largest Polish area in Detroit and the vote was against millage; the people in that area, generally speaking, send their children to a parochial school. Southwest Detroit is mostly Polish, so is the area near Dearborn on the far West side of Detroit, as is the area south of Hammtramck. In those precincts the rate went three to one against, in some cases up to nine people out of ten voted against millage. If you take a series of maps of Detroit based on issues like this, you would really see by the issues that divide Detroit along racial lines exactly where the Poles live and where the blacks live, and where population changes occur. Even in these maps which aren't that far apart in years you can trace the changes. The areas where the millage lost, but not as overwhelming, are integrated areas.

After the millage was defeated in May, 1966, a great bandwagon campaign with labor and business, called C is for Kids, was fairly effective. While it was strictly inner-city blacks and a few others who voted for the millage in the primary in May, in November it became the thing to do and the opposition almost dried up. It passed but it passed much stronger in the black areas and the integrated areas with still a residue of the Jewish community.

A significant subject is the black-Polish political coalition in Detroit. What we have discussed so far is that Poles and blacks are pretty much on opposite sides of issues. But more than occasionally they have been on the same side; both are solidly Democratic, as you know. In the 1966 senatorial primary, Mayor Cavanagh against G. Mennen Williams (G. Mennen Williams had many years of loyalty built up with blacks and Poles and in that election both Poles and blacks went for him), this coalition swept Detroit, except for the Northeast and the far Northwest. The map clearly shows great political potential in such an alliance.

The map coded on the basis of the mayor's race of last November shows the exact opposite. The inner city gave Richard Austin from 80 percent up to 95 percent. Northeast and Northwest precincts voted 90 percent or more for Roman S. Gribbs. It should be remembered that this was the first time that we had a major Polish candidate for mayor and the Polish community had, I am sure, pent up feelings of loyalty to their own candidate, the Polish candidate, just as the black community had for the first time a chance to elect a black mayor. There are white areas in Detroit where the Austin vote was significant, but city-wide the white vote was approximately 80 percent Gribbs, 20 percent Austin. The black vote was about 95 percent Austin, 4 to 5 percent Gribbs. The voting maps also show some interesting things. The inner city of Detroit is solid black, right? Wrong. Because there is an area, which includes Wayne State University (this whole corridor along Cass, Second, Third) where we have white retirees, and Southern white people. These precincts were split somewhat on both sides, but mostly for Austin.

These maps are part of our business and are very useful. In a campaign where we want to reach a certain ethnic audience and we want to do hand delivery, what we customarily do is take a map and code it from one of these maps and in that way we can go the precinct with materials for a specific ethnic group. This brings me back to the point I started on. There is block voting and it is in many ways based on ethnic considerations. It therefore has many possibilities for gaining political power, as is shown by the whole line of succession from WASP through Black Power, but it does open itself up to manipulation by politicians and companies which engage in political campaigns.

26

A Look at Some Individual Groups

The Irish Experience—Joseph B. Sullivan

If America is a melting pot, and it is, it melts exceeding slow. Ethnic voting exists because of the need to satisfy a hunger—a hunger for pride and identification, a hunger for jobs, and a basic hunger for food. It was said by Samuel Johnson that the Irish are a fair people—they never speak well of one another. Thus, I would like to discuss the Irish ethnic voter, where he comes from and why, after which, if I may, I shall attempt to relate this background history to some of the points made in John P. Casey's article.

The Irish ethnic voter was born out of a rotten potato. Driven to America by the potato famine, he landed in New York; and, immediately, another voting block, referred to as the WASP, found a new group of voters coming into New York City. The Society of St. Tammany, that great political organization which rose to power under Aaron Burr and was WASP controlled, found that if it wanted to maintain control, the best strategy was to manage and manipulate the Irish voter. So this society promised him jobs; but every ethnic group knows that as your power grows stronger and stronger, it is better to get the jobs for yourself than to have them given to you. And so the Irish took over Tammany Hall. They were a distinguished group of political leaders, beginning with William Marcy Tweed, a worthy gentleman who, at the very least, possessed geat imagination. Under Mr. Tweed's direction, the Irish started to build the New York Courthouse at an estimated cost of $250,000. Four years later, when they finished the construction and added up the bills, they found that it had come to $13,000,000. In fact, every cuspidor, and no politician could function without a cuspidor in those days, ran approximately $2,000. Indeed, William Marcy Tweed had imagination. He was followed by Lawrence Crocker, who returned to Ireland with $8,000,000, and who, in turn, was succeeded by Honest John Kelly and Silent Charlie Murphy. Now, Silent Charlie Murphy was so-called because he was not a man to commit himself on anything; in fact, he would not even sing the Star Spangled Banner for fear someone would think he was taking sides. On the other hand, he was a man who could nail together a political organization, which he did better than those before him.

The Irish leaders of Tammany could always find a good American Protestant candidate to put up, and then could turn out the Irish Catholic vote for him. However, they always made a deal beforehand, saying a particular candidate could be mayor, as long as they were granted the jobs and the contracts. And because of this, they ruled. You can be cynical about it, and I know there is a

This chapter is made up of three short papers delivered at the conference.

right to be cynical, because they were being downright dishonest. But the people found that when they had reform government, all they got was reform. Reform administrations resulted in a sterile form of government that put no one to work, never built a hospital or a school, and usually decreed that since Sunday was the Sabbath and a day of rest, there could not be any beer drinking on this day, except in the plush downtown clubs, such as the DAC. But when the Irish ethnic group in New York City, or in Boston, took over, they built. They loved contracts—contracts gave them jobs to distribute, and people did not have jobs, so they tolerated situations that today we would never have to tolerate in government. They put up with whatever was required in order to provide themselves with the basic necessities of life. The Irish were rejected; they were hated; they were given either the worst jobs, or no jobs at all. And, in their pride, they were driven together and they voted together, the same being true of every ethnic voting block in America, as is reflected on the voting maps. If you do not accept a people, you drive them together, and, in their pride, they stick together and are going to elect their own.

The Irish have a failing—it is said if you give an Irishman a job, he becomes a Republican, and too many of them have done that. If we look at the voting maps of Detroit, there is no Irish block as such. This is a good thing, because the Irish have become accepted. Maybe they became accepted when Franklin D. Roosevelt became president; when, for the first time in history of America, Irishmen attained offices of national prominence—Jim Farley, Frank Murphy, Joseph Kennedy. This was the first time in the history of this country that an Irishman was allowed to assume any reins of power. Before this time, he was merely the life of the big city machines. Why the big cities? Because the Irish came to this country with nothing at all. They had not been allowed to learn any skills in Ireland, and so they came to America knowing really nothing except how to raise a few potatoes. And in the streets of New York and Boston, there was not much room to plant potatoes. Thus, the Irish had to learn an entirely new way of life, just as the black man, brought to America against his will, had to learn an entirely new way of life. That is why they became an important ethnic voting block.

To defend themselves, they had to put men into public office. To learn how to deal with government, they had to have their own kind there to help out. There is no one more lost than the stray soul who gets into a city hall and has to ask a civil servant where to go. You must have your own people in government. And you do not get your own people in government, unless you vote together. Once you do get your own people in government, then you become accepted. Once we are all accepted, we can get away from this idea of ethnic voting. But each group, as it grows, has to rely on it. In this city today, and you can take your pick of figures, during the last mayoralty election, the experts were saying that the black vote was anything from 25 percent of the registered vote, up to 45 percent of the registered vote. You cannot really tell, when you look at the voter registration, what you have in those figures. In fact, one black candidate, who was seriously considering running for mayor, decided not to, because he felt, I am told, that there was only a 25 percent black vote, and so he did not feel he could be elected. One other candidate came to the conclusion that it was nearer the 45 percent figure. He did not happen to run either, but at least that was the result of his study. So you take your pick of figures. But the black vote sticks together.

The Polish vote as a block today for the same old reasons. The Irish vote did not stick together again until John F. Kennedy. It is often said that the only time the Irish Catholics stand together is at the Gospel. The only other time is when they have a candidate like John F. Kennedy.But here I speak of this melting pot and its failure. Maybe this is what all this chaos is about today. In many ways, we have failed the American dream and, therefore, people do vote together, because they must defend themselves. They have to exert their pride, and part of that pride is electing your own.

In the election of 1969, Richard Austin started from far behind. If he could get 25 percent of the white vote, he would be elected mayor of Detroit. Dick Austin got 22 percent of the white vote. Not enough, but a few years ago, such a vote would have been impossible to achieve. Dick Austin ran a superior campaign and convinced a lot of people he had the qualities needed to be mayor of this city. But, nonetheless, one cannot escape from the old voting patterns.

Go back to the Boston Irish, who never elected a mayor of Boston, until they had a dominant voting block, after which nobody else ever elected a mayor of Boston. You can talk good government all you like, but remember James Michael Curley, once the mayor of Boston, who was elected while he was in jail. He used to refer to the reformers, the good government people, as the goo-goos. Good government is doing the best thing for the people, taking care of the people and reflecting their needs. Criticize, all you want, the old ward healer, who went down the street and made sure his people had enough coal in the winter and a turkey at Christmas time (and why do you think the New York Courthouse cost $13,000,000?). These ward healers were the men who, today, we do not have in government, and for whom we are constantly trying to find a substitution. We say, let's get an ombudsman—these men were the ombudsmen. They provided those services the people were unable to get anywhere else. If you could not find your way around city hall, they knew how to get you in.

You get only the crumbs if you don't organize. And so the Italians, the Poles, the Irish, and the blacks did organize and did make themselves politically potent forces. The English and the Canadians, who are far more numerous in Detroit than any of the groups I just mentioned, other than the blacks, did not need to organize. They were immediately absorbed; they were American when they landed on the soil. But, where there was not immediate acceptance for those people who came from Southern and Eastern Europe, it was different, just as it was different for the Irish. Their pride drove them together and with their pride, they made the ethnic vote, and with their pride, they won those elections. That is how they became accepted, and that is the pattern we are going to see followed today, tomorrow, and until all men accept each other equally.

The Black Condition—Kenneth Hylton

The most descriptive feature of the American society today is the fact that we have a polarized political scene depending especially upon the issue involved. Our society is polarized, the rich against the poor, the young against the old, those organized against the unorganized, and, of course, white against black.

This is not an unusual thing in a society; in democratic societies, particularly, we find a very similar polarization. In the United States, however, it is unique because of the ethnic polarization and that ethnic polarization is fundamentally concerned with the vote. We have ethnic voting in this country because of the fact that ethnic voting was the easiest and quickest means of achieving political power. And as we examine American society throughout all of these epochs you will find that this is what happened with the Irish, this is what happened with the Polish community, this has happened with every minority group as it has achieved maturity in our political history. Ethnic voting is a means, an effective means, of acquiring political power.

The black community today is a politically unified community; but it is a unified community principally as a result of white oppression. It was not solidified necessarily as a means of acquiring power, it was solidified only as a result of white oppression. What do we mean by white oppression? Power in any democracy must be exercised for the benefit of the people, and it is a tragic history of American society that the political power in this country has not been exercised for the benefit of black people. So as an end result the only means of correcting this ill was for black people to assume and to acquire political power. And that is why we have throughout this country today organizations within the black community that are not tied, that are not identified with any other faction of our society. It is unity and it is blackness and it operates solely for the benefit of blackness. And this is very difficult for most whites to think about or to see. However, it was forced upon the black community and is going to remain in the black community for many many years to come.

Another example of that oppression, may be found in the restraint upon voting. For example, there are 22 million blacks in this country; however, we are the most underrepresented ethnic group in the United States. That restraint is represented particularly by the restrictions upon registration and voting.

In a representative democracy we will never be able to erase ethnic voting, and perhaps this may be good because in a representative democracy it is always a contest between those who want the political power, and those who have the political power. This is healthy. My only concern, and I have grave concern in that regard, is will the rules change? In this country whenever black people acquire political power, the rules change. Some people are not willing or ready to accept it. Black people are saying that we didn't know anything about democratic institutions when we were brought to this country as slaves, you taught it to us; we believe in it; we are going to make you practice it. And if you don't practice it, we are going to sit by and watch you destroy the democratic institutions which you have developed, for that is the only way we will be denied our rights.

The Polish Condition—Stanley Krajewski

Because of injustices in the past there is a revival of ethnicity in big ways that we are observing presently. Ethnic voting power exists and is getting stronger because people are now more open, more courageous to do the things that were unthinkable not long ago because ethnicity was considered disloyal. There is no more loyal and faithful group than the Polish. But Poles believe in living together in peace, even at the cost of suffering injustice, both social and political. A new approach is required in order to be recognized by government, church, and society. Today people don't want to suffer in quiet, but they want to be heard. There is no one better or worse in our society.

What is the situation in Detroit and the metropolitan area? Of course everybody knows about Hammtramck. Hammtramck has the reputation of being the most Polish city in the United States and the most democratic. Yet only the second point is true, it is 90 percent democratic now; it used to be 99.9999 percent democratic, but Governor Romney changed that picture and, of course, the structure of Hammtramck has changed immensely since then. It is still over 90 percent democratic, but it is not the most Polish city in Michigan or in the United States. The most Polish city right now is Warren, Michigan, where we recently witnessed several examples of political activities. They elected two district judges, they have several members in the city administration, and they even have the treasurer and one circuit judge in Oakland County. In any case we estimate that the Polish population of Detroit is around 250,000 to 300,000.

As I mentioned before, we want to be heard. But is is not an easy road; it requires effort and sacrifices and I am one who can tell you that working with Black-Polish or Polish-Black Conference, it is not an easy road, it is not an easy task, and it is not very pleasant when the outside pressures are felt. On the other hand, personally I have to admit that there is no greater joy for me than sitting down and talking together with only one aim: to understand each other as we do at our Polish-Black Conference. We must fight for human dignity because only dignified persons can be citizens who appreciate the full value and meaning of the United States, who are not an isolated minority, but who are part of America; that this is an American Pole, a proud American who is looking for true equality in every respect.

For this reason we speak of only one power: the power of voting. Let us respect our country and let us respect our name, whatever it may be. We live together, we build together, but we refuse to destroy together.

27 The American Way

Justice, Liberty, and the Vote—
William E. Bufalino

When I was first asked to participate in the Conference of Ethnic Communities of Detroit, I suggested that the Conference should have a theme song in order that we can all sing the praises of the poor, the needy, and the oppressed long after the final day of this Conference. The spirit of my remarks is captured in the words of "United Souls of America." The words are, in part, as follows:

> I don't know what this world is coming to
> But I do know that whatever we do, we've got to do it together.
>
> Different people come from different lands
> Coming here together from the House of the Creator
> Different people come to take their stand
> Coming to America for Justice and Liberty.
>
> Take the time to know my name
> And to discover that we really are the same.
> Take the time to understand
> And we can walk this world hand in hand.
>
> We've got to LIVE together, WORK together, WORSHIP together
> JOIN HANDS IN HEAVEN together, FIGHT together
> MAKE LOVE together and HAVE PEACE together.

So with these words I have given you not only an outline of what I will discuss this morning, but also my idea of what I think the purpose of this Conference is.

Defining Terms

My discussion will center and revolve around certain words, such as "power," "ethnic" (or "ethnic group"), "minority," "justice," "liberty." The general topic of our discussion is "Ethnic Power and the Vote." I would like to make one observation. We speak of ethnic power. Let us take the word "ethnic," which means "nation" or "people," and then define the word "power." By so

337

doing, we will readily be able to recognize that there are many pitfalls which we must be prepared to sidestep or avoid.

Unless it is properly harnessed, power can be an evil. And this is so even if we refer to ethnic power. When we speak of power, we mean power in any form—and that includes ethnic power.

Power and liberty are like heat and moisture. When they are well mixed, everything prospers; when they are separate, they are destructive. We will either drown or burn up. So, it is in the interest of the public at large to have a sane mixture of power and liberty. There is no stronger test of a man's true character than his use of power and authority.

Justice without power is inefficient. Power without justice is tyranny. Justice and power must be brought together so that whatever is just may be powerful; and whatever is powerful may be just. Within the four corners of those guidelines, and with a full realization of those admonitions, I feel that the ethnic power of the vote can be put to a most beneficial use for the good of all.

Now, what is liberty or justice? Whenever liberty and justice are separated, neither, in my opinion, is safe. Justice discards party, friendship, and kindred and is, therefore, represented as "blind justice": "Justice, when equal scales she holds, is blind; nor cruelty, nor mercy change her mind..." Justice is independent of all law—all party— and all religion. Justice is that which is dispensed when a judge holds the scales with an even hand—above hysteria, above politics, and above discrimination, without regard to race, creed, color, or national heritage. Justice is the constant desire and effort to render every man his due.

Very early in my study of Latin, I learned an ancient maxim—as true as it is old:

> Fiat Justitia—Ruat Coelum
> Let Justice be done—though the Heavens fall.

Justice is itself the great standing policy of civil society, and there should be no departure from it under any circumstances.

Justice is the great and simple principle which is the secret of success in all government. It is as essential to the training of an infant as to the control of a mighty nation. Justice is the ligament which holds civilized beings and civilized nations together. Wherever her temple stands, and so long as it is duly honored, there exists: (a) a foundation for social security; (b) general happiness; and (c) a solution to the improvement and progress of America. And whoever works in that temple; whoever clears its foundation; whoever strengthens its pillars, continues to raise the dome of the Temple of Justice still higher into the skies.

I am certain that all of us here recognize that the problems confronting us and their solutions are much deeper than the naked eye can see. For example the vote is a far more potent instrument for achieving legal justice than social justice. Yet we must work through our legislature because the consistent gains are in those areas which clearly involve the fair and just administration of existing laws.

Social justice, however, demands that all of us exert every effort to see that there be no withered hands stretching out for charity. It is our duty to see to it that the needy and oppressed be cared for and given the equal opportunity to help themselves. For too long, they have not had this opportunity.

Minorities

The term "minority" came into more frequent use as a description of various groups in the United States. The term "minority" reflects an awareness on the part of some groups in the United States that they are underprivileged and have less than full access to the opportunities of American life. These are people who have suffered from social or political or economic discrimination by virtue of their identification as inferiors or outsiders.

There is no question that there have been tragic injustices as a result of a widespread network of discriminatory practices which have, at times, erupted in conflict, on the streets and in the courtrooms, both civil and criminal. In order for us to succeed in our endeavors, any narrow or tightly intermeshed body of ideas, practices and movements by one segment of our population against another must vanish. Hate movements must disintegrate.

Minorities must be prepared to act. The free institutions of the United States have afforded them the opportunity to organize a coherent group life of their own. As we look back, we can be somewhat encouraged. In the past twenty years, our society has experienced a veritable revolution, as the actual diversity of our people, and the strength of our free institutions provided the instruments for destroying the inequalities of the practice and theory that make minorities of some of us.

We must strive to create a new kind of solidarity, for men cannot live in disorder. We must struggle for a reconstruction to regain all that is lost as a result of the inequality of man. We can do this by proceeding as we are today—by the contact of a diverse population and by relative freedom and equality of the social order. We should strive for a comprehensive community capable of attaching to itself the loyalties and emotions of its citizens.

The strength of the ethnic groups lay in their freedom. Their members identified themselves with it, not through external compulsion, but rather because it served their needs. Men with common antecedents and ideas were usually disposed to join together to further their religious, charitable, and social interests. Through the churches and many other organizations, such interests flourished. Through such activities, many individuals became conscious of the fact that although they were all Americans, some were of Swedish, Italian, Dutch, Spanish, Irish, and African extraction. But ethnic groups made no exclusive demands upon the loyalty of the individuals who composed them. The man who acted as an Italian when he met with the Sons of Italy was not thereby deprived of the capacity for being a good Catholic or Episcopalian when he went to church, or a good union member when he met with his local union or a good American when he went to the polling booth.

As we attempt to resolve the evils which exist, we are confronted with a paramount problem, or hazard—that of supplying the emotional and personal needs of the individual in such a manner that he will not be tempted to lose himself in blind identification with a total state or mythical race.

The United States, by the uniqueness of its diverse society, once seemed an experiment of universal significance. There is much in the experiment of which we can be proud. There are some features of it in which no pride can be taken. It is never too soon to recall the former—and never too late to eliminate the latter.

In their willingness to accept the persecuted and the oppressed, our forefathers also gave concrete evidence of their faith in the ability of all men to raise themselves to the same levels of freedom, as well as evidence of their confidence in our institutions. Our very designation—American—shows that we are accustomed to think of ourselves as one people.

We must be animated by a general philanthropy for all mankind—of whatever climate, language, or complexion—to become one people. Today, however, we must face and recognize an unhappy reality. There are those who resist this with all the strength and power they can muster. This is because of the deeprooted prejudices they hold. Deeprooted prejudices being held by the Anglo-Saxons and thousands of recollections by the minority groups will cause endless disorders. We cannot continue to prosper in the free America which our forefathers envisaged if a bitter rivalry exists. It is true that abuses and struggles leave memories which cannot readily be downed—but we should exert our efforts toward making peace and working together. We will only be frustrating ourselves if we permit segregation to sap our strength any longer. By arbitrary divisions, we prevent ourselves from applying our resources to the best effect, from using talents where they can best serve, and from achieving the unity that comes from the knowledge that our practices are in accord with our principles.

We should not create a trap to divide people arbitrarily, distracting them from the solutions of their true problems. Our economy and our society have continued to grow, and we must strive to profit from the equality of all of our citizens and even strive to add worthy new ones to our ranks.

We have earned the reputation as the Mother of Republics, the Light of Liberty and the refuge of the oppressed throughout the world. We must do nothing to lose that advantage. The role of the free ethnic groups has played an important part in the history of our country. Although at times they have differed among themselves, they have displayed, from the very beginning of our history, the ability to play a creative, constructive role in American society. They can continue to do so in the future. Given the opportunity, they will still contribute to the value, for all men, of the American experiment.

The Power of the Vote

We have a common heritage; and by working together as one people, we will be able to act as conscious and direct participants in the politics of our country. A

341

voter's primary use of his vote may be to support a candidate, a party, an issue. His vote is a weapon; and, acting alone or in concert with others, he is strong who possesses it. But the right to vote gives other satisfactions. If one can vote, he can vote "no": he can play the role of turning those out of office who would tend to abuse the powers vested in them by virtue of their office. The right to vote is a constitutional right which gives every man the potential power to improve his position within the complex of American living.

Today, the battle lines are sharply drawn. The importance of the "ethnic" or "minority" vote has been blurred because of the failure of the minority groups to communicate with each other; and consequently, they have failed to think and work together for their common good.

I believe in the capacity of men to reshape themselves and their environment. We must cling to the general doctrines of human brotherhood and equality. Some day the injustices which exist will vanish—just as the injustices of slavery have vanished. Only when the injustices of inequality and oppression vanish will we be able to find the peace and tranquility for which we all pray.

We, as Americans, have for too long clutched at the straws of indecision. There will be those who will adopt a posture of resentful defensiveness. In the brief span of the past quarter of a century, we have seen a tragic succession of horrors challenge the assumption upon which modern civilization rests—that personal dignity is inherent in the condition of human beings. We have learned much about the role of race hatred in so many brutal assaults upon our common heritage. And we have a large accummulation of information concerning the nature and effect of the various doctrines dividing men into separate categories.

We must all strive for a society free of restrictive and exclusive elements. Only by welding together as one people will we be able to strengthen our claim to our most cherished possessions: Human Freedom and Human Rights. There must not be two sets of rules. There is no room for a double standard. Each one of us is entitled to an equal application of the law. Each one of us is entitled to equal opportunities. There is a good and valid reason for taking this position. There is no difference—either under divine law or man-made law—between any one of us.

From a study of the definition of un-Americanism, or Americanism, and from a background of knowledge of history and religion, we know that all men are, by nature, equally placed on this earth by the same Creator; and the poor peasant, the Negro and the American of Italian ancestry or extraction are as dear to the Supreme Being as the mighty prince. And the Bible tells us that as we approach the Gates of Eternity we shall all, Jews, Orientals, Negroes, minority groups, hold each other's hand with an equal clasp.

We are taught, and we must believe, that equality of all men, of all races, is a divine decree; and it is universal and must, and will, elude every human interference. History teaches us that when the political power of the clergy was founded and began to exert itself; and they opened their ranks to all classes—the poor and the rich, the slave and the lord, the servant and the master—equality penetrated into the government through the church. And the being who was a slave in perpetual bondage took his place as a priest in the midst of the nobles;

thereafter, our forefathers, as they envisaged a free American nation, injected these basic and fundamental principles of freedom, equality and liberty into the paramount law of the land—the Constitution of the United States. So what reason would there be for any of us to settle for less?

Prejudice

As we attempt to arrive at a common denominator to resolve our mutual problems, we encounter a stumbling block called prejudice. You might ask:

> How do we deal with persons who are prejudiced?

> How do we deal with those who are nourished by their prejudices?

Prejudice is a disease. A prejudiced mind is a warped mind. A prejudiced person is, therefore, under a spell. We must, therefore, exert every effort to relieve them of their spell since they do not hold opinions; but, rather, opinions hold them. And, as a result, those prejudices create imaginary wrongs, thereby strangling truth and overpowering reason. We must do all that is within our power, by act and deed, to plant a seed into those warped minds so that some day that seed may give growth to deep and living roots of some degree of goodness and whatever is lawful and fair and just.

**Part VIII
What Could Be Done**

28

The Orchard Lake Testimony

Rev. Leonard F. Chrobot

Part I—Ethnic Heritage Studies—A Rationale

The American Dream. A profound and disturbing change has somehow taken place in America. It is impossible to pinpoint the exact time and place, but somehow, somewhere, imperceptibly, the American dream has become a nightmare. The disappointment is felt all the more keenly because the expectations were so very high.

The hope in America was consistently proclaimed by men of vision, men gifted with the ability to verbalize the innermost longing of the human heart. Washington, Jefferson, Adams, were among the first. As early as 1782, Michel de Crevecoeur, in his *Letters from an American Farmer*, called the American the "new Adam." "Here," he said, "individuals of all nations are melted into a new race of men, whose labours and posterity will one day cause great changes in the world."[1] Walt Whitman carried the American dream into the 19th century. And in 1908, Israel Zangwill, a Jewish immigrant, gave it almost religious meaning:

America is God's Crucible, the great Melting Pot where all races of Europe are merging and reforming . . . Germans and Frenchmen, Irishmen and Englishmen, Jews and Russians—into the Crucible with you all! God is making the American![2]

In our century Archibald Macleish wrote:

America is a symbol of union because it is also a symbol of differences, and it will endure not because its deserts and seacoasts and forests and bayous and dead volcanoes are one mind, but because they are of several minds and are nevertheless together. . . . It is where the sand and the marsh and the rock and the grass and the great trees of the eternal wind compose the frontiers of diversity that there is greatness.[3]

A Time of National Crisis. It is precisely because so much was expected from this country that the disappointment in its failure has been so traumatic. The

---

This testimony in behalf of the Ethnic Heritage Studies Center Bill was presented to the General Subcommittee on Education, United States House of Representatives, Washington, D.C., on February 26, 1970.)

streets that were to flow with milk and honey are now blocked by the rubble of the latest demonstration or riot. Our embassies, heretofore the concretization of the dream, have been burned, and our representatives, the living witnesses to the dream, have been stoned and mocked. Some of our greatest leaders have been shot down in an orgy of violence.

America is in a time of crisis, the winter of its discontent. And we search for the structure of a spring we hope will come. The greatness of a nation does not depend upon its military or economic strength; our experience of history should have taught us that. Greatness depends upon the concept of man we are able to institutionalize in our society. Good will and sincerity are not enough. The image of the "ugly American" is not so facilely dismissed.

Our history tells us of our past mistakes. Our solutions of the "Indian problem" and of the "black problem" only emphasize the Biblical warning that the sins of the father are paid by the son. We have inherited the curse of the expediency of our forefathers. Whenever, immediate comfort and material security dictate answers to human problems, we can expect to inherit the wind. There is a theory that the only lesson we learn from history is that we learn no lesson from history.

Rootless Youth in our Society. There is something very wrong with a nation in which a human being must change his name or dye his hair to merit our respect. There is something very wrong when an American girl feels compelled to say "I am of Dutch ancestry, but I am doing something to cure that." We gravely violate the dignity of a human being when we create a climate in which a young boy must ridicule the cultural heritage which has made him what he is. Insofar as we have mocked the national background of any group of people, we have added to the destruction of the American dream. Whenever we insist that a youngster deny his parents, we tamper with the very essence of our humanity.

Our own sons and daughters, suburban and sophisticated, blessed with every consumer item we can possibly deliver, suffer from an alienation which makes Sartre's *Nausea* read like Alice in Wonderland. Kenneth Keniston's description of them in *The Uncommitted* makes it understandable why they should seek escape from the pain of being in sex, alcohol, or drugs. Absence of roots can do this to a man. It makes him all shell and no substance, ready to splinter by the slightest discomfort. And the self-appointed saviors, be they Hefner of *Playboy* fame, or O'Leary with his LSD, serve as the gurus of a new but frightening age.

Language Provincialism. Part of this difficulty of Americans is their reliance upon one language. Only recently have we discovered the relationship between language and our very ability to think. Alfred Korzybski, the founder of general semantics, maintains that the structural assumptions implicit in language are of necessity reflected in how we act and what we are. He says:

A language, any language, has at its bottom certain metaphysics, which ascribe, consciously or unconsciously, some sort of structure to the world. Now these structural assumptions are inside our skin when we accept a language, any language. *We do not realize what tremendous power the structure of an habitual language has.* It is not an exaggeration to say that *it enslaves us through the mechanism of semantic reactions and that the structure which a language exhibits, and impresses on us unconsciously, is automatically projected upon the world around us.*[4]

It is simply impossible to understand another people of another culture and language unless we are freed from the limitation of our own cultural assumptions. A significant part of our difficulty in world diplomacy is the straitjacket of our one-language culture. S.I. Hayakawa says in his *The Use and Misuse of Language* that:

Words . . . are more than descriptions of the territory of human experience; they are evaluations. How we think and evaluate is inextricably bound up with how we talk. . . . How we act is determined by how we think. Even when we act without thinking, our actions are likely to follow in turn the lines laid down by our patterns of thought, which in turn are determined by the language we use.[5]

The common insistence that any people who wish to do business with us must learn our language strikes one as an outstanding example of Yankee chauvinism.

Deification of Technology. We are well aware, I think, that the decisions we make at this point in human history carry a responsibility for the future of mankind on this planet. The view of our planet from the lunar surface, however, changes perspectives for all of us. Does it really profit man to gain the moon and suffer the loss of his home?

We know so well that the problems of earth are not technological but human. And while computers feed us with sophisticated information of staggering complexity, our knowledge of our neighbor next door is still in the Stone Age. When we spend 70 billion dollars annually in the United States for defense, one wonders what we are defending. Is it worth defending? Many of our youth think not!

Education in Cultural Pluralism. How can we learn to live together unless we know who we are, and where we come from. We will survive only if we can find the best ideas about man possible, and then act upon them. John Graves expressed this idea when he wrote in *Goodby to a River*:

If a man couldn't escape what he came from, we would most of us still be peasants in Old World hovels. But if, having escaped or not, he wants in some way to know himself, define himself, and tries to do it without taking into account the thing he came from, he is writing without any ink in his pen. The provincial who cultivates only his roots is in peril, potato-like, of becoming more root than plant. The man who cuts his roots away and denies that they were ever connected with him withers into half a man. . . . It's not necessary to like being a Texan, or a Midwesterner, or a Jew, or an Andalusian, or a Negro, or a hybrid child of the international rich. It is, I think, necessary to know in that crystal chamber of the mind where one speaks straight to oneself that one is or was that thing, and for any understanding of the human condition, it's certainly necessary to know a little about what the thing consists of.[6]

Young Americans simply reject the things we have established as important in our society. They have seen the results, and they want no part of it.

American chauvinism is dying. Yankee ethnocentricism, which believes in the inherent superiority of its own group, and looks with contempt on other cultures, must finally be buried. And unless we want our cities to break up into hostile armed camps, we must return to the American dream of cultural pluralism, where diverse religious, ethnic, racial, or other groups may cleave to their own traditions within their own group, while at the same time they live together within a single economy and polity in harmony and mutual forbearance.

Black Americans have made us viscerally aware of the self-alienation and self-hatred minority groups were made to feel. Is it any wonder today that our youths burn their draft cards, make shirts out of our flag, and reject whatever symbolizes America. The very meaning of the word "America" has become negative. Only we have the power to change that image.

We are convinced that only if the Congress of the United States takes a positive stand and passes the Ethnic Heritage Studies Centers Bill to assist the many other ethnic groups which form our national ethos will progress be made even in Black Studies. A broader political base for any legislation can be achieved only if more people are involved in its results. The Ethnic Heritage Bill has the potential of institutionalizing in our society the promise carved in stone on our Statue of Liberty. We can now truly become what we have always said we were.

The Orchard Lake Ethnic Tradition. The Orchard Lake Schools, for eighty-five difficult years, have defied Yankee ethnocentricism and have represented the ideal of cultural pluralism at a time when few understood what we were talking about. The Orchard Lake Schools strongly believe in the "New Ethnicity," where every major ethnic group in our country is given the opportunity to study its history, language, literature, and art, and to teach others about the richness of its cultural heritage. Indian Americans must be made to feel proud of Indian culture. Black Americans must become cognizant of their race's contributions to the building of America. Spanish-Americans cannot be made to feel that they are second-class citizens.

The Orchard Lake Schools, students, faculty, and administration, strongly favor the passage of this Bill. We see federal funds as the only possible source of help for all of the small ethnic groups. They have already done much for themselves with their own money. But spiralling costs, especially for talented and professional personnel in these areas, will not permit them to continue. (The priest-faculty members of the Orchard Lake Schools alone contribute a quarter of a million dollars each year in their services to this cause for Polish-Americans.)

My concern today is especially for the Polish-Americans, who number some ten million citizens of the United States. They have helped build America, from the glass works of Jamestown in 1608 to the factories, foundries, and offices of Chicago, Gary, Detroit, Toledo, Cleveland, Buffalo, and New York at the present time. No youth of Polish background should ever have to feel ashamed of his national heritage in America.

In the second part of my Testimony, I will outline specifically how Orchard Lake has already implemented, is presently implementing, and is prepared to further implement the plan and program of the Ethnic Heritage Studies Centers Bill for Americans of Polish background.

Part II—Polish-American Ethnic Heritage Studies—
The Orchard Lake Plan

History of the Orchard Lake Schools. The Orchard Lake Schools were founded by a young immigrant priest from Poland who came to this country in 1869. Father Joseph Dabrowski, significantly, began his work in America among his fellow Polish-Americans and the Indian tribes of central Wisconsin. In Detroit, in 1885, he established the Polish Seminary, because he understood the need for native American leaders who would have a sensitivity for the problems of the millions of immigrants pouring into the United States from eastern Europe.

His Schools grew and prospered, and in 1909, moved to Orchard Lake, twenty-five miles northwest of Detroit, to the campus formerly occupied by the Michigan Military Academy. Today the Schools stand as a tribute to his insight into the needs of his adopted land, still training young men with a feeling for cultural pluralism, men determined to preserve the very best of the Polish people's contribution to America. The atmosphere of campus today, while very much American, is permeated by a unique spirit of appreciation for the traditions, customs, language, and culture of Poland, which is studied in the classroom by all of the students. The majority of the faculty are of second, third, and even fourth generation Polish ancestry, who contain within themselves a beautiful harmony of a sincere and warm love of America and a profound respect and admiration for the Polish background which has made them what they are. The Schools embrace three academic institutions and several related research centers.

Academic Institutions. The three academic institutions include:

Saint Mary's Preparatory, a four-year secondary program of pre-college studies in a disciplined, boarding school environment preparing young men for future study and service. Enrollment is limited to 100.

Saint Mary's College, a four-year liberal arts program offering majors in theology, philosophy, Polish, and communication arts, in a small, residential atmosphere of individual attention. Enrollment is limited to 200.

Saints Cyril and Methodius Seminary, a four-year program of graduate studies in theology preparing men for the priesthood, the permanent diaconate, and lay leadership in the Catholic Church. Enrollment is limited to 300.

The total campus population now numbers over 400. It is small in comparison to the great state universities surrounding it, but in its eighty-five years of service to America, the Schools have educated more than 12,000 men, 10,000 as laymen, and 2,000 as clerics who have served their country through the ministry of the Catholic Church. A recent study indicates that 72 percent of the alumni use Polish in their professional careers. The majority of these men, low-income sons of the Polish-American community, would never have had the advantage of such education had it not been for Orchard Lake. Students pay less than half of the cost of room, board, and tuition. The education they receive, stressing a three-fold cultural formation—Christian, American, and Polish—prepares leaders who appreciate the cultural diversity of the United States population, leaders who can create the kinds of community, especially in our inner cities from which they come, where a human being can grow and prosper.

Research Centers. The research centers of the Orchard Lake Schools, although distinct from the academic institutions, mutually support each other. They have done, and will continue to do whatever is necessary to serve the Polish-American community. They include:

Center for Pastoral Studies, which trains permanent deacons for Church work, offers programs of continuing education for priests and laymen in theology, and sponsors a program of field work in pastoral activity for students of the Schools.

Polish American Liturgical Center, which supplies Polish speaking people and their priests with homiletic and liturgical materials, and provides a special apostolate for the sick and aged.

Polish American Historical Association, which sponsors research in Polish American history, and publishes the quarterly *Polish American Studies.*

Center for Polish Studies and Culture, which develops curriculum materials for use in elementary and secondary schools dealing with the history, geography, society, economy, literature, art, music, drama, language, and general culture of Poland, and disseminates these materials to interested teachers. It is precisely this Center which is already equipped to furnish the kinds of material requested in the Ethnic Heritage Bill. It could well serve as a model for other ethnic groups in the establishment of their own centers.

What Orchard Lake Has Done. The Orchard Lake Schools have long felt that an academic institution must have a much broader responsibility than merely classroom teaching. Hence, some of the accomplishments of the Schools in recent years in the area of ethnic study have certainly answered the needs of the Polish-American community.

Development of Language Curriculum Materials

1. *Present Polish Curriculum:*

   Eighty-five years of experience of teaching Polish on a secondary, college, and graduate level have taught the faculties of the Orchard Lake Schools much about the kind and quality of material which is interesting to American youth. The language teachers are very young, very American, and very much in love with the culture of Poland: The excitement of this love is clearly contagious.

2. *Polish Language and Heritage Program (FLICS):*

   Orchard Lake, in cooperation with the Ann Arbor Schools working under a federal grant, has developed the Polish Language and Heritage Program as part of the Foreign Language Innovative Curriculum Series (FLICS). It consists of a teacher's manual and student text, with accompanying slides and tapes, of units on the history, culture, art, literature, customs, geography, social life, and architecture of Poland, and a unit on Polish American immigration. The materials have been tested on a secondary level for several years with the preparatory students of Orchard Lake and others, have been revised, and have been distributed to more than four hundred Polish teachers throughout the United States. It too could serve as a model for other ethnic groups wishing to develop materials of this kind.

3. *Language Laboratory:*

   The complete facilities of the Orchard Lake Language Laboratory are also available for the further development of tapes for teachers interested in using the audio-lingual method of language instruction. While other large language groups have many commercially developed tapes, lesser known languages must develop their own at great expense. The Orchard Lake Staff is willing to share their experience in this area, as well as furnish copies of tapes they have already developed for classroom use.

4. *Polish Room:*

   Of particular merit in ethnic heritage studies is the Polish Room, a special demonstration laboratory furnished with a collection of books, art objects, and folk art from Poland. Seasonal traditions and customs are displayed there and students participate in recreating them for their own classmates.

5. *Polish and Polish-American Books:*

   Sorely needed in the classroom by every teacher are books relating to the study of a foreign culture. Through the efforts of Prof. Robert Geryk, Director of the Center for Polish Studies and Culture, the Schools have published a bibliography of Polish books, Polish books in English translation, and Polish-American books in in the field of history and literature, and the College's bookstore has served as a supply and distribution center for such materials.

6. *Library and Archives:*
Another key factor in supplying books, filmstrips, films, and records of things Polish is the Alumni Memorial Library and its Archives. The Orchard Lake Library already has one of the largest collections in the United States, numbering 60,000 volumes, of which more than 10,000 are Polish, including many first editions and autographed copies, Polish translations of English works, and an outstanding collection of books on Polish genealogy and heraldry, and many other items of interest. In addition, it receives annually 90 different current Polish periodicals and newspapers published here and abroad, and has a historical file of such items as the *Prasa Podziemna* of World War II, and the now extinct *Dziennik dla Wszystkich* of Buffalo.

The Archives continue to grow each day with additions from estates and older people who wish to preserve some memorabilia of Poland or the Polonia for permanent safekeeping. The presence of the Polish American Historical Association gives added continuity and permanence to this dimension.

7. *Art Gallery:*
The Galeria of the Orchard Lake Schools has also provided a location for the display of Polish, Polish-American, and Slavic art, and provides a source of information about it. It has already sponsored such exhibits as Marian Owczarski, sculptor; Helen Klisz Dudzinska, painter; Richard Kubinski, posters; Donna Wessell and Helen Szpakowski, painters, and many others, and plans to continue frequent exhibits in the future.

8. *The Museum:*
In time the Schools would like to provide facilities for the permanent display of historical objects in a Museum. Its Galeria and Polish Room already contain a nucleus of material upon which a permanent collection can easily be based.

9. *Artists-in-Residence:*
Perhaps the most exciting aspect of the Schools is the Artists-in-Residence facility, which provides subsidized facilities for poets, novelists, painters, sculptors, composers, etc., to create original works of art. The stay on campus of the great Polish pianist Severin Turel several years ago was an experience which students will never forget. The more recent stay of Marian Owczarski also proved memorable.

Training Programs and Workshops

1. *Workshops on Cultural Pluralism:*
The Schools had two Workshops on Cultural Pluralism, in cooperation with the Michigan Department of Education. In 1969 the Workshop consisted of fourteen different ethnic groups (Italian, Portuguese, Arabic, Russian, Polish, Scandinavian, Dutch, Greek, French, Spanish, Oriental, Black, American Indian, and Finnish) who met on campus to hear a guest speaker on cultural anthropology, and then broke up into individual groups to examine available instructional materials and discuss target problems for the teaching of language and culture within their respective ethnic group. In 1970, the

Workshop addressed itself to the problem of how to introduce ethnic studies into social studies curricula in public schools.

2. *Conference on Racial Prejudice:*
The Schools hosted a Conference on Racial Prejudice, in cooperation with the Priests' Conference for Polish Affairs of the Archdiocese of Detroit, in an attempt to understand the problems of the inner city in relationship to the Catholic parishes of Detroit. The Conference examined prejudice from a psychological and sociological perspective, and presented recommendations on how to deal with inner-city problems.

3. *Summer Abroad 1970 Program:*
In cooperation with the Catholic University of Lublin, the Orchard Lake Schools sponsors a special intensive course in Poland in language and culture, with a guided cultural tour and an optional trip to Rome each summer, for academic credit.

Research

1. *Polish Language Teaching in the United States:*
In cooperation with the Southeast Educational Laboratory and their Bi-Lingual Design Project, Austin, Texas, the Schools initiated a research project into the amount and type of Polish language teaching in the United States. This information served the Congress in its recent passage of the Bi-Lingual Education Act—the first recognition by the Government of foreign languages—as a natural resource which should be carefully preserved. Although Polish has long been listed by the Department of Defense as one of the "critically needed" languages, little has been done to encourage its teaching.

2. *Polish Language Usage in Religious Services:*
Through the Polish American Liturgical Center, the Schools have translated, published, and distributed the new Eucharistic Prayers and the new Ordo of the Mass to all Polish priests of the United States. The Center has also undertaken the responsibility of supplying other Polish liturgical materials needed—prayerbooks, misalettes, sermon outlines, prayers of the faithful, etc. In a special apostolate to the aged and sick, the Center offers Polish materials of devotion for their use.

3. *Original Research in Polish and Polish-American Topics:*
In the realm of scholarship, the Schools have sponsored original research into history, literature, and culture of Poland and the Polish-American community, and have published translations and reprints, in cooperation with the *Eagle* Yearbook of the Schools. Many of these are already available in reprint form: (*)

The Kopernik Quadricentennial (1943)
Polonia Panorama (1946)
The 700th Anniversary of the Canonization of St. Stanislaus (1953)
Centennial of the Massive Immigration of Poles to America (1954)

The Life of John Cieplak, Bishop and Martyr (1955)
*Polish American Fraternal Organizations (1956)
*The Polish American Press (1957)
Polish Forebears Who Settled at Jamestown in 1608 (1958)
*A Seventy-Five Year History of the Polish Seminary (1960)
*American Council of Polish Cultural Clubs (1961)
*Polish American Clergy (1962)
*Polish American Parishes (1963)
Our Lady of Orchard Lake Shrine
Poland's Millenium, 1,000 Years of Christianity (1965)
Celebrating 1,000 Years of Polish Christianity, The World Polonia (1966)
*The Orchard Lake Schools (1967)
Our Lady of Czestochowa (1968)
*Outstanding Men and Women of Poland (1969)
*The Arts in Poland Since 1945 (1970)
Polish American Customs and Traditions

4. *Historical Research—The Founder's Day Symposia:*
   The annual Founder's Day Historical Symposia have, through the years, undertaken various themes related to the Polish-American experience. The results have been published continuously in the *Polish American Studies,* quarterly of the Polish American Historical Association.

5. *Visiting Artists and Scholars:*
   The Schools have long served as a host for most artists and scholars visiting this country from Poland, most of whom have either addressed our student body, or presented musical or literary programs of some kind. The recent appearance of a very young Polish Folk Rock Group (No To Co and the Alibabki) was enthusiastically received by the youngest and oldest set on campus.

6. *Professional Contact with Poland:*
   A school which teaches a foreign language and culture cannot long exist without contact with the culture's source. The Orchard Lake Schools have had close contact with the Catholic University of Lublin, the Universities of Warsaw and Cracow, and with the leaders of the Catholic Church. Annual trips to Poland by students under faculty supervision have always produced very positive results. Students have returned with a new love for America and a new-found love for the country of their ancestry.

Polish-American Public Relations

1. *Polish-Jewish Relations:*
   The Schools have cooperated with the Jewish Anti-Defamation League, especially in the Chicago area, in trying to find solutions to mutual problems of ethnic identity. The students have high respect for the work of the American Jewish Committee in the area of ethnicity.

2. *Polish-Black Relations:*
Polish Americans bear a significantly greater proportion of criticism for racial prejudice towards the black Americans because they happen to live closest to the problem. It is quite easy for white liberals who live in the antiseptic suburbs to level their charges and then return to their ivory towers.

Poland's friendliness toward minorities is a fact of history. Present racial controversies generate far more heat than light. But when the dust finally settles, we are convinced that Polish-Americans will emerge, in the long suffering tradition of their forebears, as those who weathered the storm.

The Orchard Lake Schools unequivocally support the efforts of the Priests' Conference for Polish Affairs in Detroit to find solutions to the magnitude of problems which we share with our fellow black Americans. The experience of Polish-Americans in dealing with the problems posed by a dominant culture decades ago can well serve our fellow black Americans with some important lessons in acculturation and assimilation.

3. *Polish-Canadian Relations:*
The Schools also seek to establish closer ties with the Polish-Americans of Canada. While Canada's problems differ from our own, many of the efforts we have exerted can benefit them. We have already made significant contacts with priests of Canada and their parishes. With the cooperation of Polish organizations in the United States, we will extend and strengthen the bonds we share in common.

What Orchard Lake Plans to Do. Passage of the Ethnic Heritage bill would enable us to increase work in these areas significantly, and offer services not now provided. The Center for Polish Studies and Culture would also be happy to advise any other ethnic group on methods of procedure and areas of priority. Much of its past work could already serve as a guide to other groups interested in the preservation and dissemination of their cultural legacy.

Development of Language and Curriculum Materials
1. *Distribution of FLICS Program:*
Although the Polish Language and Heritage Program is complete, work in revision and re-editing must be done to make it a more effective program. Personnel and facilities for the adequate distribution to elementary and secondary schools throughout the nation are inadequate. Further testing of the materials, especially in the so-called "Saturday Schools," where Polish is taught to children under private auspices, is essential.

2. *Translation and Publication of Books:*
Translation and publication facilities for historical, literary, and sociological studies must be provided as soon as possible. A special effort should be made to encourage new research, especially in the field of literary criticism of Polish works. Americans know very little of Poland's great literature beyond, perhaps, Sienkiewicz's *Quo Vadis.* Doctoral dissertations are especially productive of useful material.

3. *Films and Filmstrips:*
   Newest educational technology must embrace audio-visual materials for classroom use. Orchard Lake has all of the necessary resources for the production of a professional film and/or filmstrip for social studies teachers about the Polish-American experience, and Polish culture in general.

Training Programs and Workshops

1. *Summer Workshops:*
   With available funds summer workshops can be held which will prove to be invaluable for language and social studies teachers, to introduce them to existing materials, and instruct them on newest teaching methodology.
2. *Summer Sessions:*
   With the rebirth of interest in ethnicity, there is much demand for summer courses in Polish language, history, literature, art, and culture.
3. *Adult Education Classes:*
   A remarkable increase of interest in things Polish can be found in the third and fourth generation Americans of Polish background who suddenly have realized the treasures of wisdom and beauty contained within their own ethnic heritage. Formal education can contribute to "a more harmonious, patriotic, and committed populace."
4. *Seminars and Lectures:*
   The Schools plan to provide slides, films, recorded tapes, and traveling exhibits for possible use at schools and meetings of Polish-American organizations. They also will be able to sponsor lectures, dramatic presentations, music festivals, and film festivals.

Sociological Research. Sociological research among America's ethnic groups in general, and within the Polish-American community in particular, is almost non-existent. Although research in this area has begun, largely through the efforts of the National Opinion Research Center of the University of Chicago, no systematic study has yet been attempted. The preliminary outline for such a study was already presented by Dr. Lawrence Cizon, former Director of Research at Loyola University, Chicago. At Orchard Lake, such a study could provide invaluable information on the problems of our inner cities, especially those with large contiguous populations of Poles and blacks, like Chicago, Gary, Detroit, Cleveland, Toledo, Buffalo, New York, Philadelphia, and Baltimore.

Polish American Public Relations

1. *Orchard Lake–Focal Point for Polish-American Organizations:*
   Orchard Lake has long served as the spiritual and educational focal point for the organization of the Polish-American community in the United States. Meetings of fraternals, professional organizations, mass media people, and religious leaders have always been hosted by the Schools. Only limitations of staff and personnel have limited this contribution. These organizations have much power to influence the rank and file Americans of Polish background

for constructive effort and creative response to the needs of our country. The positive contribution of Polish-Americans to this country cannot be calculated. It is significant to note, however, that there has never been a riot, a demonstration, or a march of any kind, nor has there been a destructive or disruptive movement toward America, despite the fact that they are more organized than any other national group, and stronger in political influence in many sections of the country.

2. *General Information Center for Polish-Americans:*
Many ethnic groups in the United States lack any kind of centralized facility for providing general information on their own ethnic group. Orchard Lake well serves Polish-Americans in this regard, especially in view of its personnel and resources.

3. *Bi-Lingual Radio Program:*
In keeping with this desire to serve Polish-Americans, Orchard Lake now plans for a fifteen-minute bi-lingual radio program with a cultural emphasis, which will broadcast weekly. Its range of information and formation can thus be magnified many times over.

Conclusion

This Orchard Lake Plan, in its academic and non-academic aspects, is already well underway. We have 110 acres of land, 18 buildings, and a present staff of 30 priests and 20 laymen, all dedicated to the cause of the preservation and dissemination of Polish culture in the United States. The growth of the physical plant continues with the construction of a two million dollar residence facility which houses 300 students in semi-private rooms. The building has been purposely designed to function as a multi-purpose facility, especially during the summer months, when workshops and conferences can be held more easily. Future campus development includes a separate building to house the facilities of the Center for Polish Studies and Culture, and academic buildings like a fieldhouse, an auditorium, a faculty residence, and an addition to the Library. If we can serve the needs of America as we have in the past, we are confident that this plan will be realized before our centenary in 1985.

This, then, is the plan of the Orchard Lake Schools for implementing the provisions of the Ethnic Heritage Studies Centers Bill. Orchard Lake stands ready, willing, and able to devote its entire resources, personnel, and facilities for the realization of these goals. The philosophy of Orchard Lake has its roots in its history and tradition of service to those who have supported it—the Polish-American community in the United States. It stands as a monument to the faith and sacrifice of an immigrant America, a tribute to the deeply religious values carried to this country by our forefathers a century ago.

At a time when our country is undergoing profound social changes, the Schools continue to uphold the ideal of cultural pluralism—the selection of the very best from the heritages of all the groups which make up the American mosaic, and the preservation of these elements in youth to enrich our American culture. The current movement on college and university campuses to establish Black Culture programs reinforces our rejection of the "melting pot theory," in which each minority in America would lose its complete identity. In a world moving painstakingly toward more vital cooperation and more meaningful brotherhood, Orchard Lake upholds the goal of true unity without absolute conformity, demanding the right to individual differences in a culturally pluralistic society.

This is the contribution that Orchard Lake has made, and will continue to make, to a country which has welcomed our forefathers to its shores, allowed them to grow and prosper, and permitted them their ethnic ways. We still have hope in the American dream.

Notes

1. Michel DeCrevecoeur, "Letter From an American Farmer" (London, 1782), in Oscar Handlin, ed., *Immigration As a Factor in American History*, Englewood Cliffs, N.J., Prentice-Hall, 1959, p. 149.

2. Isreal Zangwill, "The Melting Pot" (New York, 1909), in Oscar Handlin, Ibid., p. 150.

3. Archibald Macleish, as quoted in Leonard Chrobot, "Philosophical Foundations for Cultural Pluralism," unpub. B.A. diss., St. Mary's College, Orchard Lake, Mi., 1960, p. 1.

4. Alfred Korzybski, as quoted in S.I. Hayakawa, *The Use and Misuse of Language*, Fawcett Books, 1962, p. ix.

5. S.I. Hayakawa, Ibid., p. viii.

6. John Graves, *Goodbye to a River*, N.Y. Knopf, 1961, p. 162.

29 Government's Role in Meeting the Needs of White Ethnic Citizens

Irving M. Levine

Recent media interest and especially *Newsweek's* October 6, 1969 report on "The Troubled American: A Special Report on the White Majority," has focused public attention on a population group whose problems have deeply concerned the American Jewish Committee. The AJC's analysis and program planning has in fact been credited by many publications as being a major influence in "turning the media on" to the white working American.

Our National Consultation on Ethnic America held in June, 1968, at Fordham University was the first national forum to discuss the life styles, problems, and attitudes of 40 million Americans whose lives and concerns were largely being neglected by mainstream American institutions. Since that time we have held a number of local consultations as well.

Since June, 1968, much new interest has been expressed, but public policy has yet to come to grips with either the "relative deprivation" faced by these Americans in relation to more successful professional and technical groupings or their often exaggerated but nonetheless real fears of black and other minority groups that are moving into a competitive posture.

Much has already been written about racial polarization, urban alienation, suburban sprawl, the inadequate response of government on all levels, the change in family authority, the meaninglessness of conventional industrial work, the irrelevance of established institutions, etc. Much less has been said about solutions that would target problem solving to this highly volatile part of the nation's metropolitan population.

The American Jewish Committee has yet to complete its pilot projects and investigations, but since it has been fortunate in early entry, it has developed some "lead time" which may give its insights some present meaning.

Some Institutional Deficiencies

Our preliminary investigations have led us to some of the following conclusions about lower middle class white ethnic Americans:

1. In the past decade there has been minimal advocacy of their deepest concerns relating to special problems they face in receiving a superior education, in developing economic flexibility, and caring for their physical and mental

359

health, in child rearing, in maintaining home, automobile and adequate credit, in maintaining a viable community, and in receiving answers relating to self and group identity.

2. There has been insufficient research into the various levels of development of groups such as Italian-Americans, Polish-Americans, Greek-Americans, etc.; how group ties affect their social, psychological, and differential interrelationships with other urban groups and urban institutions.

3. Most institutions that have traditionally addressed the needs of these groups lack the vitality of the past, and new institutions have not taken sufficient interest in them.

4. Government's present basic programs do have many positive and potentially greater benefits for lower middle class whites, but these effects are often invisible and are submerged in interpretation and administration.

5. Most of government's efforts which benefit this core population are either in generalized programs that also benefit the entire population or are holdovers from earlier periods of social progressivism. This fact makes the question, "What have they done for me lately?" relevant.

Some Suggested Federal Initiatives

The federal government's initiative in meeting the needs of lower middle class white Americans should be directed to two major purposes:

1. Fulfilling our government's obligations to a large population of taxpayers no longer capable of adequately meeting economic, social, child rearing, communal, and intergroup relations needs because of urban decay and metropolitan disorder.

2. Offering, interpreting, and delivering programs in such a way as to depolarize racial and other intergroup tensions in our metropolitan centers.

Some of the following ideas have immediacy, many others reflect longer range possibilities. They are not offered within the limited context of "political reality." It is hoped they may serve as a guide to those who would wish to construct a more orderly and pertinent social policy for these millions of frustrated Americans. By no means are they inclusive nor are they designed to fit neatly into conventional categories. They do not necessarily represent program policy recommendations of the American Jewish Committee. They are concepts which we believe merit immediate and intensive feasibility study.

Most of the following suggestions are made in the hope that major action would be forthcoming from the federal government. Some may be deemed more appropriate for other jurisdictions. In that context, all of the proposals should be read as fitting under the category of "The federal government should create, support or stimulate." Many of these proposals will have enhanced credibility if anti-inflation policies begin to work and the need for anti-recession action becomes dominant.

Increasing Real Income

1. Tax policies that more realistically account for the cost of dependents by gradually doubling the $600 dependency allowance.
2. Tax benefits for parents who send their children to private schools (elementary, secondary, and university), geared to income and number of dependents.
3. Encouragement of discount buying through government support for the creation of cooperative buying. This would serve as an anti-inflation device since lower prices and higher savings might be encouraged.
4. Subsidization through government guaranteed low interest rates and other mechanisms from home buyers and renters within lower middle class income ranges so that nobody in this income range pays more than *20* percent of his income for housing. Current 25 percent formula is too large a cut into limited income.

Social Services

1. Creation of an expanded network of health centers for those who do not wish to avail themselves or cannot afford private medical services. These clinics to be located both on a geographic and industrial basis so as to be easily accessible to workers and their families. Annual checkups for entire family should be required to maintain right to services.
2. Universal medical insurance supported through both Social Security and general revenues, including the cost of most expensive drugs.
3. Use of the Social Security system to universalize day care centers for this income group, by making available to families within lower middle income categories a "child development" grant for day care services.
4. Modifying the Social Security system to eliminate the regressive nature of the social security tax. This would be felt especially by young workers who see no benefits coming to them at points of greatest need. (A youth society is less concerned with old age security than "living.") It is suggested that among other benefits there ought to be automatic payments at the point of marriage and at the birth of the first two children.
5. To finance these new Social Security benefits (Social Security is a system that works, has the confidence of both blacks and whites and should serve as a far better model to dispense services and income maintenance than other failure-oriented "poverty programs"), an example of a suggested formula is that the federal government become a one-third contributing partner and later move to become a one-half contributing partner to Social Security funding. The other half to be paid by employer and employee.
6. New and expanded mental health facilities and services geared to deal with the lower middle class culture. There is a current lack of sophistication in understanding mental health on the part of our target group, as well as a continuing failure on the part of mental health practitioners to make a significant impact on this group's often unrecognized pathology.

Public Education

1. A considerable number of urban land grant colleges should be established to deal with urban problem solving and urban group life needs.

2. A goal for 1976, our bicentennial, should be established for a total universal higher education experience for all who wish it and can benefit from it. There should be a visible year by year timetable to accomplish the task.

3. Federal sponsorship of model educational-cultural technological centers for elementary and secondary levels which mix education, housing, physical rebirth, and new cultural facilities for declining neighborhoods. These schools would become integrative forces for racial and religious minorities. Children could experience a dual school pattern, spending a part of each week in a neighborhood-based mini school of infinite varities, and also move into large scale educational, technological, and cultural centers for other parts of the week. Computer assisted learning could become a reality in the large centers at the same time that we encourage intimacy, affective learning, cultural and religious diversity in mini-neighborhood schools.

4. Schools at all levels should be encouraged to upgrade ethnic studies with an emphasis on comparative ethnic development in America, intergroup relations and self-identity of students.

Jobs

1. A comprehensive second- and third-career program should be created which would enable lower middle class Americans to train for additional education and new career opportunities at points of greater maturity and greater understanding of occupational competency and desire.

2. Government should support systems which protect against the worst consequences of displacement based on racial competition. Government action should open up all job categories to racial minorities. At the same time it should seek to ensure those who have achieved a level of security that their status will be maintained.

3. There should be national policies and programs to pay full costs of moving workers from low employment areas to high employment opportunity areas. Resettlement and additional training costs ought to be absorbed as well.

4. Encouragement of profit sharing for workers in American industry so that a man's production is more realistically related to his sharing in the success of the enterprise.

5. Government should assist industry in the development of mechanisms to encourage humanization, human relations, and community involvement by American workers. One example: Some of the same privileges for community service and participation that are given to executives should be encouraged for the average worker as well. Federal wage subsidies or tax benefits to the company might encourage this kind of industrial reform.

6. Special study should be given to the phenomenon of the young worker, his emergence out of a new youth culture and his potential alienation from the industrial system.

7. Entrepreneurship for white workers who have underdeveloped skills and management potential ought to be more aggressively supported.

8. Studies should be encouraged to look into the consequences of the

establishment of a shorter work week. We should be ready for this step so as to spread employment opportunities to the entire society and learn to make creative use of leisure time.

Housing

1. Encourage a federal mortage policy (perhaps a large contingency fund), which would automatically make available increased amount of money at low interest rates at those times when economic conditions have depleted the supply of conventional mortage money. This fund should be designed to provide a yardstick to keep interest rates down.
2. A biannual audit of national housing needs should be conducted to develop the kinds of program flexibility so that government will be automatically geared toward building the balance of what the private market cannot fulfill. A formula to meet the full housing needs of the people, with government as "houser of the last resort" is vital.
3. Guarantees by government that homes in racially changing neighborhoods will be protected against loss of value.
4. Adequate funding for the "Model Cities" program so that there is movement toward parity among all declining neighborhoods in all parts of our most troubled cities. A greater concern for white declining neighborhoods is needed but not at the expense of removing blight from the black ghetto.
5. Federal government sponsorship of "Urban Fairs" which highlight techniques for the rebuilding of our cities and where the latest in urban technology and ideas for citizen participation can be displayed in an effective and enjoyable manner.
6. Encouraging suburban acceptance of minority and low income housing by granting "human rehabilitation" money for suburbs in the form of "impacted aid" to support local services. This would reduce the potential tax burden of lower income white suburbanites and perhaps make them less resistant to new residents. In integrating suburban communities new zoning might also be encouraged by aiding industrial developers to enter the low income housing market and thus guaranteeing a combination of a steady job along with decent housing. The leverage of suburban industrial developers to achieve zoning variances might be considerable if an industrial-growth oriented suburb felt it had to make concessions to keep industry happy and growing.

   Some suburban resistance to integrating blacks might diminish if self-interest was made more visible through the promise of significant additional government funds, through the creation of stable minority group populations, and through the understanding that industrial growth requires new worker populations.
7. Private entrepreneurs, public agencies, and voluntary organizations should be further encouraged to build "new towns." "Land banks" must be established if this movement is to have reality.

Law Enforcement
1. Encouragement through government grants to voluntary and neighborhood organizations of widespread "community organization for helping to shape safer cities." These groups would broaden citizen activity in crime control, police-community relations, rehabilitation, narcotic treatment, and tension control.
2. In its attack on organized crime, the federal government should do all it can to oppose the concept of "group guilt" or "group responsibility" for crime. Our Italian citizens bear an especially heaven burden in American life because of the "Mafia image."
3. A federally sponsored "Police-Community Relations Institute" to upgrade professional standing of this field and to give status to many constructive lower middle class white ethnic police professionals who should be recruited and vigorously trained in this field.
4. Experimenting with federal funds for security services such as those for block wardens, escort service, etc., as examples of anti-crime measures. These would also serve as constructive employment and career possibilities for thousands of urban working class people.
5. The training of local personnel in the use of new technology against burglary and other crimes and in the shaping of safer cities. This ought to be funded by government agencies to educate and help our citizens to adapt new ways to guarantee their safety and retain their continued commitment to law and order with justice.

Community and Intergroup Relations
1. Federal programs should always be articulated and publicized in the manner that would best promote amicable intergroup relations. Community conflicts could often be avoided if the announcement of programs met certain established standards which were designed to reduce intergroup tensions. A national advisory committee of people expert in this field should be established to guide government agencies.
2. Creation of a manual on "Depolarization Techniques" to be used to train federal and local officials on all levels. This manual should be done by the Community Relations Service of the Justice Department. Funds for training should also be provided.
3. There should be an increase in government grants to private agencies dealing with bridge building among various ethnic groups and racial minorities.
4. Government must look deep into the causes of violence in our society. It should also do all it can to prevent gun-buying and para-military organizations from solidifying their base. Comprehensive gun-control legislation must be passed.
5. Government must help the media interpret lower middle class America in less stereotypical and more heroic terms. The lack of adequate self-image is an important factor in group jealousy that exaggerates black potency and black power.

6. National leaders must avoid all actions and words which could pit one group against another in competition for economic advantages that may be in short supply.
7. In aiding lower middle class white Americans, government must make clear that in addition to its first priority of correcting America's injustices to Negroes and other underclass minorities, it also recognizes its responsibilities to assist other groups to make constant progress.

Fact Finding. To cope with the problems and potential explosiveness of this large group of white citizens who deeply resent those above and those below them in status, it is suggested that the federal government support additional research into the phenomena of "group life." This research should build on the studies done by the President's Commission on the Causes and Prevention of Violence. In a Commission staff report there is a telling charge of "historical amnesia" on the question of previous group conflicts in America. It states:

As probably the most ethnically and culturally pluralistic nation in the world, the United States has functioned less as a nation of individuals than of groups.

The myth of the melting pot has obscured the great degree to which Americans have historically identified with their national citizenship through their myriad subnational affiliations. This has meant inevitable group competition, friction and conflict.

It would seem we could learn much by an analysis of governmental and social policy that defused other historical polarizations.

The questions of group identity, ethnic succession, separatism, cultural pluralism, integration, and assimilation have a new urgency. Further analysis and planning for viable and constructive outlets of group identification could aid in finding the way for new yearning on the part of many people for "community" to be expressed. Community can develop into a flowering of the American dream, releasing the richness of a variety of buried cultural forces. On the other hand, if group chauvinism is allowed to fester on the level of the lowest common denominator of group conflict and overly aggressive selfish group interest, it could fragment and destroy our nation.

New Institution. It is suggested that for purposes of concentration and organization of the best resources, the federal government establish an "Institute on Group Life in America," to carry out this vital work.

Conclusion

Our society in general and the federal government in particular must recognize the dimensions of the current crisis. It is not just physical decay of our cities. It is not just a revolutionary surge by blacks and young people against established institutions. It is not just elitist impotence in solving our most serious problems. We face potential and widespread physical aggression. The combatants are lining up against each other and they are the most angry and ferocious any society produces; those at the bottom in conflict with those who have only recently put their foot on the first rung of the success ladder.

Such a struggle once seriously begun will spare no group. Least of all will it promote the stability and good name of the government of the United States.

30 Language Survey: The Peoples of Detroit Project

Valerie Komives and Blanche Goodell

Introduction

As part of the Peoples of Detroit Project carried on during 1968-1969, a survey was made of the foreign languages being taught in the Detroit Metropolitan Area. Questionnaires were sent to all public, parochial, and private schools, and to the colleges and universities. They were also sent to representatives of the ethnic groups. I was asked to make a summary of the information received and to report on it at the International Institute on April 22, 1969. I was also asked to present a shortened summary at the Ethnic Conference on June 13, 1970.

Three new language courses have been added to the list of those being taught at the time the survey was completed. These are Modern Arabic, Modern Greek, and Swahili. They have been included in order to bring the survey up to date as much as possible. There may be other changes in the list also but it was not possible to recheck the entire survey. For many reasons this summary is incomplete. Some questionnaires gave only partial information. Others were not returned at all. However, enough material was gathered to show the very considerable interest in language study in this area.

Language Survey

According to the survey taken by the Peoples of Detroit Project, there are twenty-one languages being taught in the Detroit Metropolitan Area. These may be divided into three groups:

1. those taught only in schools or colleges;
2. those taught both in schools and colleges and in special courses;
3. those taught only in special courses.

Group One: Arabic, French, German, Greek, Italian, Portuguese, Spanish, Swahili (7)
Group Two: Armenian, Hebrew, Polish, Russian, Ukrainian (5)
Group Three: Chinese, Finnish, Hungarian, Latvian, Lithuanian, Romanian, Serbian, Slovak, Swedish (9)

367

In addition, Latin is also taught in most schools and colleges, but was not included in this survey because it is not taught as a spoken language.

The special courses are those organized by independent ethnic groups and are taught either in their church or social centers or in space rented by them for this purpose.

The language classes have been divided into three groups: Elementary, Intermediate, and Advanced. The number following each group indicates the number of courses or sections in that group.

There is an important *Citizens Study of Detroit Schools* published by the Detroit Board of Education. It lists which languages are taught in each school.

Group One: Languages Taught Only in Schools or Colleges

ARABIC
Wayne State University

Classical Arabic:	Elementary, Intermediate, Advanced
Modern Arabic:	Elementary (new course)

Adult Education

Salina School, Dearborn	Elementary, Intermediate, Advanced

FRENCH
Wayne State University
Elementary (27), Intermediate (20), Advanced (17)

University of Detroit
Elementary (9), Intermediate (7), Advanced (4)

Madonna College
Elementary (2), Intermediate (2), Advanced (3)

Marygrove College
Elementary (1), Intermediate (2), Advanced (2)

Mercy College
Elementary (1), Intermediate (3), Advanced (3)

Community Colleges

Dearborn, University of Michigan Branch	Intermediate
Highland Lakes, Oakland	Elementary and Intermediate
Orchard Ridge, Oakland	Elementary and Intermediate
Schoolcraft College	Elementary and Intermediate

Adult Education

Fordson High School	Elementary
Denby High School, Detroit	Elementary

Kimball, Royal Oak   Elementary and Intermediate
St. Clair Shores   Elementary and Intermediate

High Schools
Detroit Public High Schools (22)

First Year	50 Sections	Third Year	18 Sections
Second Year	60 Sections	Fourth Year	10 Sections

Detroit Public Junior High Schools (29)

Detroit Public Elementary Schools (3)

Detroit Parochial High Schools (22)

First Year	22 Schools	Third Year	12 Schools
Second Year	18 Schools	Fourth Year	3 Schools

Suburban Parochial High Schools (16)

First Year	16 Schools	Third Year	8 Schools
Second Year	15 Schools	Fourth Year	5 Schools

Suburban Public Junior and Senior High Schools (21 Cities)

Seventh Grade	7 Schools	Tenth Grade	24 Schools
Eighth Grade	11 Schools	Eleventh Grade	18 Schools
Ninth Grade	22 Schools	Twelfth Grade	17 Schools

Suburban Public Elementary Schools (3 Cities)

Fourth Grade	1 School	Sixth Grade	3 Schools
Fifth Grade	3 Schools		

Private Schools

Grosse Pointe University School	High School	Four Years
	Elementary School	Grades 3-8

Hillel Day School	One Year
Liggett School	Five Years
Private Catholic	Four Years

Sacred Heart Academy	High School	Four Years
	Elementary School	Grades 2-8

GERMAN
Wayne State University
Elementary (20), Intermediate (14), Advanced (10)

University of Detroit
Elementary (5), Intermediate (3), Advanced (3)

Marygrove College
Intermediate (1), Advanced (1)

Mercy College
Elementary (1), Intermediate (2), Advanced (1)

Community Colleges
Orchard Ridge, Oakland Elementary (2), Advanced (1)
Schoolcraft Elementary (1), Intermediate (1)

Adult Education

Denby High School, Detroit	Elementary and Intermediate
Dondero High School, Royal Oak	Elementary and Intermediate

High Schools
Detroit Public High Schools (7)

First Year	10 Sections	Third Year	4 Sections
Second Year	13 Sections	Fourth Year	4 Sections

Detroit Public Junior High Schools (1)
Catholic Archdiocese

Catholic Central	Three Years
University of Detroit High School	Three Years
Divine Child, Dearborn	Three Years
Private Catholic	Two Years

Suburban Public Junior and Senior High Schools (11 Cities)

Two Years	4 Schools	Four Years	1 School
Three Years	7 Schools	Eighth Grade	2 Schools

GREEK
Wayne State University
Classical Greek: Elementary, Intermediate, Advanced
Modern Greek: Elementary (new course)

ITALIAN
Wayne State University
Elementary (9), Intermediate (4), Advanced (3)

Adult Education

Denby High School, Detroit	Elementary, Intermediate, Advanced
Edsel Ford High School, Dearborn	Elementary
Fordson High School	Elementary

PORTUGUESE
Wayne State University
Elementary and Intermediate   (Begun in Fall 1968)

SPANISH
Wayne State University
Elementary (25), Intermediate (15), Advanced (14)

University of Detroit
Elementary (6), Intermediate (7), Advanced (4)

Madonna College
Elementary (1), Intermediate (1), Advanced (4)

Marygrove College
Elementary (1), Intermediate (2), Advanced (2)

Mercy College
Elementary (2), Intermediate (2), Advanced (2)

Community Colleges

Oakland Community College	Elementary and Intermediate
Schoolcraft	Elementary (3) and Intermediate (1)

Adult Education

Denby High School, Detroit	Elementary and Intermediate
Dondero High School, Royal Oak	Elementary
Eastern Community Night School	Elementary
South Lake High School	Elementary and Intermediate

High Schools
Detroit Public High Schools (22)

First Year	87 Sections	Third Year	24 Sections
Second Year	103 Sections	Fourth Year	20 Sections

Detroit Public Junior High Schools (41)

Detroit Public Elementary Schools (25)

Detroit Parochial High Schools (14)

First Year	14 Schools	Third Year	6 Schools
Second Year	13 Schools		

Suburban Parochial High Schools (12)

First Year	12 Schools	Third Year	8 Schools
Second Year	11 Schools	Fourth Year	4 Schools

Suburban Public Junior and Senior High Schools (21 Cities)

Seventh Grade	12 Schools	Tenth Grade	21 Schools
Eighth Grade	14 Schools	Eleventh Grade	20 Schools
Ninth Grade	24 Schools	Twelfth Grade	14 Schools

Suburban Public Elementary Schools (2 Cities)

Third Grade	1 School	Fifth Grade	2 Schools
Fourth Grade	2 Schools	Sixth Grade	2 Schools

Private Schools

Grosse Pointe University School	Four Years
Liggett School	Four Years
Private Catholic	Four Years
Sacred Heart Academy	Three Years

SWAHILI
Wayne State University
Elementary   (new course)

Group Two: Languages Taught Both in Schools and Colleges and in Special Courses
ARMENIAN
Wayne State University (Subsidized by Armenian Groups)
Elementary (1), Intermediate (1), Advanced (2)

St. John's Armenian Church, Detroit

Pre-school and Kindergarten	Pre-school and Nursery
Grades 1-8	Class in Divine Liturgy
Saturday Class	Children Ages 7-13
Sunday Morning Classes	

St. Sarkis Church, Dearborn
Grade 2 and Grade 8

Armenian Radio Voice
Saturday Afternoon Language Class

HEBREW
Wayne State University
Classical Hebrew: Elementary, Intermediate, Advanced
Aramaic: Two Courses

Akiva Hebrew Day School
Kindergarten and Grades 1-8

Hillel Day School
Grades 1-9

Jewish Community Center
Modern Hebrew: Elementary and Intermediate for High School Age
Modern Hebrew: Elementary (5), Intermediate (5), Advanced (2) for Adults
Yiddish: Elementary

POLISH
Wayne State University
Elementary, Intermediate, Advanced

Madonna College
Elementary and Intermediate

Detroit Public High Schools (1)

First Year	1 Section	Third Year	1 Section
Second Year	1 Section	Fourth Year	1 Section

Adult Education
Fitzgerald High School, Warren   Elementary

St. Barbara School, Dearborn
Grades 1-8

St. Bartholomew Parish School
Elementary, Intermediate, Advanced

St. Florian, Hammtramck

Elementary School	Grades 5-8
High School	Two Years

Our Lady Queen of Apostles, Hammtramck
Grades 1-8

Savior on Golgotha, Polish National Catholic Church
Grades 1-4

St. Thomas School, St. Staszic Polish Language School
Elementary, Intermediate, Advanced

Transfiguration School
Grades 1-8

RUSSIAN
Wayne State University
Elementary (4), Intermediate (4), Advanced (3)

University of Detroit
Elementary

Detroit Public High Schools (4)

First Year	4 Sections	Third Year	2 Sections
Second Year	4 Sections	Fourth Year	2 Sections

Detroit Public Junior High Schools (1)
Suburban Public High Schools (2)

First Year	2 Schools	Third Year	1 School
Second Year	2 Schools		

SS. Peter and Paul Russian Orthodox Church
Elementary and Intermediate

UKRAINIAN
Wayne State University (Subsidized by Ukrainian Groups)
Elementary and Intermediate

Copernicus School, Hammtramck
Grades 1-11   History and Literature 9-11
Library Course

St. John's Ukrainian Parochial School
Grades 1-8   Advanced Grade 10

St. Josaphat Ukrainian Church, Warren
Elementary

St. Mary's Ukrainian Orthodox Church
Grades 1-8

Group Three: Languages Taught Only in Special Courses
CHINESE (Cantonese)
Chinese Community Church
Grades 1-3

FINNISH
Finnish Center Association
Elementary, Intermediate, Advanced

HUNGARIAN
Hungarian House
Kindergarten and Elementary

LATVIAN
St. Paul's Latvian Evangelical Lutheran Church
Grades 1-8   Grades 2 and 5

LITHUANIAN
St. Anthony's School, Detroit
Advanced-Language and Literature

Lithuanian Saturday School
Held at Vandenberg Elementary School, Redford
Pre-school and Grades 1-9

ROMANIAN
St. George Romanian Orthodox Cathedral, Southfield
Elementary

SERBIAN
American Serbian Memorial Hall
Grades 1-4

SLOVAK
St. Cyril and Methodius High School
Elementary and Advanced

SWEDISH
Oakland University, Rochester
Adult Education Program
Conversational Swedish

31

**New Experiment in
the Schools**

Joseph A. Wytrwal

In the play "The Tea House of the August Moon" one of the actors stated:

"It isn't easy, sometimes painful, but pain makes man think, thought makes man wise, and wisdom makes life endurable."

In our quest for wisdom, we naturally would like to know what are the ingredients of wisdom. In my opinion, an individual has wisdom when he has the facts, the experience and the third ingredient which is tolerance. When we study American history, it is quite evident that the American historians did have the facts, they also had the experience, but they lacked one important ingredient: tolerance. Recently, after studying 45 social studies textbooks used in the United States secondary schools, the Anti-Defamation League of B'nai B'rith reported that "Waspism" is still with us. In all the books examined, the nature and problems of minority groups are largely neglected. Not a single one presented a reasonably complete and undistorted picture of America's many minority groups.

Since 1776 America has moved farther and farther away from being a homogeneous nation. It no longer has all of its traditions, its culture and religious ideals and beliefs based on the English heritage. Thus when we view contemporary American society we must realize that America is moving away from ethnic homogenity, even though it is acquiring linguistic uniformity. And this linguistic uniformity does not mean, for example, that the individual ethnic groups are disappearing. It only means that the ethnic groups adapted themselves to the new linguistic reality for the expression of their old values. It also should make us aware that ethnic groups still persist, even though sociologists and historians have predicted their disappearance as early as 1920.

There are many reasons for the persistence of the ethnic groups. One of the reasons is the tyranny of the majority. It can be seen in politics, in recreation, in literary tastes, and even in religious institutions where it took the form of intolerance and bigotry. However, the ethnic groups did not lose faith in America simply because American culture, civilization, and environment offered unlimited opportunity, especially to individuals of ability and initiative. America also extended suffrage, which made one vote as good as another. Since immigrants continued to arrive in large numbers, this optimism continued.

Each immigrant, as he faced the problem of adjustment to life in America,

377

was influenced both by his particular character traits and by his psychological needs. Basically there were two types of immigrants: those whose psychological orientation was American and those whose cultural bonds continued to be with the land that gave them birth. But the more difficult the immigrants found absorption of American culture, the more they cherished their own. The more rejected they felt in the United States, the more they felt at home in their own neighborhoods and culture. Moreover, as the immigrant groups became increasingly aware of themselves as a cultural minority, they discovered that ethnic group action could be surprisingly effective in their new environment. As isolated individuals they could not accomplish much, but as members of ethnic groups, their numbers were adequate for successful ethnic enterprises.

Besides providing for food, clothing and shelter, they also had to provide their own educational, religious, and cultural institutions. In the Catholic Church existing in America, they experienced many difficulties. The church was under the control of the Irish, who had aspirations of making it the majority religion in America. The Irish clergy viewed ethnic cultures and languages as un-American and endeavored to submerge them as much as possible. The public educational system also made an attempt to destroy the heritage of the ethnic groups. They poured contempt on the past history of the ethnic groups. In teaching the immigrants to despise what they possessed, the educators sought a clear break with the continuity of their previous life. In their activity the educators revealed their own arrogance, intolerance, and intemperate intellects. And so we had an Anglo-Saxon society indifferent to the needs of immigrants, the Irish dominated Catholic Church obsessed with the idea of becoming the majority religion in America, and the public educators inculcated with the naive process of assimilation.

Only recently did we realize that ethnic groups from different backgrounds have been a powerful constructive force in the development of American society. Only recently did we realize that a strong democratic society cannot be built on a public education system that fails to teach the contributions of all racial groups to the nation. The American public needs education about the values of our diverse nationality groups and their importance to our society. New and old Americans need to be brought together more, just as much as new Americans of different nationalities need to get to know each other.

Americans cannot live significantly without the past. What is may vanish. Yet certain moments in history never vanish. There is a dimension of history in which primordial material of commitment and experience is being molded into happenings. Ethnic groups are people in whom the past endures, in whom the present is inconceivable without moments gone by. Genuine history occurs only when the events of the present disclose the meaning of the past and offer an anticipation of the promise of the future.

Chadsey High School is located on the west side of Detroit. Its local population has different nationality backgrounds and there is social and cultural diversity. Because of its uniqueness, Chadsey High School was the first high school in Detroit to develop a new approach in the teaching of American history and the contributions of ethnic and racial groups to American life. In the new course entitled "America's Heritage" students study the different national, social, racial, and ethnic groups that together make up the population of the United States. Students also consider the contributions each people has made to our national life and the circumstances of its immigration to the United States. The course also informs the student about the group from which he is descended, and gives him accurate information about others who are his neighbors, companions, and schoolmates. In studying America's ethnic groups, their hopes and fears, their aspirations and defeats, their sufferings and triumphs, the student arrives at a better understanding of American nationality.

Before the introduction of this course, Chadsey offered Black Studies, which considered the contributions of the Negro to American culture, history, and civilization. These courses had a tendency to bring about segregated classes. Thus enthusiasm and interest in Black Studies declined since no individual in school wanted to be separated or singled out. Everyone wants to be a part of the whole, and so the course in American Heritage is accepted more willingly and is helping to bring about greater understanding and tolerance.

St. Casimir School, a Catholic elementary school on the west side, also pioneered in this field. The school, originally Polish, in the last few years has become quite cosmopolitan. It is now attended by students from Polish, Negro, and Spanish backgrounds. Father Karasiewicz, the pastor, understood the change and developed a new curriculum which considers the language and culture of the Polish, Spanish, and Negro groups. Every student in the school is exposed to the culture and language of the three groups. Not only did the curriculum bring a new dimension in learning, but it made the students grateful for the immeasurable contributions others have made to their lives. They no longer were blinded by arrogance and pride. In addition, the school became a very effective institution in uniting the community for more successful and cooperative living.

Historically there have been three general attitudes among native Americans regarding the manner in which immigrant people are assimilated. These have involved: (1) Anglo-conformity; (2) the concept of the "melting pot"; and (3) cultural pluralism. The first of these assumed the desirability of maintaining English institutions and culture as the standard of American life. The melting pot theory was based on the contrasting view that the American nationality was a composite of many ethnic strains—not English, but something new and distinctively American. Cultural pluralism is based on the assumption that American society is heterogeneous and that membership in diverse, cultural minority groups is desirable.

Today we realize that American society is a pluralistic society with a plurality not only of religions but also of languages, nationalities, cultures, skills, and opinions. Today we realize that the United States is not all English or all Irish or all white or all black or all Catholic or all Jewish—it is all of them, yet it is more. Although not in a perfect way, the American people as a whole manage to live "over the heads" of every ethnic group and create the great American harmony which is more than the sum total of individuals or of different national groups.

And it is from this diversity that the greatness of America springs, and it is the triumph of America that in the midst of such diversity there is also unity; the mingling of traditions, temperaments, and cultures.

About the Authors

Harold J. Abramson teaches at the University of Connecticut, Department of Sociology.

Carol Agocs teaches at Monteith College, Wayne State University.

Frank Barna is a student at Monteith College, Wayne State University.

William Bufalino is a leading Detroit attorney and special counsel to the International Brotherhood of Teamsters.

John P. Casey is a former journalist and now a leading political public relations expert.

Rev. Leonard F. Chrobot is Academic Dean, St. Mary's College, Orchard Lake.

Anthony Connole is administrative assistant of the Chrysler Department, U.A.W.

Dan Finley teaches in the Detroit Public Schools.

Julie S. Flowerday teaches at Wayne State University, Anthropology Department.

Gustavo Gaynett is in the Latin American Secretariat of the Detroit Archdiocese.

Blanche Goodell is a former professor of Spanish at Wayne State University.

Andrew Greeley is the director of the National Opinion Research Center at the University of Chicago.

Ronald Haughton is president of the Board of Mediation of Community Disputes.

Kenneth Hylton is vice-chairman of the Michigan Democratic Party and a prominent Detroit attorney.

Christopher H. Johnson teaches at Wayne State University, Department of History.

Richard Kolm teaches at Catholic University, School of Social Service.

Valerie Komives is with Detroit's International Institute.

Helen Kovach teaches at Oakland University.

Stanley Krajewski is editor of Detroit's Polish Daily News.

Richard Kubinski teaches at Orchard Lake.

Margaret Larrie is a staff coordinator in the Detroit Public Schools.

Reginald Larrie teaches Afro-American history at Wayne County Community College.

Irving M. Levine is director of Urban Projects, American Jewish Committee.

Leonard W. Moss teaches at Wayne State University, Department of Anthropology.

Kazimierz J. Olejarczyk is president of the Michigan Polish American Congress.

Thomas F. Pettigrew teaches at Harvard University, Department of Social Relations.

Jonathan Schwartz teaches at the University of Copenhagen.

Ellen J. Stekert teaches English and is director of the Folklore Archives at Wayne State University.

Marios Stephanides is a graduate student in sociology at Wayne State University.

Joseph B. Sullivan is a leading Detroit attorney and political figure.

Djuro J. Vrga teaches at Central Michigan University, Department of Sociology.

B.J. Widick teaches at Columbia University.

Joseph A. Wytrwal is an assistant principal in the Detroit Public Schools.

About the Editor

Otto Feinstein, professor of the Science of Society Division, Monteith College, Wayne State University in Detroit, and currently acting chairman of the Division, was born in Vienna, Austria, in 1930. He graduated from the University of Chicago, spent three years at the Graduate Institute for International Studies, Geneva, and returned to the University of Chicago for his Ph.D.

He is the author of *Two Worlds of Change* (Anchor Press, 1964) and *Michigan Economic Myths: Defense Contract, Employment and Affluence* (Wayne-Monteith Monographs, 1962). He is editor of *New University Thought* and has written articles for numerous publications. From 1963 to 1966 he was the Director of the Danforth Study *Higher Education Economics—Quality and Personalism* from which his book *Higher Education in the United States*, published by Heath Lexington Books in 1971, is drawn. Professor Feinstein is also co-author (with Eric Bockstael) of *Higher Education in the European Community*, also published by Heath Lexington Books, in 1970.

Professor Feinstein is interested in the workings of nonmarket institutions and the theory and practice of resource allocation to explicit and implicit value goals of these institutions. This thread of concern runs through his works, in the economics of higher education, defense economics, and United States-Latin American relations. He is currently working on a study dealing with the impact of Vatican II on the Roman Catholic Church in Ireland.

Professor Feinstein was the coordinator for the conference on Ethnic Communities of Greater Detroit.